"My friend and CNN colleague Ron Brownstein has written a terrific book. *Rock Me on the Water* tells the amazing story of 1974 and how it changed the U.S. If you're old enough to have lived through 1974, it will bring back memories. If you're too young, you will learn a lot."
—Wolf Blitzer, anchor of CNN's *The Situation Room*

"Sweeping cultural history. . . . Enriched by interviews with the period's luminaries, including Warren Beatty and Linda Ronstadt, this astute and wide-ranging account shows how LA led the U.S. into an era when the 1960s counterculture became mainstream." —*Publishers Weekly*

"An endlessly engaging cultural history that will resonate with anyone alive in 1974." —*Kirkus Reviews* (starred review)

"Brownstein knits together the threads of history to show that, for the first time in 1974, politics and entertainment were not separate things, that the line between the two was blurred almost to the point of irrelevance. An insightful, expertly written book." —*Booklist*

"Excellent." —*Politico*

"More than just summarizing or reviewing what such films and shows were about, the author dives deep into how they were created, financed, promoted, and received. His many interviews with actors, writers, directors, and executives of that era lend such renderings veracity and energy." —*Pittsburgh Post-Gazette*

"I'm absolutely loving *Rock Me on the Water*, Ron Brownstein's riveting new book about LA, circa '74, when the City of Angels was the hub of an extraordinary revolution in film, music, culture, and politics. Really a fun read. Highly recommended!!"
—David Axelrod, CNN senior political commentator

"This is a terrific book about a pivot point in U.S. cultural history, which led to reshaping our political landscape. Ron Brownstein is a dadgum genius. Highly recommend this book."
—Paul Begala, CNN contributor and former counselor to President Clinton

"One of the very best on 1974—a hinge of cultural history for American TV, movies, and music. All in his new book *Rock Me on the Water*."
—Major Garrett, CBS News chief Washington correspondent

"In his brilliant cultural history, *Rock Me on the Water*, Brownstein drops enough names to fill the once-massive Los Angeles phone book (remember those?), elicits memorable moments from several entertainment industries, and recalls political machinations across decades."
—*Los Angeles Review of Books*

ROCK ME ON THE WATER

1974

THE YEAR LOS ANGELES TRANSFORMED MOVIES, MUSIC, TELEVISION, AND POLITICS

HARPER

NEW YORK • LONDON • TORONTO • SYDNEY

ROCK ME ON THE WATER

RONALD BROWNSTEIN

For Eileen, my LA woman

HARPER

FIRST HARPER PAPERBACKS EDITION PUBLISHED 2022.

Designed by Leah Carlson-Stanisic

Frontispiece: Walt Disney Television via Getty Images Photo Archives/Walt Disney Television via Getty Images

Library of Congress Cataloging-in-Publication Data has been applied for.

ISBN 978-0-06-289922-4 (pbk.)

22 23 24 25 26 LSC 10 9 8 7 6 5 4 3 2 1

CONTENTS

On the evening of February 21, 1974, Mo Ostin led David Geffen to the Beverly Wilshire hotel in Beverly Hills for what Geffen was told would be a business meeting with Barbra Streisand.

Dignified and reserved, Ostin had been in the music business a long time. He had started as Frank Sinatra's accountant and then ascended to become the head of the Warner Bros. music operation after the studio acquired Reprise, Sinatra's record label, in 1963. Geffen, the president of Warner's Elektra/Asylum label, was Ostin's opposite in every way: young, endlessly ambitious, brilliant, relentless, and volcanic.

Behind the doors of the Beverly Wilshire's Le Grand Trianon ballroom, an array of stars waited for the two men. Bob Dylan was there with the Band; as were Cher, Ringo Starr, Harry Nilsson, Warren Beatty, Jack Nicholson, and Bianca Jagger. So were record moguls (the elegant Ahmet Ertegun of Atlantic Records, a Geffen mentor who had flown out from New York City; Joe Smith of Warner Bros.; rival Artie Mogull of MCA), agents (Jeff Wald), and producers (Bill Graham, who had worked with Geffen that winter to mount a hugely successful reunion tour for Dylan and the Band).

Balloons and streamers hung from the ceiling, and in a carnival theme, a fire-eater, knife thrower, cyclist, fortune-teller, and two mimes were scattered through the room. Only a few years earlier, Geffen had been laboring in the mail room at the William Morris Agency, arriving early every morning to intercept a letter from UCLA informing his employers that he had not, in fact, graduated from the school, as he had told them. Now the A-list celebrities who had patiently gathered in the posh ballroom measured how quickly Geffen, still only thirty-one, had scaled the entertainment industry's highest peaks. The point was underscored when Dylan, the Band, and Cher (improbably, Geffen's girlfriend at the time) serenaded the crowd with a twenty-minute mini-concert.[1] Bob Dylan didn't play many private parties.

It was a triumphant moment for Geffen, but the party could just as easily have been a celebration of the stars and moguls who mingled around him. They, too, stood at a pinnacle. Los Angeles in 1974 exerted more influence over popular culture than any other city in America. That year, in fact, the city dominated popular culture more than it ever had before, or would again. In movies, music, and television, the early 1970s marked a creative summit in LA that transformed each of those industries. The "New Wave" that revitalized Hollywood, the smooth Southern California sound that ruled the album charts and radio airwaves, the torrent of groundbreaking comedies that brought new sophistication and provocation to television's prime time—all these emerged from Los Angeles. Working just blocks from one another in film, recording, and television studios around Sunset Boulevard, living in Brentwood and Beverly Hills or amid the flickering lights of the Hollywood Hills, a cluster of transformative talents produced a sustained burst of pop culture mastery and innovation. "There was a tremendous feeling of anything [is possible]," musician Graham Nash remembered. "What do you want to think of? We can do anything. What do you want? What do you want to do? Where do you want to go? What do you want to play? What album do you want to make? There was no end to [it]. We were in this pool of, like, magic stuff, and it was rubbing off on everybody."[2] Linda Ronstadt, a few years behind Nash in the climb to stardom, felt the same way: "LA was a lens that American culture was focused through in those days," she recalled, "like Berlin before World War Two."[3]

Those producing some of their career's greatest work in Los Angeles at this time included Robert Altman, Warren Beatty, Peter Bogdanovich, Francis Ford Coppola, George Lucas, Jack Nicholson, Gordon Parks, Arthur Penn, Roman Polanski, Martin Scorsese, Steven Spielberg, and Robert Towne in film; Crosby, Stills, Nash and Young, Jackson Browne, the Eagles, Carole King, Joni Mitchell, Linda Ronstadt, James Taylor, and Bill Withers in music; and Alan Alda, James L. Brooks, Allan Burns, Larry Gelbart, Norman Lear, Mary Tyler Moore, Carroll O'Connor, Rob Reiner, and Gene Reynolds in television. Behind them were legendary executives, agents, and managers, including Lou Adler, Clarence Avant, David Geffen, Berry Gordy, and Mo Ostin in the music industry; and in film and television, Barry Diller and Michael Eisner (first at ABC and then at Paramount), Robert Evans (of Paramount), and Robert Wood (of CBS). "I don't know what was in the air or in the water, but everything from Malibu to Hollywood was magical," said Irving Azoff, who rode the Southern California wave to fame and riches as the combative manager of the Eagles. "The restaurants were magical, the clubs were magical, the people."[4] It was an "extraordinarily creative period," remembered Michael Ovitz, a Los Angeles native who became the entertainment industry's most powerful agent during the 1980s. "The birth of phenomenal music artists, the birthing of Spielberg and of Lucas and Coppola and Scorsese—all these filmmakers came out of nowhere."[5] Danny Kortchmar, a prominent rock session guitarist and collaborator with Carole King and Don Henley, summarized it more succinctly when he recalled of Los Angeles at that time that "You couldn't throw a rock without hitting a genius."[6]

Los Angeles has had other great periods in film (the years around World War II), television (the "golden age" of the 1950s and the peak TV era that has gathered momentum through the twenty-first century), and music (the hip-hop revolution of the later 1980s and '90s). Yet, the early 1970s was the moment when all three of these industries simultaneously reached a creative peak—and 1974 stood as the absolute pinnacle of this cultural renaissance. For Los Angeles, those twelve glittering months represented magic hour.

In film, 1974 saw the release of *Chinatown, The Godfather Part II, The Conversation*, and the great Vietnam documentary *Hearts and Minds*; the filming of *Nashville, Jaws*, and *Shampoo*; and the completion of the first-draft screenplay for a space adventure called *Star Wars*. In television, the year brought together the transformative comedies *All in the Family, M*A*S*H*, and *Mary Tyler Moore* (along with the *Bob Newhart* and *Carol Burnett* shows) on a CBS Saturday schedule that has been called the greatest night in television history. That year, Joni

Mitchell, the Eagles, Jackson Browne, and Linda Ronstadt all issued career-redefining albums on Geffen's label, and Bob Dylan and the Band and Crosby, Stills, Nash and Young mounted record-setting concert tours with him. A fresh breeze blew through even the state's politics that year, when California elected Edmund Gerald "Jerry" Brown Jr. as its youngest governor in decades.

The great art produced in early 1970s Los Angeles was socially engaged, grappling with all the changes and critiques of American life that had rumbled through society during the 1960s: greater suspicion of authority in business and government, more assertive roles for women, more tolerance of premarital sex, greater acceptance of racial and sexual minorities. All these are now dominant (if still not uniform) attitudes in America, but they were not widely accepted before they were infused into the movies, television, and music emerging in this period in Los Angeles. Popular culture became the bridge between the mass American audience and once-insurrectionary ideas that developed on the vanguard of the social and political movements of the 1960s. That bridge has proven unshakeable over the past half century. Even at their moments of maximum electoral influence (the presidencies of Ronald Reagan and George W. Bush and the first years of Donald Trump's turbulent reign), conservatives often lament that they have won the political battle but lost the culture. In the struggle for control of popular culture, Los Angeles during the early 1970s was the right's Gettysburg or Battle of the Bulge: the moment when it definitively lost the war.

Very few would have predicted this outcome just a few years earlier. Even into the late 1960s, none of the entertainment industries reflected the social changes coursing around them. Hollywood, at a low ebb financially and artistically, was dominated by bloated historical epics and musicals; television, operating under the theory of what one top executive labeled the "least objectionable program," narcotized American households with a deadening array of rural comedies; and while rock music ruled the AM airwaves, the record labels had not yet accepted the idea of the album as a coherent artistic and social statement. Within a few years, all this had changed, and the artists based in Los Angeles functioned as the fulcrum of the shift. By the early 1970s, the music, movies, and television emanating from Los Angeles all reflected the demographic, social, and cultural realities of a changing America much more than the nation's politics did. At a time when Richard Nixon won two presidential elections with a message of backlash against the social changes unleashed by the sixties, popular culture was ahead of politics in predicting what America would become.

Though the city was not yet the liberal *political* bastion it would grow into, Los Angeles emerged as the capital of *cultural* opposition to Nixon. The critique of contemporary America that had been stymied in politics by Nixon's victories in 1968 and 1972 was channeled into an outpouring of artistic creativity. In their works, the artists of Los Angeles offered an alternative to the martial and material consensus of Nixon's America. Films portrayed America as suffused with hypocrisy (*Shampoo, Nashville*) and built on corruption (*Chinatown, Godfather II*); television shows (led by *All in the Family, M*A*S*H*, and *Mary Tyler Moore*) brought tensions over the Vietnam War, the "generation gap," race relations, and the sexual revolution into the nation's living rooms; and classic albums from artists such as James Taylor, Carole King, Joni Mitchell, Jackson Browne, and the Eagles, while less outwardly political than their film and television counterparts, chronicled the search for new markers of meaning in life beyond the yardsticks of suburban success that listeners had been raised on—what Mitchell, in her anthem "Woodstock," had called a way "back to the garden." Frustration over the Vietnam War, disgust at the systemic corruption of Watergate, and alienation from the constricting values of Nixon's heralded "silent majority" infused all these works like fog rolling in from the Pacific.

Across the movie, music, and television industries alike, this cultural shift rested on the same economic foundation: the rising buying power of the Baby Boom, the masses born in the period ranging from 1946 through 1964. In 1955, about 31 percent of all Americans were between ages five and twenty-five. By 1970, that proportion had grown to nearly 38 percent. Including everyone younger than twenty-five raised the number of young people in 1970 to nearly half the entire population.[7] In raw numbers, there were nearly twenty-five million more Americans younger than twenty-five in 1970 than there had been in 1955.[8] Nixon's victories had squashed the political emergence of this giant generation, but its economic force was felt as, in sequence, the music and movie industries (both starting around 1967) and the television networks (following more fitfully around 1971) reconfigured themselves to meet Boomers' cultural preferences.

Under the inescapable smog that still blanketed the city, Los Angeles in the early 1970s was poised between its parochial past and its global future. The city was not yet the cosmopolitan metropolis it would become. LA's social elite mingled at a small collection of A-list restaurants: the Bistro, Trader Vic's, La Scala, Dan Tana's, Chasen's. The music scene revolved around an equally modest roster of clubs: the Ash Grove, the Rainbow, the Whisky a Go Go, and above all, the Troubadour, just east of Beverly Hills, until its dominance was challenged by the Roxy, on Sunset Boulevard. Much of the city's social life revolved around parties in private homes, the Bel Air mansions of Hollywood producers or the funky Laurel Canyon bungalows of the rock elite. The social circuit covered only a small distance across the city's Westside. The beach was a distant wasteland, Santa Monica crowded with retirees, and Venice a dark and dangerous den of artists, junkies, and schizophrenics shouting in the street. Downtown Los Angeles was a ghost town. The big East Coast department stores had not even opened LA branches yet. The *Los Angeles Times* was just emerging from its insular, arch-conservative past to pursue its ambition of becoming a world-class newspaper. Control of City Hall finally shifted in 1973 from longtime mayor Sam Yorty, an erratic midwesterner who held power in his final years by overtly appealing to white anxiety about racial change, to African American Tom Bradley, a dignified and reserved former police officer who became the first Black mayor of a mostly white large city. The model and actress Anjelica Huston, who arrived just before Bradley's victory in the spring of 1973, wrote later that "Los Angeles was a small town then; it felt both incredibly glamorous and a little provincial."[9] Huston arrived from Manhattan, leaving a tumultuous relationship with a brilliant but erratic fashion photographer that had immersed her in the nocturnal Andy Warhol demimonde of the Lower East Side. Bright and sunny, healthful and relaxed, Los Angeles then seemed to her "the antithesis of New York," as she recalled. Unlike New York, "there were no rats in the trees, no smell of urine on Third Avenue." Huston rode horses through Griffith Park and planted wisteria, dahlias, and chrysanthemums behind her house on Beachwood Drive. "It was like a big garden to me," she remembered of LA in those years. "After those years in New York, it was like the land of milk and honey."*[10]

Huston's attitude toward LA's great rival was telling. New York's reflexive dismissal of Los Angeles as a vapid desert of silicone and sunburn always rankled some in Los Angeles. But LA in the early 1970s no longer sought validation from New York, which was spiraling into municipal bankruptcy and reeling under crime and urban decay. "I think the east was totally confounded by the west," Huston remembered. "LA could not have cared less. LA knew that it was having its moment in the sun."[11] Azoff's biggest client, the Eagles, engaged in a running feud with East Coast music critics, but the band always felt more resentment than anxiety about the skepticism it faced from those voices. Like LA's other great artists at the time, the Eagles knew they were part of something special. "My snobby East Coast New York friends . . . were trying to claim, 'We're the cultural center of the world,' and you had all this shit going on in Washington," said Azoff. "But it was here."[12]

This moment of cultural and political renaissance in Los Angeles was fragile and fleeting. From within, it was hollowed out by a raging drug culture that cut through the music and film communities like wildfire. An array of outside forces, consolidated around 1975, also

---

* Six years before Huston arrived, the Mamas and the Papas, in their seminal single "Twelve Thirty," had expressed similar emotions about the great transcontinental rivals when they sang, "I used to live in New York City / Everything there was dark and dirty," before bursting into their exuberant ode to life in Laurel Canyon: "Young girls are coming to the canyon."

truncated this moment of peak Los Angeles influence. The release of *Jaws* that year shifted Hollywood's focus from the auteur visions of the early 1970s to the summer blockbusters that revived (and, in their own way, eventually consumed) the studios. With the release of Bruce Springsteen's *Born to Run* and the rise of the punk rock movement, the center of musical energy in 1975 shifted back to New York (and from there, on to London). And the adoption by the television networks in early 1975 of "the family hour," under pressure from the first stirrings of the religious right, disrupted the edgy comedies that dominated the early 1970s and heralded the programming shift that would lead the blandly nostalgic *Happy Days* to supplant Lear's *All in the Family* as the top-rated show by 1976. Most of LA's signature artists continued to enjoy huge commercial success (in some cases, such as the Eagles and Linda Ronstadt, growing success) through the later 1970s, but they no longer drove the cultural conversation as they had earlier in the decade.

The passing of LA's cultural preeminence captured a much larger change in American life. The most memorable works of early 1970s Los Angeles—from *Chinatown* to *All in the Family* to Jackson Browne's great album *Late for the Sky*—emerged from the collision of sixties optimism with the mounting cynicism and pessimism of the seventies. They exposed the hypocrisy and inequity of modern American society, but almost all of them also clung to the hope that society could still change for the better. These works derived much of their energy from the friction between the harsh truths they laid bare and the gentle hope for a better world they nurtured, as if cradling a dying flame. But with each passing year, the hard realities of life in the 1970s—from long lines at the gas pumps to political scandals to defeat in Vietnam—made that hope harder to hold. Once the cultural balance tipped from optimism to resignation, around 1975, the LA renaissance flickered. When the last hopes that America might fundamentally transform after the 1960s faded, so, too, did LA's moment as the center of popular culture.

The early 1970s represented a confrontation between a massive younger generation intent on change and a political order controlled by older generations opposing such change. That struggle, between those who welcomed and resisted new attitudes and arrangements, has echoes today in the conflicting visions of a president who mobilizes a political coalition focused on restoring a more racially and culturally homogenous America and the huge Millennial generation (and Generation Z, emerging just behind it), who celebrate America's transformation into a kaleidoscope nation of ever-multiplying racial, ethnic, and social diversity. Just like the sixties generation, the Millennials and their younger siblings have changed the culture more quickly than they have changed politics. But America's diverse emerging generations will inevitably stamp their priorities on the nation's politics as well, even if those priorities evolve over time. Today, the Millennials and Generation Z, the two big cohorts of Americans born after 1981, represent a larger share of the total American population than the Baby Boomers did even at their peak.[13] The huge spasm of youth-driven protests for greater racial justice that erupted nationwide following the murder of George Floyd in the spring of 2020, the largest sustained wave of public protest since the 1960s, may only hint at how thoroughly these younger generations will change the terms of discussion in American life through the decades ahead.[14] One clear lesson from American history is that while the voices resistant to change may win delaying battles in politics, they cannot indefinitely hold back the future.

Perhaps the best way to understand this lesson is to explore the last time the culture was demonstrably ahead of politics in predicting what America would become. When I interviewed Jackson Browne for this book, I asked him to identify the most creative period in Los Angeles music he had experienced. Without hesitation, he answered, "Last night."[15] There's truth to this: the city's capacity to inspire invention and innovation remains undiminished. But this capacity coalesced across all the arenas of popular culture to the greatest effect in the early 1970s, and particularly in the twelve months of 1974, when Los Angeles reached the zenith of its cultural influence. In the next twelve chapters, this book follows movies, music, television, and politics in Los Angeles month by month through that transformative year. The story begins in January, when the creative lives of three longtime friends who had climbed by very different routes to the peak of the movie business converged with spectacular results.

1

JANUARY

Hollywood's Fall and Rise

Jack Nicholson and Warren Beatty did not know each other well during the 1960s. By some accounts, they did not meet until the fall of 1970, at a joint party for the casts of the movies *Carnal Knowledge* (which starred Nicholson) and *McCabe and Mrs. Miller* (which Beatty headlined), both of which were filming around Vancouver.[1] But Beatty remembers meeting Nicholson at least once before that, over dinner with Paramount executive Robert Evans at the celebrated old-school Hollywood restaurant Musso and Frank.

Once Nicholson and Beatty did meet, they bonded quickly. Beatty recalls that he "was quite knocked out by Jack" in his breakthrough role as a southern lawyer in *Easy Rider* in 1969. "I didn't know Jack very well," Beatty recalled, "but I remember I liked him."[2] Nicholson, self-conscious about his frail physique and receding hairline, was even more impressed with Beatty. "Now *that's* what a movie star is supposed to look like," he told one friend.[3] Nicholson, who assigned nicknames to almost everyone he met, reverently called Beatty "the Pro," in deference not only to his acting skills but also to his success with women.*

But during the 1960s, Nicholson and Beatty occupied opposite poles of the Hollywood hierarchy and had little reason to cross paths.

---

* Once the two became friendly, Beatty would sometimes call Nicholson "Semi-pro," in a gentle gibe at the earlier contrast in their stature.

Though Beatty was born only three weeks before Nicholson in 1937, their careers had unfolded along very different timetables. Beatty became a star with the release of his first movie, *Splendor in the Grass*, in 1961. Nicholson, who had arrived in Hollywood years earlier, didn't attract much notice until *Easy Rider*, and even that was in a supporting part; his first starring roles didn't come until *Five Easy Pieces*, in the fall of 1970, and *Carnal Knowledge*, in summer 1971.

Though Beatty was much more established when he began his friendship with Nicholson, the two interacted as equals from the start. And there was surprisingly little rivalry between them, despite their sometimes being considered for the same parts. (Robert Evans, who revered both men, tried at least fleetingly to recruit each of them to play the title role in *The Great Gatsby* and Michael Corleone in *The Godfather*.)[4] Anjelica Huston, the radiant young model and actress who began a long-term romance with Nicholson soon after she moved to Los Angeles in 1973, thought that rather than feeling competitive, the two men "sort of enjoyed" each other's success. "They enjoyed their differences, I think," she recalled. "And they both had enough to share. It's not like Jack's phone wasn't ringing, and I'm sure Warren's was."[5]

It helped that the two men gravitated toward very different sorts of roles. Beatty often gave his characters feet of clay, but they were still romantic leading men parts: even his outlaw Clyde Barrow, in *Bonnie and Clyde*, though apparently impotent, was glamorous. Whereas Nicholson initially played earthy, disillusioned antiheroes: George Hanson, the dissolute lawyer in *Easy Rider*; Bobby Dupea, the rootless piano prodigy drifting through blue-collar jobs and indifferent romances in *Five Easy Pieces*; Jonathan, the bitter womanizer in *Carnal Knowledge*. To many in Hollywood at the time, Nicholson, though the same age as Beatty, seemed to belong to a younger generation, both in the parts he chose and the uninhibited way he portrayed them. "Jack was always hipper than Warren, and everyone knew that. He just was," Huston said. "Warren was much more a product of the old school, and I think if you watch *Splendor in the Grass* and you watch the way Warren acts, it's a slightly different thing. I think Jack was on the attack, and the thing about Jack's appearance in *Easy Rider* is that he looks like he walked out of life [and] onto the screen, and Warren was never that. Warren was always a 'Movie Star.' Jack did something in *Easy Rider* that was like shorthand, it was like emotional shorthand, and so you fell in love with this guy, and he died over the course of the movie, and you're devastated because you'd lost a friend. He had that effect. I don't know that Warren ever has had that effect. He has this effect of 'Oh my God, you are handsome,' but not 'Oh my God, you'd broken my heart.'"[6]

In some ways, the two were unlikely friends. Nicholson was gregarious, sociable, happiest in a crowd; he was often surrounded by a motley pack of old friends and acquaintances he had met during his long climb in Hollywood. ("They were a band of brothers," said Huston, who was thrust, not always comfortably, into the camaraderie when she began her relationship with Nicholson. "All of these people kind of hung out at Jack's house, came over, smoke a joint, talk about whatever was going on in the day, hang out by the pool. They did a tremendous amount of . . . sports watching. It was a pleasant, laid-back atmosphere.") Beatty was veiled, reticent, best known to many of his friends as a disembodied late-night voice on the phone. Nicholson, especially during the 1960s, experimented with virtually every drug available; Beatty, always reluctant to lose control, avoided drugs and even alcohol. Nicholson was prone to regaling his friends with extended riffs on any subject imaginable. "He was a bright guy who's kind of an autodidact, and he had gotten into everything in the world that interested him with a passion," said novelist and screenwriter Jeremy Larner, a longtime friend. "He was a guy who had five-year plans and ten-year plans. He was serious, and he would lecture on many subjects."[7] Beatty had plenty of opinions, too, but he didn't dispense them as casually; he was most likely to answer a question with a question. "You don't have a conversation with Warren; he asks *you* questions," said Howard "Hawk" Koch Jr., a producer and assistant director who worked with Beatty on *The Parallax View* and *Heaven Can Wait*. "When you ask him a question, he doesn't answer."[8]

On set, Nicholson took direction easily, and he generally avoided challenging the director or demanding script changes; Beatty, painstaking and terminally ambivalent, frequently insisted on unending takes of a scene, and he routinely argued about every possible artistic choice. "You'd go up to his penthouse at the Beverly Wilshire two to three hours a day and go through a whole argument," recalled writer and director Paul Schrader. "You'd go back the next day and start at zero until, finally, you realized we will have the same argument over and over until he wins, and that's when I realized why he was such a successful lothario. [He had] the infinite patience of the pursuer."⁹ Costume designer Anthea Sylbert had an up-close look at both men in the early 1970s. She found Nicholson "the easiest man to dress— not from the way he's built—but he's extremely open and free about trying anything." Beatty was more complicated. Everything looked great on him, she noted, but it usually took more conversation to get to that point. "Socially, he's one of those people with a very short attention span," Sylbert said. "But in a working situation, he's relentless. Always asking questions about why you're doing what you're doing, whether you really think it's right. He plays the devil's advocate. He wants to know everything there is to know."¹⁰ Still, Beatty and Nicholson had some common traits. Both had a genuine reverence for film history. They shared similarly liberal politics (though Nicholson never engaged with candidates, causes, or campaigns nearly as deeply as Beatty). And both believed that sexual inhibition was strangling American society. (One of the subjects on which Nicholson liked to lecture at length was the theories of Wilhelm Reich, an Austrian psychoanalyst who preached sexual freedom as the key to both personal happiness and social stability.) In practice, this translated into a shared interest in chasing women in prodigious numbers. When Anjelica Huston lived with Nicholson, she would often overhear his conversations with Beatty, especially in the months before the two men worked on their first film together, *The Fortune*, in the summer of 1974. "Jack and he became ever closer, and around the time of *The Fortune*, they were very, very tight," she remembered. "So tight that when I would walk into the living room . . . Jack's voice would drop and/or the tone would get more hushed until I would go upstairs or whatever. They were like schoolgirls together. There wasn't much one could say about it."[11] Sometimes Nicholson and Beatty romanced the same women. Michelle Phillips, the radiant wild child from the defunct Mamas and Papas, began a serious relationship with Beatty in the summer of 1974, about a year after she ended her long-term romance with Nicholson; Beatty, a little earlier, had carried on an intermittent romance with the brilliant singer Joni Mitchell—"I did have a very nice relationship with Joni that lasted on and off, mostly off, sometimes on, for about a year and a half," he says decorously, adding, "I was somewhat in awe of her talent"—who may have had an earlier turn with Nicholson.* (For her part, Mitchell always denied an affair with either man.)[12] Carly Simon reported brief assignations with both men, her time with Beatty immortalized in at least part of the lyrics for her smash hit "You're So Vain."[13] For a period in the early 1970s, flings with Nicholson and Beatty seemed almost as much a rite of passage for rising female celebrities as a profile in *Rolling Stone* or a Christmas vacation in Aspen.

The friendship between Nicholson and Beatty was also reinforced, like a three-legged stool, by the presence of screenwriter Robert Towne. Towne was one of Nicholson's oldest friends in Hollywood. The two had met in the mid-1950s, when they were still in their teens, in a celebrated acting class taught by the blacklisted actor Jeff Corey. Towne was working in a bank, and Nicholson as a messenger for the animation division at MGM, but Towne was convinced they were both going places. "Jack and I became best friends, and when I first saw him act or work in Jeff's class, I came up to him and said, 'Jocko,' which we called him at that time, 'you're going to be a big movie star, and I'm going to write for you.' And he said, 'Yeah?' And I said, 'Yeah.' Then we eventually became roommates and friends."[14]

---

* "He had probably been a lover of Joni Mitchell," remembered Huston. "Like when we were first in New York together, we went to a Carole King concert in the [Central] Park [in May 1973], and Joni sat with us, and I was overwhelmed with jealousy. But in the retelling, how fabulous."

Over the years, as they slowly climbed into Hollywood prominence, the two remained exceptionally close. Huston remembers spending the night with Nicholson for the first time in April 1973, at his house on Mulholland Drive. The next morning, when she came down the stairs after slipping back into her slinky long dress from the previous night, she found Towne, who had arrived for an outing to a ball game with Nicholson, already in the living room looking up "appraisingly" at her. "There I was in my evening dress, long, borrowed from my stepmother from the night before," Huston remembered. "I never felt more naked in my life." Nicholson boorishly called a taxi to take her home and disappeared with Towne.[15]

Towne met Beatty much later, in the mid-1960s, at the office of the pioneering psychoanalyst whom both men used, Dr. Martin Grotjahn. Beatty read some of Towne's work and liked it and brought him in to rewrite dialogue and rearrange scenes just before production began on *Bonnie and Clyde*; Towne even followed the production to Texas in the fall of 1966, for on-set repairs.[16] The relationship between the three men was not entirely parallel. Many thought Towne treated Nicholson as a peer and looked up to Beatty. Still, Towne fought with Beatty much more, over both art and money, than he ever did with Nicholson. "Towne said that if he worked with Beatty, [Warren] was never satisfied. He would do a lot of rewriting and reediting and so on," said Larner.[17] Looking back, Towne is slightly more diplomatic: Nicholson tended to defer to writers, he recalled, but "Warren has an opinion about everything."[18]

IN JANUARY 1974, THE creative lives of these three men converged more directly than ever before. The result was two landmarks in Hollywood's early 1970s renaissance. *Chinatown*, a movie Towne had written specifically with Nicholson in mind as the lead, was nearing the completion of its filming under the autocratic direction of Roman Polanski, who had returned to Los Angeles for the first time since the murder of his wife, Sharon Tate, in 1969. At the same time, preparations for the filming of *Shampoo*, which Towne and Beatty had written for Beatty to star in, were accelerating from Beatty's suite at the Beverly Wilshire hotel.

Both projects had gestated for years. The germ of *Chinatown* had first flickered in Towne almost exactly four years earlier. He was in bed for several weeks with vertigo—friends considered Towne that rare hypochondriac who was often actually sick—when he read an article in the *Los Angeles Times' West* magazine from mid-December 1969 entitled "Raymond Chandler's L.A." The article lovingly recounted how much of the landscape that Chandler described in his classic 1940s novels about detective Philip Marlowe remained intact in Los Angeles a quarter century later. ("The best time to see Raymond Chandler's Los Angeles is when the shadows and the light allow you to see the city that was, to travel what he said were the 'mean streets' and know a little of the possibility of terror on each one.") More important, the story proved the point with photos of stately homes in Pasadena and restaurants in Hollywood that still matched Chandler's evocative descriptions.[19] Lying in his bed, the room slightly spinning, Towne suddenly realized that it would be possible to film a detective movie set in the Los Angeles of the 1930s on location around the city. "It was sort of hangovers from the thirties, and I looked at them, and I thought, Holy shit, man. You could do a movie about LA, and there are places to shoot that, with judicious filming, would be exactly what LA was like in the thirties," he remembered. "So, I thought, I'm going to do a movie about LA."[20]

Shampoo had an even longer and, appropriately enough, more tangled history. Beatty and Towne had talked about the movie for nearly a decade, having first formulated the idea even before Beatty brought in Towne for *Bonnie and Clyde*. In January 1974, to Towne's astonishment, both projects were rapidly advancing. *Chinatown* shot its final scene late in the month, bringing the cast and crew, for the first time, to LA's actual Chinatown neighborhood to film the movie's grim finale. Meanwhile, during a break in the filming of *Chinatown* over Christmas 1973, Towne, Beatty, and Hal Ashby, whom Beatty had hired as director, hammered out the final script for *Shampoo* in ten days of concentrated work at Beatty's residence in the Beverly Wilshire hotel.[21] Some of the key members of the *Chinatown* crew—notably production designer Richard Sylbert and costume designer Anthea Sylbert (who was married to Richard's twin brother, Paul)—were preparing to shift to *Shampoo* as soon as work on *Chinatown* concluded.

Shampoo was seemingly as airy and sunny as *Chinatown* was labyrinthine and dark. In Towne's screenplay for *Chinatown*, Nicholson's J. J. Gittes is hired by a mysterious woman (Faye Dunaway as Evelyn Mulwray), ostensibly to determine if her husband is cheating on her. Nicholson, in classic film noir fashion, stumbles onto much more than he expected as he discovers that Evelyn's father, Noah Cross (played by director John Huston, the father of Nicholson's real-life girlfriend Anjelica), has both engineered a massive plot to control the city's water and fathered a child with his own daughter. Polanski, in long, contentious rewriting sessions with Towne, revised the script to make it even darker.

Shampoo was a sex comedy, starring Beatty as a Beverly Hills hairdresser sleeping his way through his clientele. And yet, beneath its glamorous surface, it shared a perspective with the noir classic that Towne and Polanski had fashioned. Both movies used an earlier time in Los Angeles to dramatize the corruption and decay that so many in Hollywood believed was consuming America in the Nixon era.

After years of frustration, Towne could see his work blossoming all around him as 1974 began. "I was thirty-nine: It was great," he recalled. "I remember talking to my mom about it and saying I never thought that I would reach the age of forty and feel that I had it made, because it didn't look a year ago like there was a snowball's chance in hell these movies would get made."[22]

It wasn't only Towne who felt his fortunes brightening. Many writers, actors, and directors through the early 1970s found the studio constraints loosening, on subjects, language, style. "It was very exciting," said Towne. "We could do whatever you could think, and that was just unique." No other generation of filmmakers had been granted such freedom. "We were the first," he said.[23] This creative burst awakened Hollywood from the slumber that had numbed it to almost all the social and political tumult of the 1960s. "You could get away with more, and it was more entertaining, and everybody, older, younger, said, 'Hey, this is more fun,'" Beatty remembered.[24]

In January 1974, Beatty, Nicholson, and Towne all stood at the pinnacle of the New Hollywood that had emerged from these seismic changes. But they had followed contrasting paths to that peak. In the process, they experienced all the changes that tumbled Hollywood into cultural irrelevance during the 1960s and then rejuvenated it only a few years later with a burst of concentrated creativity unmatched since the film industry's golden age, around World War II.

JACK NICHOLSON WASN'T PLANNING a career in show business when he arrived in Los Angeles in September 1954 to live with the woman he believed was his older sister, June.*[25] Born in April 1937, Nicholson had spent his early years in small towns along the New Jersey Shore. After graduating from high school, he moved out to Los Angeles and soon got a job as a mail runner for the animation department at MGM. During Hollywood's first golden age, in the 1930s and '40s, MGM, under the imperious Louis B. Mayer, had been the first among equals, boasting "more stars than there are in heaven." It was known both for prestigious dramas (*Mrs. Miniver, Madame Curie*) and extravagant musicals (from *The Wizard of Oz* to *An American in Paris* and *Singin' in the Rain*), but as with all the studios, by the 1950s its horizons had contracted. With fewer movies in production, large sections of the massive lot were often empty. As Nicholson made his daily rounds delivering mail or fetching lunch, he saw more evidence of past glory than modern dynamism.

Yet, within months, he had seen enough to decide that acting was his future. He joined a small theater group in Hollywood and scratched out some bit television parts on *Matinee Theater* and *Divorce Court*,

---

* In a baroque twist, Nicholson learned in 1974 that June was in fact his mother, who had given birth to him out of wedlock. Ethel May Nicholson, who raised Jack as his mother, was in fact his grandmother. Lorraine, whom he believed was his sister, was in fact his aunt.

two low-budget shows with production schedules that resembled track meets.[26] This pace proved good training for Nicholson's next decade at the margins of the film industry. He recognized he needed help climbing from those first low rungs on the ladder, and at the recommendation of friends in his theater group, he won a place in the coveted acting class taught by Jeff Corey. There he met Robert Towne.

Literary and thoughtful, Towne initially envisioned a career as a journalist, but then, as an undergraduate at Pomona College, he read a collection of classic movie reviews from *Time* and *The Nation* by James Agee, the novelist, journalist, and screenwriter. "I vividly remember reading one of his reviews—which were great, as you know—which said, 'I've often been bored by a bad play, but I've never been bored by a bad movie,'" Towne recalled. "It changed [everything] for me. At that time, it was true, because B movies were very energetic and a lot of fun; even if they weren't terribly good, they were never boring. And so, I thought, What the hell. I love movies, and this guy can certainly write—and he does, too—I'm going to be a screenwriter. And I made up my mind then that that's what I'm going to do."[27]

After college, Towne found jobs in a bank and, later, selling houses. But Corey's class allowed him to nurture his artistic aspirations. Even then, Towne believed his future was as a writer, not an actor, but he found the exercises in Corey's class helped him understand "what made for effective writing."[28] And the class created a constellation of friends who encouraged and consoled one another as they moved through the triumphs and setbacks of love and work in their early twenties. From the inner ring of contemporaries in Corey's class, such as Sally Kellerman, Carole Eastman (who would write *Five Easy Pieces* for Nicholson), and Dean Stockwell, the network expanded in concentric circles with friends of friends and acquaintances made during the intermittent moments of work on television or the sets of B movies. Fred Roos, a UCLA graduate and army veteran working unhappily as an agent at mighty MCA, joined the circle when he represented the actress wife of Nicholson's friend and sometime writing partner Don Devlin. Monte Hellman, a brainy and reserved director with a Stanford degree, became friendly with Nicholson during the filming of a low-budget Roger Corman (another Corey alumnus) movie. These friends, Nicholson said later, became a "surrogate family. . . . It's like we all grew up together."[29]

Living mostly in Hollywood, scratching for their first success, Nicholson and his friends spent their days on a circuit of coffee shops, jazz bars, acting classes, small theaters, art house films, auditions, and irregular moments of work in television or B movies. "Jack and Towne and Monte Hellman and Carole Eastman—we did everything together," Roos recalled.[30] During the days, they would compare prospects and wax philosophical at coffee shops like the Unicorn, Club Renaissance, and Chez Paulette; at night, they would gather at Barney's Beanery or play darts in a bar called the Raincheck Room.[31] They read Kerouac and Ginsburg and Sartre (or at least claimed they did), listened to Dylan, smoked pot and hash, and experimented with LSD. Nicholson threw parties that floated on gallons of cheap Gallo red wine and ended, he recalled, with newly minted couples rattling the headboard in every room in his house. "I guess you could call them orgies by the strictest definition," Nicholson said later.[32] Above all, they flocked to art house theaters such as the Coronet on La Cienega Boulevard and the Beverly Canon Theatre in Beverly Hills, which played the latest missiles from the French and Italian New Wave. "You could see everything, and we did see everything," remembered Roos. "It kept us going." Hellman and a few friends even organized their own "New American Film Society," which twice a month screened hard-to-find foreign films and forgotten Hollywood gems.[33]

The one place that this young generation did not look to much for either inspiration or work was the major Hollywood studios, which they regarded as something like the pyramids, the decaying remnants of a collapsed civilization. The circle could talk "unendingly" about Truffaut, Fellini, and Godard and dissect the latest imports from Europe, but apart from a few heroes like Elia Kazan and Billy Wilder, "we would rip the studio stuff that was coming out," Roos remembered. "They would make movies they thought were for young people, but they were beach party movies," he continued. "But anything that was edgy or offbeat or avant-garde—there was no interest whatsoever."

Towne, trying to find his footing as a writer, recalls thinking that the studios in those years were producing "absolute shit." (In retrospect, he has softened his verdict on films such as *The Sound of Music*.) Accordingly, they spent little time trying to get noticed at the major studios. "You couldn't crack it," said Roos. "It was such that you didn't even try. You just knew it was a closed door, and it was."[34] *Ensign Pulver*, a loose sequel to the 1950s navy-themed hit *Mister Roberts*, was the only major studio film in which Nicholson won a part in these years. It quickly sank at the box office in 1964. Television provided steadier paychecks for Nicholson, who needed the work after his marriage to actress Sandra Knight in 1962 was followed by the birth of their daughter, Jennifer, in 1963. But Nicholson's trademark intensity, already apparent in these early years, wasn't easily contained on the small screen. Roos once arranged for Nicholson to work a few days on an Aaron Spelling show, *The Guns of Will Sonnett*. "In television they had never seen acting like Jack's," Roos remembers. "It was not television acting. [People said,] 'Who is this guy you brought in here?' I think they fired me from it."

To the extent that Nicholson and his friends found film work in the early 1960s, it was almost entirely in the low-budget B movies that subsisted at the Hollywood fringe. Producers like Roger Corman and Robert Lippert, at Twentieth Century Fox, "were open to the offbeat guy and for the wild, ready-to-conquer-the-world directors and writers," as Roos puts it. For many in Nicholson's generation, Corman became a critical source of work, if not a munificent one. The director didn't pay much, but he did offer responsibility to young people who couldn't wrangle a day pass at the major studios, including directors Francis Ford Coppola and Peter Bogdanovich. "He gave people a chance whom he thought had some talent, and he paid for it," Bogdanovich said. "He threw you in the water and said, 'Swim,' and if you didn't swim, that was it."[35]

Nicholson cycled through a procession of modest (often fleeting) roles for Corman, sometimes with dismal results (a stilted turn in Napoleonic garb during *The Terror*), sometimes more happily (a brief-but-energetic role as a masochistic dental patient in *The Little Shop of Horrors*). Both artistically and financially, these opportunities frustrated Nicholson as much as they encouraged him. But they were the best opportunities available to him in an era when, as Roos recalls, "the image of a young leading man was James Darren; it was not somebody who looked like Jack Nicholson."

For Nicholson and the cerebral Monte Hellman, the opportunity to produce something more substantial came when Roos shifted to a new role. After his stint as a mail room clerk and then an agent at MCA, he landed a job working for Robert Lippert, a cigar-chomping producer who made B movies that filled out the bottom of double bills for Fox. Roos convinced Lippert to green-light two action movies that he, Roos, would produce back to back in the Philippines. He picked Hellman to direct both of them and signed Nicholson to perform in them and to double as a screenwriter on *Flight to Fury*. When cast and crew arrived on set in the Philippines, they found the shooting conditions predictably spartan (and bug-infested), but Roos, Hellman, and Nicholson were all happy to be working at something they would leave their fingerprints on, even within the limitations of the budget and genre. Still, they were frustrated when Lippert shelved the second film they produced, *Back Door to Hell*, which Nicholson had structured more as a spoof than a conventional caper film.

The product was more polished, but the results not much more satisfying, when Hellman and Nicholson reached another deal with Corman—who, characteristically, convinced them to shoot two Westerns after they approached him with the idea for one. Once again, Hellman would direct, and Nicholson would perform in both while writing one of them, *Ride in the Whirlwind*. The duo hired Nicholson's old Corey classmate Carole Eastman to write the other, *The Shooting*. Filmed in Utah during the summer of 1965, the two movies were opaquer and more elliptical than typical Westerns, with philosophic musings outnumbering gunfights. Both films were evocative—in Hellman's direction, the vast landscapes towered over the protagonists as if mocking the futility of existence—but *The Shooting* in particular played more like an unfinished allegory than an actual story. The movie showed Nicholson's growth as an actor, and it provided the filmmakers a *succès d'estime* that acquired a cultlike following over the years. But once again, a movie Nicholson hoped would raise his profile instead disappeared almost without a trace.

In the years since Corey's class, Towne hadn't progressed much further. He had sold a few television scripts (episodes for *The Lloyd Bridges Show, The Outer Limits,* and *The Man from U.N.C.L.E.*), but other than some work for Corman, he could not point to any of his scripts on the big screen. Still, his and Nicholson's friends expected great things from both men. "Jack had this thing," said Roos. "He didn't look like any young movie star at that time, but I saw how he could take over the room just by walking in, the force of his personality and his style and his kind of irreverence. I knew that would transfer to film." And Towne, Roos thought, "was deeply intellectual, sophisticated, [had] incredible taste, and we knew what was in him to come." As Roos recognized, their problem hadn't changed much since their first days in Los Angeles: "Everybody," he said, "had to get their foot in the door."[36]

Gaining a foothold in Hollywood was never an issue for Warren Beatty, and yet he, too, found his frustration mounting through the decade. For Beatty, the early 1960s were vastly more comfortable and financially rewarding than for Nicholson or Towne, but they didn't yield much more work of consequence.

Born in Virginia to a Baptist family in March 1937, Beatty took an early interest in theater and film. After attending high school in the Washington, DC, suburb of Arlington, Virginia (where he starred in football), he spent just a year at Northwestern University before moving to New York City to try his luck as an actor. (His older sister, Shirley MacLaine, who performed under a variant of their mother's maiden name, had made the same journey a few years earlier.) Handsome, veiled, and amorphously alienated in a manner reminiscent of Montgomery Clift or James Dean, Beatty touched many of the familiar stations of the cross for aspiring serious actors in the late 1950s: classes with Stella Adler in New York and appearances on prestige television showcases (*Studio One, Playhouse 90*).

His breakthrough came in 1959, when he was noticed by playwright

William Inge, who had chronicled midcentury sexual and social angst in a succession of hit plays that also became hit movies through the mid-1950s, including *Picnic* (with William Holden and a young Kim Novak) and *Bus Stop* (with Marilyn Monroe). Inge, who was gay, was entranced by Beatty and recommended him to Elia Kazan for the lead in *Splendor in the Grass*, a screenplay Inge was writing. Kazan, a titanic figure in both New York theater and Hollywood film circles—he had directed Marlon Brando in *A Streetcar Named Desire* and *On the Waterfront* and James Dean in *East of Eden*—hesitated about Beatty, but he finally cast him as the male lead across from Natalie Wood.[37] *Splendor* was an over-spiced stew of alienation and repression with a great deal of earnest emoting and nebulous teenage dread, but it made Beatty a star, and the studio doors that were closed to Nicholson and Towne were flung open for Beatty.

He took full advantage. Beatty never considered himself a rebel; he didn't want to overthrow the studio system so much as master (or seduce) it. As with Inge and Kazan, he showed a precocious determination to court successful older men as mentors. After *Splendor's* success, those opportunities multiplied. "I was very fortunate, because my first picture was *Splendor in the Grass*, written by a great playwright, Bill Inge, and a great director, Kazan, and dealt with what I think is a uniquely American subject . . . the consequences of American sexual puritanism," Beatty remembered. "The picture was a hit, and so I was treated very nicely by people like Jack Warner and David Selznick and Sam Goldwyn, and these people who were very instrumental in the development of movies."[38]

Beatty befriended the old moguls whom Nicholson's circle tended to see as dead weight. "They were still hanging in there," Beatty said, "and I got to know that generation very well. I was completely interested in hearing how David Selznick's movies got made." He also courted veteran directors such as George Stevens (*Woman of the Year, Shane, Giant*), Fred Zinnemann (*High Noon, From Here to Eternity*), and William Wyler (*The Best Years of Our Lives, Ben-Hur*). "[Wyler] was a person I could call and say, 'What do you think about such-and-such?' and he'd say, 'They're full of baloney,'" Beatty remembered. "He would tell me of arguments that he had had with Sam Goldwyn, for instance, whom he loved. Sam Goldwyn would tell me the other side of the argument."[39] While Nicholson and his friends were talking for hours about the films of Godard, Truffaut, or Jean Renoir, Beatty was spending hours talking with the directors themselves, all of whom he met within years of becoming a star. "I was very lucky," he recalled. "I had access."[40]

For the decade's first half, Beatty lacked much competition for the role of Hollywood's bright young male star. Though actors such as Robert Redford, Dustin Hoffman, Nicholson, and Al Pacino were roughly the same age as Beatty, none of them broke through to stardom until later in the 1960s or, in Pacino's case, in the early 1970s. "Because of the success of *Splendor in the Grass* and my age, I had the field somewhat to myself until about sixty-six," Beatty said, "when other people my age started to come up. But [by then] I had been around for quite a while."

In one respect, Beatty took full advantage of this open field. Starting with a young Joan Collins and then moving on to Natalie Wood, Leslie Caron (who was married at the time), and Julie Christie, detouring tirelessly through starlets, models, dancers, and even hatcheck girls, he embarked upon a succession of romances, flings, and dalliances that became Hollywood legend. From his home in a penthouse suite at the Beverly Wilshire, which he cluttered with books, scripts, newspapers, and room service trays, he received a procession of beautiful women. He drove down Sunset Boulevard in his black Lincoln Continental, a shark inside a whale, and flirted with women in the next lane.[41]

But in terms of his film output, Beatty didn't have much to show for his years alone as Hollywood's Next Big Thing. After *Splendor*, he courted Tennessee Williams for the role of Paolo, an Italian gigolo in Williams's overheated novella *The Roman Spring of Mrs. Stone*. The movie sank quickly and earned Beatty the first in a succession of disdainful reviews from Bosley Crowther, the chief film critic of the *New York Times*. Four months later, he hit the pavement even harder with the release of the aptly titled *All Fall Down* in April 1962. The dismal response to *Roman Spring* and *All Fall Down* unnerved Beatty enough that he didn't work again for sixteen months, the first of many extended breaks throughout his movie career. But when he returned, his choices weren't any better. *Lilith*, in 1964, and *Mickey One*, in 1965, would make it four consecutive bombs he had headlined.

Mickey One was by far the most contemporary and ambitious of Beatty's movies through the mid-1960s and marked his first collaboration with director Arthur Penn. The film was energetic and stylish, and it had some ideas in its head, but it was also obscure, disjointed, and heavy-handed. Still in his twenties, Beatty buckled under the weight of playing its existential hero, appearing alternately stiff and overwrought. "I was somewhat unenthusiastic about the obliqueness of *Mickey One*," he recalls.[42]

Most critics sneered, and viewers once again shrugged. "In those days, you could open a movie in one theater, and the movie opened at the Little Carnegie in Manhattan," Beatty remembered. "So, I called the next day, and I said, 'How did we do?' The guy said, 'How did we do?' I said, 'How much money did it do?' He said, 'Well, thirteen dollars.' I said, 'Thirteen dollars?' I said, 'Is that good?'"[43]

From enigmatic existential angst, Beatty then retreated to the tepid waters of mid-sixties sex comedy. *Promise Her Anything*, filmed with real-life girlfriend Leslie Caron in London, had a more risqué frame (a Greenwich Village courtship between Caron's widow and Beatty's director of soft-core porn films), but the soul of a late 1950s powder puff romance. *Kaleidoscope*, which he filmed next in London, in early 1966, was another mess, a mangled pastiche of romance and adventure in which Beatty plays an international playboy and master gambler who is also somehow a cat burglar with world-class forgery skills. It flopped, too.

Beatty enjoyed his time with Caron in swinging mid-1960s London, but the creative energy around him only underscored how much his own career had stalled, now half a decade after his breakthrough in *Splendor*. Beatty rarely admits to doubt, and he claims he wasn't worried that his career was drifting. Looking back, he says, "I probably should have been worried," but the failures didn't rattle him at the time, he insists, "because people were offering me big commercial movies, and I was comfortable in turning them down." Others around him weren't entirely as sanguine. "He was always very deliberate, very careful," said Towne, who was getting to know Beatty after their meeting in the office of psychoanalyst Martin Grotjahn. "He knew that things had to change."[44]

THIS WAS THE STORY of Hollywood through the mid-1960s: the insider road taken by Beatty and the outsider path that Nicholson and Towne trudged along each led to a dead end. During these years, amid the rumbling changes shaking America, the film industry seemed nothing so much as exhausted. Though the blacklist that exiled some of the industry's brightest lights (along with plenty of didactic journeymen) had slowly receded in the late 1950s, Hollywood still recoiled from almost any kind of political controversy. The industry's Production Code, largely unchanged since its adoption in 1934, still severely limited portrayals of sex and anything that even hinted at what the code defined as immorality (from adultery to homosexuality); this left a huge opening for the hard, sexy, and propulsive imports from Italy and France that exhilarated Towne, Nicholson, Beatty, and cinema buffs in art houses around the country. In those years, Beatty noted, "If you wanted to see at any age a nude human being" in a movie, "you better go and look at an Italian movie or a French movie."[45]

Like an elderly neighbor drawing the blinds against a shout in the street, Hollywood looked away from the drama unfolding around it. It responded to the sexual revolution with the cotton candy, Doris Day–style comedies that had already seemed flaccid when Dwight Eisenhower was president. While protesters were marching for civil rights and chanting against the war, students were clashing with police on university quads, and cities were burning with riots, Hollywood stubbornly looked backward for inspiration. Well into the mid-1960s, it released a steady procession of World War II movies, Westerns, musicals, and above all, gargantuan historical epics. Films in those categories dominated the list of top-grossing movies through the early 1960s, including *How the West Was Won*, *Lawrence of Arabia*, and *The*

Longest Day (about D-day) in 1962; *Cleopatra* in 1963; *Mary Poppins* and *My Fair Lady* in 1964; *The Sound of Music* and *Doctor Zhivago* in 1965; and *The Bible* in 1966. Almost the sole concession to changing attitudes from the studios in those years that found a big audience was the icy violence and cool sexuality of Sean Connery's James Bond movies.

The weakness for the epic was a remnant of *The Ten Commandments*–era conviction that Hollywood's best weapon against television was grand vistas on giant screens. Twentieth Century Fox started the rush in 1953, when it released *The Robe* in the new widescreen technology of CinemaScope.[46] Though critics panned the movie, an early gust in the decade's sandstorm of sword-and-sandal biblical epics, audiences flocked to the big new screens. The other studios rushed to develop their own larger-than-life projection systems: VistaVision, Paravision, Vanascope, Vistarama, Glamorama, and assorted attempts at 3-D moviemaking.[47] "People didn't know quite what to do," Towne recalled. "Television had knocked out the commercial effectiveness of movies, and that gave rise to VistaVision, CinemaScope, every imaginable thing, and some big movies that were spectacles."[48]

This tendency toward the grandiose produced a few great movies, such as *Lawrence of Arabia* and *Doctor Zhivago* (both from David Lean), but mostly it yielded bloated, windy, and expensive potboilers that strained the patience of audiences and studio accountants alike. Even success bred failure. After Hollywood released the three beloved and highly successful musicals that topped the box office in 1964 and 1965, *Mary Poppins*, *My Fair Lady*, and *The Sound of Music*, the studio lots from Culver City to Burbank hummed for years with song-and-dance numbers. Yet the elephantine products that emerged from this assembly line (*Doctor Doolittle*; *Mame*; *Hello, Dolly!*; *Camelot*) could hardly have sounded more off-key in the world of *Pet Sounds*, *Sgt. Pepper's Lonely Hearts Club Band*, and *Blonde on Blonde*. A handful of films through the early 1960s captured the exciting new rhythms and disorienting tensions of American life: Billy Wilder's *The Apartment*, in 1960; John Frankenheimer's *The Manchurian Candidate*, in 1962; and Stanley Kubrick's *Dr. Strangelove*, in 1964. Still, through the decade's first years, Hollywood more than justified the acid verdict that Dustin Hoffman later applied to it: "New York was Arthur Miller. Hollywood was *Bonanza*."[49]

The corner office looked every bit as tired as the sound stage. Death and decline finally loosened the grip of the old moguls who had ruled Hollywood since its inception. "I remember walking into Warner's as a young agent . . . and nobody was around," recalled Michael Medavoy, later a top production executive at United Artists and Orion. "You could have fucking dropped a bomb at Warner Bros. I walked around looking in offices and seeing who's there. The guy who was there was a guy named Mervyn LeRoy, who had done a bunch of movies in the thirties and forties. But other than that, you didn't meet anybody. It was like an empty lot."[50] Barry Diller, then a young ABC executive leading the network's negotiations to acquire Hollywood films to show on air, had an upfront view of how far the studios had fallen in those years. Even as august a presence as Arthur Krim, the dignified head of United Artists and confidant of John F. Kennedy and Lyndon Johnson, needed Diller's cash to keep his books in the black. "Because the movie companies were doing so badly, I was their money juice," Diller recalled. "I was the difference between whether they would report a good or a bad year." In his overheated office with his three-piece suit, Krim would ask Diller to structure the contracts so that the movies were technically available months before ABC actually planned to show them, so he could legally report the income from the sale and show better results to UA's parent company Transamerica Corporation. "We would do things where I would agree not to air the film but to make it *technically* available . . . so he could report the income," Diller says. "Literally every four to six months, Arthur would call me and say, 'I need you to do this,' and I would say, 'Of course,' and then I got all the UA movies [for broadcast on ABC]."[51]

The weekly box office numbers measured the industry's decline. From 1950 through 1960, weekly admissions in movie theaters fell by more than half, from just over 3 million to slightly more than 1.3 million. With only occasional interruptions, the weekly admission numbers continued to sink through the 1960s, dropping to just 927,000 in 1967. Higher ticket prices cushioned the blow but could not entirely offset the public's declining interest: box office receipts in 1967 were lower than in 1956. Admissions would dwindle even further at points over the next several years and would not cross the million-per-week mark again until 1974.[52]

But even as the studios staggered, 1967 marked the turning point in the industry's fortunes, not only financially but also artistically. And a critical lever in the turn was Beatty's determination to achieve more control over his drifting career.

CONTROL HAD ALWAYS BEEN important to Warren Beatty. He quickly acquired a reputation for wrestling with directors over every aspect of his films, but even that amounted to shifting a brush stroke on someone else's canvas. When his friend Charles Feldman offered him the chance to co-produce and star in a new film, Beatty pounced. The movie, called *What's New Pussycat* after one of Beatty's signature seduction lines, was intended as a comic look at what he called "the hypersexual male. I wanted to show that hypersexuality was not necessarily a symptom of latent homosexuality, and I thought that could be funny."[53] To rewrite the script, he enlisted a young comic he had seen in New York named Woody Allen. Beatty's position in the project deteriorated from there. Allen's revisions of the script steadily increased his role and diminished Beatty's. Then Beatty objected when Feldman insisted on casting his latest girlfriend in the film. "I thought, I'll walk off the movie, and they can't afford to do it without me, and I learned within a few days that I was wrong," Beatty said. Feldman replaced Beatty with Peter O'Toole, then at his post–*Lawrence of Arabia* peak, and added Peter Sellers to the cast for good measure. "They didn't need me," Beatty said. "He had Peter Sellers, who was, at that time, you'd have to say, the biggest movie star in the world, and also Peter O'Toole, who was more important than I was . . . So, I had to do some thinking. That's when I thought, I have to be in control. I don't always have to be in control, but I want to do a movie where I am in control."[54]

Beatty's response proved a genuine hinge in Hollywood history: in November 1965, just after *Mickey One* came and went from the theaters, he bought an option on a script by Robert Benton and David Newman, two young *Esquire* magazine employees who had been inspired by the French New Wave to write a movie they called *Bonnie and Clyde*.[55] Though set during the Great Depression, their screenplay about two glamorous young bank robbers crackled with the disdain for authority and cool indifference to conventional morality that was gathering momentum through the 1960s. Benton and Newman were determined, as they put it, to make a movie "about what's going on now."[56]

The screenwriters spent two years unsuccessfully pursuing a home for their idea. Even after Beatty became involved, the movie did not advance quickly. A long list of prominent directors turned down Beatty, including some of his older-generation friends, who would have been spectacularly miscast for the material, such as William Wyler and George Stevens.[57] Arthur Penn said no as well. Beatty counted a dozen rejections. "From the beginning, everyone in the world turned him down," said Towne. "It was a joke: If he'd had a dog, the dog would have turned it down."[58] Eventually, Beatty pivoted back to Penn, whose disillusion with the film business had only deepened after producer Sam Spiegel reedited his next movie, *The Chase*, without his approval.[59] "Initially, Arthur didn't want to do it," Towne remembered, "but both their careers were floundering."

Towne joined the effort, too. Beatty had liked a script Towne had written for Corman, a Western called *The Long Walk Home*, and he brought Towne in to polish and reorganize the *Bonnie and Clyde* script. The film shoot in Texas was predictably arduous. Faye Dunaway, cast as Bonnie, was tightly wound and skittish, a racehorse stepping around broken glass. Beatty and Penn argued incessantly (though, both men felt, productively), and Beatty, as producer and star, for the first time faced the weight of balancing a dual role. Every day, logistical and financial demands swarmed around him like summer flies. Yet, with those twin burdens, he appeared happier on a movie set than ever before. "It seemed like there was a lot of responsibility, but he kind of took to it like a duck to water," said Towne.[60] Remembered

Beatty, "It was not hard. It would have been hard for me not to [play both roles]. I think I had learned a lot about making movies."[61]

When Penn and Beatty completed the shoot, the movie's challenges had only begun. Beatty haggled with censors over the graphic violence and sexual content. (Was that a button or a nipple as Dunaway's Bonnie descended the stairs? Beatty convinced censors it was the former, though he knew it was the latter.) Jack Warner never wavered in his hatred for the film, and the studio's marketing and distribution arm in New York fully shared his distaste.[62] Even after *Bonnie and Clyde* was released in August 1967, it mostly received negative reviews. Bosley Crowther, Beatty's bête noire, not surprisingly was the most scathing, but even some critics who might have been allies were cool, including Andrew Sarris at the *Village Voice* and Joe Morgenstern of *Newsweek*.[63] The turning point came when Morgenstern reconsidered and wrote a second review the next week, reversing his verdict and praising the film. This highly unusual move generated more attention than if he had initially delivered a positive notice.[64] Then Pauline Kael unfurled a monograph-length rave in *The New Yorker*. In December 1967, *Time* magazine put the movie on its cover a remarkable sixteen weeks after it was first released.[65] By February 1968, *Bonnie and Clyde* had received ten Academy Award nominations and Warner Bros., under Beatty's relentless prodding, finally released the movie into wide distribution. This time it found a big audience.

Bonnie and Clyde made the first fortune for Beatty (whose deal with Warner Bros. had been heavily tilted toward back-end profits the studio confidently expected would never exist). It also coined the on-screen persona that would become Beatty's signature: sexy and restless, captivating but elusive, a dreamer defeated by yearnings that remained always beyond his grasp and often beyond even his power to describe. Dunaway's stylish wardrobe (especially her beret, a subtle nod to the French New Wave) made her a fashion icon. Although set decades earlier, the movie caught the cultural moment of the late sixties: a society hurtling without exact destination from what it had known to something new. As with Bonnie and Clyde themselves, the destination didn't seem as important or as exhilarating as the journey. Beatty wasn't targeting the young—"I thought it was a daring movie, and people of all ages wanted to see something that was taking a chance"—but young people adopted Bonnie and Clyde as symbols of style, liberation, rebellion.[66] With its jarring violence, which carried echoes to Penn of both Vietnam and urban riots; its sleek sexuality; and its disdain for sources of authority ranging from the banks to the police, *Bonnie and Clyde* drove a big hole through the high wall that had separated Hollywood during the 1960s from the changes unfolding in the country around it.

Mike Nichols's dark, sexy film of *The Graduate*, Charles Webb's novel, as adapted by Buck Henry and starring an unknown Dustin Hoffman in his career-making role, punched another hole in the wall. Released later in 1967, *The Graduate* condensed the generation gap into a single bedroom, as Hoffman's Benjamin sought to escape the predatory clutches of Anne Bancroft's older Mrs. Robinson and the numbing conformity of his parents' generation ("Plastics!") to find love, meaning, and authenticity with the lovely Katharine Ross, the radiant embodiment of Baby Boomers' chance to change the world.

The Graduate would be forever paired with *Bonnie and Clyde* in histories of Hollywood's transformation, two landmark movies released months apart showing that *something* was finally stirring in the old-age home the studios had become.

But Penn was premature when he said, "The walls came tumbling down after *Bonnie and Clyde*."[67] Change still came slowly. After *Bonnie and Clyde*, Beatty once again took an extended absence from moviemaking, during which he romanced Julie Christie; made an early trip to Russia to explore the idea that would years later become his epic, *Reds*; and took his first systematic steps into liberal politics, campaigning for Robert F. Kennedy in the 1968 Democratic primary and then for gun control after Kennedy's assassination that June. He attended the chaotic Democratic National Convention in Chicago that August and haggled with Hubert Humphrey as if he were Jack Warner by refusing to make a campaign film for the presidential nominee until he committed more explicitly to withdrawing from Vietnam. Beatty in these months turned down most of the movies he was offered. "I just couldn't continue to make movies all the time," he said later. "I just couldn't do it. I guess it was a matter of too much compromise in the making of movies, and I thought, If I'm going to compromise . . . I'm going to compromise on the immediate issues of the day. I want to know what's happening. It was very hard in 1968 to go into a sound stage and find that more interesting than what was happening outside."[68] But when Beatty finally did step back before the cameras, in late 1968, it was to replace Frank Sinatra in a torpid George Stevens melodrama starring Elizabeth Taylor, *The Only Game in Town*. That tired film, which disappeared upon its release, only demonstrated how heavily the dead weight of the past still pressed on Hollywood even after the guerrilla raids of *Bonnie and Clyde* and *The Graduate*.

NO ONE HAD TO teach that lesson to Nicholson, who continued to slog through small acting parts and stalled screenwriting projects. He secured his second major studio role as a hippie in the musical *On a Clear Day You Can See Forever*, but it proved as frustrating as his first. The movie was limp and dated, and Nicholson's part was whittled to insignificance in editing. Corman had been Nicholson's most reliable benefactor, but even he was wavering. "I always did think Jack was a potential star," the producer said later, "but I eventually moved him to smaller parts because nobody else seemed to see him as a star. So, I thought maybe my faith was misplaced."[69] Perpetually confident through all his reversals, Nicholson finally started to question his choices. When he met director and producer Bob Rafelson (inevitably, at an art film screening), Nicholson appeared ready to abandon acting altogether for screenwriting. "He said, 'I'm finished acting,'" Rafelson remembered. "'I'm only a B-movie actor.'"[70] And Towne, visiting Nicholson at the actor's house in West Hollywood not long after, found their youthful confidence fraying. "I had told him he was going to be a movie star, and I remember it was ten to fifteen years later, and nothing was happening," Towne said. "He was doing acting exercises, sense memory exercises, and we went and walked down the street, and it was a very discouraging time. None of us had any money, and

Jack had a baby and thought it was all over with. I said, with less conviction, 'You're still going to be a movie star, Jack.'"[71]

But the tide, in fact, was turning for both men. After *Bonnie and Clyde*, studios increasingly looked to Towne as a script doctor, a role in which his intelligence and keen ear for dialogue were unmistakable: he earned his first major studio assignment, to rewrite a Sam Peckinpah script about Pancho Villa that became *Villa Rides*. The pivot for Nicholson proved his meeting with Rafelson, who had struck it rich with partner Bert Schneider by creating a hit television show on NBC around "the Monkees," a manufactured Beatlesesque rock band. Rafelson hired Nicholson to write the screenplay for a Monkees movie, which they envisioned as a deconstruction of the band's image and celebrity. The film, released as *Head*, was a disjointed, impressionistic mess derided by critics and ignored by audiences (whose interest in the Monkees was already waning). But the experience cemented Nicholson into the Rafelson and Schneider circle as they formed their pioneering film production company, BBS. "Jack was practically a partner in the company," said Rafelson.[72] And when Rip Torn withdrew at the last minute from a film the duo was producing, they slotted in Nicholson to replace him beside Dennis Hopper and Peter Fonda. The film was *Easy Rider*.

The story of two drug smugglers (Hopper and Fonda) joined on a cross-country motorcycle trip by a small-town lawyer, *Easy Rider* gave Nicholson a scene-stealing role that showcased the rebellious charisma that would define his career. The film wasn't much more than an updated version of Corman's outlaw motorcycle films, with higher production values and more ambitious social commentary, but it caught the times in every way: from its pulsing rock soundtrack to its narrative of older America squashing the young. The characters played by Hopper, Fonda, and Nicholson are all killed by small-minded locals who look like members of the "silent majority" who had elected Richard Nixon as president in 1968. Like *Bonnie and Clyde* and *The Graduate* before it, the movie sent the visceral message that escaping from the old was more important than arriving at the new: the journey was its own reward. When *Easy Rider*, which was produced on a shoestring budget, exploded as a huge hit after its release in July 1969, it established Schneider and Rafelson as rakish new power players in the movie industry and made stars of Hopper, Fonda, and Nicholson (though the first two could not sustain it). Fifteen years after he landed in Los Angeles, Nicholson had finally arrived in Hollywood.

Easy Rider knocked down the wall that *Bonnie and Clyde* and *The Graduate* had dented in 1967. It demonstrated beyond debate that there were big financial rewards for producing films that connected with the Baby Boomers, who comprised an increasing share of the studios' audience. (One industry study in 1968 found that filmgoers younger than twenty-four accounted for almost half of ticket sales.)[73] The studios' most immediate reaction was to create new divisions that would hire young filmmakers to churn out films for young audiences. But this proved like trying to bottle lightning on an assembly line. Little memorable came of these efforts. Not surprisingly, institutionalizing the youth revolution became a contradiction in terms.

But *Easy Rider* accelerated two other Hollywood transitions that proved more lasting. It coincided with the demise in 1968 of the Production Code that had bound the industry for over three decades. The industry replaced the code with the Motion Picture Association of America's rating system. The shift didn't eliminate the constraints on filmmakers, but it greatly loosened them: *Midnight Cowboy*, a story about a hustler and a male prostitute in Manhattan, won Best Picture for 1969 despite its being released with the new system's adults-only X rating. The portrayals of sex and violence, the words that actors could speak, even the subject matter for films—all opened up. For those who had labored through the drowsy gray afternoon of Hollywood in the early 1960s, it was a change as sudden as the moment when *The Wizard of Oz* shifted from black and white to color.

As important, *Easy Rider*'s unexpected success—it finished as the third-highest-grossing film of 1969—also prompted the studios to invest in a much wider circle of movies. While the formal youth divisions mostly sputtered, in *Easy Rider*'s aftermath, the industry became much more willing to finance movies from filmmakers young and old who promised to reach the emerging audience that the studio heads were no longer confident they understood themselves. As a young screenwriter, Paul Schrader (who would later write *Taxi Driver*) remembers a friend telling him to walk through the studio gates with swagger. "They didn't know what it took to sell tickets to young people, and I remember Francis Coppola saying to me, 'Just go in there and tell them you know the answer. Just tell them. They don't know. They don't know you're lying. You walk in there and you say, "This is your lucky day because you want to make money in movies, and I want to make money in movies, and I know how to get money,"'" Schrader recalled. "They would believe you because they didn't know whom else to believe. A whole dozen or fifteen filmmakers came in that gap with that sort of braggadocio, and they got empowered, and some of them actually did make money."[74]

The terms of the basic transaction between filmmakers and the studios shifted. Despite the creative upsurge, the studios' financial situation remained extremely precarious: United Artists in 1970 reported the largest annual loss in the industry's history, with Fox not far behind.[75] So, the studios offered filmmakers a new deal: more freedom for less money. For many of this period's great films, the studios provided tight, if not shoestring, budgets, but they allowed directors and writers much more creative freedom. Barry Diller saw the transition unfold around him from the late 1960s into the early 1970s. "The old mogul was ending," he remembered. "That period in the sixties had [been] its final transition. The companies were not very sound financially." The financial pressure on the studios, he recognized, had "scraped the sides off of things. Essentially, by that pressure, they cleaned out the tub, allowing this inexperienced but very energized group to come in and start, basically, a shaky but clean slate."[76]

With this increased freedom, a brilliant constellation of filmmakers advanced projects that grappled with the political, cultural, and sexual changes that Hollywood had studiously ignored through the 1960s. Some, like Beatty, had emerged from years of frustration within the studio system; more, like Towne and Nicholson, had suddenly found themselves inside the gates long shut to them. Inevitably, this sudden search for relevance produced its share of tendentious and forgettable films, but the exceptions grew more numerous and more luminous. Into the early 1970s, Hollywood hummed with a creative energy unmatched since its first golden age, around World War II.

From their contrasting positions in the Hollywood hierarchy, Towne, Nicholson, and Beatty were all drawn to the center of the revolution. As the 1960s pivoted into the 1970s, each man turned down the road that would lead him to the landmark productions of *Chinatown* and *Shampoo*.

2

FEBRUARY

The Republic of Rock and Roll

When Jackson Browne and Linda Ronstadt went out on tour together in early 1974, one of the shows Browne circled on his calendar was a late-February date at New York City's famed Carnegie Hall. But as the long days on the road dissolved into long nights driving between cities, he started wondering what had happened to the booking. One day, Browne recalled, he turned to someone and said, "We're supposed to play Carnegie Hall on this tour, right?" The other person looked back at him quizzically. "Hey, that was three nights ago," he told Browne. Such was the grind of life on the road for two singers slowly climbing the ladder to success. "I literally didn't know when we had been to New York," Browne remembered. "You get out of the bus, and you get in a room, and they wake you up and you get ready to do the gig. I really didn't think we had been in New York."[1]

Browne and Ronstadt had known each other for nearly a decade. They'd met in 1965, soon after Ronstadt moved to Los Angeles from her childhood home in Tucson. A mutual friend, the singer Pam Polland, had brought Browne, at the time a precocious sixteen-year-old songwriter from Orange County, to meet Ronstadt at the house she shared with her bandmates near the Pacific Ocean, on Hart Avenue, just south of Santa Monica. Browne played one of his youthful compositions, the aching, wise-beyond-his-years lost-love song, "These Days." "I almost fell on the ground," Ronstadt remembered. "I thought, There are some really good songwriters here, so I had to stay here."[2] The first time Browne played at the fabled Troubadour on

Santa Monica Boulevard, in 1969, it was to open for Ronstadt. Later the two were neighbors near the Hollywood Bowl, when Ronstadt moved in with J. D. Souther, a Texas-born singer-songwriter with a Clint Eastwood squint, and Browne occupied the bungalow next door.[3]

Their tour that winter of 1974 did not top the priority list for their record label, the recently formed Elektra/Asylum. The label had been created from the merger of Elektra, whose roots traced back to the folk explosion in New York City, and Asylum, the Southern California music powerhouse launched in 1971 by David Geffen, a former agent and manager of boundless ambition who combined brilliance and belligerence in equal (if volatile) proportions. Geffen, the chairman of the joint enterprise, was at high tide in early 1974. In January, Elektra/Asylum released *Court and Spark*, from the lustrous and brilliant Canadian singer-songwriter Joni Mitchell, to rave reviews. (Jon Landau, *Rolling Stone*'s preeminent critic, had immediately declared it "the first truly great pop album of 1974" in the magazine's lead review.)[4] It was Mitchell's most commercially oriented album to date, and in January she had launched a nationwide tour to support it, playing to some of the biggest audiences she had ever attracted; a few weeks before Browne and Ronstadt arrived in New York City, Mitchell had headlined both Avery Fisher Hall and Radio City Music Hall.[5]

But the jewel in the crown for Geffen that winter was the reunion tour of Bob Dylan and the Band. Geffen, in a siege of military proportions, had lured Dylan away from his longtime home at Columbia Records in New York City and convinced him to mount a full-scale tour for the first time in eight years. The result was a sensation. Geffen developed an attention-gathering idea to sell the tickets exclusively by mail, and more than 5 million requests poured in, far beyond the tour's capacity of 650,000.[6] Audiences and critics alike raved at Dylan's triumphant return. Starting in Chicago on January 3 and finishing in Los Angeles on February 14, he barnstormed through forty shows in twenty-one cities, delivering old hits with ferocious new power. A few weeks before Browne and Ronstadt arrived, Dylan had blown through New York City as well, with three raucous shows at Madison Square Garden. Then he flew out on the private jet that the celebrated concert promoter Bill Graham, who was partnering with Geffen on the tour, had chartered to ferry Dylan from date to date.[7]

Compared to all this, Ronstadt and Browne were still trying to graduate from the kids' table. Ronstadt had released her first album for Geffen, *Don't Cry Now*, in September 1973. Browne followed a few weeks later, in October, with his second album, *For Everyman*. Both albums sold respectably, but neither cracked the Top 40 on the *Billboard* album chart. And while Geffen had great expectations for both artists, in early 1974 each was still building an audience. Their tour itinerary reflected their transitional position. It brought them to big venues in Detroit, Boston, Philadelphia, and Washington, DC, but also took them far from the bright lights to small community theaters and college campuses in Oxnard, San Luis Obispo, New Haven, and Cortland, New York. At either end, there wasn't much glamour in the experience. They had moved up from the lowest rung on the touring ladder, when they had lugged their gear in and out of station wagons, but had progressed only to a Continental Trailways bus without beds that both bands crammed into for the late-night drives between shows. "The first thing that happened is we were driving all night, and the next morning we were exhausted," Browne remembered. "Like, no one slept a wink. We were sitting up all night on a bus."[8] "Touring was misery," Ronstadt said, looking back. "Touring is just hard. You don't get to meet anybody. You are always in a bubble . . . You saw the world outside the bus window, and you did the sound check every day."[9]

The performances were uneven, too. "While Browne is much more assured and confident on stage than he was a year or two ago, he's still very much like a smart kid with a grown-up gift for songwriting," sniffed Judith Sims of *Rolling Stone*. She treated Ronstadt even more dismissively, describing her as peddling "country schmaltz."[10] The young rock journalist Cameron Crowe, catching the tour a few days later in Berkeley, described Browne's set as "painfully mediocre."[11] But Ronstadt and Browne found their footing as they progressed, each alternating lead billing depending on who had sold more records in each market. By the time the cavalcade rolled into Carnegie Hall, the reception for Browne and Ronstadt was strong enough that the promoters added a second show.

In February 1974, Jackson Browne and Linda Ronstadt were still at the edge of the stardom they would soon achieve. But from their base in Los Angeles, they were riding a towering wave toward that shore. During the heyday of the folk explosion in the early 1960s, the New York City of Bob Dylan, Dave Van Ronk, and the Village Gate had been the undisputed center of the musical universe. Then the center of influence shifted to London, with the Beatles and the Rolling Stones, Cream, the Who, the Kinks, and all the bands that orbited them. San Francisco, with the Grateful Dead, Jefferson Airplane, and Santana, had its moment in a psychedelic spotlight around the Summer of Love and the Monterey Pop Festival in 1967, but as the 1960s gave way to the '70s, the center of the musical universe shifted unmistakably to Los Angeles. "It was incredibly vital," said Jonathan Taplin, who first came to LA as the tour manager for Bob Dylan and the Band and later relocated there to produce Martin Scorsese's breakthrough movie, *Mean Streets.* "The nexus of the music business had really moved from New York to Los Angeles. That had been a profound shift . . . It was very clear that something big had changed."[12]

For a breathtaking few years, the stars aligned to glittering effect in Los Angeles. The city attracted brilliant artists; skilled session musicians; soulful songwriters; shrewd managers, agents, and record executives; and buzz-building clubs. From this dense constellation of talent, a shimmering new sound emerged, a smooth blend of rock and folk with country influences. Talented young people from all over the country began descending on Los Angeles with their guitar cases or dreams of becoming the next Geffen. Irving Azoff, a hyper-ambitious young agent and manager who arrived in Los Angeles in 1972, remembered, "It was like the gold rush. You've never seen anything like it in the entertainment business. The place was exploding. I was here—right place, right time. I tell everybody, 'If you're really good in this business, you only have to be right once,' so you kind of make your own luck, but it is luck, too. It was hard to be in LA in that time and have any talent whatsoever in the music business—whether you were a manager, an agent, an artist, a producer, or writer—[and] not to make it, because it was boom times. It was the gold rush, and it was fucking fun."[13] Browne and Ronstadt emerged from the very center of this eruption. Each had been born just after World War II, at the cusp of the Baby Boom, whose massive buying power would swell record sales and concert attendance to previously unimagined heights and enshrine rock and roll as the definitive sound of American music. Both arrived in Los Angeles just as its musical renaissance began in a jangle of guitars on Sunset Boulevard in the mid-1960s. And each, in their long passage from struggling, uncertain teen to beloved rock superstar, followed the long arc of influences that created the buoyant California sound. For a time, that sound, of summer sunshine and open roads, revolutionized popular music. In their hopes, their frustrations, and ultimately their great breakthroughs, Browne and Ronstadt were the children of that revolution.

MUSIC ENVELOPED BOTH LINDA RONSTADT and Jackson Browne as they grew to adulthood. Ronstadt was born in July 1946 in Tucson, Arizona, then a dusty town deep in the desert. Her father sang in local clubs, and her mother played Gilbert and Sullivan on the piano.[14] From a very young age, Ronstadt was drawn to the radio, twisting the dials to capture distant signals that transported her to sounds and lives far beyond the sleepy hometown where she let mud dry on her bare feet to protect them from the searing sun.

"There were giant transmitters that boosted the signal from WRLS in Chicago and from Tennessee—we got the *Louisiana Hayride* and the *Grand Old Opry*. Late at night we got rhythm-and-blues stations and white and Black gospel stations. We got a ton of Mexican music. There was a lot of dance band music, Stan Kenton and Duke Ellington. When rock and roll came in, I remember it was Bill Haley and the Comets. It was before Elvis. I liked the stuff I was hearing on the late-night radio from the R-and-B stations the best," she said. And for good measure, "we had country music stations close by, too." Ronstadt was a natural mimic. "Everything I could hear I could copy," she remembered. "I copied my big brother a lot because I had a high voice, and he was a soprano."[15]

When Ronstadt reached her teens, she started haunting Tucson's small circuit of folk clubs. Inspired by Peter, Paul and Mary, she formed a folk trio with her brother and sister, but quickly began thinking about the bigger stage to the west. "People would come over from LA and play in little folk clubs in Tucson," she remembered. "They wouldn't always get a big crowd, because Tucson was a hard sell. They would say, 'We get really big crowds in LA.'"[16]

Jackson Browne was born Clyde Jackson Browne III in October 1948 in Germany, where his father worked for the military newspaper *Stars and Stripes*. When Jackson was three, his father relocated the family to Los Angeles.[17] When he turned twelve, his father, worried that his son was drifting into delinquency, relocated the family again, to a virtually all-white new subdivision called Sunny Hills, in Orange County.[18] With their move in 1960, the Browne family joined the great migration to newly built suburbs that reconfigured American life after World War II and defined childhood for millions of Baby Boomers. Sunny Hills High School, which Browne attended, had opened only a few years before, to meet the swelling demand of young families with children born in the first years after the war. Like so many of his peers, Browne chafed against the suburban conformity that his parents considered a haven. "I was popped down in a sort of very sterile, tract home community," he recalled later. "I sort of had contempt for the entire decision to move there."[19] Orange County was a seedbed for the conservative movement that emerged around Barry Goldwater and Ronald Reagan in the mid-1960s, and the adolescent Browne, with his long hair and liberal views, never felt entirely at home there.

Music created community for him. His parents had surrounded him with it from a young age. His father played Dixieland jazz on piano, and the house was always ringing with blues, jazz, and folk records. Jackson's father steered him toward trumpet lessons (though Jackson preferred piano); his mother played KPFK, the "alternative" LA radio station, at home and introduced him to Frank Zappa's music. At Sunny Hills, he gravitated toward two older students, Greg Copeland

and Steve Noonan, who were already performing and writing their own songs, including protest ballads for the civil rights movement, which became the first cause to galvanize Browne. With his friends, he frequented Orange County's modest circuit of folk clubs and coffeehouses. Soon, he started composing his own music and performing, particularly at open-mic nights.[20] He was shy and so tentative that he was often hard to hear onstage, but even then, the quality of the songs he wrote at his kitchen table late at night left his friends eager to hear his next composition.[21]

Though Ronstadt and Browne absorbed influences from many styles, it was the folk revival above all that inspired them, igniting not only their musical but also their political imaginations. Both thrilled to the music of Bob Dylan and remained riveted even after Dylan shocked folk purists by plugging in an electric guitar at the Newport Folk Festival in 1965. In conservative Tucson, Ronstadt was exposed to the history of the labor movement and civil rights struggles through *Sing Out!*, the magazine that chronicled the old-time folky left of Woody Guthrie and Pete Seeger. In Orange County, an even more conservative place, where many dismissed the civil rights movement as a Communist plot, the stories embedded in folk music provided Browne and his friends with an alternative to the history they got from their "close-minded and oppressive" teachers.[22] "All the folk music, really, contained the political reality of the half century preceding us," Browne remembered. "The immigrants and the labor movement, Jim Crow and civil rights—folk music was like our encyclopedia."[23]

Ronstadt made her first trip to Los Angeles in 1964, when she drove there with her mother to visit her aunt, a musician and music scholar.[24] She returned to LA for another visit on spring break in 1965, and at the Ash Grove, a popular folk club, she was electrified by two young guitar players, Ry Cooder and Taj Mahal. Then, at the Trip, on Sunset Boulevard, she heard the Byrds, a new band that had transfixed Los Angeles with its ethereal, jangling blend of folk and rock. Ronstadt felt like Dorothy in Oz. A few weeks later, she turned in her final exams and moved to the coast. "It was clear to me that music was happening on a whole different level in Los Angeles," she later wrote.[25]

Browne, though he began much closer to the LA scene, was initially more ambivalent about it. In Orange County, where long hair could still provoke threats (or worse) from a passing car, it took a very conscious choice to identify as a "freak." This soldered a strong bond among those who did so, such as the circle of folkies Browne had joined. "As a teenager, I was pretty happy in my little pod of friends," Browne remembered. He made the trip to Los Angeles to see Bob Dylan at the Santa Monica Civic Center in 1964 and returned the next year to see the Rolling Stones at the Sports Arena.[26] But, initially, Browne didn't feel compelled to join the scene developing on Sunset Boulevard. The venues there were primarily dance clubs, and he liked the folk and coffeehouse environment, where the crowd would listen to the music more intently. And anyway, that same Orange County circuit offered him the opportunity to learn his craft as a performer, strumming and singing on a bare stage for small crowds sipping coffee or wine. "That's where I learned to play for an audience," he remembered.[27]

But the LA pull was too powerful for him to resist for long. "I spent my last year and a half in high school going to Hollywood every chance I got," he said. In LA, Browne hung out with a band called the Gentle Soul, led by Pamela Polland, a sometime girlfriend and the woman who introduced him to Ronstadt. More and more, his weekend nights ended on a friend's couch in Los Angeles after hours of watching or playing music.

The same scene that drew in Browne and Ronstadt blinked like a beacon to talented and ambitious young musicians from across the continent. A year after LA mesmerized Ronstadt on her 1965 spring break, a young and socially awkward Canadian songwriter asked his bass player, Bruce Palmer, if he wanted to try LA after their band, the Mynah Birds, broke up. "I targeted LA," Neil Young later explained, "because that's where all the music was happening."[28] Stephen Stills, though enjoying success in New York City's folk scene, came to Los Angeles to audition for the Monkees, the synthesized rock act that producers Bert Schneider and Bob Rafelson were assembling for their television show. (Depending on the telling, Stills was either seeking a part on the show or only trying to interest the producers in songs he had written.) But Stills heard the swelling LA sound and stayed, too. Danny Kortchmar, a gritty young guitarist playing with an arty band called the Fugs in New York City, felt LA's pull as well. "I was tired of freezing my ass off every winter. I remember walking down the street in my overcoat with a guitar in one hand and my amp in the other, thinking, Ah, fuck this," he remembered. Kortchmar auditioned for a spot in a psychedelic band on the Elektra label called Clear Light, and when he got the job, he and his then wife moved into a guest room in the home of Barry Friedman, a record producer and manager who also handled artists for Elektra. Friedman lived in a bucolic section of the Hollywood Hills scented with chaparral and sage that had suddenly become the dreamy center of LA's music scene. "When I moved up to Laurel Canyon," Kortchmar remembered, "all hell was breaking. Everyone was everywhere."[29]

THE MUSIC INDUSTRY MADE room for aspiring young artists like these much more quickly than did movies or television, the other two titans of LA's entertainment business. Those industries faced very different economic incentives than the recording companies. To turn a profit, the film studios and especially the three television networks needed to attract a mass audience with mainstream tastes. Young people were only one component of this. Producing a movie or new television show required an investment that could stretch into the millions of dollars, making studios reluctant to provide opportunities to unproven young talent (at least until the breakthrough of *Easy Rider* in 1969). It didn't help that in the mid-1960s, and for many years to come, decisions in both industries were made almost entirely by older white men who might interact with young people only when they propositioned a starlet. All these considerations made the movie and television worlds slow to respond to the youth culture exploding in places like Greenwich Village, Haight-Ashbury, and on the Sunset Strip in LA.

But the music industry operated with a very different equation. Young people constituted a much larger share of their audience. And the cost of experimenting with a new artist was low: a record label might produce an album for only $25,000. It sometimes cost no more than a share of the receipts at the door to book a new band at a club. As a result, the music industry was not only nimbler than television or movies; it was also more porous. "The nature of the art form is there's just a lot more records," recalled Danny Goldberg, a rock journalist, publicist, manager, and record executive. "You could have, like, fifty or a hundred times more records released than movies, because they're so much cheaper to make and you weren't limited by the number of theaters. Tower Records had room for thousands and thousands of records. So, the ability to have more diversity was inherent in the nature of the product, and once you can demonstrate actual public interest in an artist, the concept of the gatekeeper is less important in the music business than [in] TV or movies. The music business, long before there was an internet, reacted to the crowd. And marketing was local. In Cleveland or Indianapolis, you get to know the deejay and get him drunk and whatever, 'Okay, give me a shot,' and there's a local record store, and if you could prove that you're selling in Indianapolis or Cleveland, the people in New York and LA became interested."[30]

With these dynamics, the music industry transitioned much faster to the new. In 1964 and 1965, the Singing Nun, *Hello, Dolly!*, *Mary Poppins*, *The Sound of Music*, and Herb Alpert shared space with the Beatles and the Rolling Stones at the top of the *Billboard* album charts. By 1968, the list was dominated by rock acts: Simon and Garfunkel, Cream, the Doors, Big Brother and the Holding Company, Jimi Hendrix, the Rascals, and of course the Beatles. In 1969, Glen Campbell was the only non-rocker to reach the top spot.[31]

Los Angeles through the late 1960s steadily emerged as the locus of this transformation. Earlier in the decade, the Beach Boys' creamy odes to California girls, hot rods, and surfing safaris had produced a stream of hits that rolled onto the charts as steadily as waves lapping onto a sun-kissed beach. Phil Spector, also in LA and already grappling with the darkness that would eventually consume him, blasted out a succession of raucous girl group classics powered by his unstoppable "Wall of Sound."

But by the mid- to late 1960s, few serious artists looked to follow in their footsteps. The tradition that would define the Southern California sound began instead with the Byrds, launched in 1964 by Roger McGuinn, Gene Clark, and David Crosby, three young veterans of the folk circuit united by their interest in blending folk traditions with the rock innovations of the Beatles. By spring 1965—after the release of their electrified version of Bob Dylan's "Mr. Tambourine Man," with its jangling guitars and ethereal harmonies, and after a buzz-building series of shows at Ciro's, on Sunset Boulevard, a down-at-the-mouth haunt for the Hollywood elite during the Big Band era—the Byrds galvanized Los Angeles in sound and sensation alike. The band became the center of a suddenly electric Sunset Boulevard scene that filled clubs like Gazzarri's, the Whisky a Go Go, the Hullabaloo, and the Trip.

Close behind the Byrds came the Mamas and the Papas, featuring John Phillips; his wife, the quintessential California girl Michelle Phillips; Denny Doherty; and "Mama" Cass Elliot. Like the key figures in the Byrds, all were veterans of the mid-sixties folk scene. The next band that emerged on Sunset Boulevard sold less, but generated much more critical buzz. Neil Young and Stephen Stills, who had met and bonded when their earlier bands crossed paths in Canada, formed Buffalo Springfield with Bruce Palmer and Richie Furay. Just weeks after assembling in April 1966, the band was already opening for the Byrds, a testament to how new voices could emerge far faster in music than in movies or television.[32] Like the Byrds, Buffalo Springfield combined folk and rock influences, but with a harder edge sharpened by the dueling lead guitars of Young and Stills and Palmer's pounding bass lines. Soon the band settled into a semi-permanent residency at the Whisky on Sunset, trading off headlining with another LA band, the Doors.[33] Formed by organist Ray Manzarek and vocalist Jim Morrison, a young UCLA graduate whose temperament was as volcanic as his talent, the Doors brought a dark, spectral energy to the Sunset scene, and their shows became a sensation.

Like the city they called home, these bands were all built over deep fault lines. Within a few years, Clark quit the Byrds because he didn't like traveling, and the perpetually discontented Crosby was pushed out.[34] Buffalo Springfield proved as precarious, with a struggle for control between Stills and Young (and Palmer's drug addiction) shattering the band after only two years.[35]

When Buffalo Springfield disintegrated, the component parts reassembled in new combinations. Richie Furay went on to form Poco, a pioneering country-rock band. Stills started making music with David Crosby and recorded a few demos, but their sound didn't coalesce until August 1968, when they added a third piece to the mix.

Graham Nash was a mainstay of the Hollies, the bouncy British pop group he had formed with his childhood friend Allan Clarke. Nash had come to Los Angeles to spend a weekend with Joni Mitchell, the beautiful and brilliant young folksinger he had fallen for earlier that year when they met in Canada. When he arrived at her house on Lookout Mountain Avenue in Laurel Canyon that summer day, he found Stills and Crosby there, with guitars strewn around. The latter two played one of Stills's songs, "You Don't Have to Cry," and Nash listened intently. Then he asked them to play it again. The third time, he added his voice to theirs, creating a mesmerizing three-part harmony. "When I first heard that blend that we had I started laughing in the middle of the song because it was so ridiculously right," Nash recalled. "I realized that I'd have to go to England and change my entire life. I was in the middle of divorcing my first wife. I left my friends; I left my equipment; I left my boyhood friend Allan Clarke, whom I had known since I was six years old; and I left following that sound. I heard that sound and, holy shit, I wanted it. . . . We all knew that our lives had changed dramatically."[36] Nash returned to Los Angeles permanently in December 1968, moving in with Mitchell and burrowing into the studio with Stills and Crosby.[37] In every possible way, Los Angeles entranced him. "It was free, it was warm, it was sunny, it was open, it was smiley," he said. "It was what you think it was. Coming from the north of England into Los Angeles, it was unbelievable. Then, when you add to that the community that was gathering around Laurel Canyon, [it] was insane."[38]

Winding into the Hollywood Hills, the small streets circling off

Laurel Canyon above the Beverly Hills Hotel became the emblem of LA's energized music scene, the symbol of not only a smooth sound but a rocker lifestyle that combined domesticity and debauchery in alluring proportions. Compared to New York, LA seemed on fast-forward, a few years deeper into the cultural changes of the sixties. "It was more hipped out, to be sure," remembered Danny Kortchmar. "Vegetarian restaurants everywhere. Obviously, the climate was different. The way people dressed was different. They were more flamboyant in their dress and more open, and generally it was more open than on the staid East Coast."[39]

Everything seemed a little easier in LA than in New York, even the interactions with the police. Some drug busts still occurred: a police raid on a party in Topanga Canyon famously netted a visiting Eric Clapton.[40] But mostly, the LA Police Department stayed far from the stars, especially after the mid-sixties. "I never felt any threat from any police," Nash recalled. Drugs were such a cornerstone of the social scene that even dealers could achieve their own local notoriety. Graham Nash first noticed the woman who became his wife because she was sitting in a drugstore booth with what he later described as a "famous" local drug dealer. "There were several of them," Nash recalls. Drug dealers became minor celebrities "because drugs were such a strong part of what was going on," he continued. "The drugs were kind of invisible because they were always there, so after a while [you thought], What drugs? Oh, you mean this pile?"

It wasn't just sex and drugs that filled the canyons at night: there was plenty of rock and roll, too. Musicians would bring their guitars when they went to one another's homes. When Joni Mitchell first arrived in LA in late 1967, Crosby, her lover at the time, would invite small groups over to houses in Laurel Canyon to hear her strum the songs from her still-unreleased first album. Mitchell stunned them with her beauty and talent. "We thought we hallucinated her," one of the lucky viewers remembered later. Kortchmar remembers lying around at record producer Paul Rothchild's house when a long-haired young kid from Orange County came through. "Jackson would come around, sit in the living room, and play a couple tunes," he remem-

Beach. There was a club in Santa Barbara. We would load up the car and go up there. We played pizza parlors if that's all we could get."[46] An appearance at the Troubadour's open-mic "Hoot Night" led to an agreement with agent Herb Cohen, which in turn produced a recording contract at Capitol. The Stone Poneys released three albums and had one big AM radio hit with "Different Drum," an ode to sixties independence written by Michael Nesmith before he joined the Monkees. But the Stone Poneys never found a stable audience, and the band dissolved in 1968. Forced to become a solo artist for the first time, Ronstadt was compelled to ask herself what kind of music she felt comfortable singing on her own. Her answer was the country songs she had learned from her sister in Tucson.[47]

Ronstadt's return to her roots connected her to a larger procession. Los Angeles in 1968 was a seedbed of experimentation in blending rock and country sounds. Country music had always been part of the LA musical tradition, carried there by the steady stream of migrants from the Midwest and South who came to work largely in the defense and energy industries in the years around World War II. The Bakersfield sound, developed by artists such as Merle Haggard and Buck Owens in the honky-tonks of that dusty city north of Los Angeles, offered a gravelly alternative to the slicker and sometimes soulless Grand Ole Opry tradition.

Singers on the LA scene such as Gene Clark of the Byrds started mining these country traditions in the mid-1960s, but the pivotal moment in the convergence occurred when Gram Parsons, a southerner from a comfortable (if troubled) family who had passed through Harvard, moved to the city in 1967.[48] His blending of country and rock influences reverberated through the LA music world. To the young Jackson Browne, Parsons's work in the Byrds and the Flying Burrito Brothers showed that "country [music] could be electric music."[49]

By then, the country-rock fusion had reached critical mass in LA. Apart from Gram Parsons, no one in Los Angeles tried harder than Ronstadt to cross the jagged cultural boundaries between rock and country. It was easy to underestimate Ronstadt, because of both her breathtaking looks and her sometimes paralyzing insecurity. But she had an idea in her head—or, more accurately, a sound; or, more accurately still, a collection of sounds—that she wanted to bring together in ways that she did not hear anyone else doing. "I was trying to mush up the radio," she said, "put more of an R-and-B rhythm section with a country top on it, with pedal steel and a twangy guitar."[50]

In different ways, all the LA musicians experimenting with new fusions were trying to build a bridge between deep traditions in American music—what Jackson Browne called "the soulfulness of everyday people" in folk, blues, and country—and the energy and freedom of rock and roll. "We wanted to make music that was connected to a root, not just sprung full-blown from the head of Zeus, but that had a roots underpinning with a contemporary feeling," Ronstadt remembered.[51]

In search of that new sound, Ronstadt pushed her boundaries musically and geographically. Most of the Troubadour set rarely ventured farther north than Mulholland Boulevard, the hilltop ribbon of road that divided the star-studded canyons to the south from the blue-collar, white-flight San Fernando Valley to the north. Ronstadt crossed that invisible border to play at the Palomino, in North Hollywood. Compared to the Troubadour, with its "lonesome LA cowboys," the Palomino was the place you were more likely to find real cowboys, or at least the descendants of Oklahoma and Texas cowboys who still listened to the music they were reared on even after trading the Dust Bowl for a tract house in Van Nuys and a factory job at a defense contractor. The feel at the Palomino was more honky-tonk than Hollywood. "They were drunker [there]," Ronstadt remembers. "They weren't as inclined to listen."[52] Still, the bar offered Ronstadt not only a sweaty authenticity, but also more tangible benefits: bands were paid in the cash collected at the door, a welcome (and tax-free) infusion for struggling young artists.[53]

Just before Christmas 1971, Ronstadt stepped onstage for her first appearance at the Palomino. She wore a tight red sweater, sequined blue jean hot pants, and huge hoop earrings. Doe-eyed, with a long shag haircut, and singing braless and shoeless, she asked the waitress to bring a supply of tequila for her and the band and then channeled classics from Hank Williams, Merle Haggard, Waylon Jennings, and

Jerry Lee Lewis in a voice that rattled the rafters. Even the massive photo of Johnny Cash on the wall seemed to be sweating. "I don't think some people even knew she was singing until the second or third song," Robert Hilburn, the lead rock critic for the *Los Angeles Times*, wrote in his review.[54] Compelling as her performances could be, Ronstadt was plagued by crushing insecurity—about her weight, her looks, even her powerful voice. Also, for years she was unable to find producers, executives, or bandmates who could execute the fusion she heard in her head. She recorded her first solo album for Capitol Records in 1969, but that didn't crack *Billboard*'s Top 200. Then she recorded her second solo album, 1970's *Silk Purse*, at the Cinderella Sound Studio in Nashville.

The album made clear the depth of confusion at Capitol about how to market or position Ronstadt, a confusion memorialized in the spectacularly ill-advised cover photo of her in a sty surrounded by pigs, the singer posed to look like a farmer's daughter ready for a roll in the hay. And the time in Nashville only convinced her that the artistic, personal, and political distance between Music City's version of country and the version coalescing at the Troubadour was far greater than she had hoped. "The divide was geographical," she said. "We were doing California country rock. It was very different than Nashville country. We were trying as hard as we could to copy what we heard, but it came out different, mainly the rhythm section. One of the first things I discovered when I went to Nashville is there was so much racism. I was really shocked. When we were in music, we were hippies. We were all against the war and pro-marijuana, and we wanted the police to get off our backs. Everybody was pretty united with that. I thought everybody who played music had those kinds of attitudes. I found that they didn't. People in Nashville were really nice, and they were good players, but it was a totally different place."[55]

Ronstadt couldn't find much more direction back in LA. "I felt very lacking," she remembered. "I was trying to forge an original trail, not consciously, but at that time, singing was dominated by Black gospel singing, girl groups, or Aretha Franklin and Dionne Warwick. If you couldn't sing like that, you weren't part of rock and roll. And I couldn't sing like that at all."[56] Her manager, Herb Cohen, told her she was too country for pop and too pop for country. Capitol agreed. "They wanted me to choose a category and do one or the other," she remembered.[57]

Ronstadt's fortunes started to turn in the spring of 1970, when she connected with the young producer, songwriter, and musician John Boylan. "I needed somebody who could help me do what I was trying to do; John was the first one who could see what I was trying to do," Ronstadt remembered. A New York transplant, Boylan was only about five years older than Ronstadt, but he seemed to her one of the "grown-ups" at the Troubadour. Boylan shared her assessment of her situation. "She was falling in the cracks," he thought. "Capitol didn't know what to do with her. They thought, Is she country? Is she rock? She's too freaking eclectic. Nobody knew what to do."[58]

Boylan had earned some notoriety by assembling the well-regarded Stone Canyon Band, which had helped the former child star Ricky Nelson (of *Ozzie and Harriet*) revive his music career. Ronstadt asked him to assemble a band for her. As he had with Nelson, Boylan began in the Troubadour bar. His first target was a guitarist and singer from a disbanded country-folk-rock duo called Longbranch Pennywhistle, one of what Boylan called "the hangout guys in the bar." His name was Glenn Frey. When Boylan offered him the job, Frey had only one question: Could he get paid the first month in advance?

Frey encouraged Boylan and Ronstadt to consider a drummer from Texas he knew named Don Henley, the centerpiece of a band playing around LA called Shiloh. Boylan knew the name. "Henley had pitched a song that he wrote for Linda because I remember I was at the bar one night, the night I met him, and I was sitting there, and this kid comes up to me and he says, 'You don't know who I am, but you're John Boylan,' and I said, 'Yeah.' He said, 'I sent you a record, and you never answered.' I said, 'Oh yeah, you sent me this Shiloh album. You forgot to put a phone number.'"[59]

Ronstadt knew the name, too. Hanging out one night at the Troubadour bar, she crossed through the performance space on her way to the restroom and heard a band playing her arrangement of the old Dusty Springfield song "Silver Threads and Golden Needles," "note for note."[60] It was Henley with his band, Shiloh. Ronstadt liked the rendition and filed away the name. When she left for her tour in 1971, she brought along Frey (on guitar) and Henley (on drums) as half her backup band. It was a spartan tour: college campuses, shabby motels, and loading up the amps in the station wagon to drive to the next town. When Ronstadt's original bass player and guitarist fell off along the way, she and Boylan (who remained her manager and producer after a brief turn as her boyfriend) replaced them with Randy Meisner, whom Boylan had earlier placed in the Stone Canyon Band; and guitarist Bernie Leadon, another young veteran of the Southern California folk-country scene. Meisner and Leadon, Frey and Henley, the quartet that would become the Eagles, played together for the first time behind Ronstadt at Disneyland in July 1971.[61] (The Mouse Kingdom specified in the contract that Ronstadt had to wear a bra and a skirt that would not rise more than a few inches off the ground when she knelt down.)[62] Shifting combinations of the foursome backed her in the studio and for a stand at the Troubadour, from which she harvested several cuts for her next album, the underrated *Linda Ronstadt*. From the start, Ronstadt could feel the combustion that occurred when Frey and Henley, and later Meisner and Leadon, came together. Standing at the front of the stage, she sometimes felt she was holding the microphone stand to avoid getting swept away by the waves of sound cresting behind her. "It was like standing in front of a wall of water that was mowing you down," she said. "It was like one of those mudslides in Santa Barbara."[63]

Commercially, *Linda Ronstadt* was a step back—the album peaked at a disappointing 163 on the *Billboard* pop chart, but it carried Ronstadt a long step closer to finding her sound.[64] Elements of the record, like her soaring cover of Patsy Cline's "I Fall to Pieces" (backed by Frey, Henley, and aching pedal steel from Pete Kleinow, late of Gram Parsons's Flying Burrito Brothers), beautifully anticipated the Americana movement that developed with artists like Lucinda Williams years later. But Ronstadt also belted out a knee-buckling version of "Rescue Me," a Chess Records–produced R&B hit for Fontella Bass in 1965, and a plaintive rendition of Neil Young's "Birds." These were not sounds usually heard on the same disc. "It took Linda a while to amalgamate her influences into a Linda style," Boylan remembered. "That's what was going on in those albums."[65] Late in 1972, Ronstadt finally broke away from Capitol and joined the pilgrimage of other Southern California acts (including the Eagles) to Geffen's Asylum. There she rejoined her old friend Jackson Browne, who had been the first artist Geffen signed to the label.

FOR YEARS, BROWNE FELT nearly as adrift as Ronstadt. He initially emerged with a blast of momentum after he finished Sunny Hills High School in 1966.[66] Elektra signed him to a songwriting contract that October, just as he turned eighteen, and the next year, he moved briefly to New York City, commandeering the couch of a high school buddy on the grimy Lower East Side.[67] The crowd Browne fell in with revolved around Andy Warhol's frenzied downtown club, the Dom. Browne killed time with Lou Reed and Leonard Cohen and romanced and played guitar behind Nico, the provocative former model who had become the Warhol scene's resident It Girl. Nico included three of Browne's songs on her debut album, *Chelsea Girl*, but their romance quickly flamed out, and after a few months he retreated to Los Angeles.

Browne was gaining respect as a songwriter: in addition to Nico's, his compositions appeared on albums by Tom Rush, by an early version of the Allman Brothers Band, and by his old friend Steve Noonan, and he started reaching magazine lists of emerging songwriters to watch.[68] But Browne's own career as a performer was idling. He played at clubs around LA and reached the bill (as opposed to a spot at the open-mic Hoot Night) at the Troubadour for the first time in September 1969, opening for Ronstadt. Yet he made so slight an impression that he earned only a passing final sentence in Robert Hilburn's typically enraptured paean to Ronstadt's voice and looks in the *LA Times*.[69]

Compounding his frustration, Elektra let his songwriting contract lapse. In LA, Browne was becoming the musical equivalent of a playground basketball legend in New York City: an underground sensation that everyone was convinced would someday hit the big time. But the big time remained elusively out of reach.

Browne found community at the Troubadour, but only to a point. Seeing the same people, guitar cases in hand, knocking back whiskey and tequila at Hoot Night on Mondays was both comforting and a little discouraging to him. He appreciated the fellowship and camaraderie but also viewed the place as something of a sinkhole. He "decided after about a year of hanging around the Troubadour," as he remembered, "never to go to the Troubadour again. To go sing, but don't go in the bar. Do not be seen standing around the Troubadour bar for three hours every Monday night. Don't do that. Because that's the opposite of getting your work done. You're part of a social scene, but you're not getting your work done."[70]

This work ethic separated Browne from most of the LA crowd. He treated songwriting as a job, a skill to be honed rather than a flash of inspiration to be awaited. His guiding principle about writing music was, "It's fucking hard, and if you do it all the time, you have a better chance at inspiration." Browne was a meticulous, painstaking songwriter who labored intently over every song, sometimes for months. "His songs are written so precisely," said Jon Landau, the star *Rolling Stone* critic who later became the producer on Browne's fourth album, *The Pretender*. "Every word. When he writes a song, he is focused on every single word, and he can spend a lot of time deciding whether it should be a 'the' or an 'and.'"[71]

But like Ronstadt, Browne felt that he was spinning his wheels. "I had a vague idea of what I wanted to do, but no idea how to do it," he remembered a few years later.[72] Advice descended from all directions. His friend, the transcendent guitarist Duane Allman, improbably gave him a Telecaster guitar, which was something like handing a flamethrower to a Boy Scout who has asked how to start a campfire.[73] Browne's manager suggested he sing like Otis Redding. Browne recognized the insight in this advice—it meant he needed to put "more time" in his voice—but he knew he could no more fill that role than play Duane's Telecaster. For better or worse, Browne was a breezy burst of California sunshine, movie star handsome and perpetually boyish, a sensitive surfer. As other contemporaries advanced, he felt his window closing before it had ever fully opened. "A lot of people had had faith in me, and I felt I had blown it," he told Cameron Crowe early in 1974.[74] He talked about releasing an album that he would entitle, *My Opening Farewell.*[75]

Yet, like Ronstadt, with her blend of country and rock, Browne had placed himself in a larger current that would ultimately carry him forward, even if he couldn't feel the movement from day to day. For Browne, the key development was the music industry's embrace of a new icon: the singer-songwriter telling unique truths mined from his or her own life. Dylan, followed by the Beatles, had shown that it was possible to write rock songs about something meaningful, but neither, in those years, wrote consistently about their own experiences. Others blazed that trail through the late 1960s. As the Troubadour's eccentric owner, Doug Weston, perceptively observed, the audience increasingly responded to an artist "singing songs about his own life, his own pain, his own thoughts."[76]

Few exemplified this new ideal more than the magnetic Joni Mitchell. "Nobody was making music like Joni, and everybody knew it," said Graham Nash, who remembers her playing "fifteen of the most beautiful songs I ever heard in my life, one after another," on the day they first met.[77] Other artists agreed. "Joni . . . she's on her own planet," Ronstadt thought.[78] Critics ran out of adjectives to praise the three records Mitchell released in rapid succession as the decade turned: *Ladies of the Canyon* (1970), *Blue* (1971), and *For the Roses* (1972).

But for all her acclaim from critics and fellow artists, at that point in her career Mitchell was not a top-tier commercial act. Her album sales were solid, but none had been a runaway success. Other acts initially took the singer-songwriter persona to a wider audience, notably James Taylor and Carole King. They offered music of generational transition. It was less about changing the world than changing your life. Much of the Southern California sound was about searching for greater authenticity in a society that defined success through material accumulation and social conformity. The LA music of the early 1970s represented the '60s generation folding in on itself, shifting its focus from trying to change society from the top down through politics to changing it from the bottom up through the way they lived their lives.

In songs such as Nash's "Our House" (his ode to cozy domesticity with Mitchell at a time when some young people were still decamping for communes) and "So Far Away" (Carole King's lament that no one "stays in one place anymore"), you can hear the personal becoming political and the political becoming personal. (Brian Wilson's sweet ode to marriage, "Wouldn't It Be Nice," in 1966, had been a forerunner.) The greatest works of Joni Mitchell, Taylor, and King show artists examining relationships as intently as the best filmmakers of the time were beginning to explore corruption and the abuse of power, and all toward the same end: constructing an alternative vision of how a new generation of Americans might live their lives. The period's most lasting works precisely captured the Baby Boom transitioning from footloose adolescence into the cares and rewards of adulthood. The results could be sappy and self-indulgent, drained of the drive and rebellion that energized rock and roll—many of the singer-songwriter albums seemed closer to therapy than to anarchy—but they also helped to crystallize a genuinely shared experience for millions of people. "It was a little nose to navel, it's a little self-indulgent, but it resonates because everyone else is doing it," remembered Boylan. "They were focusing a little more on themselves and their personal development and a little less on [changing society]." He used the fabled Selma-to-Montgomery march for voting rights to capture the difference: "They still cared about Selma, but they became more interested in becoming people that could deal with the world and understand what was going on, and they were helping each other through that process."[79]

This process peaked with *Tapestry*, the landmark album from Carole King, who had moved to Laurel Canyon from New York City in 1967 after splitting from her husband and songwriting partner, Gerry Goffin.[80] *Tapestry* was unreserved in its yearning for the comforts of the straight life that student protesters (and movies such as *The Graduate* and *Bonnie and Clyde*) had scorned only a few years before. Though King was a bit older than the Baby Boomers, she struck a nerve in Boomers coming in from the tumult of the sixties, moving deeper into their twenties and starting families. "She was hitting that chord of what so many people were going through," said the album's producer,

Lou Adler. Over its first year, it sold three million copies.[81] "As far as the magnitude, I could never have imagined," Adler remembered. "I never thought about records in those numbers, twenty-five million. We talked about five hundred thousand was a big seller, and a million was a gold record. From that point on, everything went through the roof."

JACKSON BROWNE, MEANWHILE, WAS still trying to find his way through the door. He took a step forward when the prominent local disc jockey B. Mitchel Reed invited him to sing for a free clinic in Long Beach in 1969. "I'd been to the free clinic," Browne remembered, "and so [had] everybody [else] that ever got clap."[82] At the event, he met the two other young singer-songwriters who were performing together in the band Longbranch Pennywhistle: Glenn Frey and J. D. Souther. The three hit it off. Browne was living in his first apartment in Echo Park, with his sister living next door. When she moved out, Frey and Souther moved in. Then Browne downsized into a room beneath the apartment Frey and Souther shared. The room wasn't really an apartment, more like a basement, but the rent was only thirty-five dollars a month, friendlier to his budget at the time. In such close quarters, each absorbed ideas from the others. Frey later said that he learned how to write songs by listening to Browne methodically working on a lyric or melody on the piano over and over again one floor below him.[83] For his part, Browne remembered, "Glenn Frey was the first person I heard play a Chuck Berry song on acoustic guitar. That's how the music began to morph. He sat down and played 'Sweet Little Sixteen' on acoustic guitar, and I said, 'Oh my God. You can do that?'"[84]

The turning point for Browne came when he produced a demo tape for David Geffen in the spring of 1970. Browne sang his love song "Jamaica Say You Will" with Souther playing drums and Frey on bass behind him.[85] Geffen signed him as a client for his management agency and then added him as the first artist on his Asylum label in 1971. But Geffen was in no hurry to push Browne on the market. He sent him in the winter of 1970 to tour with Laura Nyro, but mostly he told Browne to cool his heels.[86] Geffen loved Browne's songwriting, but didn't think he could sing well enough yet to carry an album. He gave him a year to take voice lessons, polish his songs, and sharpen his sound.

Finally, in September 1971, Geffen sent Browne into the studio to record his first album, the eponymous *Jackson Browne*.[87] After years of writing songs alone on piano or guitar, Browne was finally making music with a band.[88] The recording, with an A-team of local studio musicians churning efficiently behind him, proceeded smoothly, and the album was released in January 1972, almost exactly the same time as Linda Ronstadt's self-titled third album. After all the years of disappointment, Browne was anxious as the release approached: one night, shortly before the album launched, he and Geffen took LSD together to listen to the completed record, Geffen beaming with confidence and Browne still shadowed by doubt.[89]

Browne was still developing as a singer and arranger, but the album confirmed the songwriting promise he had displayed since high school. Younger than Carole King, James Taylor, Joni Mitchell, or Graham Nash, Browne did not echo their odes to domesticity. His songs still celebrated the road, the journey, searching. ("I heard that highway whisper and sigh," he sings on "Looking into You." "Are you ready to fly?") Still, from this divergent path, he wound his way to the same question posed by the slightly older LA singer-songwriters who preceded him: What did it mean to live a meaningful life as the 1960s' dreams of social transformation faded? What constituted personal contentment when political dreams dissolved? Browne placed himself in the steps of other Baby Boomers who shared the "dream . . . that one day the search will be through," as he sang, but who now stood with "embattled illusions . . . looking in my life for a truth that is my own."[90] The album showed that Browne could not only compose compelling lyrics and melodies but also examine as intently as any of his contemporaries the contradictions and choices facing his generation as it advanced into adulthood.

Propelled by an immediate radio hit, "Doctor, My Eyes," a rocker whose infectious beat lightened its world-weary lyrics, Browne's first album cracked the *Billboard*'s Top 50, much higher than Ronstadt had ever reached.[91] Browne went on tour to support the record by opening for another artist in Geffen's management stable, the formidable Joni Mitchell.[92] Graham Nash remembers David Crosby playing a cassette of Browne's unreleased album for Mitchell when the three were driving somewhere in late 1971. Who's that, she asked? Only your next boyfriend, Crosby responded.[93] He was prophetic. On their tour, Browne and Mitchell soon began a tumultuous romance.

ONE NIGHT IN 1971, Linda Ronstadt's own romantic ramblings took her to Lucy's El Adobe Café, an unpretentious Mexican spot on Melrose Avenue much beloved by the Troubadour crowd.[94] Her date was a lean, intense young man in his early thirties named Edmund Gerald "Jerry" Brown Jr. The son of the state's former Democratic governor Edmund G. (Pat) Brown, the younger Brown had been elected as California's secretary of state a year earlier. He had pursued Ronstadt diligently after she rebuffed his initial invitation, even finding her phone number after she changed it.[95] The date proceeded pleasantly enough until Ronstadt, an inveterate reader, brought up a book she was reading that called for legalizing prostitution. After Brown told her that he planned to run for governor when the incumbent, Ronald Reagan, was expected to step down in 1974, Ronstadt told him he should run on legalizing prostitution. "He just looked at me like I had four heads," she recalled. "But I meant it sincerely. I wasn't trying to shock him." Years later, the two would reunite for a more extended (and public) romance. But at the time, that was the end of their connection. "We were fish and fowl," she said.[96]

Ronstadt was not the first person, nor the last, to feel that way about the alternately inspiring and infuriating Jerry Brown Jr. Brown had ascended in politics on the same wave of generational transition that simultaneously transformed the movie, television, and music industries in Los Angeles from the late 1960s through the early 1970s. Born in 1938, the third of four children, he was reared in a San Francisco neighborhood crowded with upwardly mobile young Irish-Catholic families like his own. He moved to adulthood as his gregarious, backslapping father climbed the political ladder from election as San Francisco's district attorney in 1942 to California's attorney general in 1950 and, finally, to California governor in 1958. Smart and serious, and a good debater, young Jerry seemed bound for the same escalator: the class prediction at his eighth-grade graduation was that he would become the state attorney general for New York (of all places).[97] But Jerry stepped off the path in August 1956: after a single year at Santa Clara University, he enrolled in Sacred Heart Novitiate seminary, south of San Francisco, intending to become a Jesuit priest.[98] He found the experience spiritually rewarding and intellectually stimulating, but ultimately constricting.

Brown was a few years older than the oldest Baby Boomers, but the four years in the late 1950s he spent at Sacred Heart placed him in "suspended animation," as his younger sister, Kathleen, described it. When he left the seminary to return first to the University of California at Berkeley and then to Yale Law School, he stepped into the swirling maelstrom of the 1960s—events he probably would not have experienced as directly if he had been four years further into his career by then. He did a tour in Mississippi registering voters during the civil rights movement, picked produce with farmworkers (and raised money for Cesar Chavez, their leader), and as the decade proceeded, gravitated toward the antiwar movement. After his "four-year hiatus and hibernation, he comes out, and he's more my generation in a sense," said Kathleen Brown, who was born in 1945, on the cusp of the Baby Boom. "The antiwar movement, the civil rights movement was anti-institutional. It was revolutionary. It was change now, and it was [against] all of the people who said, 'Move slow and we can get there, but it takes time, and we have to do it the right way.' Whether it's the war, civil rights—we were all *impatient*. We were the kids . . . and Jerry embodied that."[99]

After Jerry Brown finished law school in 1964, he left his father's clubby San Francisco for Los Angeles, which he recognized as the state's future.[100] Working rather indifferently at a boutique law firm, Brown in the late 1960s still looked and lived like a graduate student on extended study, vaguely reminiscent of Dustin Hoffman's Benjamin in *The Graduate*. Even then, he had an ascetic charisma and intensity, but he was unformed. "He was interesting, he was very bright," said Tom Quinn, a young journalist who would become Brown's most trusted political adviser, "[but] he was a little scattered."[101]

Supporting Minnesota senator Eugene McCarthy's 1968 presidential campaign was Brown's first step into electoral politics. McCarthy touched a chord in Brown and other bright young men and women like him who went "clean for Gene" that year. In the fall of 1967, Brown helped found a California peace slate committed to electing antiwar delegates to the 1968 Democratic National Convention, an unmistakable act of resistance at a time when the party still assumed President Lyndon Johnson would seek the nomination.[102] When McCarthy entered the Democratic primaries to press the antiwar case against Johnson, young Brown joined his campaign (while his father cleaved to LBJ). After Robert F. Kennedy was murdered on the night of the California primary in June 1968, the great, grinding machinery of the Democratic Party, the big-city mayors and unions and county chairs, consolidated behind Hubert Humphrey, Johnson's vice president, and rolled over McCarthy as a tank might roll through a poetry reading. Jerry Brown went to Chicago for McCarthy, but he could only watch Humphrey's nomination (amid the chaos of the antiwar protests there).[103]

Though disappointing, the 1968 campaign still pushed Brown toward a career in politics. He said later that while he (like most activist Baby Boomers) initially thought he could create more pressure for change from outside the political system, the struggle over Vietnam convinced him that critics needed to run for office.[104] But the only offices Brown could find to pursue kept him far from debates about Vietnam or anything else of much magnitude. Relying heavily on his family name, Brown was elected first to the Los Angeles Junior College Board, and within a year, he ran successfully for California secretary of state.

In 1971, Brown arrived at a State Capitol frozen in an earlier time. Sacramento's culture married the ward heeler to the frat boy. At restaurants such as Frank Fat's and Posey's Cottage, lobbyists funded and lubricated the city's entire social life. Almost all the legislators were men. Sexual harassment was endemic. Any woman—a secretary, lobbyist, reporter—was fair game.

In this ocean of corruption, Brown inherited an office drowning in trivia. The secretary of state's usual responsibilities included regulating notaries, managing the state archives, and advising localities on the relative merits of incorporating as a town versus a city.[105] Brown himself often got lost in detail: soon after taking office, he demanded carbon copies of all official correspondence the office produced.[106] Even holding statewide office, Brown could be maddeningly scattered and unfocused. "He could disappear for an afternoon, with no one really knowing where he is or what he's doing," remembered Richard Maullin, a former Rand Corporation analyst who met Brown in Columbia in 1966 and then joined Quinn as one of Brown's closest political advisers.

But Brown also saw something past the piles of paperwork on his desk. "Jerry had this theory—more than that, a *belief*—that the office could be important," Quinn remembered. "His reading of the election law statutes said it was the chief election officer. He felt that meant something."[107] Long before Watergate, Brown transformed his office into a lever for opening government. Just weeks after settling in, he sued oil companies for hiding their contributions against a 1970 ballot measure promoting mass transit.[108] In 1972, Quinn discovered that the official arguments included in the state ballot pamphlet for and against a ballot proposition intended to grant new tax breaks to business were written on the same typewriter while an oil company lobbyist supervised; Brown exposed the fraud and then mandated the insertion of a new argument against the initiative. The state's disclosure forms for campaign contributions and expenditures by lobbyists hid much more than they revealed. "Nobody had ever audited these financial statements at all, and people put down things like 'Fifty-thousand-dollar fund-raiser at Tom Quinn's house,' with no breakdown of who wrote the checks," Quinn remembered.[109] Brown's office redesigned the disclosure forms to provide unprecedented detail on the money flowing into the legislature and refused to back down after the Democratic leadership in the State Capitol erupted over the increased exposure.

Unsurprisingly, his fellow Democrats loathed Brown. They considered him lazy, callow, sanctimonious, and a hypocrite, someone who condemned those fighting in the political trenches as corrupt and compromised while he quietly benefited from his father's connections to raise money and attract supporters. "Everybody was disdainful of Jerry Brown," remembered Willie Brown (no relation), a rising Democratic assembly member at the time and, later, a powerful speaker.[110]

Even then, Jerry Brown was a party of one. He lived in Malibu and then Laurel Canyon and spent little time in Sacramento. He would fly in, strafe the legislators with contempt, and then retreat to glittery LA for dates with Liv Ullmann, Natalie Wood, or Ronstadt. "Jerry was not social at all," Willie Brown recalled. "Jerry had no real friends, period, and he had no desire to pick up the tab or to have a tab picked up, period."

Brown didn't mind the legislative leadership's contempt: he welcomed it as a foil that would highlight his reform credentials and connect him to the same antiauthority impulses flowing through popular culture. The very shrewdness of that calculation underscored how misguided it was for others, despite his unusual pedigree in the seminary, to view him as an ivory tower idealist. He was also a very practical politician. Brown the younger both rejected and emulated his father: he was a philosopher prince who recoiled from many of the conventions of old-style campaigning. (Like John F. Kennedy, he would not wear a hat.) But he could also roll up his sleeves and dirty his hands. And though he was so reluctant to take advice from father Pat that the old man was left lamenting to visiting reporters that his son would not talk to him, the younger man had clearly learned from the older his exacting attention to political detail. Brown carefully used the 1972 presidential campaign, even though it ended in Richard Nixon's landslide, to build his own contacts around the state.

Tom Quinn thought Jerry Brown began running for governor as soon as he reached the community college board in Los Angeles. Brown held the first formal meeting of his steering committee to plan the race in June 1972. He made his candidacy official on January 28, 1974, just a few weeks after Linda Ronstadt and Jackson Browne went out together on tour.[111]

EARLY IN THE LONG gestation of Jackson Browne's first album, Linda Ronstadt heard a song he had written called "Rock Me on the Water." The composition was among his finest. A departure from the country rock conquering LA at the time, "Rock Me" was a rock-gospel blend with evocative lyrics that veered from spirituality to sexuality and back again. The song reflected what Browne later called "stuff that came from the very center of me: the desire for love and peace and release and reconciliation with the spiritual" amid all the social tumult of the 1960s, crystallized for him in works he read from radical critics of American society such as Eldridge Cleaver. It was thoughtful, catchy, and commercial. Yet, when Ronstadt asked if she could include it on the album she was recording at the same time, Browne never hesitated. It didn't worry him that her version might reach listeners before his. "Are you kidding, Linda Ronstadt wants to sing your song?" he said, looking back. "It didn't matter when we're going to do our songs. It was that a broader audience was going to hear it. So, I wasn't in competition with Linda at all."[112]

Browne's enthusiastic sharing of his brilliant song captured a large part of what made Los Angeles unique at its peak moment of musical influence: LA in the early 1970s was a Republic of Rock and Roll. When London had been the center of the rock universe in the mid-1960s, no one misunderstood the hierarchy. The Beatles were at the top. "They were ninety percent, and we were all ten percent," said Peter Asher, who was close friends with Paul McCartney and later worked for the Beatles' Apple Records.[113] Graham Nash agreed. "In England there was an attitude kind of that if you didn't know John, Paul, and George, you weren't anybody."[114] The Stones and perhaps Cream at their Clapton-is-God peak might be a half step down, the Who on the rung below them, and then everybody else scrambling below, but no one had any confusion about who stood where.

LA could not have been more different. Like the city itself, its music universe was open and inclusive. "It was a collective," said Asher.[115] LA's music felt "collaborative maybe for the first time," agreed Lou Adler, who had first hit the LA music world as a precocious young songwriter penning compositions for Sam Cooke, among others, in the late 1950s. "I remember in the fifties it was very competitive, and that could be because there were singles. Where are you on the charts? By seventy, I'm doing Carole King; James and Joni come in to do the backgrounds on one of their tracks. Carole goes to play piano on one of their tracks. George Harrison stops by and plays on a Cheech and Chong record. So, it's really just 'Let's make music,' as opposed to 'I'm going to make music, and I'm going to be a success.'"[116] The thoughtful guitarist Danny Kortchmar felt the change in the climate immediately after he relocated to LA from New York. "It was very democratic," he said. "It was a community of musicians. We all felt that we'll all rise together. Nobody was competitive in terms of wanting to keep somebody else down."[117] Nash felt the same way. "The only competition was 'Holy shit, that's a great song! Fuck, where's my guitar?'" he said. "You would be inspired to be as good as you could be because you were surrounded by people that were making great music."[118]

This instinct surfaced in ways large and small. Kortchmar remembers musicians he had idolized lending him guitars soon after he arrived. Artists would share notes on one another's songs: after Browne heard Ronstadt's version of "Rock Me," for instance, he rerecorded the album version of the song as a more up-tempo single that drew on her interpretation. (Each of their singles of "Rock Me" reached *Billboard*'s Top 100, his six months after hers.) To a remarkable extent, LA's A-list talent appeared on one another's records. James Taylor and Linda Ronstadt sang background vocals for Neil Young on "Heart of Gold," his only No. 1 hit. On Browne's first album, Crosby and Nash sang background vocals, and Elton John played the piano. On Browne's second album, Joni Mitchell and Elton John played piano, and Don Henley and Bonnie Raitt sang harmony. Glenn Frey played guitar on a Ronstadt album long after he had left her band to form the Eagles. Crosby and Nash sang with Joni Mitchell; Robbie Robertson of the Band, who had relocated to Malibu at David Geffen's prodding, played guitar for her. "I think people just liked hanging out with each other in the studio," remembered Asher.[119] Nash and Crosby, with their beautiful harmonies, were always among the most sought-after background vocalists. "There's a lot of people on a lot of people's records because we loved music and we loved songs," Nash recalled. "Joe Walsh called me one day, and he goes, 'I got this kid called Danny Fogelberg. He's got this great song called "Part of the Plan," but I keep hearing your voice. Let me send it over to you.' So, he sent it over to me, and it was a great song, so I wanted to do it. That used to happen all the time."[120]

The scene was burning with the excitement of creation. The artists played together, got high together, slept together. Joni Mitchell had a fling with Crosby, a much more serious relationship with Nash, and then involvements of varying duration (and turbulence) with James Taylor and Jackson Browne. Ronstadt cut a swath through the Troubadour bar; so did J. D. Souther, one of her more serious beaus.

For years, the Troubadour club was the central switching yard in this network. It was where Elton John had established himself in America, and it helped to break out Neil Young and Joni Mitchell, Kris Kristofferson and James Taylor. The bar at the front of the club was part singles scene, part hiring hall, part support group. Some joined Jackson Browne in viewing Troubadour society as a dead end, but most found community and encouragement there. Boylan considered the Troubadour "the center of our universe. Everybody hung out there." It was alive, unpredictable. "You could see anybody there any night," he says.[121] Joni Mitchell would stop by; Warren Beatty romanced Carly Simon backstage there.[122] Jack Nicholson or Peter Fonda would not raise an eyebrow when they breezed in. One night, Boylan remembers sitting at a table with Johnny Cash, on a visit to LA, when the country-rock pioneer Doug Dillard stumbled by, wasted on booze or drugs, and invited himself to join the group. It might have been a tense moment—Cash wasn't known for his calm—but soon after he crashed the table, Dillard started "singing some tune everybody knew," Boylan recalled, "and everyone would then suddenly fill in, come in, and sing along."[123]

One drink became two, and drop-bys extended into the early morning hours, time melting away like the ice cubes in the drinks. "The bar was the hangout," Ronstadt remembered. "I can't drink—drinking is not what I do—but everybody just came and parked themselves in the bar and hung out. You'd watch who came in and who came out. And then, at night, when it was closing time, we'd all sing in the corner. It would be me and [Doug's brother] Rodney Dillard and Boylan sometimes, Chris Hillman, Herbie Peterson. We'd close the place down."[124]

All the regulars at the bar were jostling for the same things, and sometimes they collided. But to Ronstadt, like others on the scene, LA always seemed more communal, more welcoming than New York City, where "there was a lot less forgiveness if you weren't quite happening."[125] The crowd at the Troubadour commiserated and cooperated more than it competed. "In a weird way, it was kind of supportive," Ronstadt said. "There were a lot of snide remarks that always went around—you could find that in any hairdressing salon—but mainly it was pretty respectful. J. D. [Souther] and those guys and Glenn [Frey] and Jackson [Browne]—they really respected each other's music and gave a lot of encouragement to each other. Joni Mitchell was there, and I watched her every night. I saw Elton John do his first American appearance, and it was amazing. Jennifer Warren, who was a great singer. Bonnie Raitt—the first time she played at the Troubadour, I was there . . . and that was humbling. I felt like I was in the freshman class, and they were in the senior class."[126]

In this fluid environment, hierarchy dissolved, especially in the scene's early years. Boylan remembers those who had achieved their first tastes of success mingling easily with those still pressing their faces against the glass. "Of course, there were people who had made it and those who still hadn't, but everybody thought everybody was going to make it eventually," he recalled. Nor did LA distinguish between those who sought the prestige of acclaim from rock critics and FM radio audiences and those who wanted AM radio hits. Almost without exception, the Los Angeles artists wanted *everything*. Glenn Frey spoke for his entire generation of LA musicians when he said, "We wanted it all. Peer respect. AM and FM success. Number one singles and albums, great music, and a lot of money."[127] (He omitted only sex and drugs.) "In Los Angeles, most of the artists . . . wanted to have hits," recalled Jon Landau, whose critical imprimatur was among the most coveted. "Moviemakers who made all those unusual films, innovative films—*they* wanted to have hits. LA culture was about hits, among other things, and so they wanted to be innovators, but they didn't want to be, for the most part, innovators who went unheard."[128]

From every direction, walls fell. The record company executives and the talent, the producers and the engineers, the agents and the managers, the session players and the visiting virtuosos—they all gathered in the same clubs, listened to the same bands, tried the same drugs, mingled at the same parties. "What really was special at the time," Jackson Browne remembered, "was that people who worked in record companies and people who produced records and people who sang on records and made records—[they] were all hanging out. They were all spending time together, whether it was the Troubadour or Dan Tana's, next door, or going to somebody's house. That's how bands got hipper, and record companies got hipper, too, because they were going down the same paths."[129] In London or New York, the boundaries around each of those groups—between suits and stars, or moneymen and artists—might have been more sharply defined, the borders between them more heavily fortified, but erasing lines was the essence of Los Angeles. "It was open here," Browne remembered.

Openness became the defining characteristic of LA's emergent Republic of Rock and Roll. Even the movie industry, long resistant to change, cracked open the door to new voices in those years. But the hierarchy remained much more firmly established in the last of the city's entertainment giants, the television industry. Television was buffeted by the same gales of generational and demographic change that reshaped the music and movie businesses, but it responded more slowly than either. And when change did come, it arrived largely at the hands of two older white men whom no one would have picked as the agents of revolution.

3

MARCH

The Greatest Night in Television History

On Saturday night, March 16, 1974, at 8 p.m. Eastern Time, the situation comedy *All in the Family* aired its final episode of the 1973/74 television season. The story marked a milestone in the show. Mike Stivic, the long-haired, liberal son-in-law of reactionary bigot Archie Bunker and his wife, Edith, has finally graduated from college. Archie, a staunchly conservative Richard Nixon–loving dockworker, and Edith, his daffy but benevolent wife, think this means that Mike and their bubbly daughter, Gloria, will be moving out of the Bunkers' small home in Queens, New York, where they have all been uneasily cohabitating while Mike attended school. Edith spends the episode dreading the departure, but Archie is swelling in anticipation of converting Mike and Gloria's tiny bedroom into a den, where he can puff a pipe like "Tex Harrison" in *My Fair Lady*. But then Mike, an aspiring sociologist, accepts a fellowship for more study, which means, to Archie's loud disappointment, that no one is going anywhere. The family endures to fight another day.

Two weeks before *All in the Family* signed off for the summer, the three half-hour comedies that aired right after it on CBS's Saturday night finished their seasons on March 2: *M*A*S*H*, an adaptation of a hit movie that portrayed an irreverent mobile medical unit in the Korean War; *The Mary Tyler Moore Show*, following the romantic and professional travails of a thirty-something single woman in Minneapolis; and *The Bob Newhart Show*, about a psychiatrist in Chicago drily navigating through an eccentric circle of family, friends, and patients.

The Carol Burnett Show, the hour-long variety show that closed the CBS Saturday night lineup, airing from 10 to 11 p.m. Eastern, ended its season a few weeks later, on April 6.

The 1973/74 season had been a triumph for CBS, which posted nine of the ten-most-watched shows in America, according to the final Nielsen ratings.[1] And Saturday night was the jewel in CBS's crown. For the third consecutive season, *All in the Family* topped the Nielsen ratings as the nation's most highly watched show. *M*A*S*H* finished fourth; *Mary Tyler Moore*, ninth; *Bob Newhart* (at twelfth) and *Carol Burnett* (at twenty-seventh) came in a few steps behind. This was the only season those five shows, all produced within a few miles of one another on the Westside of Los Angeles, ever appeared together on the same night. Some critics would later call it the greatest night in television history. It was an eminently justifiable verdict.

The shows boasted an incredible concentration of talent both in front of and behind the camera, particularly the three landmark programs that aired at the top of the lineup. *All in the Family*, the creation of producer Norman Lear, was brought to life by Carroll O'Connor as Archie, Jean Stapleton as Edith, Rob Reiner as Mike, and Sally Struthers as Gloria, all shepherded by John Rich, one of television's most respected and longest-tenured directors. *Mary Tyler Moore* had been created by skilled young writer-producers Allan Burns and James L. Brooks, nurtured by a writing staff that included Treva Silverman, one of television's first successful women comedy writers, and incarnated by a dynamic cast led by Mary Tyler Moore (as Mary Richards), Ed Asner (as her crusty newsroom boss, Lou Grant), Ted Knight (as Ted Baxter, a news anchor with gravel in his voice and rocks in his head), and Valerie Harper (as Mary's acerbic New York friend Rhoda Morgenstern). *M*A*S*H*, created by producer Gene Reynolds and writer Larry Gelbart, crackled to life behind brilliant performances from Alan Alda (as "Hawkeye" Pierce), Loretta Swit (as nurse Margaret "Hot Lips" Houlihan), Wayne Rogers (as Hawkeye's irreverent buddy "Trapper" John McIntyre), Gary Burghoff (as the innocent but seemingly omniscient clerk, Radar O'Reilly), and later Mike Farrell (as B. J. Hunnicutt) and Harry Morgan (as camp commander Sherman Potter).

These programs were commercial and also critical successes. From 1971, when *Mary Tyler Moore* and *All in the Family* first appeared, through 1975, those two shows and *M*A*S*H* dominated the annual Emmy Awards to a remarkable extent. Over those five years, *All in the Family* won the Emmy as Best Comedy three times, with *Mary Tyler Moore* and *M*A*S*H* capturing the other two awards, in addition to the raft of Emmys awarded to the shows' actors, writers, and directors. But *All in the Family, Mary Tyler Moore,* and *M*A*S*H* became landmarks not only because of their excellence but also because of their relevance. After years in which the television networks had deliberately, even defiantly, ignored the fissures in American life opening around them, these three shows, more than any predecessor, finally connected the medium to the moment. Though *M*A*S*H* was set in Korea, viewers could not miss the parallels to Vietnam in its brilliant satire of war's futility. *Mary Tyler Moore* sensitively chronicled the changing role of women as it tracked Mary Richards's life as a single woman in her thirties (itself a breakthrough for television). *All in the Family,* primarily through its clangorous clashes between Reiner and O'Connor (stand-ins for Lear and his father), loudly aired every contemporary issue dividing the Baby Boomers and their Greatest Generation parents, from civil rights and the sexual revolution to the Vietnam War.

All this represented a head-spinning change from what television had offered before. As recently as 1969/70, the season before *Mary Tyler Moore* and then *All in the Family* first appeared, the Top 10 Nielsen programs included *Gunsmoke, Bonanza, Mayberry R.F.D., Family Affair, Here's Lucy, The Red Skelton Show, Marcus Welby, M.D., The Wonderful World of Disney,* and *The Doris Day Show*; only *Rowan and Martin's Laugh-In,* a manic comic sketch show, connected at all to contemporary life.[2] Any of the rest might have aired as easily while Dwight Eisenhower was president.

All in the Family, Mary Tyler Moore, and *M*A*S*H* saw themselves as part of a common movement to transform television. "There was a big wave of sophistication that happened," remembered Rob Reiner. "And we felt connected to everybody."[3] Linda Bloodworth-Thomason, who went on to create and produce *Designing Women* for CBS, was just tentatively leaving journalism for a television writing career when she worked first with Gelbart and Brooks and later with Lear. "They had found a way to get all of their opinions and political philosophy into that little box," she recalled. "Even though I knew then that people looked down on television writers, Larry taught me that 'More people are going to see one *M*A*S*H* episode, Linda, than are ever going to see *Gone with the Wind*.' He said, 'If you want all the elites to just swoon over your column, that's a different story. But if you really want to affect change or affect people, you've got to get in the box.'"[4]

Each show drew inspiration from the others. It was "competition, fraternity, all that," Brooks remembered. "We all wanted to be the best."[5] Lear described Gelbart as "perhaps the greatest wit" he had ever known.[6] Brooks was awed by *All in the Family*. "We used to sit and watch *All in the Family* and just feel like pygmies next to it, because it was groundbreaking and it was great," he recalls, noting that the *Mary Tyler Moore* team watched the Saturday night CBS lineup "religiously . . . We'd get in front of the television like America did. Watch it straight through."[7] Reiner, in turn, remembers the *All in the Family* cast marveling at the artistry of the *Mary Tyler Moore* ensemble. "It was just really, really funny," he said.[8]

When CBS first placed *All in the Family* on the air on January 12, 1971, it irrevocably transformed television. After a shaky first season in which it struggled to find an audience, the show prospered, rising to become No. 1 in the ratings for five consecutive years, a record unmatched at the time. *All in the Family* commanded and concentrated national attention to a degree almost impossible to imagine in today's fractionated entertainment landscape. Archie's catchwords *stifle*, *meathead*, and *dingbat* all became national shorthand. Scholars earnestly debated whether the show punctured or promoted bigotry. Its success not only helped lift *Mary Tyler Moore* and *M*A*S*H*, but also provided a glow to other early 1970s productions from Lear and his partner, Bud Yorkin: *Sanford and Son*, on NBC (the only non-CBS show to reach the Top 10 during the 1973/74 season), and three direct spin-offs on CBS: *Maude* and *The Jeffersons*, which sprang from *All in* *the Family*, and *Good Times*, which emerged from *Maude*. Another hit, *One Day at a Time*, followed in 1975. By one estimate, Lear and Yorkin accounted for one fourth of all the shows in the Nielsen Top 15 from 1971 to 1978.[9]

It was something of a miracle that *All in the Family* reached the air at all. Before CBS bought it, ABC had rejected it twice. And before *All in the Family*, shows that tried to achieve more relevance had almost all failed, mostly because they were too laden with good intentions to attract an audience. That *All in the Family* not only reached the air but prospered was the result of two men: Norman Lear, its creator, and Robert D. Wood, the president of CBS, who put it on the schedule. That act revolutionized television, but both men were unlikely revolutionaries.

NORMAN LEAR WAS THE son of a man whose dreams dissolved quickly but whose resentments outlived him in the work of his son. Herman Lear was a small-time salesman and entrepreneur, a fountain of dubious get-rich-quick schemes, one of which (a ruse to sell phony bonds) landed him in prison for three years.[10] His wife, Jeanette, according to Norman, was self-absorbed, discontented, and like her husband, volatile.[11] Later, they would become Lear's models for Archie and Edith Bunker. Through a childhood in Connecticut and Brooklyn, Lear's parents immersed him in an environment of barely controlled chaos. The two of them, Lear would often say, "lived at the ends of their nerves and the tops of their lungs." At the peak of argument, the veins in his neck bulging, Lear's father would beat his fists against his chest and bellow at Lear's mother, "Jeanette, stifle yourself."[12]

Like many children of the Great Depression, Lear found direction and structure in the military. After drifting through a few semesters at Emerson College in Boston, he enlisted in the Army Air Force following Pearl Harbor and flew dozens of bombing missions over Germany. When he returned from the war, Lear found work as a Broadway press agent in New York before moving back to Connecticut with his wife to join his father's latest scheme: a small appliance manufacturing company.[13] After a few years, that venture predictably joined Herman's bulging ledger of failures, and the son made a decision that proved a turning point: he loaded his wife and infant daughter into a 1946 Oldsmobile convertible and pointed it toward Los Angeles, where, like many before and after, he hoped for a fresh start. The move did not immediately reveal itself as a new beginning. Lear wanted to resume his career in publicity, but he could not find work. He was reduced to selling furniture and baby photos door-to-door with a man named Ed Simmons, who was married to Lear's cousin Elaine, the one person he knew in Los Angeles. When he spent an afternoon driving around Los Angeles looking for the cheapest deal on used tires for his car, Lear figured he had hit bottom.[14]

Simmons was trying to break in as a comedy writer, and one night, Lear helped him finish a parody of a popular song he had been writing. When they found a nightclub singer to buy the song, their payday was only forty dollars between them, but that was enough to convince the two to drop their salesman's satchels and plunge into a full-time writing partnership.[15] Soon after, they sold another routine to Danny Thomas, a much more prominent nightclub comic, which in turn caught the attention of an MCA agent, who asked Simmons and Lear to develop a few sketches for Jack Haley, the Tin Man from *The Wizard of Oz*.[16] Haley, who was slated to host a new variety hour on NBC, loved the material and hired Simmons and Lear to write for the show. Having driven to Los Angeles only the year before, Lear returned to New York City in much grander style on his first cross-country flight.[17]

Through the 1950s, Lear's career advanced in step with the growth of television itself. These were the years of television's so-called golden age, when earnest dramas such as *The Philco Television Playhouse* and *Playhouse 90* would groom a steady stream of young directors for Hollywood in the 1960s. Lear was marinated in the other great television product of those years: the star-led variety shows that drew on traditions of vaudeville and radio comedy, programs such as *The Milton Berle Show* and Sid Caesar's *Your Show of Shows*. The talent that collected around these shows was blinding: the writers for the various incarnations of Caesar's shows alone included Carl Reiner, Mel Brooks, Larry Gelbart, Mel Tolkin, Neil Simon, and Woody Allen. Rob Reiner, Carl's son, was only slightly exaggerating when he later said, "It's pretty much the group that was on the *Show of Shows* and *Caesar's Hour* [that] were responsible for anything that you ever laughed at in the second half of the twentieth century."[18]

Lear and Simmons thrived in this world. After only a few months with Jack Haley, they climbed another step when the hot comedy duo of Jerry Lewis and Dean Martin plucked them to write their material on *The Colgate Comedy Hour*, a much bigger platform. After the mercurial Lewis fired them three years later, Simmons and Lear jumped to *The Martha Raye Show*.[19] Lear began to ricochet between Los Angeles and New York, mastering the breakneck pace of television production—he survived the constant deadlines, he later recalled, on Dexedrine to stay awake for all-night writing sessions and Seconal to sleep when they were over. He honed his sense of comedy, absorbing the rhythms of sketches that had to quickly grip an audience's attention between singers or dancing acts. "Because there was very little situation comedy, the shows I was influenced by [were] more the sketch shows, the variety shows," Lear recalled.[20]

His work was skilled and professional, and his shows were sufficiently successful to constantly open new doors for him. But after Lewis and Martin's, none was especially memorable. Eventually, he and Simmons ended their partnership, and Lear took up with the director Bud Yorkin, who had been a stage manager on *Colgate* and whose star had brightened after he produced and directed a highly acclaimed NBC special for Fred Astaire. Yorkin's wife, Peggy, suggested the two men take advantage of the moment by forming their own company, with Norman to write, Bud to direct, and both to produce.[21]

The two men established Tandem Productions in 1958, and weeks later they had negotiated a deal to develop both television programs and movies for Paramount.[22] Tandem quickly buzzed with the insistent energy of two ambitious men convinced their time had arrived. Within a few years, Yorkin and Lear had developed and aired television specials with Danny Kaye, Carol Channing, Bobby Darin, Henry Fonda, and singer Andy Williams, and spun the Williams special into a one-hour variety series on NBC. By Yorkin's count, the company also worked on seven movies during the 1960s, including two that Lear wrote and Yorkin directed: *Come Blow Your Horn*, a 1963 adaptation of a Neil Simon play that starred Frank Sinatra, and *Divorce American Style*, starring Dick Van Dyke and Debbie Reynolds, in 1967.[23]

Some of these films managed respectable box-office returns, but none generated much critical excitement. No reviewers saw in the Lear and Yorkin movies, or their succession of television specials with soft-edged mainstream entertainers, the profile of anything new. Looking back, one Hollywood executive described them in those years as "yeoman producers, just guys that would get their heads down and do the work." Apart from the better sections of the uneven *Divorce*, none of Lear's work in the 1960s signaled that he had much to say about the way America was transforming around him. "Here's an example, and it rarely happens, of a guy who was smarter than his career," recalled Michael Ovitz, who started his own career as a television agent before becoming Hollywood's most influential dealmaker as the cofounder of Creative Artists Agency. "Norman Lear was far more intellectually proficient than the things he was doing."[24] Within a few years, millions would agree, but not until Lear met another World War II veteran who was an even more unlikely candidate to transform the nature of television.

ROBERT WOOD'S CAREER PROCEEDED almost exactly in parallel with Lear's. Wood was born in 1925 in Boise, Idaho, but his parents relocated to Beverly Hills (the "poorer section of it," he once explained), where he was raised.[25] While Lear served in the Army Air Force during World War II, Wood spent three years in the navy, including time in the South Pacific.[26] After the war, he graduated with a degree in advertising from the University of Southern California in 1949, the same year Lear arrived in Los Angeles with his young family.

Wood started his career as an ad salesman for KNX radio, the CBS affiliate in LA. Within a few years he had moved to television ad sales at KNXT, the CBS television affiliate there. Wood was a natural salesman: gregarious, easy to talk to, a devoted fan of USC football who, throughout his life, gravitated to football metaphors to explain his decisions. After a short stint working in national ad sales for CBS in New York, he was named KNXT's general sales manager in 1955. In 1960 he was promoted to vice president and general manager of the station itself.

His elevation to that role anointed him as a prince in the CBS empire. KNXT was one of the five stations around the country that the federal government permitted CBS, like the other networks, to own and operate directly during this period. These "O&O stations," as they were known, were concentrated in the largest markets and generated enormous profits. Inside the networks, they were treated with much more deference than the affiliates that carried their programs in most markets. CBS granted great autonomy to the O&O general managers and marked them as future leaders. The network expected them to be visible in the community and to join community debates. CBS pushed the O&O managers to deliver on-air editorials, like those in local newspapers, but left them almost entirely free to decide the content.

Wood thrived in these roles. Powerfully built and bullet-headed, he was not a natural on-air television personality, but under his leadership, KNXT delivered an average of just over one hundred on-air editorials a year, almost one every three days.[27] "He was really proud of being the editorial voice, the guy who appeared in the editorials, and he was good at it," recalled Pete Noyes, a prominent news producer at KNXT in those years. "He had a great presence."[28] Wood hired Howard Williams, an editorial writer from the conservative *Los Angeles Mirror*, to help him craft the station's editorial line. "He really enjoyed it, and he took it seriously," Williams said.[29]

Wood was a gregarious boss, with a salesman's effortless capacity to make friends and create camaraderie (even if he kept his distance socially from the staff). He knew everybody's name and had time to talk to anyone. "Didn't matter who they were . . . he was your buddy: anybody in the station," said Williams.[30] He roamed the halls without his suit jacket, making conversation as he went.

But Wood wasn't just affable; he was also enterprising. His most consequential decision was approving a landmark plan from Sam Zelman, his vice president for news, to create an expanded local newscast. *The Big News*, as they called it, combined forty-five minutes of local news with the fifteen minutes of national news CBS distributed at the time to create an unprecedented one-hour block of early evening news. From the moment KNXT debuted *The Big News* in 1961, it ruled the market.

Wood's politics were consistently conservative, reflecting the center of gravity in LA media and business circles during the 1950s and '60s, in which he mingled easily. In 1962, KNXT endorsed Nixon over Pat Brown for governor when the former vice president returned to California after losing the 1960 presidential race to John F. Kennedy. (In a memo before a Nixon appearance at a Radio-Television News Association luncheon during the 1962 governor's campaign, one Nixon adviser suggested that a letter to Wood "would be good because Bob has expressed his complete support of the Boss—privately, of course.")[31] Two years later, when the first Free Speech demonstrations erupted in 1964 at the University of California at Berkeley, Wood, in one of his on-air editorials, called the demonstrators "witless agitators" and insisted that they "be dealt with quickly and severely to set an example for all time to those who agitate for the sake of agitation."[32] In 1966, Wood and KNXT endorsed Ronald Reagan in his successful drive to deny Democrat Pat Brown his third term as California's governor.

The Reagan endorsement proved one of Wood's final decisions in Los Angeles. Soon after, CBS brought him east to serve as executive vice president of the CBS Television Stations division, which supervised the O&O stations. In October 1967, CBS promoted Wood to president of the division, and on February 14, 1969, Valentine's Day, Wood was promoted again to president of the CBS Television Network, the company's highest-ranking television job.[33]

This promotion placed him atop the most powerful and profitable of the three television networks. CBS's preeminence was symbolized by its imposing Midtown Manhattan headquarters, an austere and dramatic spire of charcoal gray granite known as Black Rock. From his thirty-fourth-floor office, Wood entered a *Mad Men* world that appeared frozen in time. At the time, James Rosenfield, who later also served as the CBS network president, was a network ad salesman. He remembers long, boozy lunches with clients as the routine. If the sales team didn't have lunch with a client, it would retreat on its own to the celebrated Toots Shor's, on Fifty-First Street. At 6 p.m., the sales team and programming executives alike regularly filed into the 21 Club. "You *had* to be at Twenty-one by six," Rosenfield said. "The bar was semicircular. They had mementos hanging from the ceiling: a plane for airlines, a microphone for TV. At the bar at the immediate corner when you walked in was NBC, the far corner was CBS, and the middle was ABC."[34] This was a vastly more urbane, cosmopolitan, and cutthroat world than the domesticated cycle of Junior League dinners and weekends at the beach in San Clemente that Wood had left behind in Los Angeles.[35] But he took to it naturally. He settled into leafy Greenwich, Connecticut, transitioning easily into its country club routines. To many around him, Wood came across as the West Coast equivalent of an Ivy Leaguer, confident and smooth, if no intellectual; he was always more comfortable discussing football than philosophy.

Even from within its black-tinted fortress at the pinnacle of the broadcast industry, CBS could not entirely avoid the 1960s—but it did its best. Acutely conscious of image, William Paley, the CBS founder and board chairman, and Frank Stanton, the CBS president, expected executives to follow a common dress code (blue suit, a hat, Gucci shoes, often blue shirts and blue ties) that presented a more urbane version of the black suit/white shirt/black tie regimen Lew Wasserman demanded of MCA agents. Stanton controlled the design of Black Rock so completely that employees couldn't place a print on their office wall or a photo on their desk without approval from the building's design team. Even the furniture was positioned the same way in every office.[36] Black Rock was designed with separate elevators for the higher floors partly, the word went, so that Paley and Stanton would not have to see the employees at CBS Records, who arrived for work in blue jeans. Almost no women held positions of power.[37]

Yet, for all the power and profitability, the confidence and control, that CBS projected through the late 1960s, the ground underneath Black Rock was shifting. CBS faced disruption from the same demographic-driven transformation of its audience that had staggered the movie studios. And Wood, with his grounding in Los Angeles, felt the tremors earlier than almost anyone else around him.

IN 1961, NEWTON MINOW, the chairman of the Federal Communications Commission, memorably disparaged television as "a vast wasteland." But in those years, Minow would have been just as accurate to call television "a vast cornfield."

Through the 1960s, the networks stubbornly looked away from the simultaneous earthquakes disrupting American life: the civil rights and antiwar movements, the nightly carnage of Vietnam, the rise of the drug culture, the sexual revolution, and the feminist awakening. Like the major Hollywood studios, the three television networks, with rare exceptions, spent the decade producing programs almost entirely disconnected from the changes pulsing through society. Led by CBS, the networks mostly offered viewers a gauzy, pastoral America unruffled by racial or generational conflict, unscarred by war, and untempted by new attitudes about sex and marriage. The biggest difference between the networks and the studios was that, unlike Hollywood, television made a great deal of money while doing so.

With only three networks, shows needed to attract enormous viewership to survive: anything that drew less than one third of the viewing audience risked cancellation.[38] Scale squashed innovation. The prevailing aim at the networks and the advertising agencies was to produce what became known as "the least objectionable program" that could draw the most diverse viewership.[39] In practice, this translated into shows that would be acceptable not only to urban sophisticates but also to small-town traditionalists. So, off the CBS assembly line constructed by James T. Aubrey, the network's dynamic and dysfunctional president through the mid-1960s, flowed a procession of banal comedies celebrating the simple wisdom of rural life: *The Beverly Hillbillies* (the biggest hit in the group), *Petticoat Junction*, *Green Acres*, and *The Andy Griffith Show*. Surrounding them were variety shows and comedies led by aging figures from the 1950s and even earlier: Jackie Gleason, Red Skelton, Ed Sullivan, Lucille Ball, Danny Thomas, and for a time, Jack Benny and Judy Garland. As the Vietnam War escalated into an inferno, CBS responded with *Gomer Pyle*, an Andy Griffith spin-off with Jim Nabors as a guileless small-town marine, and *Hogan's Heroes*, a comedy set in a Nazi POW camp. (With the toothless military comedies *McHale's Navy* and *The Wackiest Ship in the Army* respectively, ABC and NBC came no closer to Vietnam than CBS did.) Each night, CBS chronicled the increasingly tumultuous strains tearing at America on Walter Cronkite's newscast and then spent the next three and a half hours of prime time trying to erase them from their viewers' minds.

The first efforts to produce programming that reached beyond this "alfalfa curtain" came from ABC, by far the weakest of the three networks, which experimented with shows targeting a younger and more urban audience, including 77 *Sunset Strip*, *Bewitched*, *That Girl*, and the high-camp television version of *Batman*, which became an unlikely hit after its January 1966 debut. But these initial ABC programs didn't connect with the social changes around them much more than the CBS rural comedies did. The network's first real step in that direction came in 1968, when ABC aired *The Mod Squad*, an hour-long drama from Aaron Spelling. Quickly a hit, *The Mod Squad* followed three disaffected young people—"One black, one white, one blonde," as the show's early advertising campaign put it—who worked as undercover cops to avoid jail time for their own past offenses. The show's message was fundamentally conformist—the three young rebels learned the value of working within the system—but it elevated contemporary concerns, such as drug abuse and police brutality, that television had rarely before addressed. That same year, NBC put on *Julia*, a gentle but well-executed situation comedy, notable mostly because it featured Diahann Carroll, the first African American lead in a prime-time comedy. In 1969, ABC followed with *Room 222*, an idea developed by writer James Brooks with producer Gene Reynolds, which tracked the travails of young students and teachers (including a leading character who was African American) at an integrated Los Angeles high school.

CBS first tapped the changing culture with *The Smothers Brothers Comedy Hour*, which reached the air in February 1967. The Smothers Brothers, Tom the leader and Dick the straight man, were a modestly successful duo who had built an audience through albums and a nightclub act that combined stand-up comedy with gentle parodies of folk music. Their CBS show didn't emerge from any conscious network desire to connect with new currents, but Michael Dann, the network's longtime vice president for programming, had a general sense that a show built around two younger stars might represent effective counterprogramming against *Bonanza*, the NBC Sunday night Western that had stampeded over all other competition for years.

Dann was right: *The Smothers Brothers Comedy Hour* was a hit from the outset and quickly became the one spot on network television that seemed conscious of the burgeoning youth culture. Cutting-edge bands such as Buffalo Springfield, the Byrds, the Who, and Simon and Garfunkel all appeared.

As the show's audience grew, Tom Smothers in particular became determined to use the platform to deliver a distinctly liberal message about contemporary issues, including civil rights, drugs, and especially, the Vietnam War. Tom "said, 'There's no point of being on television . . . at this point in time, with what's going on in this country, and not reflect what's going on,'" recalled Rob Reiner, who joined the show for part of its final season as a writer.[40]

Reiner and the stable of precociously talented young writers that the Smotherses' show attracted regularly nudged Tommy to test CBS's boundaries. "We wanted to push it further, and I remember getting into fights with Tommy Smothers," Reiner said. "I didn't realize how difficult it was for him just to get the things on that we were doing."[41]

CBS censors predictably recoiled, snipping lines from some segments and rejecting others completely. The show had supporters inside CBS—Dann was a dependable ally—but the network's senior leadership grew weary of the constant arguments with Tom Smothers. A slippage in the ratings weakened his position. Finally, Wood canceled the show in early April 1969, less than two months after he assumed the network's presidency.[42]

The *Smothers Brothers*' unhappy experience captured the difficulty of bringing change to CBS. Even as late as May 1970, the network seemed preserved in amber. On the night of May 4, 1970, a few hours after National Guard members shot and killed four students protesting the Vietnam War at Kent State University, in Ohio, the evening broadcast schedule on CBS opened at 7:30 p.m. with *Gunsmoke*, a Western that had debuted on the network in September 1955.[43] At 8:30 p.m., the network followed with *Here's Lucy*, starring Lucille Ball playing a variation on the daffy character she had first introduced to television audiences in 1951. At 9 p.m. came *Mayberry R.F.D.*, the spin-off and extension of *The Andy Griffith Show*, which had premiered in 1960. At 9:30 came *The Doris Day Show*, the eponymous vehicle for the singer and actress who had made her debut with Big Bands before World War II.

The pressure for a new approach was building, and it came, surprisingly, from the network's business staff. CBS had the biggest audiences, but ABC and NBC were successfully wooing advertisers with their arguments that they had *better* audiences: young, affluent consumers in urban centers. Rosenfield, like other CBS ad sellers, found big corporate clients such as Procter and Gamble growing more receptive to ABC's argument that the quantity of viewership was less important than the quality. "They were able to convince advertisers to buy on their demographic," Rosenfield said. Cecil Smith, chief television writer for the *Los Angeles Times*, memorably summarized the argument threatening CBS's dominance in the advertising market: "How many farmers CBS had didn't matter unless you sold tractors."[44] Even those at CBS who didn't fear competitive pressure recognized that better results with younger people would allow the network to charge more for their commercial time. At times, CBS was forced to provide discounts to its advertisers because ABC argued it was reaching consumers under fifty at a lower cost.[45] "We could demand more money if we were hitting the eighteen-to-forty-nine [audience]," said Bob Daly, a CBS business executive at the time who later became the network's president.[46] Gene Jankowski, a CBS ad executive who also later became the network's president, remembers the same discussions: "It was the sales department that said if we want to be competitive, we ought to try to get a younger profile with our audience."[47]

Wood had not been elevated to the presidency with a mission to transform the network. He arrived with no announced mandate or vision; nor did he hope to leave his mark on the culture. He didn't talk about the network as a public trust; he saw it, unsentimentally, mostly as a vehicle to sell soap and cars. "He was a sales guy," said Daly. "Sales guys go out and have a drink and make a deal over two martinis at lunch."[48] Michael Ovitz, then a young agent, recalled that no one in the creative community looked to Wood for insight. "He never read a script," Ovitz said. "And if he did, no one cared what he had to say about it."[49] Wood didn't mix easily with the network's programming staff, which was wryer and more cosmopolitan, ironic, urban, and ethnic than his natural country club environment. Daly, who revered Wood and viewed him as a mentor, keenly recognized the culture clash. The programmers, Daly recalled, "they are all Brooklyn people, mostly Jewish, and they have their style. Bob was a guy from the West Coast, and he didn't like the style as much. He wasn't that type of guy." Neither did Wood feel any urge to provide a platform for the new voices and social movements agitating for change: even after he shifted from Los Angeles to more liberal New York City, his politics remained anchored well right of center. Irwin Segelstein, a top CBS programming executive, later said of Wood, "Bob is really Archie Bunker. The radical right Irish conservative."[50] But the advertising department found Wood receptive to its arguments for a new direction. Emerging from Los Angeles and then his broader supervisory responsibility for the O&O stations, Wood was attuned to the resistance in urban centers to CBS's aging and rural offerings. "He was conscious, maybe more than a typical president, that advertisers did prefer, given their choice, an audience that was younger and more urban to one that was older and more rural," said Arnold Becker, the network's vice president for research.[51] One day in February 1970, Wood came to the sales department and said that CBS had to get younger in its programming and its audience.[52] In May he delivered the same message, in a speech to the network affiliates.[53] "We . . . have to attract new viewers . . . who are part of every generation," Wood insisted. Privately, he told CBS executives that he feared losing the younger generation to the edgier new movies emerging from Hollywood, like *Easy Rider*. "A certain genre of films were [*sic*] pulling young people away," Wood said later. "I sensed a shift in the national mood."[54] He took his first steps to redirect CBS with the fall 1970 schedule. In March 1970, CBS announced that it was canceling *Petticoat Junction* and the Gleason and Skelton variety programs.[55] Its slate of new fall shows included three variations on *The Mod Squad* theme of discontented young people working for change from within the system (always with the sensitive but firm guidance of the older generation): *Storefront Lawyers* (with Robert Foxworth), *The Interns* (with Broderick Crawford), and *The Headmaster* (with Andy Griffith). The fourth major new entry was *The Mary Tyler Moore Show*, the situation comedy about a single woman starting over in Minneapolis. Each of the first three was a ponderous failure that disappeared quickly. And while *Mary Tyler Moore* would prove to be a landmark series, building a half-hour situation comedy around the actress who had played Dick Van Dyke's winsome but unthreatening wife a decade earlier hardly seemed transformative at the time.

But Wood had planted a flag, and he acquired a dynamic ally when he replaced the powerful programming chief Dann with Dann's young deputy, Fred Silverman. Wood knew he needed a program that would make a much louder statement than those he had approved so far. He "wanted to get some show that would cause some conversation," recalled Perry Lafferty, the elegant former director and producer serving as CBS's vice president for programming in Hollywood.[56] Norman Lear, during the first two decades of his show business career, had displayed neither much interest nor much facility in generating conversation, but Lear would provide Wood exactly what he was looking for, and then some.

ALL IN THE FAMILY began as a British television show entitled *Till Death Us Do Part*, the story of a working-class British bigot, Alf Garnett; his sharp-tongued wife, Else; his daughter, Rita; and Rita's husband, Mike. It caused a sensation in Britain for its frank treatment of racism and other previously taboo topics.[57] Its potential as a template for an American show seemed obvious. Mark Golden, a CBS programming executive with a fondness for gourmet food and fine wine, had seen an episode while on a wine tour of Europe and urged the network to acquire the rights when he returned. His colleague Irwin Segelstein thought it would provide a great vehicle for Jackie Gleason, an edgier successor to his bus-driving Ralph Kramden character from the 1950s sitcom *The Honeymooners*. But when CBS tried to acquire the American rights to *Till Death*, it discovered that they had already been sold to Norman Lear.[58]

The show had reached Lear's attention from several directions. Yorkin saw it when he was in London shooting the movie *Inspector Clouseau* and recalls shipping a videotape back to his partner.[59] Lear claims he never saw an episode of the show before deciding to bid on it,[60] but he recalls discussing it on the phone with Yorkin and reading a short item about its premise in *TV Guide*.*[61] Whatever the source, the material instantly detonated with Lear: the battles between the bigoted father and the liberal son-in-law reminded him of his own struggles with his father, Herman. Lear felt he knew the story from the inside out: within days, he had written about seventy pages of notes about how he would develop the show. In late summer 1968, he acquired the American rights to the project and secured a contract from ABC to develop a pilot.[62]

Lear did not begin adapting *Till Death* with any ambition to transform television. "I have never, ever remembered thinking, Oh, we're doing something outlandish, riotously different," he recalled. "I wasn't on any mission. And I don't think I knew I was breaking such ground. I didn't watch *Petticoat Junction*, for Chrissake. I didn't watch *Beverly Hillbillies*. I didn't know what I was doing."[63] To the extent that he had an ulterior motive in pursuing *Till Death*, it was more financial than artistic: after all his years working on variety shows in which

---

* On some occasions, Lear has said he learned about *Till Death Us Do Part* from a notice in *Variety*.

he had no ownership interest, Lear was attracted to owning a situation comedy that would provide a lasting stream of revenue if it were syndicated for reruns.[64]

Lear moved quickly to write, cast, and film a first pilot for the show he initially titled *Justice for All*. For Archie and Edith (whom he had originally named Agnes), he quickly settled on Carroll O'Connor and Jean Stapleton. Neither was a household name, but both had worked steadily: O'Connor had been a character actor in dozens of movies and television shows through the 1960s, and Stapleton had worked on Broadway and in television. Lear cast two lesser-known younger actors as Mike and Gloria, Kelly Jean Peters and Tim McIntire, and shot a pilot in late September 1968.[65] ABC rejected it but didn't want to abandon the project entirely, asking Lear to recast the two younger roles and then to shoot a second pilot in February 1969.[66] But when Lear did so, ABC said no again.[67] Michael Eisner, who operated the projector for one of the screenings for the ABC executives, remembers that part of Lear's problem was timing.[68] His second pilot landed at ABC just after the network's disastrous airing of *Turn-On*, a bawdy sketch comedy show drenched in sexual innuendo that had been developed by the producers of *Laugh-In* and was canceled after a single episode. The debacle underscored the networks' struggle to find a balance between programming edgy enough to attract the younger audience they craved but not so controversial that it repelled the great gray mainstream of older viewers; after *Turn-On*, ABC had little appetite for exploring that border again so soon. Eisner recalled of the screening, "[A few] weeks later, we come in with *All in the Family*. There's *kike* in it, *spic* in it—all those words. Elton Ruhl [the ABC network president] simply said, 'I can't go back to our affiliates after *Turn-On* and [ask them to] go put on *All in the Family*, I just can't do it.'"[69]

Lear's agent pushed the pilot to Mike Dann, at that point still the head of CBS programming, and to Segelstein.[70] The project took another step forward when Yorkin, in New York to meet with Robert Wood about a different Tandem project, stopped in to say hello to Dann and mentioned the pilot ABC had rejected. Dann, who had liked the project from the first time Golden had raised it a few years earlier, expressed interest, and Yorkin obtained a videotape to show Dann the next day. Dann, as Yorkin recalled, laughed so loud during the screening that Fred Silverman poked into the office to see what was happening. They restarted the tape, and it broke up Silverman as well. As Yorkin later described it, "Fred Silverman sits down, watches it, says, 'I've got to have this. This thing is going on CBS.'"[71] The next piece came together when Wood watched the tape. He had his own hesitations: when Segelstein, Silverman, and other staffers played him the pilot, he worried that it was anti-Semitic. "We said there are three fat Jewish men sitting here: don't worry about that," Segelstein recalled.[72] Whatever his doubts, Wood quickly recognized that he had found his conversation starter. He later explained his thinking to sociologist Todd Gitlin: "I really thought the pilot was very, very funny . . . It sure seemed to me a terrific way to test this whole attitude about the network."[73] Just a year after Wood buried the Smothers Brothers, he gave a second life to Archie Bunker.

Even with Wood's support, the show faced formidable headwinds inside CBS. William Paley hated it from the outset, considering it vulgar, but Wood was determined.[74] "Bob Wood had balls," Rosenfield said. "He really had balls, and what I never understood to this day was how that happened, because Bob Wood came out of sales. He didn't have any clout with the Hollywood community. He didn't know Norman Lear, but he understood that there was an opportunity here for significant change in the medium, and he made it happen."[75] Said Becker, "Bob Wood had the guts to put it on the air, and it went on the air."[76]

With the go-ahead from CBS, Lear reshaped the cast with new choices for the younger roles. For Gloria, the Bunkers' daughter, he chose Sally Struthers, a vivacious young blonde whom Lear had seen on the Smothers Brothers and in the movie Five Easy Pieces (where she had an exuberant fling with Jack Nicholson's disaffected lead character, Bobby Dupea). For Mike, the son-in-law, Lear looked closer to home, casting Rob Reiner, the son of his longtime friend Carl Reiner. Apart from his writing for the Smothers Brothers, the younger Reiner, with long hair and unabashedly liberal views, had become the go-to casting for the industry's stilted first attempts to acknowledge the changing youth culture. He played a hippie for an episode of *The Beverly Hillbillies* and a similar character for several episodes on *Gomer Pyle*, where he improbably sang "Blowin' in the Wind" with Jim Nabors. "I was like the resident Hollywood hippie," Reiner said later.[77]

As director, Lear chose John Rich, a skilled television veteran whom he had met two decades before when Rich was one of the stage managers for *The Colgate Comedy Hour*. Coincidentally, Rich had also been approached at almost exactly the same time to direct *The Mary Tyler Moore Show* that preceded *All in the Family* on the air at CBS by four months. Rich knew Moore from his work directing almost fifty episodes of *The Dick Van Dyke Show*, and he was impressed with the pilot script from James Brooks and Allan Burns. But to him, *Mary* didn't appear nearly as revolutionary as Lear's project. "It was 1970, and the dialogue that was written then just blew me away," Rich remembered. "And I called Norman . . . I said, 'You aren't going to make this, are you?' He said, 'Yeah.' I said, 'Is anybody going to put it on?' He said, 'They say they will.'"[78]

RICH'S UNCERTAINTY, EVEN INCREDULITY, was widely shared. Even with the cast and staff solidified, and with CBS's approval, the show's future always seemed tenuous to the staff as they worked toward their January 1971 premiere. "We knew we were doing something good, but we didn't think anybody was going to go for this," Reiner remembered.[79] O'Connor was so skeptical that the show would survive that he held on to the lease for the apartment in Rome where he had been living and made Lear promise to pay for a first-class ticket back if the show was canceled.[80] Lear, too, felt that CBS's commitment was only conditional. Yes, Wood had bought the show, but he remained skittish about it. "He wanted to take a chance, but he fought me tooth and nail,"[81] Lear remembered. Asked if he considered Wood an ally, Lear said pointedly, "He wanted to be considered an ally." Above all, Lear said, Wood and CBS were simply uncertain that a show this different from their usual programming would find an audience. "That's all they worried about," Lear said. "It's as simple as 'We don't know if this works.' We know the *Hillbillies* and *Petticoat Junction*, we know that works. We don't know if *this* works."[82]

The team faced their own uncertainties about how far to push the boundaries. Initially, Lear preferred Cleavon Little for the part of Lionel Jefferson, a young African American who lives next door to the Bunkers and who often bests Archie in small wars of words (usually without Archie realizing he is being bested). Rich resisted: having a young Black character verbally one-up an old white one was incendiary enough. He viewed Little as too "threatening" to white America in that role and wanted someone with less edge. Ultimately, Rich convinced Lear to cast Mike Evans, a college student with no previous acting experience.

The nerves ran all the way to the top. During the filming of an early episode, Rich was in the control room when Wood stopped by the set. "I hope you know what you're doing," he told the director, "because my rump is on the line here."[83] Just weeks before the show was first scheduled to air, CBS still had failed to sell any advertising on it. Rosenfield was surprised one day to pick up his phone and hear Wood on the line.[84] "I've just looked at the inventory, and there's nothing but promos in *All in the Family*; there's no sales," Wood told him. "Yes, sir, I know that," Rosenfield replied. Wood continued: "You know it will be fully sponsored before air time in two weeks. Are you aware of that, Jim?" Rosenfield tried to mollify him again: "Yes, sir. I know. That's my goal." Wood cut him off. "It's not your goal," he said. "It's your absolute mandate. It will be sold, fully sold."

From the start, Lear faced an unrelenting push and pull with the CBS censors over the show's language and content. CBS's caution was evident in the time slot it selected for the show: Tuesday, a night it didn't view as pivotal, at 9:30 p.m., between *Hee Haw* and the *CBS News Hour*.[85] In advance of the premiere, Wood sent a telegram to the affiliates quoting his speech from the previous spring: "We have to broaden our base," he wrote. "We have to attract new viewers. We're going to operate on the theory that it is better to try something new than not to try it and wonder what would have happened if we had."[86]

CBS even developed an unusual disclaimer to appear just before the show's first episode, explaining that *All in the Family* "seeks to throw a humorous spotlight on our frailties, prejudices, and concerns. By making them a source of laughter, we hope to show—in a mature fashion—just how absurd they are."[87] To the cast, the disclaimer "was ridiculous because they're putting the show on the air, and yet they're trying to distance themselves from the show at the same time," Reiner remembered.[88]

CBS's ambivalence crystallized into a single choice: which episode to air first. Lear wanted to start with the third version of the pilot, which he had taped with the new cast. Viewed even decades later, the episode is explosive. Compared to anything the three major networks had aired before, its language crashes like a rock through the television screen. Summoning painful memories, viscerally connected to his characters, Lear in his mid-forties found in his script a passionate and urgent voice he had never before tapped. Within minutes, Archie is raging against "your spics and your spades"; complaining about "Hebes" and "black beauties"; calling Edith a "silly dingbat" and telling her to "stifle"; and describing Mike as a "dumb Polack" and "the laziest white man I've ever seen," the latter a direct reprise of an insult that Herman Lear used to direct at his son. Mike, as heatedly, is blaming crime on poverty and insisting that he and Gloria see no evidence that God exists. In the opening scene, Archie and Edith arrive home early from church and catch Mike kissing Gloria amorously as he carries her toward the bedroom. Archie is scandalized. "Eleven ten on a Sunday morning," Archie grumbles in his thick Queens patois.

This was all a bit much for CBS, especially the "Sunday morning" line. The network insisted it come out; Lear refused. Wood offered a compromise: the line could stay in if Lear agreed to push the pilot episode back to the second week and run the projected second show first.[89] Lear refused again. The team considered the second episode much weaker than the first. More important, Lear believed the pilot episode presented "Archie in full," with all his prejudices and animosities on open display. Airing it was like jumping into the deep end of a pool; CBS and Lear together would "get fully wet the first time out,"

as Lear later described it.[90] In what would become a common occur-
rence, Lear told Wood he would quit if CBS started with the second
episode.[91]

On January 12, 1971, the date that *All in the Family* was scheduled to
appear for the first time, Rich and the crew were performing a dress
rehearsal for the season's sixth episode in the CBS complex known as
Television City, at Beverly Boulevard and Fairfax Avenue in Los Angeles. Just before 6:30 California time, they crowded into Rich's small
control room, where they could watch a network feed as the show's
9:30 Eastern airtime approached.[92] They might have caught the final
minutes of *Hee Haw*, a last vestige of television's obsession with rural
audiences, starring Buck Owens and Roy Clark, with guest appearances that night from singer Roger Miller and baseball player Bobby
Murcer.[93] Then, at 6:30, the control room filled with the disembodied
voice reading CBS's strange disclaimer and then the sounds of Jean
Stapleton at the piano as she and Carroll O'Connor sang the show's
nostalgic theme song, "Those Were the Days." Still, it wasn't clear yet
which episode CBS had placed on the air. Within moments came the
image of Mike pursuing Gloria in the kitchen and her parents arriving home early from church, the initial scenes of the pilot. The CBS
eye had blinked. As with the movie studios a few years earlier with
Bonnie and Clyde, *The Graduate*, and *Easy Rider*, and the music industry with the Beatles and Bob Dylan before that, television's search for
a new audience had finally torn down the curtain separating it from
the tumultuous changes unfolding around it. Through that opening
over the next few years would emerge some of the greatest television
ever made.

4

APRIL

Already Gone

From behind his mirrored aviators, twenty-five-year-old Glenn Frey looked out at the largest crowd that had ever assembled for a rock concert in Southern California.[1] Frey's long brown hair cascaded to his shoulders; his bushy sideburns nearly met at his chin. On his right stood bass player Randy Meisner; on his left, guitarist Bernie Leadon. Behind them, wearing a football-style jersey, Don Henley sat at the drums. Together the four young men comprised the Eagles. As Frey stood on the stage, a large shadow passed over the huge crowd. "We got the Goodyear Blimp," he announced happily, "just like *Wide World of Sports*."[2]

The date was Saturday, April 6, 1974. Under crystalline blue skies, two hundred thousand people sprawled before Frey and the Eagles across the Ontario Motor Speedway, about an hour east of downtown Los Angeles. They had come for an all-day rock festival called California Jam. So many people flocked to the show that traffic backed up for thirteen miles on the two major freeways leading to the racetrack. After the parking lot filled, fans abandoned their cars along the shoulder of the highway; some walked as far as four miles to reach the racetrack. The bright sunshine and eighty-five-degree temperature inspired so many bikinis on women and bare chests on men that one journalist reported that "the scene at times looked more like a Sunday afternoon at the beach than a rock festival."[3]

The California Jam concert was the latest in a procession of huge outdoor rock festivals that fed on the growing buying power of the vast Baby Boom generation. Lou Adler had kicked off the trend with the Monterey Pop Festival, near San Francisco, which he promoted in 1967. Woodstock, the most famous of the mega-concerts, followed in 1969, as did the free concert at Altamont Speedway near San Francisco that spiraled into chaos after the Hells Angels motorcycle gang, hired as security by the headlining Rolling Stones, ran wild. The Summer Jam festival at the Watkins Glen racetrack in upstate New York more peacefully drew some six hundred thousand people in 1973 to see the Band, the Grateful Dead, and the Allman Brothers. Ontario's California Jam topped all of them, not in attendance—but in total receipts from ticket sales (as so many people had managed to sneak into the other big shows without paying).[4]

The concert had been planned with a precision that increasingly characterized the multibillion-dollar rock music industry. Apart from the crowded parking and snarled traffic, both as inescapable in LA life as smog, the show proceeded seamlessly. A partnership of local promoters and ABC Entertainment (which filmed the concert for later broadcast), the festival featured a state-of-the-art sound system and two stages that slid along a small railroad track; while a band played on one stage, the next performer set up on the other. The system was so efficient that the first performer, the band Rare Earth, actually took the stage fifteen minutes before the festival was scheduled to begin at 10 a.m.[5]

The Eagles weren't quite an afterthought for the promoters of this massive undertaking, but neither were they a top draw. Formed in 1971, the group had released their album, *On the Border*, almost exactly two weeks before the California Jam concert. They had been the subject of great expectations as one of the first artists signed by the dynamic young record executive David Geffen to his new Asylum Records label in 1971. The Eagles' first album had been a commercial success when it appeared in June 1972, generating three hit singles. But the group's second album, *Desperado*, had flopped with critics and audiences alike after its release in 1973. *On the Border* wasn't quite make-or-break for them, but it arrived as some wondered if the band would ever achieve the success initially forecast for it.

Those doubts were reflected in the Eagles' marginal position at California Jam, where they received sixth billing out of eight acts. They were given a forty-five-minute time slot in the late morning, which placed them lower than such modestly talented groups as Black Oak Arkansas, Seals and Crofts, and Black Sabbath, each of which had hour-long appearances in the afternoon. The headlining bands, the heavy metal pioneers Deep Purple and Emerson, Lake and Palmer, closed the show with ninety-minute sets; ELP even commanded its own special stage, which included a complicated setup for keyboardist Keith Emerson to play the piano while he (and it) were lifted from the ground and rotated in midair.[6]

The Eagles arrived in Ontario without the new guitarist they had added to the band during the recording of *On the Border*. Don Felder, a skilled (if contentious) slide guitar player who at his best recalled Duane Allman, missed the show because his wife went into labor that morning.[7] To compensate, the band invited Frey's old friend Jackson Browne, who had written most of the Eagles' first radio hit, "Take It Easy," to join them on piano. Browne sat in with the band for their opening number, "James Dean," an upbeat rocker from the new album (a song he also cowrote with Frey, Henley, and their mutual friend J. D. Souther), and for "Midnight Flyer," a country-rock tune also from the new album that featured Leadon's inspired banjo picking.[8]

About halfway through the band's set, Browne left the stage, and the four original Eagles faced the massive crowd. Just after the Goodyear Blimp passed overhead, Leadon plucked the first chords of the new album's initial single. The song, called "Already Gone," was an exuberant kiss-off, the singer telling a lover who planned to dump him that he was "already gone." With its crunching guitar chords and irresistible melody, "Already Gone" radiated confidence in lyric and mood alike (down to the defiant "All right, nighty-nite" that Frey snarled as the lyrics' final couplet). The song reflected the new direction Frey wanted for the band, a harder-rocking sound that dialed down the country influences dominating LA rock in the early 1970s and infusing the Eagles' first two records. It had also been one of the songs that convinced Frey the band needed Felder to provide more firepower on guitar. But with Felder absent, Frey had to step in at Ontario to play lead guitar on the track. He didn't miss a step. His right knee bent, cowboy boots tapping time to the driving beat, a palm tree swaying over his shoulder, Frey was lean and propulsive, a young man claiming his place in the world. With Henley pounding the drums behind him and the voices of Leadon, Meisner, and Henley swelling each chorus, Frey's lead vocals and guitar solos soared from the stage as sharp and cutting as a hot wind through the desert.

The Eagles were far from Ontario by the time the headliners performed that night, but over the next two years, their pared-down, all-American rock and roll, the sound of convertibles accelerating into the night and waves glistening in the summer sun, would take the Southern California music scene to new heights and lift the Eagles past the bloated, leviathan bands like ELP that closed the bill later that day. In Ontario, on that bright Saturday morning, questions disappeared about whether the Eagles would take flight. No one experiencing the sheer force pulsing from the stage could doubt the band's trajectory. Like the new song they rendered so fiercely that morning, the Eagles in Ontario were already gone.

AS THEIR SUCCESS GREW through the 1970s, the Eagles lived and chronicled the hazy excesses of "Life in the Fast Lane" of Los Angeles more enthusiastically than any other band. They became royalty in the LA social scene, seats at Frey's regular poker games an invitation to days of drugs, girls, and general debauchery. The irony is that none of the band's initial members had roots in LA.

Randy Meisner and Bernie Leadon had extensive experience in the Southern California country-rock scene when they joined Glenn Frey and Don Henley to play behind Linda Ronstadt at Disneyland in July 1971. But both began life far away. Meisner was born in Scottsbluff, Nebraska. A bass player with a piercingly high voice, he relocated to California in 1964 with a group called the Soul Survivors.[9] After years of subsistence living in LA, Meisner won a spot in the country-rock group Poco, but he quit soon after amid clashes with bandmates. He jumped at the opportunity when the producer and manager John

Boylan offered him a spot in the Stone Canyon Band he assembled for Ricky Nelson. This created the connection that led Boylan, a few years later, to invite Meisner to join the band playing behind Linda Ronstadt in 1971.

Leadon was born in Minnesota, but he relocated with his family to San Diego at age ten. There he gravitated to an accomplished local bluegrass scene that included the pioneering group the Scottsville Squirrel Barkers. Partly through his friendship with Chris Hillman, a Squirrel Barker who became a founding member of the Byrds, Leadon moved to Los Angeles, where he leapt from group to group as the pieces of the city's emerging country-rock scene endlessly separated and reconfigured like ice floes on the open sea. Eventually, he played behind Ronstadt for a while before joining Gram Parsons and Hillman in the Flying Burrito Brothers.[10] When the troubled Parsons drifted away, and the Burrito Brothers foundered, Leadon, too, was ready when Ronstadt and Boylan offered him the chance to rejoin her at Disneyland.

The Eagles' two central figures emerged from opposite musical (and social) experiences. Glenn Frey was a street-smart Detroit kid, an ingratiating charmer who, from a very young age, had a fast mouth and a keen eye for girls and good times. He was marinated in the smooth urban sound of Motown and the hard-driving midwestern rock of Mitch Ryder and Bob Seger. Seger, impressed by Frey's wit and ambition alike, served as mentor, inviting the kid to hang around the studio and even contribute acoustic guitar and background vocals to one of his songs. Frey first traveled to Los Angeles in the summer of 1968 to pursue an ex-girlfriend, and LA beguiled him at first look. There he would eventually reconnect with J. D. Souther, a Texas-born singer and songwriter who had been dating Frey's girlfriend's sister. The two men formed their band Longbranch Pennywhistle and hit the LA folk-rock circuit, trudging through the same itinerary of folk clubs that Ronstadt had followed a few years earlier.[11] Eventually, the two wrangled a recording contract from Jimmy Bowen, a respected former producer for Warner's Reprise Records, who had formed his own small label, Amos Records. But Longbranch Pennywhistle's only album vanished upon arrival. Jackson Browne, a friend and neighbor to both Frey and Souther at the time, thought the album might have had a shot if they had "actually spent time gestating the music," but the shoestring Amos allowed them to record only "in these really constricted three-hour sessions, where they were just knocking it out."[12] Frey felt his career had stalled before he even reached second gear.

Starting from a very different place, Henley at the same moment had reached an almost identical impasse. He grew up in the small East Texas town of Linden, a one-stoplight place that he later said looked like a set from the movie *The Last Picture Show*.[13] Born in 1947, Henley spent his youth absorbing the same rich blend of 1950s southern musical influences that shaped Ronstadt (born almost exactly one year before him) a thousand miles to his west. Henley gorged on gospel, blues, country, and Texas's distinctive Western swing. He listened to the *Louisiana Hayride* on the car radio with his father and Big Band music with his family at home. He could sing along when Johnny Cash, Patsy Cline, and Hank Williams came on the radio; the first rock record he bought was Elvis Presley's.[14] Drawn to the drums at a young age, Henley joined Richard Bowden, his best friend in high school, in a band that played Dixieland jazz. This morphed into a succession of bands performing first covers and, eventually, their own material. The final iteration was Shiloh, a quartet heavily influenced by the emerging Southern California country-rock sound. Kenny Rogers, a producer and singer, was working as a talent scout for Jimmy Bowen when he heard Shiloh in Dallas; eventually, he convinced Bowen to sign them to Amos Records. Rogers brought the band out to LA in June 1970.[15] Like Longbranch Pennywhistle, Shiloh followed the well-worn tracks of the LA club scene, but their album for Amos flopped (deservedly, Henley said), and the label itself soon collapsed. Shiloh followed not long thereafter, breaking up in 1971.[16] Like Frey, Henley was doing little more than drowning his sorrows at the Troubadour bar when the offer came from Ronstadt and Boylan to join her tour.

When Frey and Henley came together to support Ronstadt, they didn't know each other well, though they had met in passing at Amos Records.[17] Still, they quickly connected, both musically and personally, after Ronstadt and Boylan recruited them. Frey recalls talking to Henley about forming a band almost immediately after the group hit the road.[18] Ronstadt could see them moving that way as well. At sound checks, the two would practice songs they were writing. "It was going to happen: you could see it unwinding before your eyes," Ronstadt recalls. She remembers thinking from early on that she was operating on "borrowed time" to have Henley and Frey behind her. "I didn't need a band that powerful," she said. "It would blow me off the stage every night. I was lucky to have them when I had them, and they were champing at the bit."[19]

Frey and Henley realized they had found the combination they were seeking when Meisner and Leadon joined them for the first time behind Ronstadt at the July 1971 Disneyland show. After the show, the foursome spent about two weeks rehearsing some material.[20] Then they did what all aspiring rock stars in Los Angeles did in 1971: they went to see David Geffen.

CURLY-HAIRED, SLIM, MOTORMOUTHED David Geffen was the classic young man in a hurry, a combustible compound of smarts, bravado, and shamelessness. Raised in Brooklyn by Jewish parents, he moved to Los Angeles on the day he graduated from high school in 1960, to live with his elder brother, Mitchell, a law student at UCLA. LA captivated Geffen immediately, but his stay was truncated when his mother summoned him back to New York to help care for his ailing father. After his father died in 1961, Geffen enrolled at the University of Texas at Austin, which his brother had attended, but after only a few months he dropped out (the end of his formal education) and rejoined his brother in Los Angeles. Geffen's second stint in LA provided him with his first exposure to show business. He wrangled a job as an usher at CBS. Even more exciting, he was drawn into the exhilarating, if already erratic, world of the music producer Phil Spector because his brother was dating (and would eventually marry) the sister of Spector's girlfriend. Geffen hung around the studio entranced as Spector produced such "Wall of Sound" classics as his legendary 1963 Christmas album.

Geffen loved LA, but after he was fired at CBS—he got into a fight with a woman who said something nasty about John F. Kennedy on the day he was assassinated—he drifted back to New York City. There, like many young men looking for a first rung on the show business ladder, he found a job in the mail room of the powerful William Morris Agency. (He won the job in part by falsely claiming he had graduated from UCLA and then arriving early every morning for weeks to intercept the letter from the university informing William Morris that this was not the case.)[21] Geffen embarked on the familiar climb, though, to his contemporaries, he seemed to be operating at a higher speed. He became a secretary, then an assistant, and finally a junior agent in the television department.[22] Geffen watched the first flickers of the "relevancy" revolution that remade television a few years later and aspired to ascend to the movie department until an older agent told him that he was crazy to think that established middle-aged directors would ever sign with a kid in his twenties. Rock stars, however, preferred younger agents. Geffen took the advice and shifted his attention to the music department, approaching the rock world with the same precocious intensity he had applied to ascending from the mail room. Among his first major signings was Laura Nyro, an eccentric woman and erratic performer who wrote great mainstream pop songs, including "Stoned Soul Picnic," "Stoney End," and "Eli's Coming." Nyro had mystified the harder-rocking audience when she sang at the Monterey Pop Festival in 1967, but Geffen recognized her unusual talent and quickly negotiated a contract for her with Clive Davis at CBS Records. He also created a new publishing company to control her songwriting royalties, with the ownership split evenly between Nyro and him.

Another key early client came through Elliot Roberts, a friend of Geffen's from the William Morris office who had moved on to the management company Chartoff-Winkler with Geffen's help. One night in 1967, Roberts heard Joni Mitchell perform in Greenwich Village and was so awed by her talent that he asked to follow her on tour, as an unpaid audition toward representing her as a manager. On the road, Mitchell hired him for the role, and Roberts brought in Geffen as her agent. Eventually, with the help of David Crosby, whom Mitchell met and romanced during a club appearance in Coconut Grove, in Miami, she won a recording contract at Warner's Reprise Records. Mitchell and Roberts both relocated to LA. From there, Roberts regularly regaled his friend Geffen, back in New York, with reports about the exploding music community in LA, the sunshine, the captivating lifestyle in Laurel Canyon, and the money to be made.

Roberts didn't have to push very hard. Geffen was looking for a way back to Los Angeles, and he found it when Roberts encountered a problem too complex for him to untangle alone. When David Crosby, Stephen Stills, and Graham Nash sought to create their supergroup in 1968, they hired Roberts to manage them. Yet he realized he lacked the business skills (and perhaps the ruthlessness) to extricate the prospective band members from their contracts at various labels so they could record together. With the band's approval, Roberts enlisted Geffen, who seamlessly negotiated a divorce for Nash and Crosby at CBS so they could join Stills, who was under contract at Atlantic Records. (To secure CSN, Atlantic agreed to trade rights to its newly signed band Poco to CBS.) With this huge deal concluded, Geffen finally cut the cord to New York and relocated to LA, joining with Roberts to form a new management company. The two men's skills meshed perfectly.[23] Roberts, easygoing and with a prodigious pot habit, became the principal point of contact for the artists. "Elliot smoked a lot of dope, and he was funny, and he kept us human, and he kept us from screaming at each other by humor," remembered Nash.[24] Geffen represented the artists to the record companies and concert promoters. He was, in Crosby's word, a "shark" for his bands.

Geffen's own ambitions and avarice were never far from the surface, but he soon acquired the reputation as an agent who would fight for his clients to a contract's last comma. "You have to realize that Geffen was there for Geffen," remembered Nash, "but having taken that as a fact, what he did for us was fabulous. He kept all the legal stuff, all the shitty stuff that happens, away from us. 'Just leave them the fuck alone to make their music.'"[25] Jackson Browne remembers David Crosby touting Geffen to him long before Browne signed with the young mogul. "David Crosby . . . said, 'There's this guy, a great businessman, a very strong businessman, but he's one of us. That's the guy you want to get on your side, because you can trust him.' What did we know? We can't do business. We don't know how to protect ourselves in the business world. 'This is a guy that you want to meet.'"[26]

Geffen was a good manager, but he found it exhausting and somewhat demeaning to tend to rock stars with too much money and too little self-control.* As early as 1969, he started plotting to form his own record label, an opportunity that coalesced around Jackson Browne. After he signed Browne, Geffen shopped him to several of the major labels. None bit. Finally, Ahmet Ertegun, the elegant and insistent president of Atlantic Records, stopped Geffen with a question: If you believe in Browne so much, why don't *you* release his records? Ertegun wasn't betting on Browne; he was investing in Geffen's taste and drive. He made Geffen an offer impossible to refuse: Atlantic would distribute his records and give him half ownership in a new label that he would manage. Geffen agreed, and in 1971 he named the new company Asylum Records.

Asylum captured Geffen's two faces. He truly intended it as an asylum, a refuge, for musicians, but Asylum also reflected Geffen's unflagging determination to get rich. For him, the label was at least as much a financial as an artistic calculation. The half ownership of Laura Nyro's publishing rights that Geffen took as her manager earned him his first big payday when Asylum sold her catalogue to CBS.[27] The lesson he took was that the shortest path to riches in the music business was to own and sell assets. A record company was a much bigger asset to cultivate and eventually harvest than the rights to even the most talented songwriter. As a bonus, Geffen, who was keeping his management company with Roberts, thought he could lay off most

---

* No one strained Geffen's patience more than the voluble and demanding David Crosby. Early on, to establish hierarchy, Crosby wanted Geffen to carry his guitar case; Geffen refused. Much later, in 1971, Geffen got busted at LAX when he reluctantly agreed to deliver a supply of pot to Crosby in New York. Geffen later cited this incident to friends as the moment he knew he needed to branch out beyond management.

of the expenses for the firm on the new record label, swelling his profits on that front.

It was such relentless scheming that made so many wary of Geffen even as they admired his acumen and determination. Those around him quickly came to recognize his tireless instinct to identify his own advantage in any situation. "His mind was conditioned to, when he saw something, 'How does this work for me?'" remembered Lou Adler, the producer and record executive.[28] For all the charm he could focus on an artist, Geffen could be equally brutal when crossed. His telephone screaming fits became legendary. "He's a bully, sometimes in a charming sort of way, sometimes not," recalled one mostly sympathetic friend. Geffen cultivated feuds the way a farmer cultivated a field, nourishing grievances and plotting revenge. Conflict seemed to motivate him more than success.

The music itself was more a means than an end to Geffen. He wasn't one to drop the needle on each new album that arrived. "He liked music, but he wasn't a huge music fan," said Peter Asher, the British-born manager and producer. "He never talked music particularly." Jon Landau, the prominent critic, found Geffen more likely to hum show tunes than the latest hits on the radio. And he was rarely found in the studio: "I don't think David ever mixed an album in his life, ever produced an album in his life," said Jonathan Taplin, the former road manager for Bob Dylan. "He was completely bored by that stuff."[29] But if Geffen was not a huge fan of rock music, he was a fan of rock musicians. He especially liked great songs and skilled songwriters. Those were the talents he collected on Asylum. "I think he believed in the songwriters' value as the person singing the song, which I did, too," remembered Browne. Especially in Geffen's early years, most of his artists saw him as not just a suit, but a sympathetic soul: "One of us," as Crosby told Browne. "He genuinely loved and admired artists," agreed Peter Asher. "He treasured them and treated them well."[30] Early in the Asylum years, Geffen and Roberts sometimes joined Mitchell onstage during her encores to sing her poignant "The Circle Game." Closer in age to the musicians than most music executives—Geffen was born in 1943, just before the Baby Boom—to many of his young artists, he seemed more approachable, more of a contemporary. Browne at the time thought that Geffen "broke down . . . the hierarchical thing" between record companies and their recording artists: "We went swimming at his house, and he sang your songs back to you in the pool. He'd go, 'Where did you come up with that?' He'd sing the song to you, and he sang like Jerry Lewis. He was totally unselfconscious about not being a singer, about not having a good voice, and about being happy to sing. In a way, he personified the listeners, the people who would take this song into their lives and welcome it."[31] The result was there emerged what Landau called "a very uniquely identifiable—not a Geffen sound, but a Geffen *sensibility*. You could hear somebody, and you would say, 'They need to be on Geffen.' And it was based around melodious singer-songwriters."[32]

Asylum quickly announced itself as a label with great ambitions. In September 1971, Geffen unveiled an artist roster that included Joni Mitchell (moving over from Warner), Jackson Browne, J. D. Souther, folk-rock acts Judee Sill and David Blue, and what was described in *Billboard* as "a new as yet unnamed group" whose members were so obscure that the article misspelled two of their names ("Mizner" for Randy Meisner and "Glen" for Glenn Frey).[33]

Browne played a dual role in this initial lineup. Beyond his own music, he functioned as an unofficial talent scout for Geffen, who greatly respected his taste. One of the early introductions Browne arranged for Geffen was to his old housemates Souther and Frey. Geffen signed them both, but with different intentions. He saw Souther as a solo artist, but he didn't think Frey had enough talent to succeed on his own: Geffen told him he needed a band. And when Frey returned in late summer 1971 with the band that had come together behind Linda Ronstadt, Geffen signed him, Henley, Leadon, and Meisner. (He bought out the contracts of both Frey and Henley from the expiring Amos Records for five thousand dollars each.) Browne often gets credit for convincing Geffen to bet on the Eagles, but he says it didn't take much arm-twisting. "Anybody could tell the Eagles were really great," he remembered. "Come on, are you kidding me? It was Glenn Frey and Don Henley."[34]

Geffen sent the fledgling Eagles to Aspen to hone their sound away from LA's many distractions. "Teen King and the Emergencies," the provisional name Geffen gave the band for its hidden apprenticeship, captured his quickly formed assessment of its two central figures: Frey, the skirt-chasing front man; Henley, the perpetual malcontent who careened from one emergency to the next. After a few weeks in Aspen, Geffen packed them off to London to record their first album, with Glyn Johns, the veteran producer who had worked with the Rolling Stones, Led Zeppelin, and the Who.

The self-titled Eagles album that Asylum released from those sessions in June 1972 was an uneven affair. The singing, musicianship, and production were all top notch, but the sound tilted toward softer harmony and country-rock touches than the edgier Detroit rock roots Frey brought to the group. This reflected the belief of producer Glyn Johns that the Eagles were more a harmony group than a true rock band. More important, the three best songs on the album were all written at least partly by people outside the group. Songwriter Jack Tempchin contributed "Peaceful Easy Feeling." Bernie Leadon was a cowriter on "Train Leaves Here This Morning," but it bore the heavy imprint of coauthor Gene Clark, the founding Byrds member and Leadon's former bandmate in Dillard and Clark.

The album's first big radio hit, and the song that for years defined the Eagles sensibility, was "Take It Easy," which was composed primarily by Jackson Browne. Both lyrically and musically, as Henley later observed, "Take It Easy" conveyed an irresistible "sense of motion," shimmering with the promise of both new love and open roads.[35] The song's migration to the Eagles exemplified LA's bountiful culture of musical collaboration in those years. Browne had written most of the song but was not intending to include it on his own first album and never completed it. When Frey heard the fragment, "He said, 'When you finish that song, we want to record it,'" Browne recalled. Weeks passed, and Frey kept nudging. "He asked me a few more times if I was done with it, and I said, 'I'm just so busy doing my record, I can't really get to it,'" Browne said. Finally, Frey asked if he could take a shot at finishing it. Browne said no, but then, "The next time we talked, I said, 'Absolutely. You want to finish it? That would be cool, man.'" Browne had stalled on the second verse. He had the first two lines—"Well, I'm a-standing on a corner / In Winslow, Arizona"—but nothing else. A few weeks later, Frey came back with the lines that memorably finished the verse: "Such a fine sight to see / There's a girl, my Lord / In a flatbed Ford / Slowing down to take a look at me." Browne loved it at first listen. "Oh yeah," he said, smiling at the memory. "Well, doesn't everybody?"[36]

Frey's contribution to "Take It Easy" foreshadowed the band's later hits. So, to a lesser extent, did "Witchy Woman," written by Henley and Leadon, which also became a hit single (though it lacked the polished melody of "Take It Easy" or "Peaceful Easy Feeling"). But the album offered few other signs that the Eagles could write well enough to reach the top tier of rock acts, as the *LA Times*'s Robert Hilburn, who almost always championed the Troubadour bands, observed. "The group's material was a major question mark," he wrote later. "Could, in short, the Eagles write?"[37]

GEFFEN WAS SUCH A dynamic and self-promoting presence that it was easy to forget that he was only a cog in a much bigger machine, and that Asylum was just one component of Warner Music, which had grown from very modest beginnings in Burbank to surpass the industry's traditional leader, CBS Records, in total sales by the early 1970s.[38] The ascent of Warner, which included the Warner Bros., Reprise, Elektra, Atlantic, and Asylum labels, over the New York City–based CBS (centered on the venerable Columbia Records label) symbolized the tilt of musical influence from the East to the West Coast. "That was a profound shift, because Columbia had been a New York label, and [Columbia president] Clive Davis was based in New York, but it was very clear that something had changed," recalled Jonathan Taplin, the former road manager for Bob Dylan who had relocated to LA.[39] Warner, with a roster that stretched from big arena attractions such as Jethro Tull, the Doobie Brothers, and Deep Purple to edgier, more iconoclastic figures such as Randy Newman and Van Dyke Parks, led the industry in the early 1970s. But in fact, the entire music business was rising to unprecedented, and even unimagined, heights on a cresting tide of demographic and technological change.

The population bulge that swelled the number of young people; the technical advances that made sophisticated stereo systems more widely available and affordable; the emergence of FM radio as a means of marketing records beyond those that generated Top 40 AM hits— all these factors transformed the music industry from a somewhat disreputable sideshow riddled with scandal (like the "payola" payoffs to disc jockeys) into a major economic force. In 1959, at the cusp of the youth revolution, total revenue from music sales stood at $603 million.[40] In 1967, the year of *Sgt. Pepper* and the Summer of Love, total revenues for the industry crossed the billion-dollar barrier, reaching $1.17 billion. By 1970, receipts soared to nearly $1.7 billion, and in 1973 the music industry collected $2 billion in revenue for the first time.[41] The huge number of younger Boomers still entering their teens and twenties, and the willingness of the older Boomers who had grown up on rock and roll to keep spending for it as they advanced into their thirties, deluged the industry with money. Though movies still led in glamour and prestige across Los Angeles, the record industry began far outpacing Hollywood in total receipts.[42] Suddenly, the most successful albums were selling not five hundred thousand copies but five *million*; the gold record, connoting total sales of one million dollars, was supplanted by the platinum record, granted to records that sold one million *units*.[43]

Powered by this tide, and his own skill at surfing it, Geffen continued to rise. In 1972, Warner bought out his ownership half of Asylum for seven million dollars, while leaving him in control of the label.[44] The next year, Warner merged Asylum with the larger Elektra Records and made Geffen the chairman of the combined enterprise.[45] This brought under his wing another roster of prominent artists, including Carly Simon, Harry Chapin, and Judy Collins.[46]

Geffen formally separated himself from the Geffen-Roberts management company once he sold his share of Asylum to Warner, but he continued to advise the firm behind the scenes. One of his most consequential decisions there was hiring a diminutive young fireplug of ambition who rivaled Geffen in cunning and ruthlessness.

Irving Azoff had started booking bands in Champaign after dropping out of the University of Illinois. When he decided that he and his most promising clients, Dan Fogelberg and the band REO Speedwagon, were ready for a bigger sandbox, he weighed the familiar bicoastal choice of New York and Los Angeles and quickly chose LA. "New York was more a closed shop, a buttoned-down shop, and LA at that point was where bands were breaking," Azoff says. "The scene was just so vibrant. Anybody in the music business could tell that there was more going to break out here than in New York."[47]

Azoff stepped quickly into the jet stream and was essentially adopted by two stars in the rock public relations world, Bobby Gibson and Gary Stromberg. "I was the punk kid who they would take around," Azoff says. His nights would start with an early dinner at Dan Tana's or maybe the Brown Derby, still holding on to a faded glamour. More often than not, their next stop would be the Troubadour. Later might be the Whisky or the Rainbow, on Sunset, for a harder-edged sound. If a big touring band was in town, the group would make a call at the Greek or the Forum. Then they might trek to the beach for drinks at the scruffy Chez Jay, in Santa Monica (if not as edgy as Venice, home to poets, artists, drug addicts, and outpatients). "It was music every night," Azoff said. After Walsh, another of Azoff's clients, and Fogelberg had successful albums, Azoff walked into Geffen's office and talked himself into a job at age twenty-two.[48]

One of Azoff's first responsibilities at the management company was booking acts for a club that Geffen helped to develop called the Roxy. The club offered another measure of Geffen's clout, conviction, and instinct for the jugular. The Roxy emerged as a response to the dominance of the Troubadour. The Troubadour was the unchallenged domain of Doug Weston, who had opened it in 1957 and steered it to preeminence not only in Los Angeles but nationally. Tall, with long, theatrically flowing blond hair, Weston had shown great insight by recognizing the power of both the Southern California mash-up of rock, folk, and country and the intimate new wave of singer-songwriters who emerged in Dylan's wake. But he grew infatuated with his importance and began to confuse his own modest hill with the mountains that the Olympians in the LA music landscape occupied. Much like Bob Wood at CBS, who felt increasingly aggrieved that producers like Norman Lear were making millions from shows that *he* put on the air, Weston felt that he was not sharing sufficiently in the riches raining down on artists whose careers he had helped launch. His solution was to require artists, when they were starting out, to sign contracts that committed them to future appearances at the Troubadour or other clubs Weston booked, at rates only slightly higher than what he paid them as unknowns. This annoyed the artists, but it infuriated executives like Lou Adler and David Geffen. "Doug [Weston] considered himself the LA impresario, which is a hard thing to be when you had . . . Geffen and all these guys," Azoff said. "[Weston] was basically saying, 'Fuck off. My way or the highway,' and he was the taste police."[49]

Geffen and Adler were not the only ones who wanted to create an alternative to Weston. Eventually, the two of them joined with Elmer Valentine (owner of the nearby Whisky a Go Go), Chuck Landis (a club owner who had run a burlesque house), and Elliot Roberts (Geffen's longtime partner) to open the Roxy on Sunset Boulevard as the Troubadour's first real competitor in years. It was a measure of how much animosity Weston had provoked that such an unlikely alliance sublimated their differences long enough to lock arms against him. (In fact, the alliance was short-lived; Geffen, depending on the telling, either sold his stake in the club within weeks or never actually invested any money.)

The owners unveiled the Roxy on September 20, 1973, a star-studded opening night that featured Neil Young as the headliner, Graham Nash and Cheech and Chong as opening acts (after Nils Lofgren, originally slated for that role, developed laryngitis), and Elton John and Carole King in the crowd.[50] Adler, who had taken the lead in designing the club, had modeled it after the Roxy in New York during the 1940s, with a sleek elegance that consciously contrasted with the

Troubadour's faded-jeans aesthetic. Upstairs from the Roxy, Adler designed a private club, On the Rox, for marquee names in music and movies. It was a place where Warren Beatty, Jack Nicholson, and Roman Polanski could mingle with the rock gods and the executives behind them. "It was a private club, basically for Jack and I, but we let in maybe eleven other members," Adler recalled. "Most of all, it was a place where people just showed up. You didn't know who would be there."[51]

The Troubadour didn't crumble immediately, but Weston's years of dominance were over. He "had so much power that it annoyed people, and he wielded it improperly," said Azoff, who booked acts for the Roxy for a few weeks before dropping the assignment after he, inevitably, blustered into an argument with Adler. "They just took him out. He was no match for David and Lou and Elliot and those guys. They had too much clout and too much power."[52]

By early 1974, Geffen's clout in the recording industry appeared unmatched. His life in these months could have generated a one-act play, with the key figures in the cast being Bob Dylan, Joni Mitchell, Cher, and Irving Azoff. At home, Geffen had acquired a roommate in the house on Copley Drive that he rented from Blake Edwards and Julie Andrews: Joni Mitchell, on the rebound from a very bad breakup with Jackson Browne. (Most sources say she moved in with Geffen after trying to commit suicide, though she later denied this.) Living with Mitchell, even platonically, was never simple: Mitchell was a complicated woman who tended toward the turbulent in her romantic involvements. (One song on *Court and Spark*, "The Same Situation," was widely viewed as her commentary on her on-again, off-again affair with Warren Beatty; "Help Me," her account of ambivalently falling for "a sweet-talking ladies' man," may have memorialized a more fleeting assignation with Glenn Frey.) Yet no other music executive could speak of wandering into his living room to find Joni Mitchell perched behind the piano, working on the songs that became her brilliant *Court and Spark*.

Geffen's great professional cause in 1973 and 1974 was luring Bob Dylan to Elektra/Asylum, away from his longtime home at Columbia

Records. "The legend was he could sign anybody," remembered Jon Landau. "If he focused on somebody, he would go after them and communicate this tremendous intensity."[53] Dylan was to be the capstone of the Geffen legend. Geffen, as always, plotted his campaign methodically. He first targeted Jonathan Taplin, the former road manager for Dylan and the Band, as his conduit to meet Robbie Robertson, the Band's leading figure. He courted Robertson to get closer to Dylan. Geffen convinced Robertson to move to Malibu and then wooed him and his wife by taking them on a trip to Paris with him and Joni Mitchell, who memorialized the experience in her classic song about Geffen, "Free Man in Paris." "It was very clear David was moving up the stack: he uses me to get to Robbie and uses Robbie to get to Dylan," Taplin recalled.[54] Over months of courtship, Geffen promised Dylan independence, camaraderie, the intimacy of a more personal operation than Columbia.[55] To the reclusive, perpetually skeptical Dylan, Geffen presented himself more as a friend and an ally than a boss. He even helped Dylan find a house in Malibu (where his visitors included Warren Beatty, who occasionally stopped by to talk movies). As usual, Geffen got his man: outmaneuvering his fellow Warner label, Atlantic Records, he signed Dylan in the fall of 1973 and immediately sent him into the studio.[56]

While Geffen spent his days courting Dylan, his nights took an even more unexpected turn. He had lived most of his life as a gay man. He was as openly out as anyone could be in those years—to the point where some men around him felt he was carefully testing whether they might be open to a liaison—but at the opening night of the Roxy, he was seated next to Cher (Adler's doing) and was improbably stirred. The two talked until 4 a.m. He asked her to dinner the next night, she accepted, and they stayed up until the middle of the night again. From there they were off. For a gay man beginning his first serious romantic relationship with a woman, starting with Cher was like taking an interest in baseball by pinch-hitting for the Red Sox at Fenway Park. She was a huge television star—her variety show on CBS with her estranged husband, Sonny, ranked seventh in the 1973/74 season—an outsize personality, and as mercurial and flamboyant as she was sexy and exotic. (She would not, by reliable accounts, leave her house if she had a pimple.) But Geffen courted Cher with his typical thoroughness: one of his assistants waited in line to fill up her Porsche during the gas crisis.[57] Geffen managed her professional and personal separation from Bono, and he and Cher talked of marriage. It was two big personalities living large. Flying back from Aspen with them after a winter sojourn, Anjelica Huston remembers the couple traveling with so many belongings that piles of "quilts and pelts" and assorted other possessions "were left on the runway" because they could not all fit onto the plane.[58]

On every front, Geffen in early 1974 seemed to be holding aces. *Planet Waves*, the album Dylan made for Geffen, was something of a throwaway, recorded in just three days, but it still reached No. 1 on the *Billboard* charts in mid-February and stayed there for four weeks. For the week of March 9, Geffen's Elektra/Asylum controlled the three top spots: *Planet Waves*, followed by *Court and Spark* and Carly Simon's *Hotcakes*.[59] Geffen then decided to follow up on the huge success of the Dylan/Band reunion tour that he engineered that winter with an even more ambitious undertaking: reuniting the fractious Crosby, Stills, Nash and Young for a summer concert tour that would play only in sports stadiums. "Elliot [Roberts] and Geffen came to us one day . . . and they had this idea that CSNY could do an entire tour that way, and that meant big money obviously," Nash remembered.[60] Though the Beatles and Rolling Stones had occasionally filled a stadium, no other band had undertaken a tour of that magnitude before. Even the audio technology to broadcast to stadiums effectively was still tentative.[61] But the sheer size of the youth audience made it possible to imagine a tour on that scale. The original members of CSN, and especially Neil Young, were understandably hesitant about reuniting, but the money Geffen waved at them made the idea irresistible.

Geffen by now had become a man about town, one of the few music executives to build relationships in Hollywood, which still eclipsed the music scene in glamour. (Most of the Warner music executives lived in the comfortable but deeply unfashionable San Fernando Valley suburb of Encino.) Geffen had Jack Nicholson and Robert Evans on his speed dial. One day, Geffen opened the door to his house on Alto Cedro, and there was Warren Beatty with Julie Christie, who were, for a moment, looking to rent a house together. Geffen struck up a friendship with Beatty, and over time the famously skeptical and self-contained star sought him out for financial advice. In the spring of 1974, Geffen's prodding helped to convince Beatty, after years of his living rootlessly in a penthouse at the Beverly Wilshire hotel, to buy a house on Mulholland Drive. "There was a house up here, and I had been talking to Geffen about it, and he said, 'Why don't you get out of the hotel,' and I said, 'I don't want to,'" Beatty remembered. "I said, 'Maybe I'll have a house on the weekend or something.' So, there was a house up here that was owned by the bank, and I came up and I looked at it and said, 'Wooh, great lot.' Geffen said, 'You're an idiot. You should buy the house.'" Beatty bought the house. "If he gives me advice that has anything to do with finance," Beatty said, "I follow the advice."[62] The cavalcade of stars who turned out for Geffen's lavish birthday bash at the Beverly Wilshire in February 1974 cemented his ascension to the very pinnacle of LA's entertainment elite.[63]

Geffen's rise was both a response to and a reflection of the growing professionalization of the music industry as it expanded in size and revenue. "What [the artists] saw in Geffen was somebody that could dominate in the business world and represent me in that world in a way that now I needed to represent, because the industry was starting to change," remembered Lou Adler. "It was no longer just record people that were heading labels. Attorneys were starting to come in; it was becoming a big business. David was able to operate with those people."[64] Like Graham Nash earlier, the artists who collected at Asylum mostly viewed Geffen's bottomless hunger for success as an engine that would pull them along, too. "He is very competitive, and he really went to bat for things he believed in," remembered Linda Ronstadt. "David was a good talker. We just figured he would be pretty good talking us up. He was very charming. It was just irresistible charm."[65]

GEFFEN DEVELOPED A NAME not only for commercial success but also for artistic quality. Asylum was a prestigious home; musicians were excited to be included on the label. "We were like part of a stable of artists," Browne remembered. "I was very proud to be on Asylum Records, and I was very proud each time [Geffen] signed somebody else to the label."[66] Once he signed Browne and Joni Mitchell, Ronstadt remembered, "that's where we wanted to be, because that was part of our tribe."[67] The Eagles initially felt the same way. Visiting Geffen at his office, looking at the memorabilia there from Joni Mitchell and Neil Young and CSN, Frey later said, "this unspoken thing was created between Henley and me which said, 'If we want to be up here with the big boys, we'd better get our game together.'"[68]

But compared to Browne, who felt little but gratitude, the Eagles were much more ambivalent and divided about Geffen. Frey was probably closer to Browne in his overall attitude toward him, but Henley was deeply suspicious of Geffen's dual role as manager (even if he had retreated behind the scenes) and record label owner. The difference reflected the contrasting way Frey and Henley approached the world. Browne was one of many friends who likened them to Oscar and Felix on television's *The Odd Couple*.[69] Frey was messy; Henley, neat. Frey was gregarious, Henley most comfortable alone. Their personalities matched their voices. Frey's was smooth, seductive, enveloping; Henley's was more abrasive, rough-edged, skeptical. "Glenn was much more happy-go-lucky, and Don is focused," remembered John Boylan.[70]

And yet, like many great songwriting teams, the two balanced each other. Frey, at that point, was the unquestioned leader of the band, but as songwriters, he and Henley functioned as a genuine partnership. "They were a great team, in a weird way," said Ronstadt. "Don is kind of a fussbudget, and Glenn was a street fighter. And the dynamic was pretty good there for creativity for a long time. They had their ups and downs, but there was a lot of respect."[71] The two drew nourishment from very different musical traditions. Frey had been raised on Detroit rock and roll and blues; Henley, much like Ronstadt, was reared on a spicy southern gumbo of blues, country, and folk. Their lyrical styles diverged, too. Henley, who had studied literature in college, was more of what Browne called "a long-form guy," looking for ways to tell stories in songs. Frey's great gift was condensing universal experiences into a few words—the way he captured the exhilaration of a new attraction in the lines he added to "Take It Easy." ("Life in the fast lane" and "lyin' eyes" were two other resonant phrases Frey contributed to the Eagles catalogue.) "Don went to college and studied books and shit," Browne remembered. "Glenn," he continued, and then paused and snapped his fingers: "Glenn is mercurial." Frey and Henley partook of every vice available to young rock stars in the early 1970s, but they also took the work seriously, and as their careers advanced, they agonized over songs, filling legal pads with ideas late into the night. "Both of them grew up as writers in the making of records," Browne said. "They grew up in the studio."[72] Sometimes they could spend hours on a single word.[73] "Don and Glenn were both incredibly talented, but they knew what they had to do, and they buckled down and did it," said Boylan.[74]

Their first album had unexpectedly produced three chart-topping singles, but the band didn't want to be viewed as a Top 40 hit machine.[75] Their response was to structure their second record, *Desperado*, as a concept album. The idea started with Browne, whose old friend, the singer Ned Doheny, gave him a book about nineteenth-century gunfighters. Browne began talking about the parallels between the outlaws of the late nineteenth century and the rock stars of the late twentieth, and Frey and Henley, along with J. D. Souther, became excited about creating a suite of songs around the idea.[76] But critics and audiences yawned when Asylum released *Desperado* in April 1973. The outlaw conceit on the cover seemed like kids playing dress-up, and the music, like much of Ronstadt's early material, fell in the chasm between rock and country (though the title track was a beautiful song whose richness became fully apparent only when Ronstadt later covered it).

Desperado's disappointing results heightened the pressures converging on the band. Internally, Leadon and Meisner bridled at the heavy-handed leadership of Frey and Henley, who were so determined to control the band's sound and direction that they rewrote songs from the other two that they believed did not meet their standards. Frey and Henley were still locked in endemic conflict with their producer, Glyn

Johns, who viewed the Eagles as a ballad band with country tinges and steered them in that direction with lots of banjos and creamy harmonies. And though the Eagles were proud to be part of Asylum, they chafed at the inherent conflict between Geffen's role in their management (however much he operated in the shadows) and their work for his record label. The Eagles were perhaps more offended than any other Asylum artist when Geffen first sold the company entirely to Warner in 1972 and then merged it with Elektra the next year. What Geffen had promised would be a small thing, an asylum, was now a giant enterprise.[77] It didn't help that all the corporate maneuvering had put millions in his pockets but hadn't added a dime to theirs.

These frustrations boiled over in December 1973. As the band members prepared to travel to London to record their third record, they sought to make some money for Christmas. Irving Azoff helped book them a quick round of about a dozen shows across the country. But Geffen, who controlled their expenses as the head of their record label, wouldn't send a limo to take the band to the airport. Infuriated, Frey called the management company, where Elliot Roberts asked Azoff to deal with him. Frey raged across the phone: the pop band America, which was another Geffen management client but was recording for the Warner Bros. label, received a limo for its travels.[78] The Eagles had to take a taxi? Azoff was sympathetic to Geffen. "America had limousines and shit lavished on them, but David was smarter and ran the business better: he wasn't throwing limousines around," Azoff remembered.[79] But Azoff also knew enough not to draw a line over a limo. He got the Eagles their ride, but the incident widened the breach between Geffen and Frey and Henley. "These were young, cocky guys living the American dream," Azoff remembered. "Whatever amounts of drugs and alcohol were being consumed, throw that on the fire, too."[80]

IF DAVID GEFFEN HAD catalogued his anxieties as 1974 began, conflict with Glenn Frey and Don Henley would hardly have topped the list. For all Geffen's success, his frustration and disenchantment grew in pace with his position.

The relationship with Dylan that Geffen envisioned as a new peak in his professional career instead proved a prolonged headache. "I don't know if David and Bob really clicked," Taplin said. "This was more transactional."[81] The tour was a huge success, but Geffen felt slighted when Dylan didn't recognize him from the stage at the last show in Los Angeles, and Dylan was disappointed that *Planet Waves* (though hardly one of his best) didn't sell as much as Geffen had promised.[82] The two fought over how to release the live album from his tour, and battling about money with such an icon left Geffen bruised and depressed. He told friends it was one of the most excruciating experiences of his life. Dylan returned to Columbia in August 1974 and (adding salt to the wound) followed the ramshackle *Planet Waves* by delivering to Columbia a towering midcareer masterpiece as his next album, *Blood on the Tracks*.[83]

Geffen's life could be exhilarating. One night in his living room, for example, Joni Mitchell, Dylan, Laura Nyro, and the great songwriter Jimmy Webb were all singing together. But the weight of Geffen's position pressed on him. Geffen was a young man who had never finished a semester of college, and beneath his bluster, he often doubted if he was really knowledgeable enough for all those who looked to him. While everyone thought he was a brilliant businessman, he felt that he was making it up every day. He looked with increased longing at the movie business, which seemed to him, as it did to those laboring in television, the grown-ups' table in Los Angeles. His personal life remained tumultuous. Joni Mitchell had moved out, considering Geffen too focused on Dylan. (When Geffen held a listening party at his house for Mitchell and Dylan to hear each other's upcoming albums, Dylan boorishly snored through the playing of *Court and Spark*.) Geffen's relationship with Cher was a roller coaster. Reports that their marriage was imminent persisted in the press through 1974; Cher redid Geffen's wardrobe and convinced him to upgrade his wheels to a white Rolls-Royce.[84] In July the two took up residence in the mansion she shared with Sonny Bono after making a guerrilla raid to legally evict him from it. But Cher would never set the marriage date that Geffen pressed for. As the months passed, an agitated Geffen spent more and more time in the office of Dr. Martin Grotjahn, the psychoanalyst to the stars whom he shared with Beatty, Joni Mitchell, and Robert Towne.

Mitchell, with her typical acuity, eloquently captured the part of Geffen that felt suffocated by the entire enterprise and persona he had built. In "Free Man in Paris," Mitchell sang that he was "a free man" because no one was calling him "for favors" and he had "no one's future to decide." But Geffen's occasional craving to escape what Mitchell called the "star maker machinery behind the popular song" was only one aspect of his conflicted personality. He also coveted success, measured in money, power, and victory over his rivals: the trip she memorialized, after all, was not a relaxed getaway but a critical maneuver in his systematic siege of Bob Dylan. (The song initially irritated Geffen, who thought it too revealing, especially after he had paraded Mitchell through gay bars across Paris.) Still, Mitchell captured the genuine ambivalence, if not the exhaustion, that was growing within Geffen as his success mounted. Jackson Browne, the other artist closest to Geffen, felt it, too. "I always had great empathy for David because I knew what he was doing was becoming a personal champion for each of these people," Browne recalled. "He was doing for them what he had done for me." Browne thought each artist Geffen signed, whether to the management company or the record label, expected him to work his magic for them. "In some cases, he's got to remake somebody's career or take it to a level that they hadn't even thought of themselves," Browne remembered. "Each time he signed somebody else to the label, the question was whether or not he could do it for that artist." When artists entered Geffen's orbit, their expectations rose. Browne thought this was unfair because "he can't flip a switch, even though he did flip a lot of switches. It's not always going to turn out."[85]

AMONG THE ASYLUM ARTISTS disappointed in their trajectory were the four members of the Eagles. Frey especially emerged from *Desperado* convinced that the band needed a new direction. "It didn't quite succeed maybe, and they took a lot of heat for it," said Browne. "But the next thing they did . . . they really turned the corner, and they started accessing their R-and-B roots, Detroit and East Texas and all this stuff that they grew up with, and they captured all that in contemporary music."[86] The impulse wasn't only artistic: Frey had concluded that none of the country-rock bands had reached the pinnacle of commercial success and that a harder sound would speak to a wider audience and carry them into that stratosphere.[87] But their producer, Glyn Johns, continued to view the Eagles as a ballad band, not a rock band. "He said, 'You're a shitty rock band, and I'm not going to make a rock record with you,'" Azoff remembered.[88] This stalemate intensified when the band relocated to London in late 1973 to begin recording their third album. After six weeks the group had completed only two songs, both ballads: "You Never Cry Like a Lover" and "The Best of My Love."[89] At an impasse with Johns, the Eagles returned to Los Angeles feeling stymied in every direction.

Irving Azoff, five feet and three inches of blunt ambition, stepped up to sever the Gordian knot. Through early 1974, he helped free the band to set a new course. Exactly how he did so remains a matter of dispute. Geffen for years saw Azoff as the snake in the garden who enticed the Eagles away from the Eden of his management company. Azoff says, "I did not sow the seeds of discontent between David and them as much as he thinks."[90] What's clear is that in the winter of 1974, Elliot Roberts, burned out by the responsibilities of tending to mercurial artists, moved to downsize the management company he ran with quiet input from Geffen. Azoff, in his telling, was prepared to stay with the reconfigured firm until Frey and Henley informed him that the band was leaving, with or without him. "They said, 'Well, we are going to find out how much you really believe in us, because we're not staying, so you can either come or go back,'" Azoff recalls. "After a lot of soul searching, I decided that I believed in them enough to incur David's wrath."[91] Geffen did not resist the move, though he considered Azoff disloyal for facilitating it.[92] In fact, the Eagles' departure, though contentious, was hardly a catastrophe for Geffen. He didn't like losing the band from the management company, but more important, he still had them signed for several more albums for his record label. If partnering with Azoff helped the Eagles regain altitude, Geffen still stood to profit handsomely. With the Eagles as his marquee client, Azoff opened a new company he called Front Line Management (after Graham Nash told him he was always on the front line). He set up shop just a few doors down from Roberts on Sunset Boulevard.[93]

The Eagles considered Azoff a generational peer and saw him the way Crosby, Stills, and Nash had once viewed Geffen: as their shark in dangerous waters. Most important, Azoff supported the vision of the band that Frey and Henley had formulated, a vision that would steer them away from the softer country rock and singer-songwriter confessionals that dominated the Asylum roster. The band cut its ties with Johns, and Azoff connected the group with Bill Szymczyk, a genial Los Angeles–based producer who had formulated a hard-edged sound for Joe Walsh. Working with Szymczyk, the Eagles resumed recording at the Record Plant, on La Cienega Boulevard. To implement their new vision, the band invited into the studio another guitarist, Don Felder. A young Florida native, Felder had been in the Geffen orbit backing softer singer-songwriters David Blue and Crosby and Nash, who were touring together. But Felder, an ace slide guitar player, had a grittier edge than those tours allowed him to display.[94] After a single day of recording, Frey offered him a permanent slot in the band.

Even with a new producer, the recording process did not unfold much more smoothly than in London. Conflict persisted as Frey worked to tilt the band more toward mainstream rock and the equally hard-headed Bernie Leadon, with his deep roots in the Southern California country-rock tradition, resisted. "Glenn and I assumed this bulldozer attitude before we went into the studio," Henley acknowledged later.[95] Felder wondered if he had joined a band that would break up before he could unpack all his equipment. "Not a day passed during the recording of that album when someone didn't blow his top, throw something, or stalk out, slamming the door behind him," Felder recalled later. "There was one explosive argument after another."[96]

But while the process was painful, the result powerfully reset the Eagles' direction. The completed album, called *On the Border*, retained some country-rock flavors—Leadon's prominent banjo on "Midnight

Flyer," a pedal steel on "My Man"—but this became secondary to a pulsing, all-American rock beat. The new direction was evident from the album's first track. Jack Tempchin, who had penned the dreamy "Peaceful Easy Feeling" for the Eagles' first album, had written "Already Gone" with Robb Strandlund as a softer country-rock song. Frey bulked it up, highlighting biting guitar solos from Felder. In this reconfigured form, the soaring "Already Gone" kicked off *On the Border* as a statement of intent for a band that finally considered itself on the move. (The song sent the same message when the Eagles delivered their blistering performance of it at the California Jam in Ontario.) Ironically, *On the Border*'s biggest radio hit was the weepy, harmony-heavy ballad "The Best of My Love" (which surely gave Glyn Johns no end of satisfaction). Its success made clear that the Eagles would never abandon their delicate harmonies, but with songs such as "Already Gone," "James Dean," and "Good Day in Hell," the album rocked much harder than its two predecessors. "They didn't sit down and say, 'We're going to transform from a country band to a rock band,'" said Azoff. "What they wrote automatically did that. They never thought they were country rock. They always thought they were a rock band."[97]

From the start, the Eagles had a contentious relationship with rock music's critical establishment, most of which was based in New York. They always felt the victim of an eastern bias against anything happening in LA. (They even maintained a list of their ten most-hated critics.) Frey responded with casual defiance. At the start of each concert, he would come to the microphone and say simply, "We're the Eagles from Los Angeles," before hitting the first chord. "'The Eagles from Los Angeles,'" remembered Azoff. "That's what we all said. It was a defiant thing. It was like everyone from all over the country came here; it's the golden age. 'We're the sum of our parts, we're a team, we're a band, and as critically unacclaimed as it is to say, we're a band from Los Angeles. We're proud of it.' It's that simple."[98]

The Eagles' relationship never improved much with the leading rock critics (apart from Robert Hilburn, who mostly championed them), but *On the Border* was a turning point for the band with all its antagonists, from the critics to Geffen. The album peaked at No. 17 on the *Billboard* charts, but it spawned the group's first No. 1 single with "The Best of My Love." More important, it showed the Eagles honing the propulsive sound that would lift them into the upper echelons of rock royalty. Their next three studio albums, *One of These Nights* in 1975, the epic *Hotel California* in 1976, and the labored *The Long Run* in 1979, all reached No. 1, as did a *Greatest Hits* album that Geffen released in 1976. (A 2018 ranking from the recording industry trade association placed the *Greatest Hits* record as the best-selling album of all time, with *Hotel California* ranking third.)[99] The extended tour that followed the release of *On the Border* through the summer and fall of 1974 was a rollicking success. It may have been overwhelmed by drugs and groupies, but with Felder added to the mix, the band developed a sound powerful enough to fill arenas and, before long, stadiums. All the seeds of the tensions that would later divide and ultimately dissolve the Eagles were apparent—the disagreement between Leadon and Frey over the band's musical direction, the determination of Frey and Henley to retain control, the grumbling over the distribution of money, the perpetual drug use that magnified every dispute— but in the moment, it was a party on wheels. "I always went on tour with them," Azoff said. "Why would you not go on tour with them? It was the greatest party any American white male could ever have."[100]

In a way, the band's overriding message to its audience may have been that it was acceptable to party again after a decade of tumult. Although Frey and Henley were personally liberal and increasingly engaged in political activism over time, their music was almost entirely apolitical. (The song "On the Border" tried to comment on Watergate, but as Henley later acknowledged, "it was a pretty clumsy, incoherent attempt.")[101] The band promised a return to normalcy of a different sort than that offered by the early 1970s singer-songwriters in Los Angeles. As young men exulting in every excess of life on the road, they could not sing about rediscovering the pleasures of hearth and home as Carole King and Graham Nash did. But their music transcended the social tumult of the 1960s in a different way, by reverting to the eternal concerns of youth: new love, heartbreak, fast cars, pretty girls. Their songs sounded even more universal and timeless because almost none of them named its characters. In Eagles lyrics, there was no Michelle or Angie or Rosalita. It was "the new kid in town," the girl with "lyin' eyes," the "man with hands as cold as ice." Time and place receded in their songs, and all that was left was a universal situation. Bernie Leadon later shrewdly observed that the Eagles found such a large audience in part because "the country and people and young people needed to feel like things were okay" again after all the conflict of civil rights and Vietnam and Watergate.[102] The Eagles eventually came to personify all the costs of "life in the fast lane," but as stardom beckoned them in the spring of 1974, this one band seemed to encapsulate all the promise that Los Angeles offered: money, beautiful women, drugs, and a life seemingly freed from constraints. For a nation emerging fitfully from the previous decade's turmoil, the Eagles were a fresh breeze from the coast, the easy-riding, hard-partying soundtrack to Los Angeles' golden hour. And yet, even as the Eagles sang of open roads and new loves, it soon became very clear that the tumult of the 1960s was not yet confined to the rearview mirror.

5

MAY
The Ballad of Tom and Jane

The firefight began just before 6 p.m. The first volley came from a Los Angeles Police Department SWAT team that lobbed several canisters of teargas into a small house at 1466 East Fifty-Fourth Street in South Central Los Angeles. Moments later came an answering burst of automatic weapon fire from inside. Over the next hour, two SWAT teams, one deployed outside the front door and the other in the back, supported by two hundred other LAPD officers and the FBI, besieged the house with more than 5,300 rounds of ammunition and 83 canisters of teargas. Against this bombardment, the suspects inside the house responded with pounding fire of their own. The fugitives barricaded inside discharged at least 2,000 rounds at the police, one later estimate concluded.[1] It was, to that point, the largest police firefight that had ever occurred on American soil.[2]

The date was May 17, 1974. The targets inside the house were six of the nine members of a radical group that called itself the Symbionese Liberation Army. The SLA had announced its existence six months earlier, when it murdered the superintendent of schools in Oakland, California. Then, in February 1974, the group jumped onto the front pages when SLA members kidnapped Patricia Hearst, a nineteen-year-old heiress to the Hearst newspaper fortune, from her home in Berkeley, just a few minutes from the University of California campus where she attended classes. The SLA graduated from a subject of media interest to the center of media frenzy after Hearst appeared to cross over into sympathy with her radical captors, most dramatically by participating in a mid-April bank robbery, about one month before the Los Angeles shootout.

Despite the attention, the SLA was never more than a bedraggled collection of misfits. Under the leadership of Donald DeFreeze, who called himself General Field Marshal Cinque, the SLA barely attracted enough members to fill out a softball team. DeFreeze wanted to inspire a proletarian revolution, but he had no plan, no program, and no real allies.

DeFreeze had relocated the SLA to his hometown of Los Angeles earlier in May because he thought it would be safer for them than the Bay Area. Instead, on May 16, SLA members Bill and Emily Harris, with Hearst in tow, had stumbled into a firefight with employees from a sporting goods store in Inglewood after they were caught shoplifting. When the trio abandoned their van in the subsequent pursuit, they left on the front seat an unpaid parking ticket that eventually led the police to the house on East Fifty-Fourth Street. Once the police found the SLA members there, the assault was unrelenting. The police department's SWAT units, at that point, were under the direction of Daryl Gates, who would gain notoriety as the city's unbending chief of police during the Rodney King riots nearly two decades later. After an hour of ferocious fire from both sides, one of the SWAT teams threw two canisters of a more potent, and flammable, teargas, and the house almost immediately burst into flames. By 7 p.m., it had collapsed, and all the SLA members on site, including DeFreeze, were dead, some shot by police, others felled by the flames. The fire was so intense that the houses on either side of 1466 also burned down.[3]

The next morning's headline in the *Los Angeles Times* ran across all six columns: "SUSPECTED SLA HIDEOUT STORMED, 5 DIE."[4] Actually, the final death toll was six, but Hearst was not among them: separated from the main group, she and the Harrises had relocated to a motel near Disneyland, where they watched the confrontation on television, like millions of other Americans. (Hearst wasn't apprehended until September 1975, in San Francisco.) Still, the massive damage amply justified the *LA Times*'s conclusion: "Friday afternoon's battle," it wrote, "was a scene from a war."[5]

THE RUINS ON EAST Fifty-Fourth Street still may have been smoldering when Tom Hayden wrote an analysis of the confrontation nine days later on the op-ed page of the *LA Times* under the headline "An Activist Radical Views the SLA."[6]

Generally, Hayden had not been attracted to violence as a means of change. But he had been almost as alienated from American society as the SLA members. In the 1960s, he emerged as one of the most prominent New Left activists, best known for helping to stage the chaotic antiwar demonstrations at the 1968 Democratic National Convention in Chicago. He remained one of the movement's most respected and visible theorists. His credentials as a radical critic of American society were unquestioned on the left. "He was the epitome of everything to which us budding leftists aspired," remembered Ira Arlook, a prominent activist in an array of sixties causes. "He was a total hero, so you knew everything about him."[7]

If many on the left saw Hayden as the paragon of the strategist and thinker, his wife, the actress Jane Fonda, was the template for the indomitable activist. From the time she returned to the United States in 1970 after years living in France with her first husband, director Roger Vadim, Fonda burned with a born-again commitment to social change that carried her from cause to cause in a fever of impassioned, if frequently ill-informed, advocacy. When she married Hayden in January 1973, they became the First Couple of the far left, its most famous activist joined with its most renowned theorist.

As the SLA shootout erupted, Hayden and Fonda were settling into a new role. Together with a small staff working from a brownstone in Santa Monica, the two had launched an organization called the Indochina Peace Campaign. As the SLA was issuing its revolutionary manifestos and engaging in bank robberies, the IPC was working with church groups and labor unions to organize local chapters intended to pressure members of the House and Senate to end American funding for the war in Vietnam. Only a few months before the firefight in South Central, Hayden and Fonda had spent a full month in Washington, DC—he wearing a suit jacket every day, she a conservative outfit—meeting with representatives, senators, and staff from both chambers to make the case against continued funding for the South Vietnamese government. Back in Santa Monica, they were closely monitoring approaching votes in the House and Senate and waiting for instructions from a broad coalition of antiwar groups in Washington about where to focus their organizing efforts.

For both Hayden and Fonda, the work with the IPC represented a step back from the ledge on which they had been living for years. Each of them in the spring of 1974 remained a lightning rod for criticism, and each still regularly expressed views on the far frontier of political debate. But after their years of revolutionary fervor, both were looking to build credibility and leverage within the mainstream political system. In that quest, they encapsulated a larger shift among the generation of young activists who emerged during the 1960s as the most radical critics of American life. By spring 1974, it was clear to all but the most deluded that fundamental revolution, much less violent upheaval and "prolonged civil war," as Hayden once warned, was not coming to America, no matter how many manifestos self-styled revolutionaries like the SLA issued or how many bombs radical groups like the Weathermen set off.[8] "Everyone is wearing T-shirts with Che Guevara and Mao and carrying Little Red Books around, which were all one hundred percent irrelevant to what we had to do in this country," remembered Bill Zimmerman, a longtime sixties activist who moved to Los Angeles in the summer of 1974 to run the IPC with Hayden and Fonda. "It was difficult emotionally because we had all made a huge commitment to one way of bringing about social change. In a way, thankfully, groups like [the] Weathermen showed us our mistakes, that they were sort of carrying out what we were thinking but to an extreme that revealed that what we were thinking was wrong. It wasn't strategic. You couldn't bring about the objectives that we were seeking."[9]

Hayden and Fonda were at the forefront of those seeking a different way. In their search, they offered a political analogue to the changes unfolding only a few miles away in the powerful cultural industries of movies, television, and music. Each of those institutions was trying to rejuvenate itself and connect with the emerging mass audience of

Baby Boomers by incorporating more of the cultural and social critique of American life that had emerged in the 1960s. The big question threading through popular culture in early 1970s Los Angeles was what seedlings of social change from the 1960s could be sustained in the stonier political and cultural ground of the 1970s. By spring 1974, Hayden and Fonda, like many of their activist contemporaries, were applying the same question to the nation's political institutions. They were trying to establish a beachhead inside the system they had not long ago vilified. Starting from a far more radical perspective, they were nonetheless engaged in the same journey as the directors, writers, actors, producers, and recording artists who sought to reconfigure the sixties' impatience with the status quo into a message acceptable to a mass mid-American audience. Because they began their journey so far out on the fringe, Hayden and Fonda offered the most extreme example, the most daunting test, of the capacity of the sixties' movements to find a pathway back into the American mainstream. They faced, in especially pointed form, the same questions that the era's best movies, television, and music confronted: Was it possible to create a new synthesis that found space for the ideals of the sixties even as that decade's dreams of fundamental transformation dissolved? Was there a way both to accept that revolution wasn't coming to America and to shoulder more of the responsibilities of adulthood without surrendering to the numbing pieties of Nixon's "silent majority"?

Against this backdrop, Hayden viewed the SLA as something like a high school friend who shows up a decade later to embarrass you with stories about the old days. "It just looked ridiculous and underscored the change that we were trying to go through," said Zimmerman.[10] In his article assessing the SLA for the *Times*, Hayden walked a narrow line. He condemned the SLA's violence and "burning revolutionary impatience," but he presented the group as an inevitable response to the inequities in American life. He wouldn't defend the SLA's means, but neither did he want the *Times*'s readers to feel smug or reassured about its downfall. "The SLA," he wrote, "exposes what many already see as the bankruptcy of an American life-style, that of the white middle and upper class. The conversion of Patricia Hearst to the life-style of her own kidnapers [is] a morality play that threatens millions of American parents who worry about their own children."[11]

While SLA-style revolution might not be coming to the streets, he suggested, that didn't mean the sixties generation would passively accept the America it was inheriting. His argument was thoughtful, but it teetered on a base of bravado. None of the titans of the sixties left had entirely divined an effective path between those alternatives—and nothing illustrated that difficulty more than the long odyssey Hayden and Fonda had taken to that point.

THE STRANGE THING ABOUT Tom Hayden and Jane Fonda joining forces, personally and politically, was that their trajectories had moved in entirely opposite directions over the previous fifteen years. During the 1960s, Hayden had been at the fulcrum of New Left activism. He was born outside Detroit, the son of middle-class parents, a conservative father and liberal mother who divorced when he was young. As a student at the University of Michigan, Hayden was a principal author of the Port Huron Statement, the manifesto that launched Students for a Democratic Society, the premier radical student group of the decade. Hayden backed theory with action. He worked for civil rights in the South and spent four years living in gritty inner-city Newark organizing ghetto residents. He traveled to North Vietnam early in the war and became active in the peace movement; at home, he was a leading organizer for antiwar protests.

Fonda's world through these years could not have been more different. The daughter of actor Henry Fonda and socialite Frances Ford Seymour, she was reared at first in Los Angeles and Connecticut, a lonely child who struggled without success to win the approval of her famous but distant father. After her emotionally troubled mother committed suicide and her father remarried, Fonda spent much of her teen years at boarding school. As a young woman, she drifted into film without much conviction, skittering through light comedies such as *Tall Story*, the Western spoof *Cat Ballou*, and *Barefoot in the Park*, the movie adaptation of the Neil Simon play about a young married couple that made Robert Redford a star. "You can't be more white bread [than

I was]," Fonda remembered. "I was very straight and not at all aware of much."[12]

Looking for edgier film material, Fonda relocated to France, hoping to surf the fabled "Nouvelle Vague." There she caught the attention of director Roger Vadim, who married her and then sent her drifting into space as the intergalactic sex bombshell Barbarella, complete with a zero-gravity striptease.

For both Hayden and Fonda, 1968 was a pivotal year. Fonda stepped toward the flame. Confined to bed during a difficult pregnancy, she watched the student protests that convulsed Paris in 1968 and read author Jonathan Schell's celebrated reports from Vietnam.[13] Watching the Chicago protests on television that summer, she caught her first glimpse of Hayden.[14] She took out subscriptions to *Ramparts* magazine and the *Village Voice*, gorging on their radical critiques of American society and incisive investigative reporting.[15] When she returned to the United States the next year to star in the powerful Depression-era film *They Shoot Horses, Don't They?*, she was shocked by the political and social changes that had coalesced in her absence. Whether in Hollywood or Paris, Fonda had largely missed all the tumult that had defined the life of activists like Hayden for nearly a decade. Now the force of all the unrest gathering in late 1960s America hit her in a single, overpowering wave. The farmhouse outside Paris where she lived with Vadim and their daughter, Vanessa, suddenly seemed to her more a place of exile than of refuge. She returned to Paris convinced she needed to reengage with her country, and to join the movements she saw bursting around her, even if she wasn't sure how.

As Fonda leaned forward, Hayden receded. The Chicago convention protests had pushed to the extreme one influential theory among the New Left about how to change America: radicalize the population by exposing the true brutality of power, the iron fist beneath the velvet glove. But the nightsticks of Chicago mayor Richard Daley's police force had opened the heads of protesters without apparently opening the eyes of many Americans: three months after the protests, voters elected Richard Nixon as president. After Chicago's apocalyptic violence, Hayden, understandably, wanted to reconsider his next steps.

Attracted to the idea of living again in a college town (which he had not done since Ann Arbor), he relocated to Berkeley.[16]

Years after its Free Speech Movement of the mid-1960s had defined it as a hotbed of activism, Berkeley toward the decade's end remained the capital of youth culture in America. Telegraph Avenue, near the University of California campus, was the Broadway of the counterculture. Clothing shops sold tie-dyed T-shirts and bell-bottom jeans, head shops hawked incense and pipes, and record stores blasted out the latest releases from the Beatles and the Grateful Dead, all with the furtive scent of marijuana drifting on the air.

Bruce Gilbert, a young Berkeley student from Los Angeles, and his then girlfriend, Carol Kurtz, were two of the young people exhilarated by this world. "I really haven't had too many religious experiences in my life, but I have to say, coming into Berkeley at that period . . . you could feel the energy in the air there," Gilbert recalled.[17] The two were part of a small Berkeley commune called the Committee on Public Safety, or COPS, designed to offer its members group living, mutual support, and political action. It became a focal point in a local movement to increase community control over the Berkeley Police Department. Confrontations between student demonstrators and the police had grown more violent over time, culminating in weeks of running street battles in early 1969 involving not only the police but the National Guard, which California governor Ronald Reagan deployed into Berkeley over what became known as the People's Park demonstrations. Along Telegraph Avenue, students charged into battle with riot police to the sound of Bob Dylan blaring from portable speakers.[18]

Against this tumultuous backdrop, Hayden turned up one day at COPS's door. "He had heard about the COPS commune, and it was supposedly this combination of the cultural and the political, and there was sort of the nascent ideas that would become the women's movement or the feminist movement," Bruce Gilbert remembered. "There were strong women in it, they were very political and very much standing up for themselves, and there were graduate students who were just well read in everything, and there was a lot of intellectual ferment around there. But we were also kind of hippies living this quasi-proletarian lifestyle, pooling our money and sometimes our things, our cars, motorcycles, things like that. And so, Tom heard about it and was fascinated."[19] Inspired by COPS, Hayden decided to form a commune of his own, one that he hoped would become a national model.

The Red Family was the result, founded by Hayden along with a striking woman activist named Anne Weills, with whom he had started a romantic relationship; the leadership also included Weills's former husband, the journalist and political activist Robert Scheer. The collective acquired four houses near the Oakland border for communal living. With the Red Family, Hayden continued his effort to create a model for political agitation and social transformation. In some ways, it succeeded. The commune organized behind a slate of reformers who won seats on the city council, and it opened a pioneering day care center called the Blue Fairyland, but the group was whipsawed by tensions from within and without.[20] Many other activists kept their distance, in part because they were leery of Hayden's celebrity. "The Red Family never became very effective, even though it had a lot of very talented people in it," remembered Gilbert, who shifted to the new group along with Kurtz. "The rest of the Berkeley political movement viewed us as elites . . . There was an inherent distrust of leadership, that leadership was almost like it had to be inherently corrupt and so, don't let anybody think of themselves as leaders of this movement. It was a prominent feeling, and Tom both suffered from that and helped create that reaction."[21] Internally, the group fractured along multiple fault lines. Money was always very tight, and the group's commitment to renouncing monogamy as a vestige of social repression turned out to be much more volatile than hoped. "We experimented with sexual freedom, we had a free love commune, and so all the couples split up and destroyed themselves on the rocks of trying to get rid of monogamy," remembers Jack Nicholl, who also moved from the COPS commune to the Red Family.[22] Even beyond the bed hopping, the commune was caught in the full gale of the broader renegotiation of male-female relations that followed the emergence of the feminist movement. These crosswinds were especially powerful in New Left circles, where women, justifiably, felt they had been marginalized through the 1960s by charismatic and headstrong young male leaders like Hayden. The women of the Red Family demanded an equal, if not a predominant, voice in its direction. Ultimately, the group created a women's executive committee with veto power over the collective's decisions. The fact that, as all this was unfolding, Hayden was in a romantic relationship with Weills, the most dynamic and compelling of the commune's women activists, and developing a paternal bond with her young son, all while her ex-husband, Scheer, was also living in the commune's complex of buildings and functioning as one of the group's leaders, added layers of personal complexity to the underlying political and social tensions.[23] A gas leak filling the basement could not have been more flammable.

For all his interest in building a model of communal living, Hayden fit uneasily into the bridle of collective leadership. He remained an inspiring figure for many around him but tended to make decisions and engage in political projects without approval from the group. The most pointed examples concerned the Black Panthers, headquartered in nearby Oakland. Hayden believed that they should "lead" the movement because Blacks were the most oppressed group in American society.[24] But given the Panthers' dismissive attitudes about women, the Red Family's female leadership had little interest in submitting to Panther direction. Eventually, in a solemn group meeting, Hayden was forced out, with even Weills joining the effort.[25] He was crushed both politically and emotionally. He walked out of the Red Family, crumpled into his Volkswagen, and like many people looking to start over, pointed his car toward Los Angeles.

LA ALSO CALLED TO Jane Fonda when she was ready to return from her years of drawing room radicalism and offhanded hedonism abroad. For years, she had listened to leading lights of the French left decrying American imperialism and global capitalism. Now she wanted something more pungent than attending Brentwood and Beverly Hills cocktail parties that collected checks for radical causes while servants offered champagne and canapés around the pool. "I hadn't lived in it yet, but I had rented a house on the top of a hill where I was going to be able to do fund-raisers, and it just hit me: 'I don't want to be someone who lives in a house on the top of a hill doing fund-raisers,'" she remembered. "I want to be at the bottom of the hill with the people that are impacted. It was like an epiphany. I knew that that was where I was at."[26]

Over Fonda's first months back in the United States in 1970, that impulse thrust her to the front lines of causes from coast to coast. She joined Native American protesters at Alcatraz[27] and then traveled up the coast to Washington State for another Native American demonstration.[28] In Denver, she fasted for peace in Vietnam with Dr. Benjamin Spock.[29] After the Kent State shootings in May 1970, she spoke at a massive rally at the University of New Mexico, in Albuquerque. A few days later, she spoke at another large rally to protest the Vietnam War and the Kent State killings, this one in Washington, DC.[30] She helped to raise bail money for imprisoned members of the Black Panthers.[31] (Fonda kept her distance from the Panthers after that—she was hesitant to identify too closely with a group so inclined toward violence—but her initial encounter was sufficient to trigger the FBI surveillance that would shadow all her subsequent activism.)[32] The work was all-consuming. Even when she resumed her film career in the summer of 1970 by appearing as Bree Daniels, a high-class call girl, in the movie *Klute* (a role for which she would win the 1972 Academy Award for Best Actress), she rushed to antiwar work on nights and weekends.[33]

The cause that Fonda connected with most powerfully was engagement with the soldiers themselves. A Vietnam veteran she met at director Mike Nichols's house suggested she visit the alternative "GI Coffeehouses" sprouting up outside military bases around the country. The coffeehouses provided a place for rank-and-file soldiers to share experiences and discuss the war. It wasn't a surprise that soldiers were happy to meet a beautiful and famous actress, but Fonda proved a good listener and enjoyed the human connection. "They came into my life right at that time when I was like an open book," she recalled.[34] Fonda transformed her appearance. Gone were the long blond hair, alluring makeup, and miniskirts of her sex kitten years in Paris. Now she wore jeans, a navy peacoat, and the simple shag haircut she would make famous in *Klute*. It was the uniform of a confident, independent woman, but it was also, in many respects, just another costume: Fonda remained wracked by insecurity and eating disorders as she powered through her long and stressful days.[35] She felt isolated by the gulf between her affluent life and the lives of the activists around her. To trigger a crisis of confidence, it didn't take more than a Native American woman asking her, at one of the first protests she attended, where her daughter was that day. "She had her little daughter with her, and of course my daughter was at my dad's home being looked after by a nanny, and I realized, How do I bridge this? I'm so privileged. I'm white, I'm famous, I'm wealthy," Fonda recalled. "I felt like such an interloper."[36]

Still, she pushed forward, soon taking on an even more ambitious project: the "F.T.A. tour." Depending on the audience, the initials stood for "Free the Army" or "Fuck the Army." Either way, the shows, which Fonda organized with actor Donald Sutherland, were meant as a counterculture alternative to the patriotic pieties that Bob Hope served on his tours to entertain the troops. Joined by a cast that included actor Peter Boyle, activist Dick Gregory, and Broadway performer Ben Vereen, Sutherland and Fonda presented the shows to receptive and enthusiastic audiences not only across the United States, but also near bases in the Philippines and Okinawa.[37]

By any fair accounting, this was a record of remarkable commitment and effectiveness for a woman who had never finished college and who had spent much of the 1960s drifting through a life of comfort in France, but it was only one column in the ledger. Through these early months, Fonda became a kind of caricature of the right's vision of a privileged leftist. She was ardent, committed, and fearless, but also dogmatic, reckless, and turgid. It wasn't only that she repeatedly made the factual and historical mistakes that might be expected of anyone learning her politics while standing in front of a pack of reporters. It was also that she adopted and discarded revolutionary concepts with alarming frequency. At one point she declared herself "a revolutionary, a revolutionary woman."[38] At another, she insisted, "This is not America in 1970; it is Berlin in 1936, and we are all Jews."[39] When one sympathetic interviewer asked if she considered herself a Communist, Fonda replied, "I'm not flippant with that phrase. I'm not a Communist. I would be honored to be called a Communist. It's like a Red Badge of Courage, which I haven't come close to earning."[40] It was a revolutionary stew, and Fonda swept everything she heard or read into the pot almost instantly, but her inclination was always toward more spice, more heat, more absolutism—all spurred by her belittling belief that she had "wasted" the thirty-two years of her life that preceded her revolutionary reinvention.[41] As she later acknowledged, "During the first years of my political existence, I was so filled with self-loathing and contempt for what I represented that I couldn't function effectively. What got me into so much trouble was this attitude that 'I'm not left enough, I'm not militant enough.' More left rhetoric came out of my mouth during that time—I didn't even know what the words really meant. I was trying too hard to prove my credentials, to prove that I was sincere. It was very bad for both me and the movement."[42]

Even in a movie community that was coalescing around opposition to the war, Fonda's combustible intensity isolated her. Working with Sutherland, she launched an antiwar group called the Entertainment Industry for Peace and Justice.[43] The group drew twelve hundred people to its first meeting and set plans for a massive antiwar rally at the Hollywood Bowl, but it collapsed without achieving much of anything. Fonda's connections to the film industry itself withered during these months. After *Klute*, she filmed *Steelyard Blues*, a poorly received anti-establishment comedy, and then didn't release another mainstream Hollywood movie until 1977.[44] Her absence was often described as a form of "graylisting" by the studios, a softer version of the blacklist that had exiled leftists from the industry during the 1950s, but Fonda wasn't even sure, in fact, that she wanted to make movies anymore.[45] Driven to prove her revolutionary ardor, she increasingly considered moviemaking shallow and unsatisfying. Ironically, this meant she had withdrawn from Hollywood just as such generational contemporaries as Warren Beatty, Jack Nicholson, and Robert Towne, along with the cohort of great directors a few years their senior, had produced Hollywood's most concentrated burst of socially conscious films since the Great Depression.

Still, Fonda remained plagued by doubts about her ability to function as an activist. She felt as if she were constantly racing after the latest splits and fissures in the New Left, always one step behind the doctrine she needed to absorb. "I was being pulled in all directions because I was famous, so I could attract people, and I could give money and all that kind of thing, but I didn't know all the pitfalls, and I wasn't in good shape," Fonda said.[46] The antiwar movement itself was splintering as Nixon withdrew American ground troops while intensifying the bombing of North Vietnam. Even as she settled into a new home in the hills above Studio City, Fonda wasn't sure she still fit into any of the parts she had designed for herself.[47] She was ready for a new act, and she would find it in a romantic and political alliance with a man who had arrived in Los Angeles in even greater need of a fresh start.

TOM HAYDEN WASHED UP in Venice, California, like a tangle of driftwood onto the beach. After his expulsion from the Red Family collective in Berkeley, he rented a one-room apartment in a shabby building a block from the ocean, under the name of his mother's father, Emmett Garrity.[48] He wanted to disappear, and he picked the right place to try.

Venice, located just south of Santa Monica, had been declining pretty steadily since World War II. It was designed just after 1900 by flamboyant developer Abbot Kinney, as an American homage to Venice, Italy, complete with extensive canals, gondolas, and an amusement park. But over time, the canals proved difficult to maintain, and many were filled in after they became brackish and buggy. The amusement park went bust. The rich and famous who once flocked to the seaside attractions moved elsewhere, and their mansions became hotels or apartment buildings that grew seedier with each change in ownership.

During the Beat era in the late 1950s, Venice enjoyed a rough revival as an outlaw enclave of artists and poets, but by the time Hayden arrived in 1970, even that gritty glamour had faded. Artists were still drawn to Venice by the low rents and beautiful coastal light, but the great beatnik hangouts were gone.[49] The fabled coffeehouse Venice West had become a head shop; the Gashouse, another Beat gathering spot, was simply condemned and boarded up. Venice had become a community of hot plates and drug busts: longtime elderly residents eking out a meager retirement surrounded by hippies, drug addicts, the mentally ill, and the homeless. The run-down apartment building Hayden had settled into was just off the ocean, on Westminster and Speedway, a corner dominated by drug dealers.

It was here that Hayden tried to rebuild his life after Berkeley. Joan Andersson, a radical young lawyer, was one of the first people who tugged him out of his gloom. Committed, vibrant, and attractive, Andersson, in her mid-twenties, was already a veteran activist. She had helped to found a leftist legal and political collective called Bar Sinister, based in Santa Monica. Like the Red Family, Bar Sinister sought to marry social and political change. It took on cases involving racial and sexual discrimination and defended young men trying to avoid the draft; its clients included the Black Panthers. And like the Red Family, Bar Sinister earnestly and endlessly debated gender relations and the changing roles of women.

When Andersson first encountered Hayden in Venice, he was bruised and tentative. "For the first period of time that he was there . . . he really tried to change a lot about himself," she recalled. "I think he was very shaken by what [had] happened. In addition to his relationship with Anne [Weills], he was very close to her son, and it was very hard for him to no longer have that relationship. He let his hair grow long, he was a vegetarian, he got into karate, and he wasn't doing anything political for the first little while. He was kind of recovering, and I think he wasn't drinking." Hayden and Andersson dated briefly as he began to take the first steps out of his ditch. They walked her dogs, practiced martial arts, and sat on the beach, dissecting the left's uncertain future. Hayden, Andersson thought, was "very wounded" but not necessarily chastened by his expulsion. "Tom was not a person who did a lot of self-reflection," she remembered. "I don't get a sense that he thought he was wrong. I think he felt he was *wronged*."[50]

Hayden in these months sought anonymity as a balm. The radical left community in Los Angeles was not nearly as large as in the Bay Area or New York City, and no one in it matched Hayden for national contacts or reputation. Yet he did not pursue a leadership role, and the city's scattered activists did not seek him out. "There was an initial feeling of distrust of Tom by many people," said Andersson. "There was always a feeling that he was out for himself in some ways."[51]

Hayden took his first steps back toward political engagement with another new friend who helped him recover in Venice. When they met, Larry Levin was nearly as alienated as Hayden.[52] Levin had been raised in San Bernardino, the sleepy "inland empire," east of Los Angeles, but he had gravitated toward the city to join in activism for civil rights and against the war. Unlike Hayden and his circle, Levin was drawn to electoral politics, having worked for a time for Robert F. Kennedy's Senate office. After Kennedy's assassination, he spent a year in Ireland, following the growing resistance to British rule and conducting interviews, gathering materials, and producing reports for KPFK, a radical-left Los Angeles radio station.

When Levin returned to Los Angeles to resume his education at Immaculate Heart College, he rented a room in a rambling, run-down group home about three blocks north of Hayden in Venice.[53] A friend told him that Hayden was living not far away, and Levin looked him up. The two men instantly connected. Hayden liked Levin's idealism and also his roots in mainstream Democratic politics, a world Hayden knew very little about. Levin, a few years younger, revered Hayden as a hero of sixties activism and spent hours with him, walking, reading, talking. Hayden took Levin to meetings with radical activists back in Berkeley and on strolls along the shore with Andersson. "He was just trying to learn and deepen his knowledge about what was happening," Levin said. "It was just one room he had, not even a one-bedroom—a studio. And it was just books everywhere. Books, books, books. He'd be reading morning to night and then go to whatever else he was doing, the martial arts and Joanie."[54]

Like Andersson, Levin felt Hayden wanted to remain as anonymous as possible at the time. But a turning point came as Hayden, who was raised Irish-Catholic, listened to Levin's tales of the growing opposition to British rule in Northern Ireland. Levin had returned from there with a trove of taped interviews, revolutionary Irish music, and recordings of speeches from leaders of the incipient Irish independence movement. At night, he and Hayden listened to the tapes while drinking Bushmills whiskey and Guinness. Hayden grew committed enough to the cause to plan a trip to Ireland, but he was denied entry to the country because the Irish government thought he intended to travel on to Northern Ireland to agitate for the Irish Republican Army.[55] Back in Los Angeles, Hayden edged back onto the public stage by delivering, with Levin, presentations about the Irish uprising to small audiences at campuses and churches.[56]

This small step ended Hayden's period of exile. Levin, who was attending classes at Immaculate Heart, encouraged Hayden to seek a teaching position there. Historically a Catholic girls' school, Immaculate Heart had become something of a renegade institution, and in the early 1970s, it severed its connection to the Church.[57] It became the sort of place that eliminated doors and blackboards to dismantle the hierarchy between students and teachers.[58] "It was getting the reputation as an activist place," Levin remembered. With his help, Hayden developed a proposal to teach a course there on the history of Vietnam. The twist was that it would involve the students in developing pamphlets, slide shows, and multimedia presentations (including posters from Sister Corita Kent, a celebrated leftist artist teaching at Immaculate Heart) that they could take to audiences to make the case against the war. Hayden later replicated the course at the UCLA Extension school and the Claremont Colleges east of Los Angeles. He soon had nearly one hundred students pumping out slides and posters on Vietnam, which he used to make presentations about the war at campuses and churches.[59] Then, in early 1972, he attended a talk at the Embassy Theatre in downtown Los Angeles by a famous activist with her own Vietnam slide show: Jane Fonda.[60]

Backstage after her talk, the two connected with an unmistakable spark, and soon after, Hayden went to Fonda's house in Laurel Canyon to show her *his* slide show.[61] No one would have confused the scraggly Hayden with a leading man, but when he projected his slide show on the wall of Fonda's house, she felt herself falling. For the beleaguered and besieged Fonda, Hayden was "like a haven," she remembered. "He opened my heart, and that's when I fell in love with him. But what he gave me was structure; he gave me an understanding of the movement and the history of the movement and how to organize. I don't know what would have happened to me if I hadn't met him."[62] The two began a romance and joined forces, personally and politically.

IF TOM HAYDEN IN 1972 provided Jane Fonda with focus, Fonda provided Hayden with scale. His "Indochina Education Campaign" was energetic but still very small. When Fonda entered the picture, that changed almost immediately. "Jane's involvement somehow turbocharged what we were doing," Levin said.[63] She, Hayden, and Levin developed the idea of expanding their local education campaign to national scale through what they would call the Indochina Peace Campaign. They would undertake a national speaking tour with their slide shows and posters about Vietnam and barnstorm across the battleground states they expected to be decisive in Richard Nixon's 1972 reelection campaign. The goal wasn't to explicitly endorse the Democratic nominee, but they did hope to make the case against the war and against Nixon's reelection.

Even with the careful choice not to directly align with the Democrats, any engagement with electoral politics represented a huge step back toward the mainstream for Hayden and Fonda and the broader far-left circles in which they moved. Some on the left considered any gesture toward conventional politics a betrayal of the goal of radical change. But others saw the IPC as a potential path out of the isolation that solidified around the remnants of the sixties left during Nixon's first term. "By that point, anything was valuable," said Andersson. "We were desperate. One of the things that really happened . . . is we became very isolated. We felt we were very isolated from America."[64] The IPC tour was intended to reconnect the peace movement with mainstream America. Fonda certainly saw it that way: as they prepared for the tour, she cut off the long braid Hayden wore his hair in, bought him a polyester suit, and found some good, Middle American polyester outfits for herself.[65] Resistance on the left to participating in conventional electoral politics diminished also because the North Vietnamese had told a visiting delegation of American peace activists that they believed the movement needed to reconnect with the mainstream. "The Vietnamese said, 'Become Girl Scouts and Boy Scouts, blend in, and focus on Congress,'" Fonda recalled.[66]

But the next weeks underscored how big a gulf still separated her and Hayden from the mainstream they hoped to reengage. Just before they finalized plans for the fall tour, Fonda received an invitation from the North Vietnamese government to visit the country.[67] Hayden strongly encouraged her to accept, but for reasons even those close to both never entirely understood, he chose not to join her. (The cost of the trip might have been a factor, Fonda recalled.) Each would come to deeply regret that decision. "The biggest mistake I ever made was to go by myself," Fonda said, "because I wouldn't have made the mistake I made if I hadn't been alone."[68]

In July, as Levin was beginning preparations for the fall IPC tour, Fonda flew alone to North Vietnam for a two-week visit. Her principal goal was to publicize the allegation from the North Vietnamese, some foreign diplomats, and antiwar groups that Nixon was bombing the dikes indispensable to the country's agricultural production. And she did raise awareness of that charge at press conferences in Paris and New York after her return.[69] The film she brought back from Vietnam caught the attention of United Nations secretary-general Kurt Waldheim, who urged Nixon to stop the bombing. (Nixon continued to deny that the United States was targeting the dikes, but the bombing ultimately stopped.)[70]

But in the months and years that followed, this very tangible mission was entirely eclipsed by the larger message Fonda delivered while in Vietnam. During the tour, she not only urged peace, but she also repeatedly appeared to side with North Vietnam against her own country. She did this most famously during her last day on the trip, when she sat on a North Vietnamese antiaircraft gun aimed at American flyers while North Vietnamese soldiers serenaded her with song. Later, she described the decision to sit on the gun as a "two-minute lapse of sanity" that would "haunt" her until she died.[71] But Fonda's time on the gun was less an aberration than a culmination of her trip. Days before the incident, Fonda, distraught at the damage she had seen from the bombings, asked the North Vietnamese to allow her to deliver radio appeals to American pilots.[72] The request was impulsive—before leaving the States, she had not discussed with Hayden what she might say on the radio if offered the opportunity to speak[73]—and the broadcasts she delivered combined genuine empathy for the civilian suffering she saw around her with a stiff and formulaic leftism that hailed North Vietnam as a new society while lamenting "the encroachment of the American cancer" onto the region.[74] Fonda's loyalties were, at the least, conflicted long before she climbed behind the gun. "We . . . support the Vietnamese people's struggle," she declared in one broadcast. "We understand that you and we have a common enemy—U.S. imperialism. You and we have engaged in the same struggle, and your victory will also be that of the American people and of all peace-loving peoples throughout the world."[75] As she repeatedly insisted over the years, she never explicitly asked American pilots to disobey their orders, but it wasn't unreasonable for anyone who heard her to reach that conclusion when she broadcast that "the men who are ordering you to use these weapons are war criminals according to international law" and that "the use of these bombs or the condoning [of] the use of these bombs makes one a war criminal."[76]

These were highly incendiary comments, but when she returned to the States, they generated only sparks of controversy, not a full-scale firestorm. Some state legislators introduced resolutions to condemn her, but not much came of them. And while Fonda's antiwar allies may have winced at the photos of her on the North Vietnamese gun, as Levin worked to plan the fall tour, the trip caused barely a ripple for the local groups partnering with them.[77] "It wasn't a political liability to any major extent," said Bruce Gilbert from the Red Family, who had reconnected with Hayden to work on the IPC.[78]

The IPC tour launched on Labor Day 1972 in Columbus, Ohio, a location chosen precisely to demonstrate that its message of defunding the war and disengaging from Vietnam could find an audience in what Hayden later called "the middle of 'middle America.'"[79] Over the next two months, the tour traveled to ninety-five cities, sometimes making four or five appearances a day.[80] Usually the appearances started with folksinger Holly Near performing. Then Fonda and Hayden divided the message. She focused on the human cost of the war, narrating a slide show that included searing images of teenage prostitutes in Saigon who had undergone plastic surgery to look more Western for the American soldiers. Hayden offered a high-altitude political analysis that linked the war to a broader critique of American foreign policy. Antiwar figures George Smith and Bob Chenoweth, former POWs, provided personal testimony. They displayed the multimedia presentations designed by Hayden's students in hundreds of locations, from small-town city halls to art museums.[81]

Some of the events inevitably drew protests and demonstrations from veterans and supporters of the war, but mostly the tour was an enormously reaffirming experience for Fonda, Hayden, and their small staff. Fonda initially got by on charisma and star power, but over time, she became a more relaxed and conversational speaker. As evidence to her listeners that they could step forward to promote change, she offered her own belated political awakening. She would later describe the tour as "the most fulfilling experience of my life up to then," and the experience moved her on every level.[82] Personally, it bonded her to Hayden. "First of all, I was madly in love with Tom, and it's like you're glued," she remembered. "We had no money, we would sleep in people's homes, oftentimes both of us on a twin bed, sometimes on waterbeds. We were never apart, and I was just at his elbow watching him, listening to him."[83] Politically, the trip fulfilled the yearning to connect with a larger community that she had felt since returning to the States. "This was Middle America, and you could tell people were changing, and I wasn't alone; I was part of a troupe," she said. "Oh God, it felt so good to know that what you're doing really matters and that you're not alone. It is the most beautiful feeling in the world."[84]

After years of isolation and retreat, each felt a sense of personal and political renewal. With their newfound optimism, they took their personal relationship to another level: Fonda became pregnant with their son, Troy. Even the election results that fall, in which Nixon won forty-nine states and almost 61 percent of the vote in a historic landslide, did surprisingly little to discourage Hayden, Fonda, and the IPC staff. They felt they had positioned the group to make a difference in the states that could tip a close race; just because George McGovern failed to stay close to Nixon didn't mean that their efforts were in vain. Still, for all that bravado, the magnitude of McGovern's loss made clear how far the antiwar movement remained from building a political majority. Yet Hayden now found that mission less daunting than energizing. He emerged from the tour convinced that the opportunity to organize grassroots opposition to the war was much greater than they had anticipated. If anything, he felt, the tour's biggest mistake was failing to build an organization that could channel all the energy they tapped in their audiences. A few months after Nixon's reelection, Hayden and Fonda moved to institutionalize their work by opening a permanent IPC office in Santa Monica to lobby for an end to military aid to South Vietnam. And as they anchored their political action on that new foundation, they moved to solidify their personal bond as well: with Fonda three months pregnant, she and Hayden were married at her home in January 1973. During the ceremony, they sang Vietnamese songs.[85]

HAYDEN AND FONDA ESTABLISHED the IPC to rejoin the mainstream work of building a political coalition to end funding for the war, yet they remained almost completely isolated from the other liberal and antiwar activity bubbling in Los Angeles. The IPC's office was located in a two-story building at 181 Pier Avenue in Santa Monica, still largely a haven for retirees, and much of the small staff lived a few miles south, in scruffy Venice. When the veteran activist Bill Zimmerman arrived in July 1974 to run the IPC, he moved into an apartment on the evocatively named corner of Speedway and Horizon in Venice (not far from where Hayden had landed after his expulsion from Berkeley about four years earlier). Walking the short distance to the ocean, Zimmerman was wide-eyed to discover that the stretch of beach outside his apartment building had been designated as "clothing optional."[86] This was a world away from the gilded mansions a few miles to the east, in Brentwood, Beverly Hills, and the Hollywood Hills, where much of Los Angeles' liberal activism was centered. "Norman Lear and Warren Beatty, they were not coming down to Venice," said Bruce Gilbert. "We were not running in the same circles."[87]

The IPC's separation was especially striking because Los Angeles was an early center of Democratic dissent over the war. In 1967, when Lyndon Johnson visited LA for a fund-raiser at the new Century Plaza Hotel, some ten thousand mostly middle-class protesters marched down the Avenue of the Stars to condemn the war. More than a thousand Los Angeles police, wading into the crowd with nightsticks, responded with a bloody assault that foreshadowed the confrontations between police and demonstrators at the Democratic convention the next summer.[88] And when Johnson stepped aside in March 1968, Los Angeles quickly emerged as a critical source of support for the antiwar Democrats vying to replace him. Actor Paul Newman became one of the most important surrogate speakers for Senator Eugene McCarthy.

All this proved just a prelude to 1972. Los Angeles provided decisive financial and political support for South Dakota senator George McGovern's insurgent antiwar bid for the party's presidential nomination that year. Wealthy businessman Miles Rubin took an extended leave to run McGovern's political and fund-raising operation in California. Warren Beatty served throughout the year as a backstage adviser to McGovern and organized a series of splashy rock concerts around the country to raise money and visibility. Working with the producer Lou Adler, Beatty wrangled Barbra Streisand, Carole King, James Taylor, and Quincy Jones to perform at an April 1972 concert for McGovern in Los Angeles and enlisted celebrity friends, including Jack Nicholson, Julie Christie, Jon Voight, and Burt Lancaster, to serve as ushers. Even McGovern's loss to Nixon in the general election barely slowed the momentum from this awakening. The fund-raisers and activists who emerged from the long political struggle against the war—Stanley Sheinbaum, Harold Willens, industrialist Max Palevsky, Miles Rubin, Norman Lear, Ted Ashley of Warner Bros., joined occasionally by stars such as Beatty, Newman, and Robert Redford—continued to work together in informal alliances and shifting combinations on causes ranging from the environment to nuclear disarmament to the 1973 campaign of Tom Bradley, who won election as Los Angeles' first African American mayor. The press labeled this glittering new axis of financial and political power the "Malibu Mafia," and its members became an indispensable stop for almost any liberal political candidate or cause looking to raise money in Los Angeles.[89]

Hayden and Fonda watched all this from a distance. "Just instinctively, my comfort zone was with Middle America and working-class people," Fonda said. "I didn't feel comfortable hanging with celebrities on this issue."[90] The couple's intermittent attempts at building common cause with the more conventional LA left usually flopped. Michele Willens, the journalist and activist daughter of Harold Willens, remembers accompanying her father to a meeting with Fonda at a tennis club in Beverly Hills. "She was just starting to get political, no smiles, very stern, looked emaciated," Michele Willens recalled. Fonda asked Harold Willens to help support a protest she was planning. "She said, 'We're going to go on a fast,'" Michele Willens remembered, "and my dad said, 'You look like you've *been* on a fast.'"[91]

The estrangement between Hayden/Fonda and the Los Angeles liberal establishment was reciprocal. For most in the LA left, Hayden and Fonda operated too far out on the fringe. Particularly problematic was that their goal in Vietnam extended beyond ending American participation to openly advocating a North Vietnamese victory. For those "who were a little more mainstream, like the Malibu Mafia," Bill Zimmerman recalled, "Tom and Jane and those of us working with them were behind sort of a radical barrier . . . so there wasn't a lot of cross-fertilization."[92] Rather than contributions from the big liberal donors just a few miles away, Hayden and Fonda relied mostly on small benefit concerts to fund their new organization.[93]

And soon enough, the pair was embroiled in another raging controversy that underscored the distance separating them from more conventional opponents of the war. In spring 1973, Fonda reacted angrily when some of the first returning American prisoners of war reported that the North Vietnamese had tortured them during their captivity. To *Newsweek*, she declared that only "guys who misbehaved and treated their guards in a racist fashion or tried to escape were tortured. . . . And the guys are hypocrites. They're trying to make themselves look self-righteous, but they are war criminals according to law."[94] Inside the IPC organization, these were not outrageous sentiments;[95] Fonda recalls hearing Hayden use those exact words in a meeting before she repeated them publicly.[96] Yet, not only had Fonda and Hayden gotten their facts wrong—they later would acknowledge some prisoners had been tortured—but they seemed oblivious to the monumental callousness of a famous actress denigrating American service members returning after years of captivity and deprivation. Fonda's comments ignited a much greater backlash than her photo on the antiaircraft gun of the previous summer. The South Carolina Legislature passed a resolution asking theater owners not to show her films (not that she had any recent ones to offer). In Maryland, legislators debated whether to remove her tongue or execute her.[97]

This time, the backlash extended to her backyard. When she came to speak at the University of Southern California in April, members of the Young Republicans and other young conservative groups hanged her in effigy.[98] In early May 1973, the battle shifted to the Los Angeles City Council, where a flamboyant Republican council member and former marine named Arthur K. Snyder offered a resolution to censure Fonda for her remarks. Characteristically, the actress leaned into the opportunity for confrontation. Heavily pregnant, she attended the city council meeting ready to speak against the motion. When the council, clearly wanting no part of the spectacle, instead sent Snyder's resolution to a subcommittee, Fonda immediately detoured to hold her own press conference before the gaggle of reporters who had assembled for the hearing. There, while allowing that not "all" prisoners were dissembling, she repeated her allegations that returning POWs "selected by the Pentagon" were lying about "systematic tortures."

Through all this, the television cameras whirred. It was exactly the sort of chaos the city council was sensibly hoping to avoid. A week later, on June 27, before an audience that included two dozen members of the Veterans of Foreign Wars and a very pregnant Fonda—she would give birth to her son only about ten days later—the city council voted 9 to 3 to uphold the committee decision to bury the resolution.[99] Fonda had stared down the city council in her hometown, but the pandemonium she provoked, and even pursued, along the way, only reaffirmed the sense in liberal Los Angeles that she and Hayden were careening along a course that few others wanted to follow.

EXACTLY HOW THEY SET that direction remained a mystery even to many around them. Much like the Red Family collective in Berkeley, the IPC was, in theory, a collective organization that, in practice, Hayden often sought to mold to his will. He still resisted disagreement from any source. "It's true, he could turn against people who didn't agree with him and be vindictive," Fonda said. Hayden was tough, stubborn, and sometimes drank too much. "He wasn't always an easy guy," agreed Ira Arlook, who joined the IPC after the 1972 tour to lead its organizing efforts outside California. "Tom was in many ways very strange emotionally, very strange emotionally. He had a lot of alcohol issues, to put it mildly, which he struggled with and, ultimately, for the most part, overcame, but it was a long, hard slog and very damaging."[100]

Yet, even with his rough edges, Arlook concluded, Hayden still inspired those around him with the power of his thinking. "He was a very studious person, and he had a very unique mind, the way he would synthesize things and the conclusions he would draw." To those working long hours for little pay at IPC, Hayden offered the reassuring (if overstated) encouragement that the arc of history was bending in their direction, with America's failure in Vietnam the potential fulcrum for fundamental change at home and in the international order. "From the beginning," Bruce Gilbert recalled, "one of the things that attracted me [to Hayden] . . . is that he could pull in these strains of thought or feeling about the wheel of history and contemporary culture and movements, even if they were nascent at the time, and give you a coherent view of the way things were, the way things are, and where they're going in an articulate way that made you go, 'Yes, that's what I've been feeling.'"[101]

Fonda was one of the activists Hayden clearly inspired. To those watching closely in the fishbowl of the IPC's small offices, their relationship was complex. As the organization's most visible asset, Fonda wasn't shy about expressing opinions, especially about how she would be deployed, but on questions of political strategy, she followed her husband's lead. In the intimate circle of their marriage, Hayden viewed Fonda more as a disciple than an equal. "He thought I was superficial, and he let me know it," she remembered. The effect, unsurprisingly, was to reinforce the insecurity that had afflicted her since she began her activist career. "I didn't think I deserved input," Fonda said. "I know that some of my friends—Carol Kurtz, for example—were upset [about how Tom treated me]. He didn't listen to me, but I think he was right not to listen to me."[102]

Hayden showed his arbitrary instincts in an episode that offered a window into how personal and political dynamics intertwined in their marriage. A few months after his wedding to Fonda, he bought a house for them in Ocean Park, south of Santa Monica. On bed rest while pregnant with their son, Troy, Fonda never saw the house before Hayden purchased it.[103] She loved her home in Laurel Canyon and was reluctant to leave it. It was a relatively modest wood-frame house, but it had a pool, so Hayden found it too ostentatious for his political taste. "I just remember Tom sitting there one day saying, 'This is some operation you got here,' disapprovingly," Fonda said. Fonda, who later described herself as "both in love with and in awe of Tom," thought Hayden was testing her commitment to the cause with the new house and bit her lip about the move.[104] "I wanted to prove to myself and to Tom that I didn't need the affluence that I had been raised to expect, so this was part of my proving to me and to him that I could," she recalled.[105]

Hayden didn't make the test an easy one. The house he purchased, on narrow Wadsworth Avenue, was a weathered two-story wood-frame structure near the ocean. Cockroaches ran out of the oven when Fonda turned it on.[106] The neighbors, closely packed along the block, were mostly blue-collar workers (though some other political activists were sprinkled among them). Fonda had company even inside the house because Hayden decided they didn't need all the space. Looking to minimize expenses on their modest IPC salaries, Jack Nicholl and Carol Kurtz, two more Red Family members who reunited with Hayden to work on the IPC, moved in on the first floor. At times, Fred Branfman, another prominent antiwar activist, camped out with his wife in a room off the front porch. One visiting interviewer found Hayden and Fonda living upstairs in a bedroom with a mattress on the floor.[107] Fonda's Oscar for *Klute*, flaking and worn, functioned as a bookend.[108]

Fonda grew more contented with the house over time. "We were surrounded by friends," she remembered. "It was the greatest place for my kids to grow up. I was proud of myself."[109] But it was never an easy fit. The house's open access to the street left little security for public figures as controversial as Hayden and, especially, Fonda. "It was not a very secure place for her to be," said Kurtz. "I just remember there were situations where people were just showing up at the house, and they shouldn't have been, and there was no protection."[110] Because the house didn't have a washer and dryer, Fonda became surely the only recent Academy Award winner to wash her clothes at a Laundromat. One day, someone stole them all.[111]

Yet she was all in on the IPC effort. "She was working every day," said Paul Ryder, a young IPC staff member at the time, "and when we would divvy up assignments, she'd get assignments like everybody else." If the group was five thousand dollars short in its budget, she would make calls to raise the money. If it launched a media blitz, she would sit for interviews. "She had a brutal work ethic," Ryder remembered. "Her position, given her immense visibility, was different from everybody else['s]. At another level, she just regarded herself as a necessary cadre doing necessary work."[112] Fonda never complained about losing her star status or expressed anxiety about disrupting her career. "She didn't show any sign of that," said Zimmerman. "She was fully committed to working on the war."[113] Kurtz remembers coming upon Fonda backstage before an IPC event in San Diego while she was pregnant. She was so exhausted that she had curled up to sleep while the crew was setting up around her. "Then they announced her name, [and] she gets up, walks out, and gives a speech," Kurtz remembered. "She had been sound asleep. That was her."[114] The firestorms that detonated around her after her trip to Vietnam or her remarks about the returning POWs never dented her determination. "I think IPC was pretty much her whole life," said Nicholl. "She was steely about it."[115]

NO ONE ON THE activist left could ignore the magnitude of Nixon's victory in 1972. As Bill Zimmerman recognized at the time, the scale of the landslide painfully demonstrated how limited an audience they had built for their brand of radical change. Massive public protests against the war had not convinced anything approaching a majority to renounce Nixon. Violent revolution, always a fringe idea, had descended into farce with the fragmenting of the radical Weathermen. The movement's most thoughtful leaders, like Zimmerman, increasingly concluded that they could never reach their ends of sweeping social change with their current means of street protest and disdain for the conventional political system. Clearly, those who hoped for that change needed another path. "The seventy-two presidential race was really a fulcrum for a lot of us," Zimmerman said.[116]

Despite the scale of Nixon's victory, the surprisingly warm reception Hayden and Fonda received during their 1972 tour through "the middle of 'Middle America'" solidified their belief that they had found an alternative path. The IPC became one of the crucibles in which the 1960s generation of activists hammered out their return to mainstream U.S. politics. In the same way that artists in movies, music, and television asked which aspects of the 1960s legacy could be grafted onto American culture in the '70s, Hayden, Fonda, and the activists around them tried to adapt their youthful ideals to the new political realities. Through 1973, the group settled on a strategy of organizing grassroots chapters in key states and districts to bring pressure on Congress to cut off continued U.S. funding for the South

Vietnamese government. The new approach acknowledged that not only the political landscape, but also the lives of the activists looking to remake it, had changed since the 1960s. "It was the pragmatic, strategic initiative that Tom articulated in a way that people who were still caring and [who] weren't screwed up on drugs or [who hadn't] dropped out entirely could respond to," recalled Brewster Rhoads, a senior at Williams College in 1973, whom the IPC recruited to run a chapter in Massachusetts. "And increasingly, people . . . had jobs, they had real lives, they were buying houses and shit, so the idea of doing something as traditional as grassroots lobbying was seen as 'Okay, we tried this other stuff. Let's do this.' I even cut my hair."[117]

Hayden was initially skeptical that anything as traditional as lobbying Congress could succeed, but gradually he warmed to the shift. The transition was eased for him when he learned that Larry Levin, his old ally and acolyte from Venice, had taken a job in Washington as executive director of the Coalition to Stop Funding the War, a broad alliance of church, labor, and pacifist groups. After Levin had mailed one of the coalition's newsletters to the IPC office, he answered the phone one night to find Hayden and Fonda on the line. They were ready to join the effort. "Something had taken place there," Levin recalled. "When I was brought into it, the consensus had been reached, and they were trying to figure out how to proceed."[118]

The choice by Hayden and Fonda to join the coalition continued the journey in from the political frontier that they had started with their national tour in 1972. On the left, some called them sellouts and insisted that only a mass movement outside the political system could really bring change. But by 1974, those voices were growing faint, and the movement of Hayden and Fonda out of their camp further diminished them. Tom Daschle, at the time a young Senate aide and, decades later, the Democratic Senate majority leader, thought their enlistment in the lobbying effort legitimized it for many grassroots activists who might otherwise have scorned it. "They elevated the level of attention and the degree to which people were willing to listen, especially on the left, on the progressive side," he remembered. "They had quite a following and were recognized for their organizational abilities."[119]

Fonda and Hayden crossed a symbolic threshold when they spent an entire month in Washington, DC, beginning in late January 1974. They hadn't been totally domesticated. Just before they left Los Angeles, Fonda had headlined a rally in a steady rain outside City Hall urging Nixon's impeachment.[120] And when they arrived in Washington a few days later, she joined a group of 250 protesters who marched to the State Department to try to present Henry Kissinger with an "Ignoble War Prize for 1973," a bitter comment on the Nobel Peace Prize he had been awarded the year before.[121]

But after that, Hayden and Fonda buttoned their collars and lowered their heads. After a short initial squib from the Associated Press, their tour through Washington attracted almost no press attention. This was by design: it was intended not to inspire a public movement but to quietly make converts in Congress.[122] Living in a borrowed apartment near Georgetown, Hayden and Fonda commuted almost every day across town to Capitol Hill. Over the next four weeks, they met with about fifty senators and House members, but the core of their efforts were the seminars they held for congressional staff, delivering their multimedia presentations on the war for Republican and Democratic aides. The movement's leadership was happy to keep Hayden and Fonda away from the public spotlight because they remained a magnet for criticism from the right,* but their private briefings proved a huge success. For Levin, directing the overall lobbying effort against the war, the effect was dramatic. "They transformed our relationships

---

* On March 18, soon after their lobbying trip ended, Republican representative William Dickinson of Alabama, a flamboyant conservative, led a phalanx of Republicans onto the House floor to deliver speeches condemning Hayden and Fonda. One of the Republicans, Rep. Skip Bafalis of Florida, quoted a returning POW who had said that Fonda should be hanged as a traitor. "Drastic punishment?" Bafalis asked rhetorically. "Not really" (Skip Bafalis, floor statement, 93rd Cong., 2nd sess., Cong. Rec. [March 18, 1974]: H 6991).

inside the House," he remembered. Before the seminars, the coalition was just one more supplicant knocking on members' doors; after the seminars, staffers came to see the IPC's grassroots organizing as a potential asset. "After Tom and Jane," Levin recalled, "they'd be calling us for meetings, instead of us calling to beg them for meetings."[123]

After so many years of estrangement, Hayden and Fonda threw themselves into Washington. When they weren't on Capitol Hill, they went to meet with Clark Clifford, Johnson's last defense secretary, who had grown critical of the war. At night they joined strategy meetings over potluck dinners at the home of John Holum, McGovern's foreign policy adviser, sitting on the floor while staffers and advocates debated legislative tactics. Fonda thought it made sense to shift focus from protesting to lobbying, but she remained uncomfortable doing it herself. (In Washington, she remembered, "I always felt like I was trying to talk to my father. I always felt intimidated.") Hayden took more easily to the political world. Arlook could see him soaking up the experience, the way he always did when trying to work through an intellectual puzzle. "He wanted to immerse himself," Arlook said. "He had to be here. He had to talk to everybody. He had to feel it because he had been totally alienated up to that time."[124]

Hayden and Fonda were coming in from the cold, but they still kept one foot outside the door. A long interview in *Playboy* that spring captured their conflicted instincts. In one breath, Hayden rejected the term *radical* and insisted that "if you want change, you have to be part of the mainstream, part of a kind of normalcy."[125] A moment earlier, he delivered a dense, quasi-Marxist pitch for a "revolutionary process" of international economic transformation in which "private property is no longer legalized or tolerated, at least with respect to the massive and vital industries."[126] At one point, Fonda indicated her greatest frustration with the Senate Watergate hearings was that they didn't investigate the possibility that a "grand conspiracy" of conservatives engineered all the assassinations of the 1960s.[127] And she denounced the returning prisoners of war reporting torture almost as unreservedly as a year earlier and refused to criticize North Vietnam for its own repression.

More bumps followed on the path to the mainstream for Hayden and Fonda, but the IPC's about-face with regard to a congressional lobbying strategy in 1974 represented a lasting turning point for them and the broader universe of 1960s activists they represented. That summer, the coalition won key congressional votes slashing funding for the war. Those victories, Nixon's resignation in August, and the huge gains for mostly liberal Democrats in the November 1974 election (including Jerry Brown's election as governor in California) all encouraged Hayden to plunge deeper into mainstream politics. A few months after the election, he decided to challenge John Tunney, the bland Democratic senator from California, for the party's nomination in 1976.[128] Bill Zimmerman, making his own transition from activist to operative, signed on as Hayden's campaign manager.

Fonda likewise climbed in from the ledge professionally. She signed with Columbia to costar with George Segal in *Fun with Dick and Jane*, her first film since *Steelyard Blues* and her most inoffensive and conventional part since the mid-1960s. "*Fun with Dick and Jane* was a testing of the waters, really, about whether there would be protests outside of every theater because of the whole Vietnam and POW thing," said Gilbert, who was transitioning into the movie business as Fonda's partner and producer.[129]

No meaningful protests developed, and Fonda resumed her career. "When I went to work on *Dick and Jane* . . . I really sensed that I had made it home," she said later.[130] Once again, Fonda became a top critical and box office favorite, with roles in films such as *Julia*, *The China Syndrome*, and *On Golden Pond*. Closest to her heart was the 1978 Vietnam epic *Coming Home*, which had grown out of her engagement with the war. With Gilbert, she conceived and developed the film, which looked at the war's effects on the lives of American soldiers and their families. Her role would garner her another Best Actress Oscar.

Hayden lost the 1976 primary to Tunney but performed respectably and used his increased visibility (along with money Fonda provided from her resurgent career) to build the Campaign for Economic Democracy, a broadly based grassroots liberal advocacy and organizing group. With that new platform, he finally launched his own political career by winning a seat in the California State legislature in 1982, where he served effectively for almost twenty years.

Neither Hayden nor Fonda ever entirely surmounted their radical moments, but after the turning point of 1974, both found pathways back to productive careers in the central current of American life (even after they divorced in 1990). Fonda and Hayden didn't see the fundamental political transformation of the United States they had once anticipated, but like their fellow sixties activists, they could point later in life to enormous cultural changes—suspicion of centralized authority, loosening sexual mores, a reconsideration of gender roles, more concern for the environment, greater tolerance of alternative lifestyles—that they had set in motion decades before. Those changes came not so much frontally through politics as sideways through culture, and no institution proved more important in advancing them than Hollywood, which, for a critical window in the early 1970s, turned to the '60s critique of America as the spark for its own creative and financial revival.

6

JUNE

From *Chinatown* to Jerry Brown

On June 21, 1974, the day the *Los Angeles Times* ran its rapturous review of the newly opening movie *Chinatown*, the headline for the newspaper's late afternoon edition screamed in big block letters, "NIXON TOLD ME TO DO IT—COLSON."

The screenwriter Robert Towne started writing *Chinatown* long before the Watergate scandal engulfed Richard Nixon and led to prison terms for White House aides such as Charles Colson (who was convicted for his role in the scandal's cover-up). Yet the atmosphere of official deceit and deception that extended from Lyndon Johnson's presidency into Richard Nixon's and culminated in Watergate permeated Towne's story. In Towne's script, Chinatown was more a state of mind than a place. It symbolized the inscrutability of evil and the inability of even the most well intentioned (like J. J. Gittes, the detective whom Jack Nicholson played) to pierce the hidden layers of power, the wheels within wheels, turning far from view and from understanding. Towne viewed his script as a testament to "the futility of good intentions." Like America itself in the age of Vietnam and Watergate, Nicholson as Gittes knew less than he thought as he excavated the secrets of Faye Dunaway's Evelyn Mulwray, and he understood even less than he knew. "It was [about] a guy who was a smart-ass who . . . realized you may think you know what's going on, but basically you don't," Towne said, looking back at his masterpiece. "It was [true] in regard to what was happening with Evelyn Mulwray and what was happening in the country. You don't know what's going on."[1]

Once the actual filming began in October 1973, the movie unfolded in parallel with the Watergate scandal. Nixon's vice president, Spiro Agnew, facing corruption allegations from his years as Maryland's governor, resigned almost exactly as director Roman Polanski shot *Chinatown*'s first scene. The Saturday Night Massacre, when Nixon fired Special Prosecutor Archibald Cox and provoked the first real consideration of impeachment, came only a few weeks after filming began. The real-life conspiracy loomed over Towne's fictional one. "When I was shooting the film, I was amazed sometimes, listening to the news programs, by the parallels between what I was hearing and what I was shooting," Polanski said at the time.[2] When *Chinatown* was released in late June 1974, only about a month before the House Judiciary Committee voted on the articles of impeachment that prompted Nixon's resignation in early August, *Newsweek* described it as a "Watergate with real water" and recognized "this is really a story about the decadence of the 1970s."[3] On the *Chinatown* shoot, Watergate "enveloped all of us," Hawk Koch, the film's assistant director, recalled. "That's a good word for it. It *enveloped* the movie. We were thrilled to be doing the movie because of what it was about. We were thrilled to be part of it."[4]

The connection was equally intense, though more ironic, between Watergate and Warren Beatty's film *Shampoo*, which finished shooting about ten days before *Chinatown*'s release. Beatty's decision to set *Shampoo* on Election Night 1968 meant the filmmakers were documenting Nixon's rise precisely as he fell from power. Towne, who wrote the *Shampoo* script with Beatty, considered Nixon "a vile son of a bitch,"[5] and Beatty, a diehard Democrat, viewed his election as a disaster (though he retained a grudging respect for Nixon's personal resilience). But *Shampoo* treated Nixon with subtlety. The film never shows his Democratic opponent, Hubert Humphrey. The televised clips of Nixon that appear through the film all present him in a positive light. In a key scene, set the morning after the election, Beatty's George and Jack Warden's Lester, the wealthy businessman whose wife, daughter, and mistress George has slept with in the previous twenty-four hours, stop their argument long enough to listen to Nixon promise to bring the country together. The irony of how far Nixon had veered from that aspiration by the time the movie opened is left unspoken.

Critically acclaimed from the moment of its release, *Chinatown* is widely acknowledged as one of the greatest movies ever made. *Shampoo*, though not reaching those heights, was a huge box office hit and marked another landmark in early 1970s popular culture. Though different in tone and ambition, the movies represented matching parts, with each reflecting the disillusion with political and social change common by 1974 among those who had once hoped the 1960s would transform the world.

The irony is that only two weeks before *Chinatown* was released and just days before *Shampoo* completed filming, one of the first political candidates to reflect that same 1960s critique of American life reached a political milestone. While *Chinatown* and *Shampoo* lamented the implausibility of change, on June 4, 1974, a thirty-six-year-old candidate who had held elected office for only five years raced past two much more experienced rivals to capture the Democratic nomination for governor in California on a theme of political reform. The young politician was Jerry Brown.

ROBERT TOWNE, AS WAS his style, took his time writing *Chinatown*, even after he first developed the idea of setting a movie in 1930s Los Angeles while reading the *Los Angeles Times West Magazine* around Christmas 1969. The next big step came the following spring, when Towne traveled to Oregon to help his friend Jack Nicholson with a balky script. Nicholson was making his directing debut with *Drive, He Said*, a Jeremy Larner novel about campus radicalism and basketball that Nicholson and his friend, the casting director and producer Fred Roos, had been trying to develop for years before Bert Schneider, at the production company BBS, gave them the green light. The atmosphere on set was irritable; Nicholson felt the pressure of directing for the first time and was also breaking up with his longtime girlfriend, Mimi Machu. Towne's responsibilities on the film didn't extend too far beyond emotional support of the harried director, so he used the time to visit the library at the University of Oregon. There he read

Raymond Chandler's Philip Marlowe detective novels for the first time. He also discovered journalist Carey McWilliams's classic 1946 muckraking book, *Southern California: An Island on the Land*, which recounted how Los Angeles had obtained (or stolen) the water from Owens Valley to fuel its growth.[6]

Even after Towne returned from Oregon, other projects initially intruded. First, he spent months adapting the Darryl Ponicsan novel *The Last Detail*, the story of two navy lifers, Billy Buddusky, played by Nicholson, and "Mule" Mulhall, played by Otis Young, who escort a young sailor to an eight-year jail sentence for stealing forty dollars from a charity box on his base. Towne's script fully exploited Hollywood's newfound freedom to unleash a torrent of profanity, and the story inherently condemned the heartless bureaucracy that would lock up a dimwitted but harmless young man (played by Randy Quaid) for eight years over such a trivial offense. But Towne's portrait of the two military men, and the navy itself, is surprisingly affectionate. The navy might be rigid, even harsh, but Towne's script made clear that Buddusky and Mulhall would have been lost without it. "I don't know what I would have done without the navy," Mulhall says at one point. These were not sentiments often heard about the military in liberal circles circa 1970. "They loved the military," Towne said, looking back. "It was really quite wrong to say otherwise. They owed their lives to the navy, those guys."[7]

Nicholson's commitment raised the project's profile. He had followed his breakthrough in *Easy Rider* with star turns in *Five Easy Pieces* and *Carnal Knowledge*, each of which drew reverent reviews (and his first Best Actor nomination for *Five Easy Pieces*). His grin seemed to eat Hollywood, and his expressive, unmannered acting captured the fresh breeze blowing through the industry; *Newsweek* in 1970 put him on its cover as the embodiment of "The New Movies."[8] Yet, even with Nicholson on board, and Hal Ashby signed to direct, Columbia Pictures, which held the rights, still balked at the script's rapid-fire profanity. While the two sides argued over the script, shooting on the film didn't begin until November 1972.[9]

During the impasse, Towne continued to work as a highly sought script doctor. Francis Ford Coppola, whom Towne had met when each worked with Roger Corman during the 1960s, enlisted him to rewrite the classic garden scene in *The Godfather*, in which Marlon Brando's Don Corleone and Al Pacino's Michael declare their love for each other without ever speaking the words. But with *The Last Detail* on hold, Towne turned more of his attention to *Chinatown*. "Since we were stuck in limbo on *The Last Detail*," Towne recalled, "I went to Jack and said, 'What if I wrote a detective story set in the LA of the thirties?' He said, 'Great.'"[10]

Towne was so committed to the opportunity that when Robert Evans, the Paramount production chief, offered him $175,000 to resuscitate Truman Capote's stillborn script for *The Great Gatsby*, a film that Evans initially envisioned as a star vehicle for his wife, Ali McGraw, Towne refused.[11] Instead, he borrowed money from his agent to continue concocting *Chinatown*, and when that money ran out, he convinced Evans to forward him $25,000 to complete the movie in return for an option on the finished product. "After an hour of him telling me the story, I understood it less," Evans reported later, "but how could I turn down the top script doctor in town when he's willing to work for scale plus change?"[12] Evans picked *Chinatown* as the first movie he would develop under the unusual arrangement he had negotiated with Charles Bluhdorn, the blustery chairman and chief executive of Paramount's parent company, Gulf and Western. Their agreement allowed Evans to produce one movie a year under his own banner while retaining his job as Paramount's production chief.

From the outset, Towne wrote with Nicholson in mind for the lead, as he had promised his friend fifteen years before in acting class. *The Last Detail* raised the stature of both Towne and Nicholson when it finally went into production, but *Chinatown* still represented an entirely different level of ambition for both men. For Nicholson, the role of J. J. Gittes, the cynical but classy private eye drawn into a scandal involving incest, political corruption, and stolen water, was his first chance to play a true romantic lead. For Towne, who had made his name polishing or adapting the work of other writers, it was his first chance to paint on a canvas entirely his own. Until *Chinatown*, he observed at the time, he had been considered "a relief pitcher who could come in for an inning, not pitch the whole game."[13]

Initially, Towne, who was born in San Pedro in 1934, was motivated mostly by a desire to capture the mood of Los Angeles in the 1930s, a period that, as he later put it, was "just beyond my recall."[14] As he began developing *Chinatown*, he immersed himself in reminders of LA's past, driving at night through Silver Lake and Echo Park, wandering through the magnificent art deco Union Station downtown as the sultry Santa Ana winds blew, and haunting garage sales and junk stores from Venice to Santa Barbara.[15]

But Towne's ambitions widened as he worked. Pieces of the complex plot collected from disparate sources: A disputed building project near his house enlightened him to municipal corruption. Carey McWilliams's book provided the story of how rich developers engineered a project to transfer water from the Owens Valley to the undeveloped San Fernando Valley, outside LA, where they had surreptitiously bought up land at bargain prices.[16] (The conspiracy actually occurred in the early 1900s, but Towne moved the story forward to 1937, the year of Nicholson's birth, and also the period more connected to the great noir movies and detective novels.) A former girlfriend of Towne's told him a terrible story of being propositioned by an older man who was visiting the Fox lot for an audition. The older man turned out to be her estranged father, who didn't recognize his own daughter after many years apart. From that seed sprouted the incest plot between John Huston's Noah Cross and his daughter, Faye Dunaway's Evelyn Mulwray.[17] The movie's central metaphor came from a Los Angeles Police Department vice cop who sold Towne his beloved sheepdog, Hira.[18] After the man told Towne he worked in Chinatown, the writer asked him what he did there. "Probably as little as possible," the cop told him. "I said, 'How's that?'" Towne recalled pressing. "He said, 'Look, you can't tell what's going on because we can't crack the language. There's so many dialects and things like that, we can't tell, frankly, if we're helping prevent a crime or helping somebody commit one, and so the best thing to do is nothing.' I said, 'Nothing?' He said, 'Yeah, nothing.' And that was the origin of the significance of Chinatown." In Towne's script, Nicholson's Gittes repeats that line almost verbatim when Evelyn Mulwray asks him what he did in Chinatown when he worked for the DA's office before becoming a private eye. "As little as possible," Nicholson replies.

By 1972, Towne was deeply engaged in *Chinatown*. Envisioning Nicholson in the role helped him frame the pitch and pace of the dialogue. "I always considered Jack my collaborator then, whether I talked to him about the scene or not, because all I had to do was imagine him doing it," Towne recalled later.[19] Still, the words did not come easily. Towne worked fast as a script doctor but agonized over his original scripts. In every way through 1972, he appeared to be spinning his wheels. The script advanced slowly. *The Last Detail* remained stalled. His girlfriend at the time grew so frustrated that she threw him out of the house. "It was my house," he recalled plaintively, "but as a writer I was fairly fragile, and I skulked out of my own house."[20] Towne retreated to the weathered Banning Lodge on Catalina Island with his dog, Hira, and his early model IBM Selectric typewriter, and continued wrestling with his script through the fall of 1972. "No script ever drove me nuttier," he later recalled, "as I tried one way and another casually to reveal mountains of information about dams, orange groves, incest, elevator operators, etc."[21] Even after he returned from Catalina, he bounced around between friends' apartments as he tried to untangle his story.[22] Finally, he finished his first draft in early 1973: a 180-page behemoth that left Evans and the other executives at Paramount perplexed.[23] "People didn't understand the script," said Peter Bart, a former West Coast correspondent for the *New York Times* who had joined Paramount as Evans's deputy.[24]

Most important, the draft didn't satisfy Roman Polanski, whom Evans (with help from Nicholson) had recruited as *Chinatown*'s director. Polanski was living in Rome at the time, and he initially resisted returning to Los Angeles, where the Manson family had slaughtered his wife, Sharon Tate, only four years before. "I had too vivid memories of all those events of '69, and I didn't feel like going to work there," he said later.[25] But each of Polanski's two previous films had bombed, and he needed the money, so he took the job.[26] Polanski met with Towne for the first time at the Nate'n Al's Delicatessen in Beverly Hills.[27] Polanski thought Towne's script was "brimming with ideas, great dialogue, and masterful characterization," but that it also required "massive cuts, drastic simplification, and the pruning of several subsidiary characters, all of them beautifully drawn but contributing nothing to the action."[28]

Polanski and Towne then spent eight weeks over the spring and summer of 1973 reconfiguring the script, working in a home Polanski rented, above Sunset Boulevard in the Hollywood Hills, belonging to actor George Montgomery.[29] The house set the right mood for the work: pretentious and slightly run down, with a garden waterfall and faux Spanish notes in the architecture, it struck some visitors as something lifted from a Chandler novel.[30] (Montgomery had himself played Marlowe in *The Brasher Doubloon*, a 1947 film version of Chandler's *The High Window*.) But progress still came very slowly. Towne's strategy to deal with complaints about his scripts was to delay making changes, as if he could wait out the other side. This sometimes worked with Beatty, but not with Polanski. "Polanski is not going to deal with a procrastinator; he just isn't," said Anthea Sylbert, the celebrated costume designer who first worked with the director on *Rosemary's Baby* before their reuniting on *Chinatown*.[31]

The knottiest problem with the script was the structure: Towne had struggled for months with sequencing the revelations about the public (stealing the water) and private (incest) scandals. Finally, he and Polanski reduced each scene to a single sentence, which Towne cut out on strips of paper that he hung on a board in the downstairs bedroom where they worked.[32] They then moved the strips around to test how the scenes might work in different sequences.

The two spent long hours together. Most days, they started around nine thirty or ten in the morning, and they wrote until seven or eight at night. They tightened dialogue, reordered scenes, and streamlined the plot. Relations remained cordial enough for Polanski and Towne to go out on the town after work. "I don't think there was a day that we worked that we didn't go out and play at night," Towne remembered.[33] But the working relationship was fraying. "We fought every day," Towne said.[34] Nicholson sometimes joined for the evening's entertainment, but otherwise, he kept his distance from the struggle (which had the effect of bolstering Polanski, given that he had more intrinsic leverage as the director). The most stubborn disagreement was over the ending: Polanski, with his own traumatic past—in addition to his wife's murder, he had grown up in a Jewish ghetto in occupied Poland; his mother perished at Auschwitz—wanted something even darker than what Towne was contemplating. When shooting on the movie began that October, they had not reached an agreement on how it would end. By then, each man had had enough of the other.[35] Polanski didn't exactly ban Towne from the set of *Chinatown*, but he didn't need to. "I never tried to bar [Towne] from the set," Polanski said later. "He just didn't come because we weren't on speaking terms anymore by the time I started the picture." Towne had essentially reached the same conclusion: after all their disagreements, he felt, "At that point it was wiser to just let him shoot the movie."[36]

While Polanski and Towne jousted over the script, the production designer, Richard Sylbert, joined at times by the assistant director, Hawk Koch, had scouted a rich array of location shots for the movie. It turned out Towne was right: enough of Los Angeles before World War II survived to convincingly reproduce on film.

Once filming started, the movie progressed on a brisk but bumpy trajectory. Tiny and tousle haired, Polanski was an autocratic director accustomed to dictating every detail about a scene, from where the actors stood to how they delivered their lines. "Of all the directors I've worked with, and I've worked with some goddamn good ones," Koch recalled, "Roman more than anybody else is totally controlling, doesn't want anybody else around. Roman . . . knew before we started shooting . . . where he wanted to put the camera, why he wanted to put the camera there, where he wanted the actors to be. Actors were really his pawns."[37] Polanski's direction extended to movements, gestures, intonation. "Roman would go, 'Jack, turn your head, move your shoulder like this. Okay, roll the camera,' and Jack would say, 'I'm uncomfortable like this,'" Koch recalled. "But Roman would tell him, 'It looks great, Jack!' And he'd say, 'Action.'"[38]

Nicholson, fluid and supremely self-confident, rolled with Polanski's dictatorial tendencies, finding them more amusing than threatening. Polanski's methods might have grated on John Huston, an extremely accomplished director in his own right, who was playing the film's villain, but like Nicholson, Huston mostly went with the flow. (His one quirk was invariably to mispronounce Gittes as "Gits," a deviation that Polanski incorporated because it captured Noah Cross's boundless arrogance and entitlement.) "I think they were fully in for it," said Anjelica Huston of her father and boyfriend. "You don't go halfway with a director like that. If you know what he's like, you pretty much know what you're in for, and I'm sure both of them respected the fact that he was the director."[39] Anthea Sylbert, like Koch, responded well to Polanski's decisiveness. "I adore him," she said. "I actually found it easier to deal with directors who had a strong point of view than wishy-washy directors. Because there was a clarity about what they were trying to achieve that one could understand and help them achieve."[40]

Polanski clashed more explosively with the tightly wound Dunaway. Publicity photos taken during the production by the celebrated film photographer Steve Schapiro routinely show Polanski and Nicholson laughing or leaning in closely to share confidences. But every shot of Polanski and Dunaway is cold and tense, with the actress towering over the diminutive director in strained conversation. "They were at loggerheads a lot," remembered Anthea Sylbert. "Over anything."[41]

Dunaway was difficult for everyone. Towne had originally envisioned Evelyn Mulwray as a kind of "California Yankee" who moved with the easy confidence of someone who has grown up in money; young Katharine Hepburn was his model for the character.[42] Dunaway created a much more fragile woman, brittle and skittish, who held herself so tightly it seemed she might snap at any moment. No one complained about the characterization, which was inspired; the problem was Faye Dunaway the actress was every bit as stressed and difficult as Mulwray the character. Dunaway was congenitally late. Anthea Sylbert remembers her repeatedly missing appointments for fittings until Sylbert finally confronted her. "It was a day that *Women's*

Wear Daily was there, wanting to do a piece on the costumes, and she was something like three quarters of an hour late," Sylbert remembered. "And she came swanning in, and I said, 'Get up and get into the fitting room right away, and if you ever do this again, the fitting will be canceled because I'll assume you don't care about it.'"[43] Dunaway worried constantly about her appearance, questioned her lines, demanded new makeup between almost every take.[44] She called for so many applications of Blistex ointment on her lips that the crew created a giant tube of it and presented it to her at the end of filming.

But Polanski contributed more than his share to the tensions. He was an unrepentant sexist, openly contemptuous of women's intellectual capacity. "You must admit that most women one meets do not have the brain of Einstein," he had once told *Playboy*. "It causes an absolute outrage if you say that women on the average are less intelligent than men, but it happens to be true."[45] Anthea Sylbert remembers her one argument with Polanski centered on the kind of nail polish Evelyn Mulwray would wear. Polanski wanted her to wear red nail polish; Sylbert, who had extensively researched the period, said a woman from her class would not do so. "He said to me, 'Are you getting dumb like the others?' He thought I was the only smart woman he ever met . . . He said, 'People know Hollywood in California through the movies, and in all the movies they wear red nail polish.' It was an argument I couldn't win."[46] Polanski's preference for very young girls, which later would lead to his arrest and flight from America, was also evident to some around him during the filming of *Chinatown*.[47] Dunaway thought he sought out young girls because they wouldn't challenge him.[48] She also thought he was trying to make her performance more vulnerable by bullying her on the set.[49]

Probably the strangest moment during the filming came on the one day when Anjelica Huston visited the shoot. Huston had begun her romance with Nicholson a few months earlier, in the spring of 1973. She arrived on the set as the production was shooting a scene in which her father, John Huston as Noah Cross, asks Nicholson if he is sleeping with his daughter, Evelyn Mulwray. As the production paused for lunch, Anjelica Huston remembers sitting at a long outdoor table on a beautiful California afternoon, with her father at the head, she on his right, and Nicholson and Polanski sitting to his left. "My dad turns to Jack and, in a rather loud voice, says, 'I hear you've been sleeping with my daughter,'" Anjelica Huston remembered. Then, after a theatrical pause, John Huston continued, "Mr. Gits." "Of course, everyone was electrified at the first half of the sentence, and then he continued," Anjelica Huston said. "They were just rehearsing—ha-ha—at my expense."[50]

All the movie's details were done to perfection. Richard Sylbert picked a color scheme for the production that constantly evoked drought: "burnt grass, dead leaves, parched earth, a desert without water."[51] All the government offices that Nicholson's character encounters were designed in "the color of shadows in various shades." Anthea Sylbert thought Nicholson's Gittes imagined himself a star, so she dressed him in the style of movie stars from the period. "I figured he was probably somebody who looked at what the Hollywood group was doing and wearing—that was his inspiration," she said. Evelyn Mulwray, as a child of money, would be "more subdued," Sylbert thought.[52]

Apart from the tension with Dunaway, the production proceeded steadily, with Polanski keeping things disciplined and organized: shooting most days ran from about 7 a.m. to 6:30 p.m. Polanski didn't linger over multiple takes of every scene the way Warren Beatty did.[53] "He knew exactly when he got it, and once he got it, that was it," Anthea Sylbert remembered.[54] Polanski held themed parties every Friday night at the George Montgomery mansion he was renting—Japanese food one week, Mariachi bands and margaritas the next. Nicholson sometimes treated his fellow cast members to dinner at the venerable Mexican restaurant El Cholo, happily holding forth on every subject imaginable.[55] The movie even took a break for Christmas.

The production operated under the benign protection of Robert Evans. He was an unusual, flamboyant figure. A gravelly voiced former actor, he lived in a celebrated mansion known as Woodland, just above the Beverly Hills Hotel, and established himself as the center of a fast-living social scene that included Beatty, Polanski, Nicholson, Richard Sylbert, and an infinite, interchangeable supply of aspiring starlets and models. Afflicted with sciatica and, over time, a consuming addiction to cocaine, Evans did much of his work at home, lying flat on his back. "He had a certain kind of sophistication, like black magic," remembered Anjelica Huston. "There was something so debonair and dark and kind of mysterious and suave about him."[56] Yet, for all his eccentricities, Evans had a great eye for movies. "The truth is Bob was an idiot savant for movies," said Barry Diller, who eased Evans out of his executive position and into a full-time producing role when he took over Paramount in 1974. "Bob was great at pure movie instinct. I mean great, not good."[57]

On *Chinatown*, Evans played the peacemaker in every direction. He shielded Polanski from studio interference. "Polanski was mostly off on his own," remembered Sylbert. "Bob Evans was one of the people who was very good to creative people and didn't interfere."[58] Evans also negotiated a truce between Dunaway and Polanski. The estrangement between Polanski and Towne that kept the writer from the set was another problem Evans helped defuse by inviting Towne to watch the dailies each night at his home.[59]

The production neared the finish line as 1974 began. Finally, in late January, the only scene Polanski had left to shoot was the grim finale.* To complete it, the cast and crew assembled for a few nights on Chinatown's Ord Street, just north of LA's City Hall. The movie's ending had been the greatest point of dispute between Polanski and Towne. Towne wanted an ending that was bittersweet: Dunaway kills her monstrous father but is still separated from her daughter because she is sent to prison.[60] Polanski, wanting something more tragic, rewrote Towne's finale so the movie now concluded with an ending as sharp as the drop of a guillotine. Dunaway's Evelyn Mulwray is shot through the eye and killed by the police as she tries to escape with her

---

* After concluding principal photography, Polanski shot one additional scene: the moment in the movie when Nicholson is hurtled against a fence by a wall of water. The scene was shot in a single take because the water hit Nicholson so hard that his shoes left a dent in the wire mesh fence behind him (Koch, author interview; also, Polanski, *Roman*, 354).

daughter. (Like many who worked on *Chinatown*, Anthea Sylbert saw the shadow of the past shaping this choice. "I think it was the murders that made him say Faye had to get killed," she said.)[61] Nicholson's Gittes, by now her lover, is helpless to save Evelyn or the daughter, who is enveloped by Huston's Cross as Dunaway's Evelyn slumps lifelessly against the steering wheel of her Packard, her shattered eye gaping, the horn blaring like a cry of despair. As Nicholson's Gittes turns to lunge at the police lieutenant who directed the shooting, one of Gittes's associates at his detective agency leads him away while delivering the movie's immortal concluding line, "Forget it, Jake—it's Chinatown."

Polanski made a brilliant choice to demand that the movie's final scene unfold in Chinatown, which beautifully compounds the power of Towne's metaphor. In Gittes's memories, Chinatown is a place of almost mythic inscrutability. After Gittes makes love with Mulwray for the first (and only) time, she asks him why he is so reluctant to talk about his past there. "I was trying to keep someone from being hurt," he tells her obliquely. "I ended up making sure that she was hurt." This lament foreshadows the movie's grisly conclusion: Gittes initiates the final tragedy by calling the police to arrest Mulwray, whom he mistakenly believes has killed her husband. Even after he realizes his error and tries to help her escape with her daughter, he cannot reverse the forces he's triggered. Gittes, as with the earlier woman he tried to protect, precipitates tragedy with his arrogant overconfidence in his own understanding. Once again, he knew much less than he thought he did. "You may think you know what you're dealing with," Noah Cross chillingly tells Gittes earlier in the movie, "but believe me, you don't." It was a sobering message from Towne and Polanski at a moment when Watergate, the Pentagon Papers, the ITT scandal, and a cascade of other government and corporate misdeeds constantly reminded Americans that they knew much less than they imagined about the workings of power in their country. *Chinatown*'s grim final moments anticipated a world just coming into focus as the production completed: a political environment in which most Americans would assume, as their default instinct, that their public and private leaders were lying to them, covering up, colluding at their expense. Set far in the past, it pointed to a future of rising alienation and distrust.

After a couple of days of preliminary work, Polanski was ready to shoot *Chinatown's* final scene on a chilly, starless night in late January 1974. It was a difficult shoot. Dunaway, perhaps taking her final measure of revenge for the months of conflict with Polanski, remained in her trailer for hours with her makeup man, delaying the filming. (John Huston had kept himself warm through the long delay by drinking and was a little tipsy by the time filming started, which added another complication.) By the time Dunaway emerged, Polanski had only a few hours of darkness to work with before the sun came up the next morning. And in that limited time, he needed to shoot a demanding scene that presented complex logistical challenges, including disconnecting streetlights (since they hadn't existed there in the 1930s) and using a crane that rose high above Ord Street for the sweeping final shots.

It took about three dozen takes to capture the scene. Everyone worked with one eye on the horizon because they knew they couldn't film after the sun rose. Through Polanski's viewfinder, the tragedy unspooled again and again: Evelyn Mulwray struggles with her father, tries to escape with her daughter, is shot by the police, and Gittes is led away by his partner, who tells him to "Forget it, Jake—it's Chinatown." Take by take, burrowing deeper into the night, they all edged closer to a Hollywood landmark, a single, searing scene that crystallized the alienation, distrust, and frustration millions of Americans felt in a world of big government and big business that appeared as opaque and inscrutable as the Chinatown Towne had conceived and Polanski, Nicholson, Dunaway, and the rest had brought to life. By the time Polanski was satisfied and called a wrap on the scene, and with it the production, "the light," Koch remembered, "was almost coming up."[62]

SHAMPOO STARTED FILMING IN mid-March 1974, about six weeks after *Chinatown* wrapped. The idea for the film, as was typical for both Beatty and Towne, gestated for a very long time before the cameras rolled. Towne recalls that they first formulated the concept even before Beatty enlisted him to work on *Bonnie and Clyde*.[63] They would update the premise of an old English play, *The Country Wife*, about a compulsive womanizer who cuckolds London's upper-crust men without suspicion because they think he's a eunuch. Beatty and Towne modernized the concept into the story of George, a Beverly Hills hairdresser who juggles multiple affairs while shielded by the assumption that he is gay. Beatty saw *Shampoo* as an opportunity to document the consequences of "American puritanism." He recalled, "I wanted to make a movie that dealt with sexual freedom and the social consequences of sexual freedom."[64] But the project idled for years, and Beatty grew so frustrated by Towne's slow (or nonexistent) progress on the script that, at one point, the two stopped speaking for months.[65]

Both moved on to other projects. Beatty worked with director Robert Altman on the revisionist Western *McCabe and Mrs. Miller*, which costarred Beatty's girlfriend, Julie Christie. It was a turbulent shoot, and Beatty and Altman clashed incessantly. Beatty, ever diplomatic, says now that he found Altman creative and interesting. "Bob was a very, very talented person at getting the best out of other people and himself . . . He was a lot of fun, and so we wrote it from day to day and improvised so much of it, but the intention was always there."[66] Though critics, especially over time, viewed *McCabe* as a modern classic and an important corrective to Hollywood's myths about the West, at the time, it attracted only mixed reviews and modest interest from audiences.

By 1971, Towne had finally produced a completed draft of *Shampoo*, but Beatty considered it too unfocused and decided to write his own version.[67] He worked both to organize the script and to introduce a political element, by centering the story's events on November 4, 1968, the day Richard Nixon was elected president. Beatty had campaigned that year for Robert F. Kennedy, and after Kennedy was assassinated in June, he did some work to support Hubert Humphrey, the eventual Democratic nominee against Nixon. Towne's script had sprawled across months and even years, but Beatty, correctly, thought the story would be more powerful if attached to the specific moment of Nixon's election, which marked such a stark dividing line in the politics of the 1960s: "I wanted it to be the political apocalypse of 1968, which had a profound effect on me," Beatty later told biographer Peter Biskind.[68]

Even after Beatty finished his new script, *Shampoo* remained adrift. Other obligations intruded, notably the 1972 presidential election. Beatty was a key early convert to George McGovern's long-shot, antiwar presidential campaign. After a few attempts at public campaigning for McGovern during the Democratic primaries, Beatty realized he preferred a backstage role and established himself as a trusted adviser. As McGovern unexpectedly surged toward the nomination, Beatty probably achieved more influence than any Hollywood celebrity had ever amassed in a presidential campaign. He forged an especially close alliance with McGovern's youthful campaign manager, Gary Hart, but he was respected by much of McGovern's staff, who found him serious, thoughtful, and easygoing, yet bold in his ideas. His use of star-studded concerts in Los Angeles and elsewhere to raise both money and visibility for McGovern was pathbreaking. His attempt to broker a last-minute deal for Hubert Humphrey to join McGovern as his vice-presidential running mate, though ultimately unsuccessful, showed solid political instincts. "Warren was a real adviser, political advice, ideas, strategy," Pat Caddell, McGovern's pollster, recalled years later. "He wasn't in the loop per se, but he was in the loop floating in and out . . . Warren, of course, was on the phone with everybody every day, too. He really played a fairly significant role."[69] Beatty would work diligently for McGovern until the lopsided end.

In 1973, Beatty returned to Hollywood to make a thriller called *The Parallax View*. The movie brought him together with director Alan J. Pakula, who was working through what he came to call his "paranoia trilogy." First came *Klute*, Pakula's 1971 film that won Jane Fonda her first Academy Award, as a prostitute caught in a murder conspiracy. Nineteen seventy-six would bring *All the President's Men*, with Robert Redford and Dustin Hoffman as Bob Woodward and Carl Bernstein unraveling Watergate. The middle entry, *The Parallax View*, was a complicated story about investigative reporter Joseph Frady (played by Beatty), who stumbles onto a private company (the Parallax

Corporation) that assassinates presidential candidates and other political leaders. The story was drenched in paranoia, connecting distrust of big business and big government: after each Parallax assassination, a shadowy group of officials, meant to evoke the Warren Commission, declares the killing the work of a lone gunman.

The Senate Watergate hearings, chaired by courtly senator Sam Ervin, began during the production, and the cast and crew would watch them during breaks in the filming. Like Polanski a few months later, during *Chinatown*, Pakula was struck by the parallels between the scenes he was filming and the news about Watergate he heard on his car radio as he drove to work each day.[70] The problem was he often wasn't sure what he would be filming when he arrived on the set. The production started with major portions of the script still in flux. "We wrote that movie as we shot it," Beatty recalled. "Whenever I think of *Parallax View*, I think of Alan and me and [costar] Hume Cronyn sitting around a card table in the middle of the set because we didn't know what we were going to do next."[71] A writers' strike compounded the problem, because no writer was supposed to accept assignments during the work stoppage. But, as usual, Towne was there for Beatty. Despite the strike, he surreptitiously rewrote the script. "I wrote that," Towne acknowledges. "I had to, because there was a strike and nobody could touch it, [but] we were friends, and I would normally have never done that."[72] Even with Towne's intervention, the final product was provocative but muddled.

After *The Parallax View*, Beatty was finally ready to tackle *Shampoo*. He hired Hal Ashby as the director that fall. Ashby, a prodigious pot smoker, was laid-back but talented and even-keeled. "He was a very strange guy, but he was just a genius," said Paramount executive Peter Bart, who had worked with Ashby a few years earlier on the cult classic *Harold and Maude*.[73] Beatty, Ashby, and Towne spent the ten days over Christmas in the Beverly Wilshire crafting a final script from the competing versions Beatty and Towne had produced. Despite both men's reputation for procrastinating, Towne recalled, "We didn't procrastinate that week." Towne would type in one room and then bring the pages into the other for Ashby and Beatty to review. "I would rewrite the scenes, and he would come in and look them over," Towne re-membered.[74] Having Ashby involved defused conflict between Beatty and Towne, whose relationship mixed dependence and resentment in perpetually oscillating proportions. (Beatty says he learned from Stanley Kubrick that it was better always to have three people involved in any argument, because it diluted the personal tension.)[75] Working nonstop, the trio produced a final script that was funny and sexy but also surprisingly wistful.

The story follows Beatty as George, a hairdresser who operates out of a Beverly Hills salon, but who dreams of opening his own shop. George has an innocent actress girlfriend (Jill, played by Goldie Hawn), but also engages in a herculean succession of seductions. His ex-girlfriend (Julie Christie as Jackie) is the mistress of a wealthy busi-nessman (Jack Warden as Lester), whose frustrated wife (Lee Grant as Felicia) is also sleeping with George. The script presents George as a kind of Beverly Hills gunslinger, riding through the canyons on his motorcycle, a hair dryer tucked in his belt like a .45. Like all the characters in the film, George appears equal parts glamorous and vac-uous. All these lives collide on Election Day 1968.

Production on *Shampoo* began in mid-March 1974, with several of the key figures from *Chinatown*, including Richard and Anthea Syl-bert and art director W. Stewart Campbell, proceeding directly from that set and onto the set of *Shampoo*.[76] Immediately, they recognized they had left behind Roman Polanski's autocracy for something much more fluid. Ashby, who had directed *The Last Detail* from Towne's script, held the title of director, but Beatty, as the producer and star, and Towne, as the writer and Beatty's confidant, shared authority with him. "Roman was more of a dictator director," said Anthea Sylbert, the costume designer. "Hal Ashby is more 'ah, ah, ah.' In fact, if the truth be known, it was as if Warren were co-directing. So, there was a democracy going on in *Shampoo* that did not exist on *Chinatown*."[77] Frequently, Ashby, Beatty, and Towne would be seen huddling around the camera. "Hal Ashby is a very laid-back, pleasant guy as a direc-tor," said Tony Bill, the budding producer whom Beatty had recruited to play Johnny Pope, a director trying to seduce Goldie Hawn's Jill.

"The only thing I noticed that might be different than most movies was there was more of a triumvirate between Warren, Hal Ashby, and Bob Towne when it came time to discuss a tape or change a line or something like that. Most sets have a little huddle, and probably more huddles happened on that movie than most that I had been on."[78] Exactly who was in control at any given moment was sometimes difficult for the cast to ascertain. Beatty tried not to overtly undercut Ashby, whom he liked, but there was also no question that as the producer, the star, and the cowriter of the script, he was the final arbiter. And Towne was the adviser whispering in Beatty's ear. "It wasn't that they were against [Ashby]; it was that they were supervising him," Sylbert said.[79]

Sylbert recalled one incident that encapsulated the dynamic. For a critical scene, Sylbert had designed for Christie's Jackie a remarkable, shimmering dress that demurely rose up to her neck in the front but was cut down to the crack of her rear in the back. Christie complained to Sylbert that it was too staid. "I look like the queen mother," the actress told her. Sylbert refused to change the dress. Ashby, an amiable sort who resisted confrontation as much as Polanski reveled in it, suggested a compromise: maybe Anthea could lower the neckline in the front a little bit? "No, I can't," Sylbert responded. At an impasse, Sylbert brought in Beatty. "I said, 'She doesn't want to wear this dress,'" Sylbert recalled. "'I will design a whole other one, but I won't change this one.' He said, 'Let's test it.' And I brought it to the stage, and when [Julie] came out of her dressing room, every guy on the crew started to whistle. Warren said [to Julie], 'You're wearing this, and that's it.'"[80] (It was the right call: the dress's decorous front and risqué back perfectly symbolized Jackie's precarious position as a seemingly proper lady who was, in fact, sleeping with Lester for his money.)

Beatty fully indulged his preference for multiple takes during the production, which frustrated some of the cast and crew.[81] Still, the filming proceeded mostly smoothly, with little of the overt tension evident on *Chinatown*. As on *Bonnie and Clyde*, Beatty moved easily between his roles as star and producer. The production "went well," remembered Anthea Sylbert. "He's a very good producer because as much as he questions, he's also very clear. I think he was making a comedy with a point—that it was necessary that it be funny, but it was also saying something. I think he was trying to say that, underneath, there's a corruption going on, and who can you trust? Everybody is having an affair with the other person sitting next to them."[82]

It was in this way that *Shampoo* represented a bookend to *Chinatown*. Each film documented the decline in early 1970s America by exposing the corruption and decadence of an earlier era in Los Angeles. One movie is about concealment, the other about display, and yet they reach the same bleak destination. In both movies, idealism is dashed. Nothing escapes the rot of corruption. Richard Sylbert, the production designer for both films, recognized their mirror-image nature. In *Chinatown*, he wrote later, the vices are hidden; in *Shampoo*, they are all displayed. "What you hide in Chinatown, you show in Beverly Hills," Sylbert explained.[83] *Chinatown* portrayed corruption on a grand scale: a vast public conspiracy (to steal water) and a monstrous personal offense (the incest). *Shampoo* found its center in smaller moments of intimate betrayal and self-deception. Yet George's dashed hopes for love, juxtaposed with Nixon's election, seemed to capture how the dreams of personal and political transformation that so many harbored during the 1960s had all been extinguished.

The movie presents Nixon's election as the collective result of Americans' personal corruption and hypocrisy. All the televised snippets from Nixon and his vice president, Spiro Agnew, about rebuilding respect, upholding law and order, promoting unity, and restoring the nation's "moral code" are deeply ironic by the time audiences hear them in the movie. And yet this message is delivered in a tone more of sorrow than anger, one that underscores the complicity of the electorate in choosing leaders capable of such immorality. Lester, the businessman who symbolizes America's establishment, is presented as a figure worthy of understanding, not disdain, when he tells George, "I don't know what's right or wrong anymore."

This tone of ambivalence imbues every aspect of the film. *Shampoo* celebrates sexual freedom yet ripples with an undercurrent of regret over its consequences. One of the movie's most memorable scenes occurs when Lester, still thinking George is gay, asks him to act as a beard and escort Jackie to a Republican Election Night party at the Bistro, a hot Los Angeles restaurant at the time. The party is stiff and lifeless, an ambulatory morgue of old white men and their bored wives numbing themselves with cocktails. A huge photo of Nixon (as well as a drawing of Ronald Reagan) hangs on the wall. Newscasters updating the election results chirp from television sets. Jackie, in the dress cut down to her rear, quickly gets drunk and belligerent because Lester is there with his wife, Felicia. (Like Lester, Jackie doesn't know that George is sleeping with *her*, too.) When a senator asks Jackie if there's anything she wants, she points at George. "Well, most of all, I want to suck his cock," she says. Towne remembers that the line surprised even Beatty when he read the script. "I remember Warren saying to me at the time, 'Can we do that?'" said Towne, who answered, "Of course we can."[84] The line is a testament to the new freedom both in film and sex that emerged from the 1960s, but it conveys as much resignation as rebellion: Jackie is so agitated because she is in the timeless position of the mistress who can't be acknowledged at a public event. Her boldness is fueled by weakness. It's a common dynamic through the movie. Everyone is having lots of sex, but no one appears particularly happy about it. Even unshackled from the constraints of what Beatty called "American puritanism," all the major characters are unfulfilled. *Shampoo* celebrates America's newfound sexual freedom, but it acknowledges that unbridled freedom might not be a sustainable model on which to build a successful adult life. It only deepened the point to have Beatty, Hollywood's most celebrated embodiment of unbridled freedom, deliver the message.

The presence in the film of Christie, the central point in the vast constellation of lovers and assignations Beatty had mapped over the previous fifteen years, deepened the sense that *Shampoo* was a commentary on the actor's own life. Beatty originally envisioned the movie as a defense of the serial Don Juan, whom psychiatrists at the time often diagnosed as a repressed homosexual.[85] But he and Towne were sufficiently self-aware to highlight George's flaws. He is indecisive, unfocused, self-absorbed. The movie's most meta moment comes the morning after Hawn's Jill discovers George having sex with Christie's Jackie, his ex. In the living room of her small house, Jill confronts him about his infidelities. George at first hems and haws (in Beatty's patented halting delivery), but then, in a rush, confesses to everything. "Let's face it: I fucked 'em all," he tells her. "That's what I do . . . I don't know what I'm apologizing for . . . It makes me feel like I'm going to live forever." The speech seemed to be a justification for Beatty's own life, or Towne's, or the life of any man who took full advantage of the opportunities that the sexual revolution had created in Hollywood. "It came from me," Towne recalled, "but it was for the two of us, really. . . . It was something we both believed."[86] When they first shot the scene, Beatty delivered his speech standing, while Hawn sat on the couch. Watching it, Towne realized it looked like Beatty was bullying the diminutive Hawn. So, he told Beatty they should reshoot the scene with him sitting down and her standing over him as he delivered his unashamed mea culpa. Ashby didn't think they needed to reshoot the scene, but Towne and Beatty insisted, so they did it again (with Towne also changing the language of the speech between takes).[87] In the revised version, George seems not only defiant but also vulnerable, sad.

For all the sexual calisthenics, a sad, elegiac quality hovers over the entire movie. Both the political and the personal are coming to an end. *Shampoo* shows the vibrancy of the sixties when George and Jackie flee the arid Election Eve dinner at the Bistro for a raucous, psychedelic party in the Hollywood Hills. (Sylbert said later that she patterned some of the movie's fashions on her memories of the giant parties John and Michelle Phillips threw in their Bel Air mansion before they split up.)[88] They arrive to hear the Beatles' "Sgt. Pepper" pulsing through the sound system (a counterpoint to the wan jazz band heard draining the life from "Yesterday" when George and Jackie arrived at the Bistro). All around them is teeming with life. When Lester arrives at the same party a few minutes later, with Jill and Johnny Pope (the director played by Tony Bill), he seems like Alice through the looking glass. Wandering through the house, he encounters a woman nursing a baby and smoking a joint, couples lounging naked in a Jacuzzi; a topless girl passes him as a strobe light flashes. The excitement of a life less constrained is virtually shimmering around him. The moment seems to crystallize when he sees a couple exuberantly making love on the floor of a building beside the tennis court. "Now, that's what I call fucking," Lester says with admiration to Jill and Johnny Pope, but then he realizes that the couple writhing in ecstasy are George and Jackie, and he flees in horror (with Jill close behind when she sees them, too). The freedom is exciting for Lester, until it threatens something he cares about, or at least something he covets.

From then on, *Shampoo* is a steady story of loss. George, who thought he could have everything, ends with nothing. Jill leaves him. His hopes of opening a salon are dashed. Most important, on the gray, cloudy morning after the election, Jackie goes off with Lester even after George, belatedly, on a hillside overlooking her house, asks her to marry him. She leaves George alone on the hill and drives back to her house to meet Lester, who has left his wife. Jackie gives one last, plaintive look toward the hill and then slides into Lester's Rolls-Royce and is driven away toward her cold and gilded future. Jackie doesn't die like Evelyn Mulwray, but Beatty's George is left as hollowed and haunted as Nicholson's J. J. Gittes: The woman he loves is gone to him. Money and power prevail. On this morose morning after, all the grand dreams of the 1960s deflate. The hope of political change crashes with Nixon's victory. The hope of personal transformation collapses, too.

Shampoo ends at the moment of disintegration; it doesn't try to answer what comes next. But as the dreams of transformation from the 1960s faded, that was precisely the issue facing the Baby Boomers moving deeper into adulthood. The questions began close to home with the issues that *Shampoo* raised: Was it possible to combine more personal freedom with stability and commitment? But the questions also extended to politics: was it still possible to achieve social change as the era of mass political protest faded? On June 4, 1974, about a week before *Shampoo* finished filming, and a little over two weeks before Paramount released *Chinatown*, one hint of an answer came from a lean and intense former Jesuit seminarian who carried into the political arena much the same critique of American society that coursed through both those landmark films.

WHEN JERRY BROWN FORMALLY entered the race for the Democratic nomination for governor of California in January 1974, he joined a sprawling field. Quickly, though, the race effectively settled into a three-person contest among Brown, San Francisco mayor Joseph L. Alioto, and Bob Moretti, the powerful state assembly speaker.

From the start, Brown stood apart in this company. Everything about him exuded change. Young and lean, slightly graying at the temples, reserved in manner, moody, sometimes cold, often abstract in his language, prone to philosophical tangents—he was unlike any politician the state had seen. He opened his campaign office in an abandoned record store on the corner of Sunset and Vine, in the heart of LA's music industry. He ate health food. He dated movie stars. He postulated about philosophy, history, and ethics. He took reporters to Lucy's El Adobe Café, a funky Mexican restaurant on Melrose Avenue, and jousted with them late into the night, chips and drinks piling up across the table. "He was very challenging right away," remembered Bill Boyarsky, a *Los Angeles Times* reporter. "Always arguing with you. Every time you'd ask him a question, he'd argue or want to have a discussion. I think he thought journalists were second-rate intellectuals and [that] he was definitely, to use the old cliché, the smartest guy in the room."[89]

Brown's political strategy was as novel as his style. He focused his campaign on young people, minorities, and socially liberal white professionals. He tilted his schedule toward those audiences, and he courted them with a new formula. He was passionately liberal on social issues and causes: he was a staunch supporter of the farmworkers, an unabashed opponent of the death penalty, a committed environmentalist, and an advocate for decriminalizing marijuana.[90] He stressed his earlier opposition to the Vietnam War at every opportunity. But while leaning left on issues relating to values and lifestyle, Jerry Brown also presented himself as fiscally conservative: from his announcement on, he said he wouldn't raise taxes. One of his campaign's cornerstone promises was his pledge not to move into the opulent new governor's mansion Ronald Reagan had built.

Then Brown hammered a third central plank onto his platform: in the season of Watergate (and *Chinatown*), he shrewdly centered his campaign on a program of campaign finance and lobbying reform. Working with two citizens' groups, Brown's staff drafted a ballot initiative called Proposition 9, to impose new state ethics and campaign finance rules and to create a powerful Fair Political Practices Commission to oversee them. As the Watergate scandal grew, Brown portrayed the initiative as the castle wall against corruption in California. He condensed its impact into a memorable slogan: lobbyists would be limited to buying legislators the equivalent of "two hamburgers and a Coke." The state's powerful labor unions opposed the initiative because they thought it would limit their clout, so Alioto, a traditional labor Democrat, opposed it, too. Moretti was publicly supportive but privately hostile. Both the candidates running to succeed Reagan in the Republican primary for governor also condemned it. In a year defined by scandal and disillusionment, Brown's rivals in both parties ceded the terrain of reform to him. "It was brilliant, and we had nothing to compare it with," remembered Grover McKean, an adviser to Moretti. "There was just no way to defend the legislature. It was a hopeless task. Jerry took that issue and ran very well with it."[91]

In his two principal rivals, Brown found perfect foils. A generation older than Brown, San Francisco mayor Joseph Alioto was dynamic and charismatic, with a certain Rat Pack swagger. He unreservedly embraced the political formula that dominated the Democratic Party in the years before and after World War II: he was mostly conservative on social issues (especially crime) and leaned toward hawkish positions on national security, but he was also an unwavering supporter of social programs such as Medicare and Social Security and a believer in using government spending to create jobs. After Nixon routed George McGovern in 1972, Alioto emerged as a leading critic of the sixties-flavored New Left that coalesced around McGovern.

Bob Moretti was rougher-edged personally and much younger than

Alioto, but he started politically from a very similar place before following his party's general tilt to the left through the early 1970s. As
he ascended in the state assembly, eventually succeeding the towering
Jesse Unruh as speaker, Moretti worked effectively to advance legislation on causes Jerry Brown only talked about, including blocking oil
drilling in the Santa Barbara channel, protecting the California coast
from development, toughening air pollution laws, and raising taxes on
rich school districts to provide more funds to poor ones. But Moretti
also continued Unruh's grimy accommodations with lobbyists. And
as a chain-smoker and dogged womanizer, he seemed a full generation older than Brown, though he was born only two years before him.

Alioto and Moretti detested everything about Brown, from his philosophical musings to his oddball interests. Their disdain converted
the California Democratic gubernatorial primary that spring into an
extended exposition of the conflict between the emerging Baby Boom
and its Greatest Generation parents (even though the generational
contrasts in their ages didn't exactly line up). Both men thought they
had earned their way to the top and that Brown had coasted; they
thought they were virile and that he was somewhere between ethereal
and effeminate. They were doers; he was a mere thinker. Brown had
read a lot of books, and he used a lot of big words, but was he tough,
street-smart? Could he get things done? Alioto "gave off the feeling
that it was due him," remembered Doug Faigin, Brown's press secretary.[92] Moretti "thought Jerry was a dilettante," said McKean, "while
he was the guy in the trenches, a manly man and all that shit."[93]

It was the psychodrama in a million Baby Boomer families—the
weekly collision between Archie Bunker and Mike Stivic on *All in the
Family*—unfolding along the California campaign trail.[*] Moretti and

---

[*] The most acute expression of this generational conflict remained surprisingly
tangential to the election. Brown was running to succeed Ronald Reagan, who
was born twenty-seven years before him. Reagan had been elected governor both
in 1966 and 1970 as the genial but unbending barrier against all the changes
unleashed by the 1960s. He launched his first bid for the governorship a year
after the Watts Uprising in 1965, and in his announcement speech, he warned,

Alioto constantly questioned not only Brown's record and his ideas but also his manhood. Alioto said Brown was campaigning like "some kind of vestal virgin of campaign reform."[94] On another occasion, Alioto, ostensibly complaining about Brown's refusal to debate, insisted that he "continues to campaign in the closet."[95] Late at night, as reporters clustered over their drinks on the campaign trail, Moretti more explicitly dangled hooks about Brown's sexual orientation. He had talked to women who had dated Brown who said he had never made

---

"Our city streets are jungle paths after dark" (Lou Cannon, *Governor Reagan: His Rise to Power* [New York: PublicAffairs, 2003], 144). Both in the campaign and as governor, he unendingly targeted "hippies" and student demonstrators. Reagan backed administrators cracking down on protesting students at San Francisco State College (while Alioto tried to mediate) and sent in not only the California State Highway Patrol but also the National Guard to quell the demonstrations in Berkeley's People's Park that drew Tom Hayden and his allies. Reagan told shocked middle-class and middle-aged audiences that the unrest in Berkeley was driven by a "minority of malcontents, beatniks and filthy-speech advocates" who writhed together in orgies "so vile that I cannot describe them to you" (Cannon, *Governor Reagan*, 272).

In the early 1970s, Brown shied away from directly challenging Reagan's backward-looking vision. In his secretary of state race, he even ran an ad criticizing violent student protesters (Quinn, author interview). As secretary of state, Brown largely avoided conflict with Reagan, and when he did criticize him, it was from the political right, for not cutting spending effectively enough (Press release, 8/31/72, "Brown Charges Reagan Mismanagement," Box B-29-3, Miscellaneous, Llew Werner Files, 1973–1983, press releases folder, Edmund G. Brown Papers, University of Southern California Library, Special Collections, Los Angeles and Southern California Regional History, Los Angeles). Even in the gubernatorial campaign, Brown largely ignored Reagan. In the June 1972 meeting to begin planning for his governor's race, Brown told his advisers that he had been very deliberate about "never attacking Reagan in open forums" (Report on Meeting of Tuesday, 6/13/72, Box C-5-3, Governor's Office, 1975–1983, Press Unit, Press Releases, Speeches, Addresses and Remarks, 1975–1983, January 1975–June 1978, Edmund G. Brown Papers, University of Southern California Library, Special Collections, Los Angeles and Southern California Regional History, Los Angeles). But for all this deference, the enormous gulf between Reagan and Brown was apparent throughout the campaign; in every possible way, Brown embodied the transition from Reagan's confident World War II generation to the more idiosyncratic and impatient Baby Boomers. All Brown's advisers understood that Reagan was an important part of the backdrop as the unusual young candidate urged voters to turn the page toward a new generation.

a pass at them. What could explain that? "There's something wrong with that guy," Moretti would mutter at the press.[96] Brown's staff eventually had to confront the other campaigns with their own files on Alioto (who had faced extensive allegations of links to organized crime) and Moretti (whose womanizing in Sacramento had been legendary) to force a truce.[97]

As a politician, Brown that spring was an unfinished product. He wasn't a natural backslapping campaigner like his father; he fit the self-image of the college-educated Baby Boomers as cool, reserved, cerebral. The other candidates thought that once voters took a closer look, they would reject him as inscrutable and just plain weird. "I wish I could meet every voter in this state personally," Moretti would tell audiences. "But since that is not possible, I wish every voter could meet Jerry Brown."[98] But the backlash against Brown that Alioto and Moretti anticipated never arrived. Brown wasn't a magnetic presence, but he developed his own quirky charisma. "He was a little green and inexperienced, but people liked him," remembered Tom Quinn, his top campaign strategist. "He came across as unpolished but very likeable and very sincere."[99] The biggest problem for Brown's campaign was that staffers never knew which Jerry would show up on any given day. "He was like the little girl with the curl," said Doug Faigin, his press secretary, referencing the Henry Wadsworth poem. "When he was good with people, he was great. He would be charming, he would be empathetic, he would be hitting just the right note, people would love him. If he was off, it wouldn't be terrible, but it wouldn't strike that spark."[100] As the campaign progressed, it wasn't only Brown's daily performance that became unpredictable. He spent more time over the months with an obscure, somewhat mystical Frenchman named Jacques Barzaghi. Brown's other aides knew little about Barzaghi, a former seaman and actor whom Brown appeared to have met at the home of a Hollywood director.[101] Brown would show up at the campaign headquarters in the morning, questioning the schedule, wondering why his message for the day was focused so intently on some narrow policy issue or a minor contrast with his opponents. He wanted to be bigger, more visionary. When his senior advisers Tom

Quinn and Richard Maullin heard him deliver these complaints, they assumed he was channeling Barzaghi. Sometimes the two young men felt as if they were holding the end of a rope that kept Brown from spinning entirely into chaos.

But the rope held through primary day: Brown mostly followed the path Quinn had charted, sticking to his broad theme of reform and change, minimizing specifics on other issues and largely ignoring his opponents. Brown had not only recognized something larger than either of his principal rivals, an urge for political reform and generational change, but he had also personified it. Alioto and Moretti never really comprehended what hit them. In the June 4 primary, Brown won almost two fifths of the vote, while Alioto and Moretti each took almost exactly half that. Proposition 9, Brown's signature ballot initiative, triumphed by more than two to one.

Brown's victory over Alioto and Moretti in the 1974 California gubernatorial primary marked a generational hinge in the Democratic Party. Along with the victory that year of Gary Hart, George McGovern's 1972 campaign manager, in a Colorado US Senate race, it represented one of the first skirmishes between the party's traditional New Deal ideology, expressed in various ways by both Alioto and Moretti, and the very different set of concerns that the sixties generation would bring to politics. Brown's victory showed the emergence of a new formula aimed not at the working-class white voters who had anchored the party since the New Deal, but at white-collar professionals, young people, and minorities with an agenda and persona that stressed social change while maintaining a skeptical distance from government. "The truth is he was different, and that's what the campaign was all about," said Faigin.[102]

To those closest to him, it was clear that Brown viewed himself as the arrival of something new. "He very much saw himself being on the leading edge," remembered Maullin.[103] This was apparent when Brown received a visit in his Laurel Canyon home about a month before the primary from David Broder, the star political reporter of the *Washington Post* and the dean of the eastern establishment press corps. Brown was expansive when Broder arrived. While "a woman friend fixed dinner in the kitchen," he sat on a lawn chair in his garden, enjoying the view and cool breezes that had attracted so many rock stars to the canyon over the past decade. Broder, like many visitors, found Brown "cool, reflective, rather withdrawn and ascetic." To Broder, Brown called himself "a politician of the '70s," shaped not by John F. Kennedy's Camelot but by disillusionment over "the Vietnam War, the Great Society, and Watergate."[104] It was a telling trinity. No Democrat of an earlier generation would have connected Lyndon Johnson's Great Society to Vietnam and Watergate as a source of disillusion, but "he saw government as [as] much of a threat as any other big institution," said Mickey Kantor, a Democratic strategist.[105] Brown's sister Kathleen recognized the same instinct. "Jerry's prism, as my prism, was that the establishment and the institution got us into this war, resisted civil rights, and we changed it."[106]

In that way, Brown shared the same instincts as the filmmakers revitalizing Hollywood through movies that portrayed America and its institutions as corrupted from within. His gubernatorial campaign distantly echoed the themes, in particular, of *Chinatown*, which reached theaters with its riveting portrait of systemic rot less than three weeks after Brown won his primary. In the summer of Watergate, all these political and cultural currents converged. But even as Hollywood reached its peak moment of critiquing American society, the industry started to shift back toward a more conventional focus on entertainment, ironically because of the growing influence of younger moviemakers who emerged from the same sixties experiences as Jerry Brown.

7

JULY

Hollywood's Generational Tipping Point

On July 4, 1974, Steven Spielberg dispatched his cameras to film the Independence Day parade in Edgartown, Massachusetts, on the island of Martha's Vineyard. It was not where he had expected to be.

Spielberg, bushy haired and slim at twenty-seven, had arrived in Edgartown almost exactly two months before to begin filming his adaptation of *Jaws*, the grisly best-selling novel by Peter Benchley. Spielberg had been heralded as a rising star since 1968, when Universal Pictures made him the youngest director it had ever placed on contract. But while his work on television had been widely praised, his first feature film, *The Sugarland Express*, had disappointed when it was released a few months earlier, in March. With *Jaws*, a sensation as a novel that had been the subject of a spirited studio bidding war eventually won by the elite producing team of Richard Zanuck and David Brown, Spielberg knew that everyone expected a much bigger splash.

The production team on *Jaws* originally sketched out a brisk shooting schedule that would allow the cast and crew to finish on Martha's Vineyard before the height of the summer vacation season. Spielberg was confident enough that he would be back in Los Angeles by July that, in May, he had staged and filmed his own Independence Day parade along Edgartown's Main Street.[1] But when the real July 4 rolled around, Spielberg was still in town, deploying cameras to a bank, a church, and a cheese shop along Main Street to capture the town's actual parade.[2] Everything had taken longer than he had expected. In particular, the production team was struggling with the operation of the three two-thousand-pound mechanical sharks that it had trucked across the country from Universal's headquarters in the San Fernando Valley. The models were designed to run along a huge submersible steel platform with greased rails that made the shark appear as if it were swimming. On July 1, the first time the crew lowered the submersible platform into the ocean, it sank.[3] That was just the beginning of Spielberg's trials with his sharks. Weather, tides, and prickly locals in the famously insular vacation town all compounded his production troubles. He had no way of knowing, as he watched the July 4 parade unfold, that he would not leave Martha's Vineyard for over two more months.

Two days later and about 950 miles to the south, director Robert Altman had gathered the cast and crew of his next movie for an Independence Day cookout at the comfortable ranch house he had rented on the edge of Nashville.[4] Balding and beefy, with a salt-and-pepper goatee, Altman stood behind a grill on the steamy afternoon dispensing slabs of steak and tumblers of scotch. The big crowd at Altman's barbecue reflected the kaleidoscopic nature of the movie that had brought him to Tennessee: a sprawling look at the world of country music entitled, simply, *Nashville*. Like Spielberg on Martha's Vineyard, Altman, at forty-nine, felt pressure to deliver a hit. After long years of churning out television dramas, he had achieved unexpected commercial success with his irreverent feature film *M*A*S*H* in 1970. But despite steady praise from critics, only one of the six movies he had completed since had performed well at the box office. He expected *Nashville* to be his magnum opus, his summary statement on America as it approached its bicentennial.

Jaws and *Nashville* unfolded in tandem. Both were shot in the summer of 1974 and then edited over the following fall and winter. They were released nine days apart in June 1975 and were the subject of competing covers that month, one week apart, in the two major national news magazines, *Time* and *Newsweek*. *Nashville* wasn't the last film infused with the sixties critique of American society, but it culminated the revolution that began with *The Graduate* and *Bonnie and Clyde*: in a single, teeming story, it encompassed all the big themes of early 1970s cinema and tried to wrestle them to a kind of conclusion. By contrast, *Jaws* marked the beginning of something else. It changed Hollywood forever by demonstrating that a captivating story, supported by mass marketing and mass distribution, could produce blockbuster receipts on a scale almost unimaginable before.

The simultaneous development of *Jaws* and *Nashville* captured the tipping point in Hollywood's generational transition. *Nashville* was among the last great statements from the brilliant generation of directors, like Altman, born in the 1920s and '30s. *Jaws* was one of the first great statements from the brilliant generation of directors born in the 1940s. The irony was that the older generation produced a big, contemporary social commentary, while the younger generation made a big, throwback popcorn movie.

ROBERT ALTMAN HAD SPENT years traveling over rocky ground by the time he reached Nashville in the summer of 1974. He was born in the heart of mid-America, in Kansas City, Missouri, and ricocheted between improbable business ventures and two broken marriages before finding a foothold as a director of television drama in the late 1950s. Altman quickly established himself as an assured and efficient director, briskly spinning out episodes of programs ranging from *Bonanza* to *Combat!*. After stumbling attempts at feature film directing through the late 1960s, he finally broke into the top tier when he became, almost by default, the director of *M*A*S*H* after more than a dozen other directors passed on the project.[5] A scabrous comedy about a mobile hospital unit during the Korean War, *M*A*S*H* was an uneven satire—biting in some segments, flabby and cartoonish in others—but it earned good reviews and found a big audience as an irreverent commentary on the Vietnam War, which Hollywood still would not confront directly.

Two decades after he arrived in Los Angeles, Altman was an overnight sensation. The headquarters for his Lions Gate Films in Westwood, near UCLA, became a druggy hangout for aspiring filmmakers, much like the offices of Bert Schneider's BBS, a few miles to the east, on La Brea Avenue. For all his eccentricities and excesses, Altman was a diligent craftsman who worked quickly and steadily. But, if anything, his rise allowed him to become even more headstrong than during his television years. He reveled in snap decisions. On set, Altman avoided rehearsals and often disregarded the script, preferring to spend just a few quick moments sharing ideas for each scene before the cameras rolled. "There would be a discussion in the room for a small bit of time before the shoot, but other than that, a good deal of it was as fluid and spontaneous as it could possibly be," said Joan Tewkesbury, a screenwriter who first worked with Altman as a script supervisor on his revisionist 1971 Western with Warren Beatty and Julie Christie, *McCabe and Mrs. Miller*.[6]

Altman was a polarizing figure with a devoted coterie of collaborators as well as a reliable circle of movie critics who reverently promoted his work, notably the influential *New Yorker* critic Pauline Kael. But people outside Altman's circle, and often even those within it, found him rude and arrogant. Peter Bart, the Paramount executive, considered Altman impossible. "He was a nightmare to work with because he was arrogant, he was drunk," Bart recalled. "Mean-spirited guy, and we had cosmic fights. He admitted to me something that was very interesting and that is, when he made a picture, usually halfway into it, he would begin to get bored with it and begin to turn against the characters in the movie. He said to me once, 'That's why, if you notice . . . by the end of the movies, you don't like them [the characters] very much. That's my fucking fault.'"[7]

Though none of Altman's films after *M*A*S*H* had truly scored at the box office, they were highly regarded for being quirky and always provocative, if sometimes ragged. They usually conveyed mood more effectively than they developed plot, or even character, but Altman's distorted, sometimes disjointed narratives, which delighted in the loose ends they defiantly dangled, seemed to capture the fractured sensibility of the times. His movies repeatedly subverted genres. *McCabe*, with a rapacious corporation triumphing over Beatty's lone schemer, inverted the classic Western's celebration of heroic individualism; Altman's updating of Raymond Chandler's *The Long Goodbye*, with Elliott Gould as a chain-smoking, mumbling, oddly passive Philip

Marlowe drifting through an opaque contemporary Los Angeles, upended the hard-boiled detective story. Altman, after years of struggle, found his niche in Hollywood by reversing the pictures of America that the movies had sketched since his childhood. Although he was two decades older than the oldest Baby Boomers, his flurry of early 1970s films radiated with the rejection of underlying rules—about success, authority, sex, the relations between men and women, the fundamental nature of America's character—that emerged from the protest movements of the 1960s. Altman told stories that encouraged his audiences, sometimes explicitly, sometimes implicitly, to rethink the stories on which they had been reared. In a burst of concentrated creativity, he constructed a successful career on an act of sustained deconstruction.

In that, he was far from alone. In Hollywood during the early 1970s, the boldest statements about America, the most piercing social critiques, came from a large group of other directors who were, like Altman, born decades before the Baby Boomers: Arthur Penn (1922), Sam Peckinpah (1925, the same year as Altman), Alan Pakula (1928), and Hal Ashby (1929). The youngest followed a few years later: Mike Nichols (1931), Bob Rafelson (1933), and Roman Polanski (1933).[*]

In their personal styles, these men had little in common, but they were united by a conviction that films could, and should, comment on the society around them. Beginning in 1967 with *Bonnie and Clyde* (from Penn) and *The Graduate* (from Nichols), they produced, over roughly the next decade, a remarkable body of work that portrayed America as adrift and rotting from within, deceived not only by its leaders but even by its most cherished myths. They advanced their

---

[*] Robert Towne (born in 1934) and Warren Beatty and Jack Nicholson (both 1937) largely overlapped in sensibility with these men and contributed to some of their most important works. Sydney Pollack, born in 1934, also directed several films early in his career infused with strong social commentary (especially *They Shoot Horses, Don't They?* and *Three Days of the Condor*), though he is better known for more mainstream entertainments, including *The Way We Were*, *Tootsie*, and *Out of Africa*.

chosen themes across a wide array of genres. One was the "neo-noir" thrillers that put a cynical modern spin on classic detective stories, including Altman's *The Long Goodbye*, Polanski's *Chinatown*, and Penn's *Night Moves*. Another group of movies followed shadowy conspiracies and spiderwebs of surveillance involving government or big business or both: to this genre, Pakula contributed his paranoia trilogy *Klute*, *The Parallax View*, and *All the President's Men*. Penn's *Bonnie and Clyde* and his earlier *The Chase*, like Peckinpah's *The Wild Bunch* and *Straw Dogs*, portrayed sudden, unpredictable violence as an intrinsic component of the American character. Relationships disintegrated under the strains and pleasures of the sexual revolution in *Five Easy Pieces* (Rafelson and Nicholson), *Carnal Knowledge* (Nichols and Nicholson in 1971), and *Shampoo* (Ashby with Beatty and Robert Towne).

In these films, characters drift away from lovers and family, unable to make genuine connections with other people and often unable to verbalize, or even understand, their own emotions. Authority is mindless, cold, remote. Film traditions are evoked only to be trampled. *The Wild Bunch* is a Western without a single entirely admirable character on any front of the multisided conflict. In Penn's *Little Big Man*, starring Dustin Hoffman as the self-proclaimed last white survivor of Little Big Horn, the heroic clichés of earlier Westerns become the basis for tragedy or farce, often at the same moment. In *Chinatown* and *The Parallax View*, the seemingly heroic investigator understands much less than he thinks he does, bringing disaster to others (in *Chinatown*) and himself (in *The Parallax View*).

It was the cracks in the foundation of the movie industry that created space for these men and their films to emerge as the 1960s turned into the 1970s. Suddenly, studio executives, movie critics, and audiences alike were ready to hear what they had to say: the ground shifted just enough to clear away the interference from the signal they had been broadcasting. In these directors' hands, Hollywood wrestled more concretely than it had before with the world around it, just as the television networks did through the vision of producers and writers like Norman Lear, James Brooks, and Larry Gelbart. But in Hollywood, as in the television industry, that window did not stay open for long. Even as Altman's generation of directors reached the pinnacle of their influence in the film industry, the next wave of change was gathering at the studio gates, and it would sweep Hollywood in a very different direction—beginning, fittingly enough, with a movie that forever changed how its audiences looked at the ocean.

WHEN STEVEN SPIELBERG FIRST arrived in Los Angeles in 1965 as an undergraduate at California State University in Long Beach, he did not find Hollywood scrambling to open its doors for him—or for any other young people. "I discovered nobody really wanted anything I had to offer, that it was still a middle-aged man's profession," he said later. "The only young people on the lot were actors."[8] Spielberg was not alone in this perception. "It was us versus them," remembered Tony Bill, a young actor who wanted to transition into producing. "I think it was a given that if you were a young person, the world was against you."[9]

Except for the actors and actresses before the camera, older men dominated every institution in Hollywood. The gray tint was especially pronounced among directors and producers. Peter Bart, who became a production executive at Paramount in 1967, remembers, "There was a whole structure that you had to hire these old guys as directors."[10] The studios, hollowed out by the industry's losses of the late 1960s, felt just as moldy. "When I started, you still had vestiges of the old studio system," said Michael Ovitz, who joined the William Morris Agency after graduating from UCLA in 1968. "You had people that had roots in the old system." As a young agent, Ovitz reached the same conclusion David Geffen had around the same time: there was no point in trying to represent movie stars, because the older men controlling the budgets in the studios wouldn't deal seriously with agents so much younger than they. "I couldn't do it in movies; there was no chance," he remembered. "If you were a young agent in the film business, you didn't have a prayer." The same hierarchy governed the talent agencies, public relations companies, and law firms serving the industry: the grayer the temple, the bigger the office. "People liked their jobs," remembered Ovitz. "It was the biggest problem with the film business. People had good jobs, good perks, and they wanted to stay."[11]

The doors cracked open for the Baby Boomers through the early 1970s. As Hollywood became painfully aware of the generation gap with its audience, more of the older men in charge realized they needed younger people involved. "There started to be a movement," said Mike Medavoy, at the time one of the very few younger agents successfully working with the studios. "The older guys were starting to die off, and new guys were coming into the business. So, you had new guys, new ideas, new writers, new everything."[12] Young people who had been shunned only a few years earlier suddenly could get their calls returned and lunches on the schedule. "It was crazy, because one's qualifications almost were only that you shouldn't know too much about what you're doing in order to get trusted with a movie," said Bill.[13]

Though most of Hollywood's power brokers recognized the need to involve more young people in decision making, few welcomed the shift. "Don't kid yourself," said Ovitz. "It was a transition, and those guys hung on as long as they could." But through the early 1970s, cracks finally emerged in Hollywood's generational stone wall. United Artists named David Picker, still in his thirties, as its president in 1969;[14] in 1974, it hired Mike Medavoy, just thirty-three, as its vice president for production.[15] Universal, maybe the stodgiest studio under the fiercely methodical leadership of Lew Wasserman, entrusted its youth production arm to a creative, if volatile, former record executive named Ned Tanen and eventually named him head of its overall film division.[16] Warner Bros. hired John Calley, an intellectual young producer, as its production chief in 1969.[17] Bearded and thoughtful, Calley became the emblem of the generational change inside the studios. Holding court in a modernist office without a desk and championing younger directors such as Martin Scorsese, Calley was "a total kind of jazz hipster," remembered Jonathan Taplin, the former rock manager trying to establish himself as a movie producer with Scorsese's *Mean Streets*.[18]

Across Hollywood, the Baby Boomers steadily ascended. "It was very clear what was happening," said Paul Schrader, the screenwriter and director. "There was a hole opening here, a gap, and into this gap a generation came . . . It affected all forms of entertainment commerce. It affected the agencies and the TV stations and the music business. It affected everything, and there was a period there where it was an open crapshoot."[19] Tony Bill and the married couple Michael and Julia Phillips elbowed their way into the ranks of top-tier producers with *The Sting* in 1973. The first sales accumulated for younger screenwriters: Willard Huyck and Gloria Katz, David Ward, Walter Hill, John Milius, and Schrader. Younger talent gravitated to younger agents like Ovitz and Ron Meyer at William Morris; Medavoy (before he moved to the other side of the desk); and Jeff Berg, who started his career as an assistant to Freddie Fields, a pillar of the old Hollywood establishment at Creative Management Associates. Tom Pollock, a young attorney who had spent 1968 working on the presidential campaigns of Robert Kennedy and Hubert Humphrey, opened a law firm with two friends that focused on representing the talented young filmmakers emerging from the film schools at UCLA and USC. Each of these transitions reinforced the other: younger executives hired younger filmmakers, which created more opportunities for younger managers, agents, and lawyers.

One aspect of the change overshadowed all the others and quickly emerged as its symbol: the rise of the next generation of movie directors, a group that became known as the Movie Brats. The infusion of directing talent that transformed and reinvigorated Hollywood arrived in two waves. First, through the late 1960s came three directors born in the mid- to late 1930s: William Friedkin (1935) and Francis Ford Coppola and Peter Bogdanovich (both born in 1939). Then, through the early 1970s, a surge of directors and writers born in the 1940s followed them: Brian De Palma (1940), Martin Scorsese (1942), Terrence Malick (1943), George Lucas (1944), John Milius (1944), and Steven Spielberg and Paul Schrader (both 1946).

It was the emergence of these younger talents—even as so many directors in their forties or early fifties, like Altman, Penn, and Pakula, were producing the most vital work of their careers—that made the early 1970s so memorable in Hollywood. The younger and older directors volleyed compelling films across the generational divide like howitzers over a canyon. Just the two years of 1973 and 1974 saw the older generation release *The Parallax View* (Pakula); *The Long Goodbye*, *Thieves Like Us*, and *California Split* (Altman); *Chinatown* (Polanski); *Pat Garrett and Billy the Kid* (Peckinpah); and *The Last Detail* (Ashby). During those same two years, the younger directors responded with *Badlands* (Malick); *Mean Streets* and *Alice Doesn't Live Here Anymore* (Scorsese); *The Conversation* and *The Godfather Part II* (Coppola); *The Exorcist* (Friedkin); *The Sugarland Express* (Spielberg); *Paper Moon* (Bogdanovich); and *American Graffiti* (Lucas). It was a remarkable confluence of talent, perhaps the only moment in Hollywood's history when two such distinct generations of directors simultaneously produced so many great films.

The two camps didn't interact much. "They thought of themselves as thinking differently and living differently, and their values and interests were different," said Peter Bart.[20] Nor did they share many common experiences. Most of the Altman generation had honed their skills as directors on television or on Broadway, or both; most of the younger generation had studied at film schools and graduated directly to moviemaking.* The younger generation were more self-consciously students of film, more inclined to debate tenets of auteur theory, more likely to feel a thrill about re-creating the trademark effects of the directors who came before them. These were unashamedly the children of the movies who did not look to television or theater for their guideposts and who were as likely to find inspiration in forgotten Hollywood horror and noir as they were in the classics of Fellini, Godard, and Truffaut. Like so many Baby Boomers, they were diligent pupils: Bogdanovich calculated that from 1952 to 1971, he saw "something like 6,000" movies (all of which he catalogued on index cards).[21]

---

* The most notable exceptions were two younger directors who straddled the generational divide: Friedkin worked in television and Bogdanovich briefly in theater before both graduated to feature films. Spielberg also spent a few years as a precociously young television director for Universal.

Schrader wrote a book about the *Transcendental Style in Film*. Their movies, as critic Foster Hirsch perceptively noted as early as 1973, repeatedly referenced earlier movies in a form of "calculated homage."[22] For them, a great shot, a great scene, a great film, was its own reward. The older generation prized craft, too, but they tended to see it more as a means to an end: they were drawn most to movies that said something about the society around them.

It was this contrasting impulse that led to the most conspicuous, and unexpected, divergence between the older and younger generation of great filmmakers. The younger were more likely to modernize Hollywood's myths than to debunk them. Their passion was to entertain, not confront. "Their interests were film for its own sake," said Bruce Gilbert, the former leftist activist who became Jane Fonda's partner and producer on *Coming Home, The China Syndrome*, and *9 to 5*. "They were film geeks, they studied film and went to film school, and they were just in love with the idea of movies. There was a smaller subset of that generation, of which I'm part, that saw this as a means to a cultural end . . . so we tended toward movies that were about something. But I don't think they were socially aware. They had a singular focus of movies for movies' sake."[23] Those priorities produced the defining paradox of Hollywood in the mid-1970s: the great wave of movies infused with the countercultural energy of the sixties receded precisely as the first Baby Boomers ascended to the director's chair.

The shift was subtle, and the initial films from the younger generation of directors still wrestled with larger social concerns. George Lucas's first film, *THX 1138*, was a suitably bleak science-fiction vision of an authoritarian future. Scorsese, who was the most connected of the younger directors to the rock-and-roll scene, also displayed flashes of social commentary in his earliest work. *Boxcar Bertha*, the first movie Scorsese directed in Los Angeles, was a Roger Corman production with all the sex and gore that implied, but the film also lionized unions and offered a thirties-style portrait of class conflict that Woody Guthrie would have recognized. *Alice Doesn't Live Here Anymore*, Scorsese's 1974 film for Warner, wobbled at points in its message, but with Ellen

Burstyn in the title role, it became one of the first studio features to acknowledge the changing role of women.

Of the emerging generation, Coppola made the most important social statements on-screen. After directing the juvenile comedy *You're a Big Boy Now* and the elephantine musical *Finian's Rainbow* for Warner, he convinced the studio to finance *The Rain People*, his stripped-down portrait of a housewife fleeing domestic monotony. Like *Alice*, *The Rain People* wobbled in its perspective on women's changing position, but it did show that Coppola was alert to the possibilities of movies to engage with the world around them. With *The Godfather* and, even more explicitly, *Godfather II*, he used his epic tale of the Corleone family to paint America as endemically corrupt and increasingly soulless in the generational transition from Marlon Brando's Don Vito Corleone to Al Pacino's Michael Corleone. Amid brilliant filmmaking and gripping popular entertainment, the two *Godfather* films presented as powerful an indictment of American society, with its crooked politicians, police, and judges, as any that the older generation had ever filmed. "I feel that the Mafia is an incredible metaphor for this country," Coppola, somewhat grandly, declared in 1972. "Both the Mafia and America have their hands stained with blood from what it is necessary to do to protect their power and interests."[24] In between those two epics, Coppola in April 1974 released *The Conversation*, a taut, unnerving mystery starring Gene Hackman. Coppola had written the movie years before, but his portrait of Hackman as a surveillance expert facing a crisis of conscience over his work vibrated with the same Watergate-era paranoia as *The Parallax View* and *Chinatown*, each of which debuted a few months later, in June 1974.

But Coppola proved the exception among his contemporaries. Over time, the next generation steadily moved away from this kind of socially engaged filmmaking. Stephen Farber, a tart-tongued critic, saw the shift emerging as early as spring 1974. "Whereas the last generation of important American filmmakers . . . had and continue to have strong social concerns, many younger writers and directors have little or no interest in social issues," he wrote in the *New York Times* in March 1974. "Some of them come from film schools in which the auteur theory has been enshrined as gospel, and where courses of study concentrate on arcane meanings in the melodramas of Alfred Hitchcock, Howard Hawks, Don Siegel and Douglas Sirk. When they enter the industry, these young filmmakers want to remake the simple-minded genre movies that they loved as children and that the academics have finally made respectable."[25]

Farber pointed to Coppola's two partners in Paramount's short-lived Directors Company as the directors who "set the example" for this retreat from relevance: William Friedkin and Peter Bogdanovich. Friedkin spent most of the sixties in television before directing a succession of indifferently received films late in the decade, including *The Birthday Party* and *The Night They Raided Minsky's* (from a script cowritten by Norman Lear). His career drifting, Friedkin feared being labeled an art house director and publicly declared his intention to return to Hollywood's "roots" of films with strong characters and dynamic plots.[26] He showed a sniper's eye for that target in 1971 with *The French Connection*, a riveting crime story starring Hackman. Friedkin hit again with *The Exorcist*, whose visceral terror shattered box office records in 1973. His films exploited the greater freedom of expression that the Hollywood revolution of the previous decade had provided, but they showed no real interest in the social themes that had emerged through those cracks in the system.

Bogdanovich, the last of the new generation of directors born in the 1930s, was even more disconnected from the socially conscious movies that flourished over these years. Born between the Altman/Nichols/Penn/Pakula and Scorsese/Lucas/Spielberg generations of directors, Bogdanovich identified with neither. "I wasn't interested in anything that was being made," he recalled, looking back.[27] He felt alienated from the alienation integral to so many of the era's movies. "I admire many of the young directors, but they don't move me," Bogdanovich told the *Los Angeles Times* in 1972. "A lot of the modern stories are about alienation, so they tend to alienate the audience. Purposely. But I don't like that; I really want to be swept along."[28] Instead, his passion was for the American film classics of the 1930s and '40s:

directors such as John Ford and Howard Hawks, stars like Cary Grant, Jimmy Stewart, and Humphrey Bogart.

The Last Picture Show, Bogdanovich's breakout 1971 film, marked a pivotal moment in Hollywood's turn away from the Altman generation's critical perspective on America. The movie, which follows the lives of both young people and their middle-aged parents in a dying West Texas town in 1951, is bleak and beautiful. Shot in crisp black and white (at the suggestion of Orson Welles),[29] deepened by an alternately jubilant and mournful Hank Williams soundtrack, it is an astonishingly assured product for such a young director. Though set in the past, it seemed on the surface very much a product of the modern Hollywood, its opening an explicit sex scene between two teenagers.

But in its sentiments, *The Last Picture Show* rejected the social critique that Altman's generation embraced. Bogdanovich's tale of young people stumbling into adulthood could be seen as a response to *The Graduate*, which depicted the need for its youthful protagonists to throw off a materialistic and misguided older generation to find happiness and meaning. But in *The Last Picture Show*, the older generation is as trapped and unfulfilled as the younger generation, and much more thoughtful about its condition. The younger generation has no claim to greater insight or even more authenticity; the older generation's dreams and aspirations are every bit as valid and heartfelt. The movie throbs with a sense of loss; it feels like an old friend is being buried when the town's final movie theater (the last picture show) shuts its doors. The small town the film brings to life isn't just suffocating and arid, it's supportive and neighborly. At a moment when so much of popular culture portrayed America's past as something to escape, Bogdanovich defiantly affirmed the worth of what came before. "I didn't feel that way," he said. "The past is present to me."[30] It was a sentiment that would prove surprisingly resonant with the precocious young directors poised to revolutionize Hollywood.

THE FIRST OF THAT younger generation to craft a big, mainstream hit was George Lucas, with *American Graffiti* in 1973. The movie re-created

Lucas's youth. He was born in the small California town of Modesto in 1944, just before the Baby Boom began in 1946. His father, who ran a stationery business, was a staunch conservative, and Lucas grew up immersed in the rituals of small-town Americana. He loved television and consumed comic books, joined the Cub Scouts and patrolled the outfield in Little League.[31] As a teen, he developed a passion for tinkering with cars, cruising at night, and careening through back-road drag races. School moved him less. He drifted through high school, but after a serious car accident ended his dreams of becoming a racer, Lucas turned more seriously to his other great passion, photography and film. He applied for admission to the University of Southern California to study film and was admitted for the fall 1964 semester.

While campuses around the country exploded in protest over Vietnam, Lucas spent the middle sixties mostly in the dark, absorbing the movies of other directors and carefully cutting his own. (He drew notice first for his skill as an editor.) He expressed a vague sympathy for the social causes of the 1960s, but he found moviemaking much more captivating. "The central thing in my life was that I wanted to make movies," he later told biographer Dale Pollock. "I didn't want the distraction of causes, much as I believed in them."[32]

Lucas forged an early and critical alliance with Francis Coppola and followed him to San Francisco when Coppola established his American Zoetrope studios there in 1969.[33] Coppola had convinced John Calley at Warner Bros. to bankroll American Zoetrope in the post–*Easy Rider* era, when studios threw money at developing young talent whom they hoped could reach young audiences. Coppola envisioned Zoetrope as a collective that would provide emerging filmmakers the freedom to make personal statements, and he assembled a roster of bright young things, mostly from USC and UCLA, to develop projects. Lucas led that list. Coppola persuaded Calley to bankroll *THX 1138*, which Lucas had expanded from a student short into a full-length screenplay. But when Lucas and Coppola showed Warner the finished product in May 1970, the executives there disliked it so much that they not only recut the picture, but soon after also canceled their overall development deal with Zoetrope.[34] *THX* arrived and disappeared in a blink when Warner Bros. released it in 1971.

By then, Lucas was moving in a very different direction. *THX*'s bleakness put him in the mainstream of the older directors (and even Coppola) gleefully deconstructing myths and excavating America's flaws. But Lucas started to feel that in joining that movement, he was wearing someone else's clothes. Though he nodded sympathetically toward all the right causes, "George was not at that time political," said Tom Pollock, Lucas's attorney in those years. "His values are kind of small-town Republican values."[35] Like Bogdanovich, Lucas grew alienated from the alienation. In response, he developed a script based on his experiences as a teenager in Modesto.

American Graffiti was a project self-consciously out of time. The film, written by Lucas with his contemporaries, the married couple of Gloria Katz and Willard Huyck, follows four friends through a long summer night of cruising and flirting as they face decisions on what to do after high school, all set to the rousing backbeat of AM radio hits; Lucas never identifies the precise date, but the advertising campaign from Universal, which bankrolled the movie, placed it in 1962, just before all the earthquakes that rattled America through the 1960s. The perfect bookend was that Lucas filmed *American Graffiti* in the summer of 1972, as Richard Nixon steamrolled toward reelection on an implicit promise to stop those upheavals. Lucas, in his story of four friends on the cusp between youth and adulthood, captured on film the America that was poised to reelect Nixon, the America that saw change as something that happened somewhere else. ("Why can't things stay the way they are?" Lucas scribbled in his first notes for the screenplay.)[36] *American Graffiti* shared with *The Last Picture Show* an affectionate posture toward the past. The film didn't whitewash the more innocent years before the mid-1960s, but unlike most of the decade's culture, it suggested that something was lost in the transition into a society that maximized personal freedom. "It affirmed and exalted everything about America, about American movies, about American culture, pop culture," said Sean Daniel, a young film enthusiast who joined Universal soon after as a production executive.[37]

When the film reached theaters in August 1973, it immediately found an enthusiastic audience and eventually ranked as the year's third-highest-grossing film (trailing only *The Exorcist* and *The Sting*). Reviewers raved (perhaps a bit excessively for a film that intermittently veered toward the juvenile), but it took the far-right *Human Events* newspaper to correctly identify the counter-revolutionary message of Lucas's apolitical posture. "*American Graffiti* has . . . shown up those blowsy New Left films for the shallow and damnably unrealistic shams that they were," wrote reviewer Alan Crawford. "It has once again made kids real. . . . In direct contrast to the very With-It '60s films, the kids in *American Graffiti* accept their problems as part of life, something within themselves not to be blamed or foisted upon a society 'that made us what we are.'"[38]

After Lucas finished the movie, his father asked him to speak to the Modesto Rotary Club. Lucas returned to the small city where he had biked through Fourth of July parades and presented his film as an answer to the critical stories that had become so common in Hollywood, especially from the older directors. "I decided it was time to make a movie where people felt better coming out of the theater than when they went in," the hottest young director in Hollywood told the assembled Rotarians of Modesto. "It had become depressing to go to the movies."[39]

Hardly anyone noticed at the time, but Lucas had defined the mission statement for much of the Movie Brat generation of directors. Altman's generation prized nothing more in their films than exposing their audiences to what they considered uncomfortable truths. Lucas wanted his audience to shriek with fear and gape in wonder, to cheer at heroes and hiss at villains. And with *Graffiti* completed, he began writing the screenplay for a project he believed would do all those things across a bigger canvas than he had ever contemplated before. The project was a space epic inspired by the Saturday morning movie serials of his youth that Lucas called *Star Wars*.

STEVEN SPIELBERG NEVER ISSUED a manifesto of artistic intent as unambiguous as Lucas did in Modesto, but he clearly shared the sentiment. Even more than Lucas, Spielberg largely ignored the sixties—

the protests, the music, the drugs, the sex.[40] His style was always to ingratiate, not overthrow. Once Spielberg established his footing in Hollywood, he spent so much time with a circle of older agents and producers that his friends staged an intervention to steer him to socialize more with young people.[41]

Born in Cincinnati in 1946, Spielberg through his youth bounced from New Jersey to Phoenix to a suburb of San Jose as his electrical engineer father, Arnold, climbed the ladder at RCA, General Electric, and IBM at the dawn of the computer age. Through a friend of his father's, Steven wrangled an unpaid summer job at Universal during his final years in high school. He then parlayed that into a kind of floating observer status after he entered college. Spielberg spent years haunting the set, shadowing directors, learning from editors. In December 1968, just before he turned twenty-two, Universal finally signed him to a directing contract; the *Hollywood Reporter* declared he "is believed the youngest filmmaker ever pacted by a major studio."[42] For the next three years, Spielberg served his apprenticeship directing episodes for Universal's huge television production business. Even though he operated within the inherent limits of shows such as *Owen Marshall, Counselor at Law*; *Marcus Welby, M.D.*; *The Psychiatrist*; and Rod Serling's *Night Gallery*, Spielberg's talent was unmistakable. Joan Darling, who a few years later became one of the few female directors on television, and her husband, Bill, a screenwriter, were blown away by his command and confidence when she appeared in an episode of *The Psychiatrist*. "He just was so gifted that when we met him and we worked with him on that show, there was no doubt in either Bill's or my mind that he was going to rule the world," she said.[43] Reviewers agreed: Spielberg's television episodes frequently earned raves in the Hollywood trades, most unusual for the small screen.

By 1971, Spielberg had shown enough promise that Barry Diller, the ABC executive who had created the network's Movie of the Week, agreed to Universal's recommendation that Spielberg direct one. Operating on a very tight schedule, Spielberg delivered *Duel*, a propulsive thriller about a maniacal (but never seen) truck driver trying to run down an Everyman driver as they speed down remote desert roads.

With *Duel*'s success, Spielberg finally amassed enough cachet to direct a feature film after several early attempts had stalled. For his first project, he chose a script he had been developing for years. Based on a true story, *The Sugarland Express* follows a young Texas woman, Lou Jean Poplin (played by Goldie Hawn), who convinces her husband, Clovis (William Atherton), to break out of prison just four months before his release to help her reclaim their toddler son, whom she fears the state will place permanently with foster parents. After their plans quickly go askew, the couple kidnaps a Texas Highway Patrolman (Maxwell Slide, played by Michael Sacks) and commandeer his patrol car to drive to Sugarland, where their son is living with his foster parents. Soon they are trailed across the highway by an armada of Texas law enforcement and cheered by people who line the road as they pass through on their doomed mission. The film tries to walk the tightrope between tragedy and farce and sometimes stumbles in the transitions, but it offered more evidence of Spielberg's talent, particularly in his assured handling of big set-piece chase scenes.

It also signaled that, like Lucas and Bogdanovich, Spielberg was not enlisting to tear down institutions. The crowds who lined the roads may have viewed Lou Jean and Clovis as folk heroes fighting an uncaring bureaucracy, but Spielberg didn't. "You see, to me, the real villain's Hawn; she's the heavy for me—I mean, I intended it that way," Spielberg said while promoting the movie.[44] He could have presented the couple as a modern-day Bonnie and Clyde, glamorous rebels against the system; instead, he showed them as dim-witted and misguided (though essentially harmless). The movie's most sympathetic figure is the Highway Patrol's Captain Tanner (played powerfully by Ben Johnson, also the moral foundation of Bogdanovich's *Last Picture Show*), who tries (but fails) to end the confrontation without anyone dying. "For me, anyway—nobody else sees it that way—but I think the heroes are the police," Spielberg said later, while promoting the film.[45] This was not a sentiment commonly heard in any context among Baby Boomers at the time, but it was revealing of the attitude toward American institutions that would infuse the early years of Spielberg's work.

The most fully sympathetic character in Spielberg's next movie,

Jaws, is also a law enforcement officer, Roy Scheider's police chief, Martin Brody. Tanner and especially Brody embody what Spielberg would describe as his classic protagonist: "Mr. Everyday Regular Fella," an ordinary person thrust into extraordinary circumstances. As Spielberg developed a more identifiable voice through the 1970s, he offered a view of America that was not oblivious to the critiques of the 1960s, but stopped well short of endorsing them. In his films, the suburbs might be conformist, but they are not imprisoning. Government might be murky in its motivations, but it is not malign. Like Bogdanovich and Lucas, Spielberg steadily grew alienated from the alienation. "I'm not really that preoccupied with being the spokesman for the paranoid Seventies, because I'm not really that paranoid in real life," Spielberg said at the time.[46]

Spielberg drifted further from the social critiques of the Altman generation as he worked to develop *Close Encounters of the Third Kind,* an updated version of a film he made in high school about alien visitation. Spielberg and Michael and Julia Phillips, who had acquired the rights, first pitched the movie to Columbia in the fall of 1973, during the height of the Watergate crisis.[47] Spielberg's initial proposal very much reflected the ethos of alienation ascendant in Hollywood at the time: he described the film as "UFOs and Watergate."[48] With that perspective, in December 1973 he accepted the Phillipses' suggestion that he hire Paul Schrader to write the screenplay.[49]

Only in the context of a film that combined sci-fi spectacle with anti-institutional paranoia is it possible to imagine a collaboration between Spielberg and Schrader, and even then, it's difficult to picture a more mismatched pair. Though Schrader was only five months older than Spielberg, the two men's sensibilities and formative experiences could hardly have been more different. Raised in Michigan by severe Calvinist parents, Schrader was forbidden to watch movies; even Disney films, his mother told him, supported an "evil industry."[50] He made up for lost time once he enrolled at Calvin College, a seminary in Michigan, and started soaking up foreign films. Obsessed with movies, he spent one summer in New York City taking film courses at Columbia University. Through a friend, he was introduced to the influential film critic Pauline Kael, who arranged for him to be admitted to the film school at UCLA.

Schrader had always been a strong brew: volatile, long-winded, strangely obsessed with guns. In 1972 his life blew up entirely. He had no job—he quit a fellowship at the American Film Institute in protest over budget cuts—and no money and had recently left his wife for a woman who then left him. For weeks he lay in bed all day, started drinking around five, and then drove through the darkness in his Chevy Nova, with a revolver in his glove compartment, often ending his night sleeping in porn theaters or the car.[51] After several weeks of this, Schrader dragged himself to a hospital emergency room in May 1972 with severe pains in his stomach from what he learned was a bleeding ulcer. A news event during his weeks of solitary driving deepened his sense of encroaching chaos: a mentally ill man named Arthur Bremer shot and paralyzed George Wallace during the Maryland Democratic presidential primary. With his own disarray mirroring the country's, a powerful vision settled on Schrader as he lay in the hospital. "While I was in the hospital, this idea of the metaphor of a taxicab occurred to me, the yellow steel coffin flowing through the sewers of the city with this young man trapped inside who looked like he's surrounded by people, but he's absolutely alone," Schrader recalled. "Once the clarity of that metaphor occurred to me, I knew I had to write that in order not to become him."[52] All the elements converged; when Schrader left the hospital, he finished in two weeks the script for what became the classic film *Taxi Driver*, as dark a vision of modern America as anything produced by the older generation.

The Phillipses had optioned the *Taxi Driver* script (on a recommendation from Brian De Palma, another satellite in their social circle) for a token one thousand dollars, but initially they couldn't stir much studio interest in Schrader's bloody story. So, Schrader was game when the Phillipses offered him an opportunity to work on their other property, *Close Encounters*. Schrader spent five months writing a script, but when he completed it, around the time of the release of *The Sugarland Express*, in the spring of 1974, Spielberg hated it.[53] With his own intensely religious background, Schrader had started from the assumption that any meeting with an alien species would be a deeply religious experience for people on Earth. His draft imagined that a government scientist whose job was to debunk UFO sightings would become the one to make contact with the aliens; in Schrader's vision, he would become, in effect, a modern apostle Paul, converting to belief on his own Road to Damascus. Spielberg, however, wanted a common man, "Mr. Everyday Regular Fella," as his hero. The conflict came to a head in spring 1974 at the Phillipses' home in Malibu. "I remember there's this meeting up at Point Dume with Steven and Michael, Julia, and myself, and Steven had read the script," Schrader recalled. "He was not happy about it." The argument escalated until Schrader finally told Spielberg, "I refuse to write a script about the first person to leave our planet so he can go to another world and set up a McDonald's stand." Spielberg looked back at him. "That's exactly what I do want," he said. The exchange ended Schrader's improbable partnership with Spielberg. "That's when I knew there would never be a middle ground," Schrader recalled.*[54]

Spielberg didn't have much time that spring to untangle the script for *Close Encounters.* He was already completing his preproduction work on *Jaws*, an adaptation of the celebrated novel, which producers Richard Zanuck and David Brown had hired him to direct.[55] In May 1974, he brought his *Jaws* crew and cast to Martha's Vineyard in anticipation of a brisk 55-day shoot.[56] Instead, Spielberg stayed on Martha's Vineyard 159 days. What happened in between transformed the movie industry.

WITH *JAWS*, STEVEN SPIELBERG built a new era in Hollywood with the tools of the old one. *Jaws* wasn't the first movie to demonstrate that the ceiling for box office success was rising as the Baby Boom swelled the size of the youth population: *The Godfather, The Exorcist,*

---

* Ironically, Julia Phillips finally sold *Taxi Driver* to Columbia in part by promising that Spielberg would finish the picture if its director, Martin Scorsese, who was not nearly as established at that point, could not deliver it.

The Sting, and even *American Graffiti* had all shown that already. What *Jaws* inaugurated was the era of the summer blockbuster, the mass-marketed, mass opening action/adventure thriller that relied heavily on cutting-edge special effects. The problem at the time Spielberg made the movie was that the technology for those effects was rudimentary. In frustration, he sometimes called the special effects department the special *defects* department.

With computer graphics far in the future, Spielberg and his team faced bracingly physical challenges on *Jaws*. The movie's foundation was to create a shark convincing enough to frighten audiences. Initially, producers Richard Zanuck and David Brown assumed they could train a great white shark to perform at least a few simple maneuvers (while relying on miniatures for the rest).[57] That idea didn't last long. Spielberg sensibly recommended that they obtain footage of real great white sharks for some underwater scenes; the producers hired an Australian couple famed for their shark footage and had them film an ex-jockey inside a shark cage, so the shark would look bigger and more menacing.[58] But this covered only a fraction of their requirements. Spielberg needed a mechanical shark. To build it, he lured out of retirement Bob Mattey, a special effects whiz who had constructed the giant squid in *20,000 Leagues Under the Sea* two decades before.[59] Mattey's hiring perfectly crystallized *Jaws*'s position as a hinge in Hollywood history: Spielberg was poised to propel the film industry into its big-budget, big–box office future, but he could not get there without a major assist from its past. Mattey was dogged and creative, but he faced unending problems with the three mechanical sharks he constructed, especially once they were exposed to actual seawater. The sharks initially didn't work that often, and when they did, they didn't look very convincing. Spielberg was forced to continually delay the shooting of the scenes that required them.

The shark struggles were only the most visible complication that swelled the production schedule and budget. Rain and cold in June slowed completion of the scenes on the beach. Once the movie's three heroes, Roy Scheider as police chief Martin Brody, Richard Dreyfuss as oceanographer Matt Hooper, and Robert Shaw as the shark hunter

Quint, set out after the shark on Quint's boat, the *Orca*, the difficulties multiplied. Shooting scenes on the open ocean required a huge operation to ferry the crew, cameras, film, food, and makeup. As Spielberg shot the *Orca* in her lonely and increasingly embattled pursuit of the shark, he insisted on keeping the horizon clear of other boats. He had good reason: it wouldn't help the sense of menace if families were enjoying a pleasant summer sail at the edge of his shots. But practically, it was a huge challenge to maintain a clear line of sight off Cape Cod, particularly as the filming moved into the Vineyard's high season, which meant bigger crowds and more boats. Many days, Spielberg and the crew sat in their boats for hours, hoping that the shark would work and the summer sailors would disperse. At one point, the *Orca* sank for real; the next day, she caught fire.[60] Locals hired by the production to ferry supplies went on strike, demanding more money.[61]

Everyone seemed ambivalent about the material. The first screenwriters Spielberg asked to punch up Peter Benchley's screenplay drafts turned him down, bad-mouthing the project as "a dumb horror film."[62] Richard Dreyfuss, his star rising after *American Graffiti*, took repeated meetings to convince; he told Spielberg he thought the movie "would be a turkey."[63] Shaw described the book as "a piece of shit."[64] Even Spielberg once lamented to his champion Sid Sheinberg at MCA, "Why are you making me do this B movie?"[65]

But no one on the set doubted Spielberg's talent or tenacity. As in his television work, his precocious filmmaking skill was evident throughout. He stayed cool and focused as the weather, the tides, and the reluctant shark all shredded his schedule. Spielberg's technical mastery was indisputable. He responded to the limitations of his special effects team by constantly finding ways to heighten tension without showing the shark (most notably, by unnervingly shooting scenes from the shark's perspective). In the famous stampede-out-of-the-ocean scene, Spielberg's camera simultaneously tracks forward and zooms back (emulating a fabled Hitchcock technique) to underline Chief Brody's despair over another attack.

The politics of *Jaws* was less sharply defined. Spielberg nodded toward the Watergate-era distrust of politicians: the town's oily mayor, fearing the loss of the summer season, insists on keeping the beach open too long, a decision that leads to the death of another young boy. (The local newspaper editor is equally culpable.) And while *Jaws* punctured Quint's arrogant machismo, it also saw the limits of Dreyfuss's smug scientist, the embodiment of the book-smart Baby Boomer. As in *Sugarland*, the true hero, the source of stability, and the character easiest for the audience to identify with is the law enforcement officer, Roy Scheider's police chief. Spielberg's commitment to the decency and resourcefulness of Scheider's Everyman is much deeper and sustained than any fleeting gestures toward political alienation or outrage.

The *Jaws* shoot was an ordeal for all involved. The delays and mounting bills set off alarms back at Universal's headquarters and rose to reach the ears of its imposing and unsentimental chief executive, Lew Wasserman. "I've been the executive on a movie that goes over budget at Universal with Wasserman, and it's really unpleasant," said Sean Daniel. "Wasserman and [Sid] Sheinberg were television guys, so their approach was 'You got the shot, fuck it, move on.' Spielberg said, 'I don't have it yet.' The shark was sinking, the ocean was rough, whatever, and Steven dug in until he had the takes that he thought he needed."[66] Zanuck and Brown, under fire, looked at finishing the movie in Los Angeles or just shutting down the production for a few months until the summer season had passed and the special effects team had fixed the sharks.[67] Instead, to their credit, Wasserman never pulled the plug, and the producers let Spielberg push through. By the time he finished filming on September 15, Spielberg had shot four hundred thousand feet of film, and the movie's budget had more than doubled, to ten million dollars.[68] Within days of *Jaws*'s release the next summer, that looked like a bargain.

WHEN ROBERT ALTMAN FIRST sent Joan Tewkesbury to explore Nashville, she felt as if she were "going to a foreign country."[69] Tewkesbury, who had written the screenplay for a recent Altman film, *Thieves Like Us*, didn't know exactly what she was looking for; as usual, Altman had not provided her much guidance. He had never been to Nashville, and he knew almost nothing about country music.[70] The initial idea to explore that world came from United Artists, which wanted Altman to direct a script called *The Great Southern Amusement Company*, set in the country music scene, but he hated it.[71] So, he told UA he would develop his own country-themed project after *Thieves*, and he sent Tewkesbury to Nashville to find one.

After a few days in Music City, Tewkesbury felt as alienated as Linda Ronstadt had when she recorded there a few years earlier. "It was one step away from bib overalls and big hair," Tewkesbury said. She spent some time following the tourist circuit with a public relations agent for the music industry and returned to Mississippi feeling as if she had spent a weekend on a Disney ride. "I came back from the first trip, and I said, I don't know what the fuck this is," Tewkesbury remembered.[72] So, she went back a second time, shed the minders and tour guides, slipped through bars and recording studios on her own, and took copious notes on a yellow legal pad.[73] This time a movie coalesced for her—about ambition, missed connections, dreams, and delusions. "As I went through on my own, I realized Nashville was very much like Hollywood had been in the early forties, when I was growing up," she said. "Everybody wanted to be in the movies, everybody wanted to be famous. Everywhere you went in Nashville, somebody had a hit tune that they wanted to play for you. What began to gel was those themes: ambition, wanting to get out of a small place to get to a bigger place."[74]

Tewkesbury returned to LA and sketched an extraordinarily large canvas. She created so many characters that to keep track of them all, she constructed a graph that she hung on her wall, with the day and time of the action written on one axis and the name of each character on the other. They would cross paths, interact, and then recombine in different groupings. The first draft she completed had eighteen characters and ended with one of them (the hopelessly untalented singer Sueleen Gay, eventually played by Gwen Welles) committing suicide.[75] Altman hated the script. He told Tewkesbury it needed a larger point. His first answer was to insist that the movie end with an assassination, of the fragile country star Barbara Jean. "By then we had had all those assassinations, and he said, 'Nobody has killed off a girl.' He said, 'Let's kill off Barbara Jean,'" Tewkesbury recalled.[76] Then, as Watergate consumed Nixon, Altman pushed Tewkesbury to add more political themes to the movie. "He was rabid about what was going on in the country," she said.[77] By the time she finished the rewrites, she had progressed from eighteen characters and a suicide to twenty-four characters and an assassination.[78]

Altman's directing style was loose and instinctive. As filming approached, he shuffled the cast. Keith Carradine was set to play one member of a folk trio, but when Gary Busey unexpectedly dropped out,[79] he was shifted to the more central role of the womanizing Tom Frank (whom Tewkesbury envisioned as a cross between Warren Beatty and country singer Jerry Jeff Walker).[80] When Susan Anspach, who had been cast as Barbara Jean, withdrew, Altman plugged in Ronee Blakley, a singer who had virtually no acting credits.[81] He picked Henry Gibson and Lily Tomlin for central dramatic roles, although at that point they were known almost entirely for their light comic work on television's *Laugh-In*. Altman asked the cast members to pick out their own wardrobes. More significantly, he asked them to write their own songs, partly because the rights were expensive for the country standards that Tewkesbury included in her first draft, but also to connect the music more intimately with the characters. He was undaunted that only Blakley and Carradine had much songwriting experience.

Altman's songwriting edict led him to another characteristically idiosyncratic decision: the hiring of Richard Baskin to oversee the movie's music. Just two years out of college, Baskin connected to the movie when his sister asked him to write songs for her friend Gwen Welles, who had been cast as Sueleen.[82] He agreed to do so on the condition that Welles introduce him to Altman. Baskin knew almost nothing about the real Nashville—he owned a single country record, and that was by Ray Charles, hardly part of the country mainstream—but Altman liked him and hired him anyway as the movie's music director. "He was like, 'Who are you, kid?'" Baskin remembered. "But he was willing to take a chance."[83]

This was filmmaking without a net. Altman gave Baskin a copy of the script when he hired him, but no other guidance about what he expected. He never even told him whether he wanted the songs to play straight or as satire. "I think the way Bob worked," Baskin said, "was that his kind of context was so large that you really couldn't make mistakes."[84]

Altman didn't impose much more structure after shooting began on July 10.[85] With his television training, he shot fast: he knew what he wanted and would usually be satisfied after a few takes. The pace was intense: Baskin could barely keep ahead of the shooting schedule as he wrote songs and rehearsed the local musicians he had hired to play them. Altman gave enormous leeway to the cast. Geraldine Chaplin, as a pompous BBC reporter, wrote her own addled monologues. Altman told the actor playing Kenny, the seemingly straitlaced kid who ultimately shoots Barbara Jean, to decide why he did it.[86] The cast bunked together over the long, hot southern summer as if they were off at camp. Every night, Altman invited the cast to watch the dailies with him, over plenty of pot and scotch.[87] "I never saw him take a drink or do drugs while we were shooting," remembered Baskin, "but at five-oh-one, when they called 'wrap,' he had a joint and a drink in his hand."[88] Then he got up early the next morning and did it all again.

With so many moving pieces, the set could seem like barely contained chaos, but Altman unquestionably had a direction, a vision. "He had the stories, he had the characters, and they perfectly played into his sensibility, which was his improvisational, let-it-all-happen thing," said Baskin. "But that's a little misleading. 'Let it all happen' in the context of a master director who knows what he's doing is different than some amateur letting it all happen."[89] Tewkesbury described Altman's process on *Nashville* in virtually identical terms. Altman didn't abandon scripts as completely as he sometimes suggested—he certainly didn't on *Nashville*—but he was always open to actors offering new interpretations, nuances, even monologues for their characters, so long as it fit his general construct. "It was always fluid," she said. "[As a writer,] you got your feelings hurt because you loved certain things [in the script]. But in working with him, it was this collaborative operation, and everybody had a voice in it."⁹⁰

Nashville had no central story or even a central character. It became a kaleidoscope of America nearing its bicentennial in 1976. Altman later called it "my metaphor for America" and the "culmination" of his work to that point.⁹¹ It was, even more fundamentally, the culmination of Hollywood's early 1970s renaissance. *Nashville* wasn't the best movie Hollywood produced in those years: both *Godfather* movies and *Chinatown*, arguably, would rank above it for sustained excellence. Nor was it the last movie that embodied those early 1970s themes and styles: *One Flew Over the Cuckoo's Nest*, *Network*, *Coming Home*, and others all upheld those traditions later into the decade. But *Nashville* encapsulated more of the major themes of early 1970s American cinema than any other movie. Across its complex mosaic, Altman explored misplaced hero worship; the dangers of blind obedience to authority; the inability to make personal connections; ambition and greed; the threat of free-floating violence; and endemic personal and political corruption—here portrayed not on the epic scale of *Chinatown* or *The Godfather*, but in petty and achingly personal terms, as when Michael Murphy's political operative and Ned Beatty's oafish local attorney coerce the hapless Sueleen to strip at a fund-raiser of leering old men. If *Jaws* was Spielberg's encounter with the great white shark, *Nashville* was Altman's great white whale, his attempt, like Herman Melville with *Moby-Dick*, to condense all the great questions of his time into a single story. Tewkesbury is spot-on when she says the movie's "effect is cumulative. You come to it viscerally. It's a single story without ever telling a single story. It's like being in the middle of the ocean: you're in a shipwreck, and all this shit is floating around you."⁹²

Watergate sluiced around the movie and seeped into its bones. Altman hated Nixon. Tewkesbury remembers walking with him in New York City on the night of Nixon's reelection and getting caught in a huge storm. An umbrella turned inside out blew past them on the street. "That's a symbol of what's coming," Altman told her.⁹³ Under his prodding, *Nashville*'s political element kept growing. Tewkesbury wrote in a fictional third-party presidential candidate named Hal Phillip Walker. Walker is never seen, but he sets much of the movie's plot, such as it is, in motion when Murphy, his slick young aide, arrives in Nashville to recruit country stars to appear at a rally for him that serves as the movie's climax. Walker's words, broadcast from loudspeakers on a van that crisscrosses through the action, ring through the movie both eloquent and empty, a droning hum that conveys both the possibility of political change to inspire and the certainty that, upon closer inspection, it will disappoint.

On the evening of August 8, 1974, Nixon announced his resignation. Poetically, the production that day was shooting its concert scene at the Grand Ole Opry, the building that represented the capital of country music and the beating heart of Nixon's America. As film critic Jan Stuart recounted in *The Nashville Chronicles*, his indispensable account of the movie's making, newspaper ads highlighting Gibson and Tomlin, the most famous cast members from their work on *Laugh-In*, had drawn a crowd of more than four thousand people.[94] Roy Acuff, fiddler, singer, and patriarch of the Grand Ole Opry, opened the filming by imploring the crowd to welcome the visitors. But Acuff, who had performed at the Opry since the 1930s, seemed wary of the Hollywood outsiders, and his mood darkened that evening when the cast and crew gathered around a television to watch Nixon resign. In tears, Acuff approached a group of actors standing offstage.[95] "Look at what you've done to our president!" he cried. Then he stalked off to his dressing room, where he mournfully played the fiddle for the next two hours. The next morning Altman stopped the filming to watch Nixon depart the White House for the final time after his resignation. Altman himself left Nashville a little over three weeks later, after completing the movie's unnerving final scene on a stormy August 31.[96] That scene was the rally for Hal Phillip Walker at Nashville's ornate Parthenon monument, when Kenny, the blandly pleasant young man, shoots Barbara Jean for no apparent reason, an act that seemed entirely logical in Altman's vision of America unraveling at the seams.

NASHVILLE REACHED THEATERS THE following year, on June 11, 1975, and *Jaws* shortly after, on June 20. The media recognized the release of both movies as major events. One week apart, *Time* (*Jaws*) and *Newsweek* (*Nashville*) put the films on their covers. *Nashville* got an early critical boost, as so often happened with 1970s movies, from Pauline Kael in *The New Yorker*. Altman had invited her to see an earlier cut of the movie in January, and in the magazine in March, she disgorged a rave of Homeric proportions. "Is there such a thing as an orgy for movie-lovers—but an orgy without excess?" her review began. "I've never before seen a movie I loved in quite this way. I sat there smiling at the screen, in complete happiness." Kael found echoes of Whitman in Altman's capacious vision: "The picture says, This is what America is, and I'm part of it. *Nashville* arrives at a time when America is congratulating itself for having got rid of the bad guys who were pulling the wool over people's eyes. The movie says that it isn't only the politicians who live the big lie—the big lie is something we're all capable of trying for."[97]

Not all critics were so moved. Some on left and right alike saw *Nashville* as overly condescending in its portrait of the American mainstream. "The film is . . . the mere posturing of a pretentious and unabashedly presumptuous boor," complained Alan Crawford, the same reviewer at the right-wing *Human Events* who praised *American Graffiti*.[98] From the left, Robert Mazzocco, in the *New York Review of Books*, found the movie undermined by Altman's air of "self-congratulatory befuddlement" that saw no possibility of rescuing a culture "careening into nutsville."[99] But the dissents were very much the exception. Kael and *Newsweek* both predicted big box office success for the film.

Those predictions were rooted in an earlier model of Hollywood success, when movies built on strong critical notices and expanded their distribution slowly from major theaters in a few big cities. But *Nashville* was a nearly three-hour movie with no central figure and no linear plot and with a perspective on its characters and milieu that was ambivalent at best. The mystery, Tewkesbury thought, wasn't why it didn't clean up at the box office, but why anyone thought it would.

Altman himself thought some viewers were frightened away by the movie's critical raves—"The word *masterpiece* frightens people," he complained—others, by its tough portrayal of contemporary America.[100] "*Nashville*'s indictment made too many people nervous," Altman said.[101] Mostly, he pointed to a different explanation for the movie's sluggish performance. "Commercially, the biggest problem with the movie," he told one interviewer, "is that it doesn't have a shark."[102]

Indeed, *Jaws* delivered a shock-and-awe demonstration of the power of the new model for releasing a film. Universal mounted an unprecedented advertising campaign by seeking to buy thirty-second ads on every network prime-time program for the three days leading into the film's release. The ad campaign set a new standard in sophistication for Hollywood: the spots on male-themed shows emphasized themes aimed at men, and vice versa for women-themed shows.[103] With all this firepower behind it, Universal released the film in more than four hundred theaters, an unusually large number, and solidified a new model for mass-marketed mass distribution.

Reviewers were divided on the actual product. The *Washington Post*'s Gary Arnold loved it: "Brilliant young director Steven Spielberg has taken the premise of Peter Benchley's best-selling but rather pedestrian novel . . . and streamlined it into a new classic of cinematic horror and high adventure."[104] So, too, did Pauline Kael, who compared Spielberg's work to that of the legendary Soviet director Sergei Eisenstein. But in the *New York Times*, the acerbic Stephen Farber likened it to "a whole rash of grade-B movies about giant ants, tarantulas and rats on the warpath."[105] All the critics might as well have hurled their sharpened pencils against a great white itself. The movie chewed through the competition. Less than three months after its release, in September 1975, *Jaws* surpassed *The Godfather* as the highest-grossing film of all time.[106] By the end of 1975 alone, it had grossed $260 million, or more than twenty-five times as much as *Nashville*. Those numbers could only make inevitable the movie industry's long march from the personal works of social criticism that marked the early 1970s to the blockbusters that have ruled Hollywood ever since.

NASHVILLE AND *JAWS* CAPTURED Hollywood in transition. Altman's generation typically made movies with a blowtorch, convinced they were burning away illusions about America that Hollywood had enameled; with that demolition behind them, Spielberg's generation built new myths from shards of the old and the new. "They were excited about making movies," remembered Tony Bill. "In a way, by the time the antiwar movement petered out, I think people might have been worn out by being critical of this culture. It was such a pervasive and exhausting time to be critical. I think maybe it was when we got that out of our system, so to speak, you just wanted to relax and do something that was personal rather than universal."[107] The younger generation created indelible characters and even manufactured, in Lucas's case, an entire cosmos. They stirred the imaginations of millions, in countries around the world, but with few exceptions, they did not create art that challenged their audiences to question their lives, their relationships, or their country.

In the hands of the Spielberg/Lucas generation, the movies would follow the same arc as music did from the mid-1960s to the early 1970s: from a roar of defiance to a recognition that a house "with two cats in the yard" might not be so bad after all. The movies of the second generation also converged with the message of *All in the Family* and many of the era's other landmark television shows: that it was possible to reconcile the Baby Boomers' desire for new personal freedoms with older generations' priority on stability and order. As the Baby Boomers deepened their hold on Hollywood, the movies, like television and music, both cemented the new social consensus and tamed its most threatening aspects.

8

AUGUST

The Icarus of Los Angeles

Bill Zimmerman, the veteran peace activist working for Tom Hayden and Jane Fonda as director of the Indochina Peace Campaign, had been living in Los Angeles for only a few weeks when Hayden asked him to drive to a small apartment building in the San Fernando Valley. Zimmerman had never been to the Valley before, but he found the building, and the apartment, and used the designated knock on the door that he had been given to signal his arrival.

When the door cracked open, Zimmerman saw, through the thin sliver of space, a tall, handsome man peering back at him nervously. The man was movie producer Bert Schneider, a powerful and wealthy Hollywood operator. Ever since they provided the money to produce the seminal youth movie *Easy Rider*, Schneider, with his partner, the director Bob Rafelson, had been considered among the most dynamic figures in the "New Hollywood." BBS, the company Schneider and Rafelson started with Steve Blauner, a childhood friend of Schneider's, became the vanguard of Hollywood's youth revolution, producing landmark films like *Five Easy Pieces* and *The Last Picture Show*. The BBS offices, at 933 North La Brea Avenue, were the focal point of Hollywood's counterculture, a place to screen the latest avant-garde foreign film or to score the best drugs. Musicians, writers, yogis, directors, politicians—all passed through; even Thomas Pynchon, the famously reclusive novelist, once called Rafelson to come hang out and talk movies.

Schneider lived in an opulent home in Benedict Canyon, a place he kept stocked with celebrities, radical political activists, and young women, all lubricated by a seemingly bottomless supply of marijuana and cocaine. Living across the canyon, the young actress and writer Candice Bergen, who later engaged in her own romance with Schneider, remembered watching a parade of willowy topless girls sunbathing by his pool.[1] Though Schneider generally avoided the spotlight, he had a movie star aura of his own. He was very tall and imperially slim, handsome with wavy blondish-brown hair and penetrating blue eyes. "Just as a man, he was so gorgeous and so sexy," said Jane Fonda. "I had a crush on him."[2] Anjelica Huston thought that "he was actually built like a praying mantis, but a very attractive praying mantis, I should add. He moved slowly and gracefully and quietly, and he had a kind of Zen approach."[3] Schneider threw parties that were legendary for combining his passions of moviemaking, radical politics, drug use, and sexual adventuring. On any given night, the cast that gathered in his house might include Jack Nicholson, who functioned as virtually a fourth partner in the early years of BBS; the radical protester Abbie Hoffman; actors Dennis Hopper and Peter Fonda; and Huey Newton, the leader of the Black Panthers, the cause that galvanized Schneider above all others. One night at Schneider's home, Warren Beatty found himself in a friendly argument with Newton. Beatty remembers Newton insisting that the country would soon reject Richard Nixon, with Beatty cautioning that Nixon might not be so easy to dislodge. The men settled their debate by betting one hundred dollars and then, theatrically, climbing a ladder to stash the bills in a chandelier in the foyer. (Some two decades later, Beatty found the money still there when he looked at renting Schneider's old house after his own was destroyed in the 1994 Northridge earthquake.)[4]

But when Zimmerman found him in late August 1974, in a small apartment in the unfashionable San Fernando Valley, Schneider was anxious and disheveled. Letting Zimmerman in the door, he excitedly waved a small derringer pistol he had been given. "Do you know how to work this fucking thing?" he demanded. Zimmerman didn't, but he thought he could figure it out if he stayed calm, which clearly Schneider was not. Zimmerman wasn't sure if Schneider was on drugs, but he was undeniably agitated—and he had good reason to be.

In August 1974, most of the left in Los Angeles, as elsewhere, was celebrating Richard Nixon's resignation. "Guess what, folks? He's gone," Graham Nash had declared to a roar of applause at Roosevelt Stadium in Jersey City, where that summer's gargantuan Crosby, Stills, Nash and Young reunion tour had stopped on August 8, the night Nixon announced he was stepping down.[5] Irving Azoff and the Eagles were at the Paradise Island casino in Nassau during a break in their tour and filed into the bar with a large crowd to watch Nixon's speech. "They were cheering in the Bahamas," Azoff recalled.[6] At an IPC retreat that month in Lake Arrowhead to plot out the final stage of the legislative campaign against the Vietnam War, "excitement was high," because of Nixon's resignation, remembered Paul Ryder, one of the young activists working with the group.[7] But while most on the left were exulting, Schneider was sinking into a rapidly escalating crisis.

The immediate chain of events that had forced him to hide in the Valley began when Huey Newton erupted in a series of violent attacks through early August 1974 and then skipped out of his court hearing in Oakland after his arrest. Newton fled to Los Angeles, where Schneider soon arranged for him to be spirited to a house in Mexico that the producer owned.[8] Once Schneider had stashed Newton there, he began looking for a way to fly him into Cuba, which he expected to provide him asylum. That was why Schneider asked Hayden and Fonda to set up a meeting for him with Zimmerman, who had gained renown as a daredevil pilot the year before, when he airlifted food and medical supplies to the Native American activists facing a siege from the FBI during their occupation of Wounded Knee. It was also why Schneider was hiding with a derringer in a nondescript apartment in the Valley: his first attempt to find a pilot had put him crosswise with a group of Cuban exiles in Los Angeles, who were now threatening him if he didn't deliver the payout they expected.

But the chaos engulfing him when Bill Zimmerman arrived at his door was also a logical culmination of Schneider's journey since he had arrived in Los Angeles almost ten years before. Over those years, the highest aspiration for many involved in LA's cultural revolution had been to break boundaries and shatter conventions, to live without constraints. No one barreled through the barriers more energetically or obsessively than Bert Schneider. He rewrote the rules of movie-making and then constantly navigated toward the farthest frontiers of sex, drugs, and political radicalism. It had all brought him enormous professional success and impassioned connection with Newton and the Black Panthers, but it had also wrecked his marriage, and before many more years, it would send him spiraling out of the movie business and into a maelstrom of drug abuse that isolated him from almost all his friends and family. Sitting in the small apartment listening to Schneider's fanciful plans for spiriting Huey Newton to Cuba, Bill Zimmerman could see both the focus that had made Schneider a Hollywood power and the frenzy that would soon topple him from his perch. "On the one hand, he was a brave guy willing to take a chance to support someone who was, (a) his friend and, (b) an important person for the movement," Zimmerman said. "On the other hand, he was nuts. He was crazed."[9] In a place and time defined by excess, no one climbed farther out onto the ledge than Schneider, or fell harder to the ground below.

BERT SCHNEIDER SPENT HIS youth surrounded by hedges, not ledges. He was reared in New Rochelle, a leafy suburb north of New York City, the middle son of Abe Schneider and Ida Briskin. The father spent his entire career at Columbia Pictures, starting as an office boy for Harry Cohn, Columbia's irascible founder, before ascending through the company's financial hierarchy all the way to chief fiscal officer.[10] Eventually, he became president after Harry Cohn died in 1958. Abe cast a long shadow in the Schneider household: all three of his sons followed him into the movie business, with Stanley Schneider, the eldest son, eventually becoming Columbia's president as well. Bert had a rebellious streak. He was expelled from Cornell University for what he later described as "bad marks, gambling and girls," but even he surrendered to his father's gravitational pull: after Cornell, he took a job in New York City, at Screen Gems, Columbia's television arm.[11] Like his father, he quickly showed a facility for finance and climbed the ladder there. Schneider married Judy Feinberg, a local beauty from Scarsdale, started a family, and put down his own roots in the suburbs.

Like Schneider, partner Bob Rafelson, the son of a hat manufacturer, was raised in an environment of comfort, in his case, on Manhattan's Upper West Side. Rafelson followed the Beat-era path of rebellion, playing in a band in Mexico, smoking pot, and haunting readings by Jack Kerouac. He was drawn to film from an early age, disappearing for hours into movie theaters even as a kid.[12] Rafelson was working in New York for the producer Dan Melnick when he first met Schneider. "This young fellow approximately my age kept coming over for meetings, and he took note that it was I who was doing the hustling in Melnick's office," Rafelson remembered. "So, we said, 'Let's go out for lunch,' and lunches led to long, long walks in Central Park."[13] On those walks, Rafelson posed the same question that Jack Nicholson, Robert Towne, and their friends were asking in Los Angeles: Why were American movies so lifeless while Europe was bursting with energy and ideas? It was in these conversations that the two ambitious young men first considered the idea that they could fill that gap with a production company of their own.

Both men eventually headed to Los Angeles and formed their first company, called Raybert. Rafelson developed the idea that generated their initial fortune: a television show about four zany, Beatlesesque musicians called "the Monkees." Acceptable to older generations, attractive to younger ones, *The Monkees* struck a buoyant chord, drawing solid television ratings and selling millions of records on the side.

But television was always a way station for Rafelson and Schneider: their sights never wavered from the big screen. They moved into film in 1968 with *Head*, the dizzying deconstruction of the Monkees' image that Schneider produced and Rafelson directed from a script he wrote with their buddy Jack Nicholson. The movie perplexed critics and audiences alike, but it carried Schneider and Rafelson over the bridge, which was more imposing then than now, between television and movies. So, Schneider and Rafelson were ready when Peter Fonda and Dennis Hopper, frustrated by Roger Corman's hesitation and ambivalence, presented their idea for the biker movie that became *Easy*

Rider.[14] Schneider wrote a check to finance the film—Rafelson says he mortgaged his house to help meet the cost[15]—and kept the production on track, despite the frequently erratic behavior of Hopper, who was directing. (Some believed that Schneider and Rafelson cast their ally Nicholson in a critical supporting role after Rip Torn pulled out partly to keep an eye on their volatile director.)[16] After production completed, Schneider deftly eased out Hopper from the editing room, when he appeared incapable of cutting the movie into a length that could be released.[17] "Dennis said, 'This movie is perfect, and I'm not touching it,'" said Henry Jaglom, an eccentric actor and aspiring filmmaker who became part of the circle around Schneider and Rafelson. "And it was four hours and forty-two minutes."[18]

The huge box office and critical success of *Easy Rider* made Hopper and Fonda celebrities, hailed as the voice of a new generation. Nicholson, after all his years of struggle, became a star, too. Though Schneider stayed firmly in the background, the film's success also testified to his unique ability to steer a movie into port amid all the waves that constantly threatened to capsize it. "You think this guy can really make a movie?" Schneider asked Rafelson after listening to Hopper's initial pitch for *Easy Rider.* "I don't think he can make a movie without you as the producer," Rafelson answered. "You produce and, yes, he can make a movie."[19]

As the buzz around *Easy Rider* built, Rafelson and Schneider seized the moment. Just before it was released in July 1969, they added Schneider's childhood friend Steve Blauner to the partnership and started BBS.[20] Then they signed a unique distribution deal with Columbia, still under the leadership of Schneider's father, Abe. Columbia agreed to release six BBS movies at a budget of a million dollars per movie. Any cost above a million BBS had to cover out of its own pocket. Whenever it could finish a movie for less, it could keep the difference. Most important, Columbia gave BBS the most prized commodity in Hollywood: final cut over its films. To underscore their independence, the partners moved their operation off the Columbia lot and bought a building on 933 North La Brea Avenue, just west of Hollywood. Almost immediately, the BBS building became the raucous embassy from the new Hollywood to a studio system still deeply ambivalent over its rise.

FROM THE START, THERE was no cooler way to kill an afternoon than to hang in the BBS building with Bob and Bert. On the top floor were the executive offices for Rafelson, Schneider, and Blauner, complete with a sauna. One floor down was a state-of-the-art screening room and editing facilities. A rotating cast of filmmakers, including Tony Bill, Peter Bogdanovich, Hal Ashby, and even Michelangelo Antonioni, rented space on the second floor. "It was a hangout place," said Jonathan Taplin. "It was like one of those record company offices where you could go and smoke pot in the office. Schneider smoked a lot of dope. It was very loose, very 'Oh, you have to be comfortable, artists have to rule, most of the business is bullshit, and I'll protect you.' The same kind of vibe, that 'I'll stick up for the artists against the suits, but I'm cool. Take your shoes off, whatever.'"[21]

The offices became a magnet for misfits and rebels. Novelists (Pynchon, William Burroughs) and political activists (Newton, Tom Hayden, Abbie Hoffman, Daniel Ellsberg) regularly shuttled through.[22] Strange characters would drift in selling the latest pathway to self-enlightenment, the newest social cause, or just the best pot and, later, cocaine. "It was a hotbed of political insurrection," said Rafelson. "It just was. Not only political, but cultural. You had wacko gurus and dope dealers, serious dope dealers." As Taplin recognized, the overall sensibility BBS projected was closer to rock and roll than to old Hollywood.

BBS was not only a great place to hang out; more important, it was also a great place to make movies. After the transcendent success of *Easy Rider*, its next films included *Drive, He Said*, directed by Nicholson; *Five Easy Pieces*, directed by Rafelson and starring Nicholson; and Peter Bogdanovich's *The Last Picture Show*. *Drive* flopped (despite some arresting moments), but the other two were huge successes, with *Five Easy Pieces* providing the first true star vehicle for Nicholson, who was riveting as Bobby Dupea, an amoral and downwardly mobile drifter fleeing convention and responsibility. BBS became known for

its deference to directors (though not without limits) and its willingness to bet on unusual ideas and the offbeat talents that produced
them. "They really let me make the picture the way I wanted to," Bogdanovich recalled.[23] Rafelson thought Schneider a natural at coaxing
the best from filmmakers who might otherwise spiral into disarray.
"Having talent isn't much if you don't have someone who can exercise
it, and that's what Bert did," Bob Rafelson said. "He was a genius, in
fact, at taking an idea and making it [happen], putting the buttons
and the cloth together."[24] At a time when Hollywood was struggling
to reach the growing audience of young people, BBS appeared to have
cracked the code.

The BBS films were not political per se. The company's movies spotlighted solitary alienation, not collective action. As one critic perceptively noted, the BBS movies reduced "general dissatisfaction with the
political, social and cultural climate of the time into the existential
problems of specific individuals."[25] Nicholson's Bobby Dupea in *Five
Easy Pieces* personified their style. A talented pianist, he abandons his
upper-middle-class family and his music for a life of blue-collar work,
transitory romances, and aimless drifting. He runs not because he
believes he has found a better way to live, but because he considers it
the only chance to escape the corruption and rot he's convinced will
destroy him if he grounds himself in conventional society. Dupea ex-
presses an inchoate despair closer to *Rebel Without a Cause* and the
formless discontent of the 1950s than to "The whole world is watching!" and the concentrated protest of the 1960s. But the BBS films still
struck a contemporary chord. Its movies captured the jagged edges
and unraveling seams of America remaking itself.

If the BBS sensibility could be condensed into a single scene, it is
the moment in *Five Easy Pieces* when Nicholson faces the implacable
waitress at a diner who will not give him his omelet with tomatoes
instead of potatoes, or his side order of toast. When Nicholson sent everything on the table crashing to the floor, he captured the frustration
of millions of young (and not-so-young) Americans straining to sweep
away social conventions that had outlived their time.

In Hollywood, BBS was unique at a time when the studio system was still constrictive and constrained. "BBS was a beacon in this world," said Fred Roos, who worked with Nicholson to develop *Drive, He Said* and served as casting director on *Five Easy Pieces*.[26] BBS provided the closest equivalent to what would later be called independent film. "Bert was willing to do things nobody else was willing to do," said Henry Jaglom. "As the son of the studio head and as a rebel, he had this combo which was beautiful and very sincere. In my whole lifetime out here, I've never met a second person like him."[27]

The deal BBS cut with Columbia (limited financial exposure in return for maximum creative freedom) became a template for the shift in authority from studios to filmmakers. Behind that autonomy, BBS built a powerful machine. Blauner kept the trains running on time, managing the administrative and business details. (When Richard Wechsler, the co-producer of *Five Easy Pieces*, once asked Nicholson what Blauner did, Jack replied, "Pencils and erasers.")[28] Rafelson was the creative spark, but Schneider was the business visionary, the undisputed sun around which BBS orbited. Schneider liked movies (though, like Bogdanovich, his taste ran more to American classics than the European imports that most of his circle admired), but deal making was his real art, and empire building his passion. He knew numbers and spreadsheets, but he also knew people, when to coax them and when to bluster. He was shrewd, a good listener, and attentive to detail. These skills made him a very effective negotiator. "He could be charming," said Roos, "but he could also be tough."[29] Schneider projected a buccaneer confidence about besting the system, which inspired those around him, and he didn't mind risks: when Bogdanovich asked to shoot *The Last Picture Show* in black and white, Schneider initially hesitated, but within days, he convinced Columbia to accept the choice, unconventional as it was. "Later on, I asked him why he had let me do it so easily, without an argument," Bogdanovich recalled. "He said, 'I thought it would be a novelty.'"[30]

But after its hot run from 1969 through 1971, the company's momentum slowed as the seventies progressed. Rafelson's *The King of Marvin Gardens*, which reunited him with Nicholson after their triumph in *Pieces*, came and went with little notice in 1972. The party on

La Brea was as alluring as ever, but profit became more elusive. BBS lost its edge for many reasons, but near the top of any list was that, for Bert Schneider, movies were fading next to his other passions: sex, drugs, and political revolution.

WHEN SCHNEIDER FIRST ARRIVED in Los Angeles with his wife, Judy, they were a conventional, if unusually attractive, couple. "Particularly when we all were out here together, and I got to see them in this context, they were like this golden couple, some kind of a blessed aura around them," remembered Bob Rafelson's wife, Toby.[31] During his first LA years, Schneider still sipped martinis and smoked a pipe. A walk on the wild side was the occasional joint.[32] He arranged for regular tennis games and had Friday night bridge lessons at his house for a foursome that included Nicholson and Henry Jaglom. "That's how petit bourgeois we were aiming at," Jaglom remembered.[33] It was as if Schneider were re-creating the New Rochelle of his parents, with a few palm trees and a swimming pool rolled in, like a new backdrop for a movie scene.

But Schneider never entirely slouched into suburban satisfaction. Toby Rafelson, a perceptive observer, thought he felt trapped by the expectations of replicating the success that both he and his wife had been raised in: the nice house, beautiful kids, Saturdays at the country club. "They came from similar families with similar patriarchs, in a way, married to strong women," she said. "So, there was a kind of dynastic feeling to the whole group, to both families and then to the merged families . . . It's a heavy burden when you become the current symbol of all of your family's history."[34] The rebellious streak that Schneider had displayed in college, and then mostly suppressed after, resurfaced as the success of *The Monkees* and then *Easy Rider* exposed him to more of LA's temptations. Like many Hollywood men born just before the Baby Boom, Schneider appeared determined to make up for lost time when the sixties revolution in cultural attitudes created opportunities that had not been available during his own twenties, in the 1950s. Marijuana became a major part of his life, punctuated by the occasional psychedelic and, later, supplanted by cocaine. "He was not engaged with dope when I met him," said Bob Rafelson, "but within a few years he outdid us all."[35]

And with the drugs came sex. Both powerful and attractive, Schneider engaged in nearly constant affairs, some brief, others more extended. The philandering broke up his marriage in 1971. (The Rafelsons later divorced as well.) When he found a new house in Benedict Canyon, he soon filled it with a procession of political radicals and lissome girls lolling by the pool.[36]

Living across the canyon was Candice Bergen, who watched the beautiful people come and go through a telescope. Schneider, thirteen years her senior, pursued her, and within weeks of his breakup the two began a relationship. Bergen, a luminescent young actress and model who was also working regularly as a photographer and writer, saw Schneider as a force of nature. He seemed to have more hours in the day, more energy, more enthusiasm, than anyone she had met. Within weeks, he had taken her on a weekend to the Bay Area to meet Huey Newton, Joan Baez, and Baba Ram Dass, the former Harvard professor Richard Alpert, who had become a celebrated New Age spiritual teacher.[37] When they returned home, Abbie Hoffman was waiting on the couch.[38] Huey Newton would spend days at the house plotting strategy with Schneider (and soliciting his checks) for Bobby Seale's 1973 mayoral bid in Oakland.[39] Schneider glided confidently through all of it. "I seldom saw a situation he couldn't handle," Bergen wrote later. She was swept along in his current.[40]

In the fall of 1971, the fierce *Los Angeles Times* gossip columnist Joyce Haber predicted marriage for the couple, but the centrifugal force in Schneider's life could not be contained in a single relationship.[41] He preached liberation but simultaneously sought control. He argued to Bergen that monogamy was a bourgeois concept. "You have to understand that I'm a love object for every woman who walks into my office," he told her.[42] At the same time, he bad-mouthed her movie opportunities: no script was good enough.[43] Besides, if she went off on location, he explained, she needed to understand that he would see other women, something she dreaded. He defined freedom in a way that made her feel trapped. "He wanted to be in control," said one friend of both.[44] Bergen finally gave up, and the couple split in 1973, leaving a trail of angry fights and broken furniture at Schneider's house. As when he separated from his wife, Schneider was undeterred. He kept his compass pointed toward the farthest frontiers of experience. During 1974, the year he turned forty-one, friends remember him dating—if that word can be applied—a very young girl who was a student at the high school his own children attended.[45]

Besides the drugs and sex, Schneider dabbled in almost every variety of self-help and consciousness-raising that sprouted at the tail end of the 1960s. Bergen remembers the bookshelves at his house groaning with volumes about finding spiritual insight.[46] Together they traveled to Big Sur, pilgrims in his Porsche, to soak in the hot tubs at Esalen. Bergen endured grueling sessions of Rolfing; Schneider had a personal gestalt therapist.[47] Besides seeing Baba Ram Dass, he made trips to visit Richard Baker, the celebrated Zen master in San Francisco.[48] Toby Rafelson suspected his immersion in these movements was the final piece in his reinvention as the augur of a new, advanced, consciousness. "I think he needed to be aligned in his mind with a higher purpose," she said.[49]

Schneider saw himself as a rebel who could subvert the system all the more effectively because he had mastered it. "He was the genius," said Bob Rafelson. "He was the treasurer of Screen Gems at the age of twenty-four or something. He knew all that shit, and he was a tough, tough son of a bitch. At the same time, he loved talented people, and he mixed with them as genuinely as they would mix with one of their own kind. Bert was too weird not to be loved by the artists. He was a suit, but, boy, was he a fucking weird guy in a suit. And I knew that right from the day I met him."[50]

There was an undeniable exhilaration to it, but the journey contained an ugliness that deepened over time. The most obvious was a dismissive, even contemptuous attitude toward women. Schneider and the BBS crew treated women as disposable, interchangeable, conquests. They graded them in demeaning terms that sometimes seemed like a movie script parody of locker-room bragging. But there was also a casual disdain that could surface with regard to anyone who wasn't evolved enough to share Schneider's definition of liberation, which translated into the freedom to do drugs and sleep around. "Everybody was square compared to him," recalled writer Jeremy Larner. "Bert was the kind of guy who would let you know, if you weren't sexually liberated, that you had missed out on the revolution."[51] Peter Bogdanovich saw this attitude up close. He thought BBS almost didn't make *The Last Picture Show* because the partners considered him too straitlaced. "Bert told me later that I was so square that they thought maybe I wouldn't be the right mix," Bogdanovich remembered.[52]

Schneider was known for deferring to directors and supporting their vision, but in his personal and business relations, he maneuvered constantly for his own advantage. Jeremy Larner experienced this side of Schneider when he moved to release a new version of his novel *Drive, He Said* as a tie-in to the movie. Schneider fought him fiercely: he insisted that the new edition include the movie script (and thus promote the film more directly). Larner, who held the rights, refused. "He wanted to control it," he said of Schneider. "Externally he was very happy and inclusive, but if there was anything to be negotiated, he wanted control of it."[53] Toby Rafelson saw the same instinct: "I think it was just very important to him never to be at a disadvantage."[54]

Schneider's political journey was as extreme as his personal odyssey from Westchester to Esalen. Jaglom remembers Schneider first expressing interest in politics during Robert F. Kennedy's 1968 presidential campaign, hosting meetings at his house and making contributions.[55] But Kennedy's assassination severed Schneider's connection to mainstream liberal politics. After that, he lurched much further to the left, becoming active in antiwar demonstrations and traveling to Washington for the national moratorium in November 1969 (and writing a big check when the organizers couldn't pay their phone bill).[56] He helped to finance Abbie Hoffman and befriended Jane Fonda when she began her activist career, at a time when few others in Hollywood would associate with her.[57]

But even the antiwar cause was a bit conventional and tame for Schneider. His most passionate attachment was to the militant Black Panthers. He initially connected with the Panthers through Fonda, during her own short period of working with them.[58] He financed, with contributions of several hundred thousand dollars, the two giant "survival conferences" the Panthers organized to distribute food and clothes and to build support for Bobby Seale in his Oakland mayoral race. (Seale made the runoff, but he lost decisively to a Republican incumbent in May 1973.) He helped fund the legal costs from the Panthers' constant confrontations with the law, and he became especially close with Huey Newton, the Panthers' charismatic but volatile and violent leader. Leading-man handsome and surprisingly soft-spoken in social situations, Newton, through Schneider, became a familiar figure in Hollywood. Sometimes he came to raise money and preach revolution; more often, he turned up to hide from rival Black Panther factions or to dip his pan into the river of drugs and starlets that flowed around his producer friend.[59] Jaglom remembers a New Year's Eve at Schneider's house with Newton when they passed cocaine around the room in a crystal bowl.[60]

Others on the left had been drawn to the outlaw posture and radical rhetoric of the Panthers, too. Fonda had lent Newton a penthouse for a press conference in New York (disastrously, it turned out, when the images of Newton seated on an antique French chair became a symbol of trivializing "radical chic").[61] Hayden had written in a *New York Times* op-ed that Newton's ideas should become the basis for nothing less than rewriting the U.S. Constitution.[62] But many pulled back over time as evidence accumulated of the Panthers' criminal behavior, violence against their own members, and systematic abuse of women: when Newton wasn't spouting theories of revolution, he was brutally pursuing control of all the vice rackets in Oakland and targeting an extortion scheme at local Black-owned businesses.[63] Yet Schneider never wavered. "Everything Huey did was justified because of his upbringing, because of the oppression of the white folk," remembered Jaglom. "It was nuts. It was bullshit. It was drugs. It was brainless craziness."[64]

No one could have contributed as much money to the Panthers as Schneider did without feeling a genuine political connection. Schneider, with his own dreams of revolution, thrilled to their message of confrontation.[65] But the association with the Panthers also spoke to his deep need to live on the edge: it "satisfied a great part of his lust for independence and for freedom," Rafelson thought.[66] Michie Gleason, Schneider's assistant in the mid-1970s, felt that Newton was a validation of Schneider's rebel commitment, living proof that he would go further than anyone around him. "Huey was like a trophy wife for him in some ways," she said. Indeed, Schneider's connection with Newton was so intense that some, then and later, thought it crossed into the romantic and erotic, though this was never conclusively proven.[67]

No other cause stirred Schneider as much as the Panthers. But if any came close, it was the trial of Daniel Ellsberg, a military analyst at the Rand Corporation, in Santa Monica, indicted for leaking the Pentagon Papers, a secret history of the U.S. involvement in Vietnam. Schneider contributed to Ellsberg's defense and regularly hosted him, his wife, Pat, and their attorneys at his home to plot strategy.[68] And he developed an idea: BBS still had one movie left on its no-questions-asked distribution deal with Columbia. Schneider decided to make a documentary about Ellsberg, the Pentagon Papers, and Vietnam.

WITH THAT DECISION, BERT SCHNEIDER took the first step toward filling the biggest blind spot in Hollywood's artistic revival. Through the early 1970s, the studios completed dozens of movies about previously taboo subjects and also became a hotbed of political activism against the Vietnam War. But over those years, the film community did not make any movies explicitly about Vietnam.

While the conflict was raging, the sole Hollywood movie that addressed it was John Wayne's pro-war *The Green Berets*, in 1968. Other films that envisioned a more critical perspective never achieved traction.* The closest the studios came to the war were a few smaller

---

* Richard Condon, the author of *The Manchurian Candidate*, failed to raise money for a film he proposed in which a group of student radicals plot to wipe out a small town in New Jersey in retaliation for the massacre by American soldiers at My Lai, in Vietnam. Stanley Kramer, the stolid director of earnest, middlebrow message pictures (*The Defiant Ones, On the Beach*), contemplated a Vietnam movie after *Guess Who's Coming to Dinner*, but he backed off "because . . . I was never

films about returning veterans, such as Elia Kazan's bleak *The Visitors*, which closed eight days after its release in 1972.[69] Jane Fonda, who began her own long march to film *Coming Home*, her sweeping story about returning veterans and war's costs, soon after Schneider started working on his Vietnam film, found the industry's reluctance to touch the war easy to explain. There was, she said, simply no heroic story to tell: "We lost, and it ripped families apart, and it ripped the country apart, and it led to Watergate, and it's nothing but a dark hole for the United States."[70]

Schneider didn't know the documentary world, but Bob Rafelson did. He recommended that Schneider meet Peter Davis, an old friend of his working as a producer at CBS. Davis, an LA native, had a Hollywood pedigree. His father, Frank Davis, was a producer at MGM. His mother, Tess Slesinger, was a novelist and screenwriter. His wife, Johanna Mankiewicz, was the daughter of Herman Mankiewicz, who cowrote *Citizen Kane* with Orson Welles. Davis blended his filmmaking roots with an interest in journalism and landed at CBS as an associate producer and writer in 1965.[71]

At CBS, Davis made his biggest splash in 1971, with his landmark documentary *The Selling of the Pentagon*, an exposé of the military's attempts to influence public opinion. Narrated by Roger Mudd, the film drew rave reviews and a shelf of awards, but it also provoked an intense backlash from the Pentagon; Spiro Agnew, Nixon's attack dog vice president; their allies in Congress; and conservative publications.[72]

---

able to draw a bead on the subject" (Julian Smith, "Look Away, Look Away, Movie Land," *Journal of Popular Film* [Winter 1973]: 29–31). Even after the runaway success of *American Graffiti*, George Lucas failed to attract financing for a movie about Vietnam that he wanted to direct from a John Milius script called *Apocalypse Now* (David Rensin, "George Lucas, Skywalker," in *Very Seventies, A Cultural History of the 1970s from the Pages of "Crawdaddy,"* ed. Peter Knobler and Greg Mitchell [New York: Fireside, 1995], 236). Hal Ashby, a busy director in those years, later said that possible Vietnam projects simply never came up. "I cannot recall any serious conversation by individuals contemplating such a project," he remembered (Ralph Applebaum, "Positive Thinking," in *Hal Ashby: Interviews*, ed. Nick Dawson [Jackson: University Press of Mississippi, 2010], 63).

CBS defended Davis when congressional committees sought to obtain his notes and interview tapes in an effort to prove he had misleadingly cut the interviews,[73] but Davis could also feel that the network wasn't eager to repeat the experience. "They were both proud of me *and*," he recalled, "didn't want to see it happen again."[74]

Davis was working as a producer at *60 Minutes* when he received a call in the spring of 1972 from Rafelson: would he be willing to leave CBS to make a movie about the Pentagon Papers? Davis was interested enough to learn more about the project, so he arranged to fly to Los Angeles for a meeting. Schneider turned on all his charm. When they met at the BBS offices, he introduced Davis (who instantly felt out of place in his suit and tie) to Tom Hayden, whom Schneider envisioned in a consulting role for the film. Later that weekend, Davis found himself at Schneider's house in Benedict Canyon watching *60 Minutes* on Schneider's huge bed with a group of people that included Jane Fonda. The whirlwind had the desired effect. "I was dazzled," Davis recalled.[75] Schneider took a liking and a leap—he offered Davis the job directing the film. "You know you're not going to be able to make this for a hundred and fifty thousand," Davis told him. "No, I was thinking more like a million dollars," Schneider responded. "I think I can make three of them for that," Davis replied. He gave CBS his notice and moved out to Los Angeles in the summer of 1972.

Schneider originally intended to build the movie around the Ellsberg trial, interviewing witnesses for each side as they came out to Los Angeles.[76] Davis quickly determined that this was impractical: even the defense, much less the prosecution, was uninterested in allowing a documentary crew access to their witnesses. Davis also eased Hayden out from the consulting role Schneider envisioned, but even as he dropped his producer's ideas, he found Schneider a stirring partner. "He was an inspirer," Davis said. "Everybody who worked for him— Dennis Hopper, Peter Bogdanovich, even Bob himself—did their best work for BBS." Davis found a description from Rafelson apt: Schneider didn't know filmmaking, but he knew filmmakers. "When he saw somebody he thought he had faith in, [his view was] 'All right, let that guy do it,'" Davis said.

To construct the film, Davis focused his reporting on three questions: Why did we go to Vietnam? What did we do there to the Vietnamese? What did that in turn do to us?[77] Shortly after Nixon's reelection in November 1972, Davis and the crew flew to Vietnam for about six weeks of filming. On his first day there, addled with jet lag, he had the insight that shaped the film.[78] With his researcher, he was in the small village of Hung Dinh, viewing a giant crater from a bomb that American planes had dropped there. He could see the remains of a bicycle wrapped around a tree, colorful shards of a cooking bowl, severed limbs from a child's doll. He thought about how he would film this scene if he were still at CBS. He might start with a close-up on the bicycle, pull back for the bowl and the doll, and then, after about ten or twelve seconds of silent images, settle on a correspondent, a white man who looked like him, standing in pressed fatigues and explaining in measured tones what the viewers had just seen. At CBS, the seconds of silence were considered "dead air," because the goal was to reach the authoritative voice of the correspondent as soon as possible. But Davis thought the reassuring figure of the correspondent would lift the viewers out of the war. He decided to flip the equation and eliminate any narration. "I was like, 'Okay, I'm going to make two hours of "dead air" and see what happens,'" he said.[79]

When Davis returned to the States to continue filming, he wrote letters to key officials who had planned and executed the war. Three agreed to interviews: Clark Clifford, the former defense secretary under Lyndon Johnson, who had become a critic; Walt Rostow, LBJ's second national security adviser; and retired general William Westmoreland, the former commander of American forces in Vietnam. The meeting with Westmoreland in June 1973 was Davis's final interview for the film and the most memorable. He flew with the crew to Westmoreland's home in Charleston, South Carolina, where the general was mulling whether to run for governor. Davis first had to talk him down—Westmoreland was threatening to pull out of the interview because his aides thought *The Selling of the Pentagon* had been unfair to the military. Davis reluctantly agreed to let the general review anything used in the movie, in case he said something he didn't exactly mean. Upon those rules, the interview proceeded, with Davis leading the general through detailed questions he had sequenced on a legal pad. Then he asked Tom Cohen, a documentary director himself, who was working on the crew as a sound engineer, if he had anything to ask the general.[80] Cohen looked at Westmoreland and asked an ingenuous question: I've been in the U.S. Army, he said, so I have an idea what American soldiers are like, but I don't know what the Vietnamese soldiers are like. Can you explain them? Westmoreland answered, "The Oriental doesn't put the same high price on life as does the Westerner." Davis and Cohen were both stunned, and then terrified when the film ran out as Westmoreland was answering. They reloaded and repeated the question, and Westmoreland said the same thing with only slightly different phrasing. Suddenly, the general yelled, "Cut!" and stopped talking. Davis remembers thinking, Surely now he will come to his senses. But Westmoreland then repeated the sentiment a third time. Davis had the signature moment of his film.

After a summer spent just sorting and cataloguing the two hundred hours of film he had shot, Davis began in the fall of 1973 to shape the mass into a rough cut. It was now almost eighteen months since Schneider had hired him, but the producer still had not asked to see anything. "He was one floor above us," Davis recalled. "I don't remember him ever coming into the screening room."[81] Finally, Schneider asked for a look. He arranged a screening at BBS for the afternoon of Christmas Eve 1973, for about fifty friends from politics and Hollywood.[82] The showing was a disaster. Davis's rough cut was five and a half hours long, still unstructured, "an almost random assemblage of footage we had culled from the 200 hours that we had shot," Davis later recalled.[83] Leaving the screening, Stanley Sheinbaum turned to his wife, Betty, in the elevator and said simply, "That was forever." Schneider offered a six-word verdict: "It's incredible, but it's a mess."[84]

More editing and more screenings followed through the early months of 1974. After one of them, with the film still unfocused, a director friend of Schneider's confronted Davis about the stakes in fixing Hollywood's first real attempt to grapple with Vietnam on film.

"We're only getting one crack at this," the director told Davis, "and you're blowing it." Davis couldn't disagree.[85]

But gradually the film took shape. Davis's brother-in-law, Frank Mankiewicz, a top Democratic operative, suggested the title *Hearts and Minds*, drawn from President Johnson's frequent declarations that the United States could not win the war without winning the hearts and minds of the Vietnamese people. (Johnson had a saltier, private variation on the saying: when you've got someone by the balls, he liked to say, their heart and mind will follow.) By March, Davis had pared the film down to about two hours, and it was accepted for the Cannes Film Festival in May. Through the spring, Davis moved with growing confidence to finish the movie, but as the film solidified, Schneider's relationship with Columbia Pictures deteriorated.

After big losses, Schneider's brother Stanley was forced out as Columbia's president in June 1973, and their father, Abe, was sidelined into the ceremonial position of honorary chairman. The new regime, led by Alan Hirschfield and David Begelman (a former agent later toppled in a celebrated forgery scandal), didn't like the unique deal Schneider had wrangled from his family members at Columbia and moved to cancel its contract with BBS.[86] The studio became even more uneasy when Schneider finally showed them the film in the spring of 1974, a few weeks before Cannes. According to Schneider, Begelman called him just hours after the screening to complain that the company could face reprisals from its bankers if it distributed a movie so critical of the war.[87]

The prospect that Columbia would ever release the film grew more remote with each passing month. Then tragedy struck Davis: in July his wife, Johanna, was killed when two taxis collided outside their apartment in Greenwich Village and one jumped the curb, striking her. The future of *Hearts and Minds* remained very uncertain in August 1974, when Schneider was suddenly swamped by a crisis engulfing his other great passion, Huey Newton and the Black Panthers.

HUEY NEWTON ALWAYS LIVED on the edge, but in the summer of 1974, he spiraled entirely out of control. Heavily using cocaine and increasingly paranoid, in July he exiled Bobby Seale from the party (in part because of disputes over a movie Newton wanted Schneider to produce) after physically attacking Seale at a meeting of the Panthers' Central Committee.[88] A few days later, on July 30, 1974, Newton ordered his massive, six-foot-eight, four-hundred-pound bodyguard, Bob Heard, to shoot two plainclothes police officers he believed were following him; Newton and the bodyguard were arrested that night. Out on bail, Newton on August 6 shot a teenage prostitute in Oakland after he flew into a rage over her come-on line, "Hey, baby," which reminded him of a hated childhood nickname ("Baby Huey"). More violence followed in the middle of the month. First, he beat two women who angered him at one of the after-hours clubs the Panthers controlled.[89] Then, on August 17, Newton brutally pistol-whipped an African American tailor he had summoned to his lakefront penthouse suite to fit him for some suits.[90] The tailor's wife called the police, who arrested Newton in his penthouse. While doing so, they found evidence tying him to the August 6 shooting of the prostitute, who would die later that fall.[91] Newton again posted bail on both charges, but on August 23, he failed to show for his scheduled court appearance and headed south. The strange saga of Huey Newton and what the participants sometimes called "the Beverly Hills Seven" had begun.

Dressed as a woman, Newton showed up at Schneider's door late one evening, shortly after he skipped his court appearance. At this point, he faced criminal charges for multiple acts of violence, his attacks on the Black tailor and the teenage prostitute, who could hardly have been described as enemies of the revolution. Nothing explained the attacks beyond Newton's own rage and arrogance, but when he arrived at Schneider's house, the producer didn't hesitate. Both personally and politically, Schneider had grown so deeply attached to Newton that he never questioned the morality of helping him escape. He arranged for his partner Steve Blauner, who was also close with Newton, to transport the fugitive to Yelapa, Mexico, a remote island off Puerta Vallarta where Schneider had a small house—some described it as merely a hut—on a larger property owned by Benny Shapiro, an avuncular-looking but shrewd music manager best known for representing Miles Davis.[92] Then Schneider started searching for a way to permanently resettle Newton in Cuba.

At that point, the operation became a comic opera. "These guys fantasize about being Navy SEALs," recalled Bill Zimmerman, the veteran antiwar activist soon enlisted for his skills as a pilot. "They're all macho guys who think that because they've been a success in the movie business, they can do anything, and it was nuts. It was a clown show in many ways."[93]

Nimble in the music business, Benny Shapiro was quickly in over his head in the field of fugitive exfiltration. He located a Cuban pilot in Los Angeles whom he recruited to fly Newton from Mexico to Havana. (By one account, he found the pilot through his coke dealer.)[94] What Shapiro didn't realize, Zimmerman quickly came to understand, was that any Cuban in Los Angeles was an exile who hated Castro, what the revolutionaries called a *gusano*, or "worm."[95] Once Shapiro revealed the mission to the pilot, he backed out, while complaining that he still expected the money Shapiro had promised him. Shapiro, who considered himself a tough negotiator, brushed off the pilot and next put Schneider in touch with a Mafioso in Las Vegas who smuggled pot from Mexico in a small plane. But the mobster also backed out when he learned the details of the assignment.[96]

That's when Schneider learned that Zimmerman, the veteran activist working for Hayden, was a pilot. Schneider called Fonda, who talked to her husband, which is how Zimmerman found himself, late one afternoon about two weeks after Nixon's resignation, standing on the corner of Pico Boulevard and Ocean Avenue in Santa Monica waiting for Tom Hayden to pull up in his light-blue Volkswagen Beetle. Zimmerman stuffed his lanky frame into the car's backseat because there was a woman he didn't know sitting next to Hayden in the front, and Hayden pulled away and started driving along Main Street.

Hayden was not enthusiastic about joining the cast of Schneider's "movie." His relations with Schneider, despite their shared interests, had cooled, but Hayden had strongly supported the Black Panthers and viewed Newton as an important symbol. Zimmerman agreed but told Hayden he would not fly into Cuban airspace without ironclad assurances from Castro's government that it would not shoot him down.[97] Hayden said he figured as much, which is why he had brought along the woman in the front seat. She was Joan Andersson, the activist attorney who had been Hayden's first girlfriend after he washed up in Venice and who had some previous contacts with the Cuban government. They agreed that Andersson would fly to New York City to seek permission for the flight from Cuban officials at the United Nations, while Zimmerman would travel to the Valley to explain the situation to Schneider.

Schneider was hiding over the hill in the Valley because the situation between Shapiro and the *gusanos* had deteriorated. The Cubans were demanding the money that Shapiro had promised them and threatening him and Schneider if they didn't get it. Schneider arranged for the Black Panthers in Oakland to send down some "soldiers" to protect his house and also to guard Shapiro.[98] While Schneider went to hide at his friend's apartment in the Valley, Shapiro tried to defuse the situation with the Cubans. He arranged for a sit-down at Canter's Delicatessen, on Fairfax Avenue, in the heart of LA's historic Jewish neighborhood. In case of trouble, Shapiro brought two of the Panther "soldiers" to sit at another table. Shapiro later told Zimmerman that one of the Cubans became so incensed when he refused their demands for the money that he pulled a gun under the table; when Shapiro grabbed for the gun, it went off, sending a bullet into the ceiling. After the Cubans left, he was livid at his Black Panther bodyguards, who had remained motionless through the entire episode. "Where the fuck were you?" Shapiro erupted at them. "You're supposed to be here to protect me." The Panthers explained that because they didn't realize the meeting would be so confrontational, they weren't "dressed" for it, meaning they were not carrying guns.

Zimmerman, meanwhile, had found Schneider in the Valley, and the two developed a plan. Zimmerman explained that he would need to buy a plane for a one-way flight to Cuba. Schneider agreed to foot the bill. He explained that Andersson needed to travel to New York to obtain permission from the Cuban government for the flight. Schneider said he would fund her travel expenses as well.[99] For the next few days, Schneider and Zimmerman waited. The *gusanos* gradually backed off when it became clear that Schneider would not pay them and that he had also acquired formidable protection from the Panthers. But Andersson returned from New York with a mixed message. The bad news was the Cuban government would not provide permission for Zimmerman to fly Newton to the island. (Cuban officials worried about allowing a fugitive to arrive by air at a time of intense international concern over plane hijackings.) The consolation was that they would accept him if he arrived there by other means. As Zimmerman refused to fly under these circumstances, the crew started searching for a way to move Newton by boat.

Enter Artie Ross. Ross was a friend and protégé of Schneider's who was currently working for him on a documentary Schneider was producing about Charlie Chaplin. More relevant to Schneider's immediate needs, Ross, with a friend, had built a three-hulled boat called a trimaran a few years earlier and sailed her through the Panama Canal from California to Miami, where she was sitting at a dock.[100] This put the boat in a good position to execute the plan Zimmerman had developed for moving Newton. Zimmerman had once lived on the island of Cozumel, off the east coast of Mexico, and he explained to Schneider that if they transported Newton there from Yelapa, on Mexico's Pacific side, it would be relatively easy to sail him to Cuba. Schneider asked Ross to take Newton from Cozumel to Cuba in his trimaran, and Ross agreed. With Schneider's money, Ross upgraded his boat, adding sonar, radar, and a diesel engine.[101] But when he set out from Miami to Mexico, the boat snagged on a giant underwater statue of Jesus off Key West and sank.[102] Ross barely made it back to shore.

The *Mission: Impossible* team, this wasn't. Zimmerman and Andersson, who were falling in love amid the chaos (and later married), watched with a mixture of bemusement and horror. "As the plan unfolded, we were trying to make it more doable, more practical," Zimmerman remembered. "But every night, we'd go home and say, 'These people are crazy.'" Still, Schneider was nothing if not tenacious. He regrouped, recognizing that Newton was growing more volatile during his long hideout in Mexico. Schneider scrambled and finally found a

Swedish marijuana smuggler in Miami who agreed to scoop up Newton and his girlfriend, Gwen Fontaine (later his wife), in his sailboat
and transport them to Cuba.

The smuggler, not surprisingly, was another eccentric: he never
revealed his name to anyone involved and called himself only "the
Pirate." He found Newton and Fontaine without incident in Mexico
and set out for Cuba, but there were more misadventures to come.
When the boat reached the mouth of Havana harbor, the Pirate explained that he would sail no closer. He put Newton and Fontaine in a
small inflatable motorized boat and pointed them toward land, about
twelve miles away. That was the moment Newton chose to reveal that
he didn't know how to swim and had never been in a boat before. The
smuggler gave him some rudimentary instructions and sailed away.
Newton pointed the boat toward land, but he couldn't navigate the
gusty winds. The boat drifted miles off course and then capsized in
the surf. All their luggage sank. When Newton and Fontaine struggled onto the shore, drenched and breathless, they were surrounded
by soldiers with guns: they had wandered into a Cuban military facility. Newton revealed his identity, but when Cuban officials tried to
confirm it with another Black Panther already living in Cuba, the Panther refused to do so because he was an ally of Eldridge Cleaver, whom
Newton had exiled from the party. Newton and Fontaine spent a week
in jail before Cuban authorities finally corroborated Newton's identity
with the Panthers' lawyer in San Francisco.[103] Only then could Bert
Schneider exhale.

ABOUT THE TIME SCHNEIDER spirited Newton to Mexico in late
August, he also submitted the completed film *Hearts and Minds* to
Columbia.[104] The response remained frosty. More legal and public re-
lations skirmishing between the two sides followed through the fall.
Doubts grew over whether the movie, despite its strong critical buzz,
would ever be released. "First an Undeclared War, Now an Unseen
Film," insisted the *New York Times* in a November 1974 article.[105] To
Davis, still in shock over the death of his wife, Schneider never wavered.
"I think he loved being in the scrap," Davis remembered. "First of

all, he liked [the movie], and secondly, he loved thumbing his nose at Hollywood.[106] Finally, Schneider concluded that the only way to save the movie was to buy it back from Columbia, but for that, he needed a million dollars he didn't have. He found the funds from an unexpected source: Henry Jaglom, the eccentric writer, director, and occasional actor. At BBS, Schneider had financed Jaglom's first movie, the ethereal if often incomprehensible *A Safe Place*, which had flopped so badly that, for years, Jaglom was unable to secure studio financing for anything else he proposed. So, his business partner Zack Norman had raised a million in small amounts "from doctors and dentists" looking for a tax shelter to fund Jaglom's second movie.[107] Ironically, that movie, called *Tracks*, dealt with a returning Vietnam veteran (ultimately played by Dennis Hopper). But when Schneider told him about the impasse with Columbia over *Hearts and Minds*, Jaglom used his million to buy back the movie.[108] Warner Bros. agreed to step in and distribute the film. Finally, on December 20, *Hearts and Minds* opened in Westwood, just in time to qualify for Academy Award consideration.[109]

Some reviewers found it heavy-handed and simplistic in its condemnation of the war—"We're bludgeoned by the point of view," wrote Roger Ebert.[110] "We don't like the feeling of manipulation we get"—but mostly the response was powerful. Vincent Canby, the *New York Times*'s influential film critic, called it "one of the most all-encompassing records of the American civilization ever put into one film" and included it on his Top 10 list for the year.[111] Another *New York Times* writer predicted that *Hearts and Minds* could become the American equivalent of *The Sorrow and the Pity*, the titanic French documentary about collaboration with the Nazis.[112]

When *Hearts and Minds* received an Oscar nomination for Best Documentary, Schneider realized he might have a giant worldwide television audience to address on the awards broadcast. A few days before the ceremony, he reached out to Cora Weiss, the prominent peace activist, to ask the Vietcong to send a message that he or Davis could read from the stage if *Hearts and Minds* won, as most people in Hollywood expected. Weiss solicited a telegram for Schneider from Dinh Ba Thi, the Vietcong's chief delegate to the Paris peace talks.

Peter Davis knew none of this. Since his wife's death the previous summer, he had minimized his time apart from his children and didn't arrive in Los Angeles until the day of the Oscars ceremony, on April 8, 1975. Davis went directly from the airport to the BBS offices on La Brea Avenue. There Schneider showed him the telegram and asked him to read it from the stage if they won. Davis looked it over and refused. "I made a film that doesn't have any narration," he told Schneider. "This is a little bit of a narration."[113] A few hours later, *Hearts and Minds* won the Academy Award for Best Documentary (on the same night *The Godfather Part II* swept past *Chinatown* for most of the major awards). Accepting the statuette, Davis made a few graceful remarks, thanking the crew, remembering his wife, and telling his two young sons back in New York to "go to bed now."[114] Then Schneider, resplendent in a three-piece white tuxedo, his curly hair piled on his head, stepped up to the microphone. First, he thanked his brother Stanley, who had been deposed as Columbia's president almost two years earlier and then died of a heart attack in January. Then he observed that "it is ironic" for *Hearts and Minds* to receive the award "at a time just before Vietnam is about to be liberated." Next, he read the telegram from the man he described as "Ambassador Dinh Ba Thi." The text itself was anodyne: "Please transmit to all of our friends in America our recognition of all they have done on behalf of peace . . . ," but as Schneider recognized, it was an incendiary act to transmit a message from a foreign power that was still at war against the South Vietnamese government allied with the United States and to present the impending defeat of that ally as a "liberation."[115]

Sure enough, Schneider's gambit stirred a flurry of action backstage. Bob Hope, the host, and Frank Sinatra, who was there as a presenter, huddled in outrage. Hope quickly scribbled a brief statement disassociating the Academy from Schneider's remarks, which Sinatra read from the stage. Some in the crowd booed.[116] Warren Beatty, who had just presented the Best Picture Award, mumbled under his breath to Sinatra, "You old Republican, you."[117]

The exchange between Schneider, the drug-taking pioneer of the new Hollywood, and Hope and Sinatra, two aging conservatives from the whiskey-and-soda generation, seemed like a final skirmish between the forces of change and tradition that had shaken Hollywood at the turn of the 1970s. But, in fact, both sides of the confrontation had passed their peak influence. This was less obvious for the youthful Schneider than for Hope and Sinatra, but the moment when *Hearts and Minds* won the documentary Oscar was the last true high point of Schneider's career, though he was only forty-one at the time. His decision to read the telegram was a mistake that would shadow Davis's movie. Warner Bros. pushed Davis to hold a painful press conference the next week, to insist that the film wasn't a propaganda vehicle for the North Vietnamese.[118] Later, Davis regretted that he had not fought harder to prevent Schneider from reading the telegram. The *Hearts and Minds* Oscar was also a coda for BBS: by the time Schneider claimed the award, the firm had dissolved. Rafelson wanted to make his own films. Schneider wanted to focus on politics. At that point, he "was [a] full-out revolutionary," Bob Rafelson recalled. "That's what he wanted to do. It was another phase in his life."[119]

Initially, Schneider tried to maintain his connection to Hollywood. Shortly after the Academy Awards, he completed his documentary on Charlie Chaplin. It was well received but not a major cultural event like the early BBS films. Schneider's first attempt at producing a mainstream movie after BBS was a fraught affair. *Days of Heaven* garnered acclaim and is now considered a classic, but the film went way over budget and provoked epic battles between Schneider and director Terrence Malick. Schneider produced only one more movie, and then, a dozen years after he revolutionized the movie industry with *Easy Rider*, his career as a producer was over.

Schneider retained his political interests even as his ties to the movie business frayed. In the 1980s he traveled to Nicaragua and hosted Daniel Ortega, the leader of the revolutionary Sandinistas, at his house in Los Angeles. He also stuck by Newton after he returned from Cuba in July 1977 to face trial for his 1974 crimes. (Though Newton beat the charges against him, he never regained his earlier prominence and was killed on an Oakland street in 1989 by two crack dealers from whom he had earlier stolen drugs.)[120] But Schneider didn't have the discipline or insight ever to become as effective a political force as Hayden or Fonda or even the mainstream Los Angeles liberals he disparaged. "His identity was always with that of the revolutionary," said Toby Rafelson, "but his intellect and his potential for rational thoughts and compassion was stunted from an early age on."[121]

Schneider's behavior over time became more volatile, more destabilized by drugs. He grew isolated from friends and even his family. "Bert went further than any of us, and it was combined with drugs and psychedelics . . . and he became more and more crazy," said Jaglom. "That's the only way to put it. He became more and more distrustful of everybody, paranoid. He didn't speak to me for the last thirty years of his life. It was terrible, because I loved this man more than I loved any man in my life besides my father and brother."[122] As Schneider spiraled into deeper disarray, Jack Nicholson became virtually the only one of his old friends he trusted. "Jack was the only one, finally, who could deal with Bert," said Jaglom. "When something was needed, Jack was there."[123]

By the time Schneider died in 2011, relatively few Hollywood powers remembered him, and for those who did, he was a cautionary tale. In his rise, he embodied the most glittering promise that Los Angeles sold in the early 1970s: the possibility of liberation from every rule, the chance to transcend both the numbness of corporate hierarchy and the constraints of conventional morality and monogamy. At the peak of his power, wealth, and glamour, Schneider was a sunburst, but in his long fall, all that melted away. He was destroyed by the promise of unlimited freedom that beat down on Los Angeles as unstintingly as its desert sun. For the generation that transformed movies, music, and television, Bert Schneider lived and died as the Icarus of Los Angeles.

9

SEPTEMBER

Three Roads to Revolution

The revolution that CBS president Robert Wood and producer Norman Lear ignited when they collaborated to bring *All in the Family* to the airwaves in January 1971 reached the peak of its influence in the television season that began in September 1974. From Los Angeles, a small group of producers, writers, directors, and stars generated a torrent of smart and funny comedies that not only drew high ratings and (mostly) critical acclaim, but also connected viewers to the changes unfolding around them far more than only a few years earlier. In a manner that had been almost completely absent during the 1960s, the present again became present on television.

Once *All in the Family* and *Mary Tyler Moore* achieved even modest traction with viewers during their first season, Wood moved rapidly to complete the overhaul of the network that he began in 1970. With Michael Dann, who had resisted the changes, replaced by Fred Silverman, who embraced them, Wood took a scythe to CBS's desiccated fields of older, rural shows. In March 1971 he announced the cancellation of thirteen shows, including *The Beverly Hillbillies*, *Hee Haw*, *Green Acres*, *Hogan's Heroes*, and *Mayberry R.F.D.* Even *Ed Sullivan*, after twenty-three years on the air, got the hook.[1]

Much of what replaced CBS's aging, rural lineup also proved instantly forgettable, but CBS accumulated a growing roster of sparkling comedies that opened a window onto contemporary life. In 1972 came *Maude*, an *All in the Family* spin-off starring Bea Arthur as Edith Bunker's liberal cousin; the brilliant war comedy M*A*S*H, created by producer Gene Reynolds and writer Larry Gelbart; and *The Bob Newhart Show*, developed by MTM Enterprises. In 1974 came *Rhoda*, a *Mary Tyler Moore* spin-off that returned Valerie Harper's acerbic character to her native New York City; and *Good Times*, which moved Florida, Maude's African American maid, played by Esther Rolle, to Chicago. (In the genealogy of television spin-offs, this made Archie Bunker a grandfather.) *The Jeffersons*, yet another *All in the Family* spin-off, featuring the Bunkers' African American neighbors who had moved up "to a de-luxe apartment in the sky" (as the theme song had it), joined them in January 1975. Other networks followed down the same path. *Sanford and Son*, adapted by Lear and Bud Yorkin from another British comedy, reached the air on NBC in 1972, starring raunchy stand-up comic Redd Foxx. When that also proved a big hit, NBC followed with *Chico and the Man*, starring the electric young Hispanic comic Freddie Prinze, in 1974.

Over the 1974/75 season, these contemporary comedies dominated the television ratings. Lear alone had five shows in the top ten: *All in the Family* (first), *The Jeffersons* (fourth), *Good Times* (seventh), and *Maude* (ninth), all on CBS; *Sanford and Son*, for which Lear's partner, Bud Yorkin, served as day-to-day producer, finished second. *Chico and the Man* (whose run ended after only three seasons when Prinze committed suicide) ranked third that year. *M*A*S*H* finished fifth, *Rhoda* seventh, *Mary Tyler Moore* eleventh, and *Bob Newhart* seventeenth. Together these shows expanded the bandwidth of television comedy to encompass a much wider range of experiences and issues than it had ever before reflected. African American and Hispanic protagonists took their first steps onto center stage. So did shows about single women at least as focused on career as marriage. Characters debated the same issues viewers read about in the headlines. "Everybody was a little bit by the seat of their pants, which was really exciting, because you felt like you were breaking all this ground and doing stuff that had something to do with something," said Elliot Shoenman, who began his television career writing for *Maude*.[2]

For the pioneers of the new contemporary comedies, these were paradoxical years in Los Angeles. After years of despairing over television's banality, many critics swooned over the new generation of comedies. And with only three networks (and a modest public television option) dividing the audience, the best shows generated enormous viewership. Joan Darling, one of the first female directors to work regularly in television during the 1970s, remembers asking Norman Lear if he ever missed movies.[3] No, he told her, because the audience was so much bigger on television. *All in the Family* alone reached more than twenty million households and probably twice that many individual viewers a week.

But it was grueling work. Producing twenty-two, twenty-four, or even twenty-six episodes a year, the cast and crew of the major television shows sprinted to keep pace. "An ongoing series," Larry Gelbart, the brilliant comic writer behind *M*A*S*H*, once said, is "factory work."[4] Lear recalled that the writing staff for his shows would rarely have scripts finished more than three or four weeks before they were due to be filmed.

The shows that filmed before a live audience, such as *All in the Family* and *Mary Tyler Moore*, operated on an unforgiving schedule: one day to read the new script, three days to rehearse and revise it, and then one day to perform the show for the cameras and audience, before starting the process again. Nights were long. Barbara Gallagher, who worked as a production assistant on *Maude*, would routinely stay with the cast in the rehearsal hall until 9 p.m. and then meet with another secretary to retype changes to the scripts until nearly midnight. "Then I would go home and sleep and get up at five a.m. to go meet Norman [Lear] at CBS to go over the script and take it down to the rehearsal hall for the next day." The rewriting process was endless. *All in the Family* always shot twice, before two separate audiences, so they could select the best bits from both performances; sometimes they even tweaked the script between tapings.

All the shows operated with very lean staffs. The typical pattern was for the producers and lead writers to develop the story ideas, hire freelance writers to flesh out the ideas, brutally rewrite the scripts the freelancers turned in, and then continue to rewrite through rehearsals as the cast learned what did and did not work.

The relentless pace of production meant that the television elite mostly lived and worked in a self-contained world that was completely isolated from the movie and music industries. Even the brightest lights on television recognized that compared to the stars and power brokers of Hollywood, they very much represented the kids' table in the Los Angeles hierarchy. Rob Reiner remembers looking up to movie stars such as Jack Nicholson and Warren Beatty as "gods" far beyond his reach. "I would see Warren Beatty, and . . . he was going out with Julie Christie at the time, and I'd be 'Oh my God, wow, just to be like that. Could I be that? Could I be in that world?' They were the royalty. We were peons." Despite the huge audiences, "there was a huge division between films and television," Reiner recalled. "If you did television, you couldn't do film. You were looked down upon."[5] Joan Darling, as a neophyte director, remembers absorbing the same warning. "A lot of people were afraid to do television because it meant they would never do movies," she said. "It was much, much harder."[6] Jodie Foster, as a child actress, starred for a year in an ABC adaptation of Peter Bogdanovich's film *Paper Moon* before crossing into films with Martin Scorsese for *Alice Doesn't Live Here Anymore* and *Taxi Driver*. She remembers her mother telling her she was fortunate the show was canceled because if it had been extended and marked her as a television actress, she never could have developed a film career. "You did not do TV," Foster said of young actors hoping to break into movies. "There was no feature actor that went over and did television ever. That would be acknowledging that your career was over."[7]

It wasn't only television actors and directors who felt as if they were on the wrong side of the velvet rope in Los Angeles. As a young agent handling television at William Morris into the early 1970s, Michael Ovitz could not even approach film agents in the company about possible opportunities for his clients. "They had a separate movie and television operation," he remembered. "You couldn't talk to a motion picture agent. They were above it all, and they had important clients."[8] As far as the people working on movies were concerned, "they weren't in the same business" as those producing television, recalls Barry Diller, who was unexpectedly plucked from his executive role at ABC and named as chairman and CEO of Paramount in September 1974. "Television people were plumbers, and movie people were artistes."[9]

EVEN NORMAN LEAR, THE most powerful producer on television, could not cross the divide. "I think back then TV was lower class," he said. "If you were writing for the screen, that was more important than writing for television. If you were directing for the screen, that was more important than television."[10] Through his political activism, Lear had grown friendly with movie stars as luminous as Warren Beatty, Burt Lancaster, and Paul Newman, yet it never occurred to him to ask them to guest star on any of his shows. For a writer, director, or actor "who was doing film, it was stepping down to do television," Lear said.[11] The biggest star ever to cameo on *All in the Family* was a past-his-prime Sammy Davis Jr., who appeared in a celebrated episode where he plants a kiss on Archie Bunker's cheek.

Yet only the very finest Hollywood movies matched the best television in capturing America's evolving attitudes and shifting fault lines in the early 1970s. Three shows above all emerged as landmarks in television's transformation: *All in the Family, Mary Tyler Moore,* and *M*A*S*H*. Each was part of the renaissance at CBS driven by Wood and Silverman. Each attracted huge audiences and shelves full of awards.

But while the three shows are forever linked in television history, they displayed very different personalities. *M*A*S*H*, under Larry Gelbart and star Alan Alda, was vaudeville, rapid-fire and knowing, the equivalent of Groucho Marx riffing on Vietnam through the guise of Korea. Led by writer/producers Allan Burns and especially James L. Brooks, *Mary Tyler Moore* was gentler, character driven, and like its star, much more reserved: its changes were subtle and internal, and its commentary tightly focused, less concerned with swelling social changes than with the daily abrasions of human interaction. *All in the Family* was the steamroller, reflecting Lear's restless ambition and pile-driving determination. For all the brilliance of *Mary Tyler Moore* and *M*A*S*H*, it is difficult to imagine either achieving its ratings success or cultural impact without *All in the Family* clearing the path. "Once we had digested *All in the Family*," Jack Schneider, a senior CBS executive, said later, "nothing else was an issue."[12]

Each show represented a different way in which television finally connected to the changes unfolding around it. Together, for the small screen, they represented three roads to revolution.

M*A*S*H HAD A SMOOTHER path to the air than either *Mary Tyler Moore* or *All in the Family*. The commercial and critical success of the M*A*S*H movie, directed by Robert Altman in 1970, made the series something of a pretested proposition. When Fox decided to adapt the film for television, it assigned the show to Gene Reynolds, a former child actor and television director who had recently transitioned into producing with his pathbreaking ABC show about an integrated Los Angeles high school, *Room 222*.

Thoughtful and meticulous, Reynolds made two critical decisions that allowed M*A*S*H to blend comedy and drama to greater effect than any television show before it (or, for that matter, almost any since). The first was in selecting a writer. Reynolds's first choice was Ring Lardner Jr., a member of the formerly blacklisted Hollywood Ten, who wrote the movie's screenplay.[13] When Lardner passed on the project, Reynolds remembered an old friend, Larry Gelbart. At that point, Gelbart was not an obvious choice: he had not worked in American television or even lived in the United States for nearly a decade, but in the fraternity of television comedy writers, he was revered; Norman Lear, for one, considered him the wittiest of all.

Born in Chicago in 1928, Gelbart was a true prodigy: he was writing regularly for network radio programs while still in high school and was hired as a gag writer for Bob Hope before he turned twenty-one.[14] From Hope, Gelbart jumped to the legendary television writing staff for Sid Caesar, and after a relatively short stint there, he devoted much of the late 1950s to writing his play *A Funny Thing Happened on the Way to the Forum*, with songs by Stephen Sondheim. After *Forum* won the Tony in 1962 for Best Musical, Gelbart, burned out by the television business, moved to London to help supervise a 1963 production of the show there. He stayed the next nine years, keeping busy by writing and producing a show for the frantic British comedian Marty Feldman. But when Reynolds approached him with *M*A*S*H*, Gelbart was ready for something meatier. Familiar with the networks' succession of antiseptic war comedies during the 1960s (*Hogan's Heroes*, *McHale's Navy*), he had only one concern: while America was still fighting in Vietnam, he didn't want to work on a show that would "trivialize that effort by simply doing another gang comedy set in an army background."[15] Reynolds assured him he felt the same way.

The other key decision Reynolds made was casting Alan Alda, as the show's lead character, the charismatic surgeon Benjamin Franklin "Hawkeye" Pierce. Reynolds viewed Hawkeye as a tough balance: highly literate but impertinent. Alda, who had built a respected career in television, films, and the stage without achieving a true breakout role, offered just that combination of intelligence and irreverence. He initially expressed the same hesitation Gelbart had: with Vietnam still burning, he didn't want to enlist in *McHale's Navy*. Reynolds and Gelbart assured him that wasn't their intent. Both men, in fact, on their most philosophical days, saw the show as something of an existential dilemma, albeit with a lot more jokes: under grueling conditions, the mobile army surgical hospital's doctors labored to repair wounded young soldiers so they could return to the fight and risk death or maiming again. The surgeons were Sisyphus with a scalpel. "What we wanted . . . was to do a show which fundamentally had as its subtext the wastefulness of war," Reynolds said.[16]

With this underpinning, the show's contemporary echoes were impossible to miss, especially in its early years, while American troops remained in Vietnam. Gelbart, in fact, saw the show as a way for him to comment on the war after sitting out the protest movement of the 1960s while living in London, an interlude he called his "hiatus of conscience." "I wasn't very active in expressing my feelings about the war, except for the odd demonstration [by the American embassy] in Grosvenor Square, which hardly counts," he later told sociologist Todd Gitlin. "I was drawn toward something that would let me get this sort of tardy . . . negative vote in."[17]

M*A*S*H was a relatively peaceful oasis. It debuted on September 17, 1972, only about seven weeks before Richard Nixon's landslide reelection. After struggling its first year on Sunday night (when it was ground down between two shows that symbolized Nixon's "silent majority" consensus, ABC's *The FBI* and NBC's *Wonderful World of Disney*), *M*A*S*H* thrived as soon as it was placed between *All in the Family* and *Mary Tyler Moore* on the brilliant 1973/74 CBS Saturday night. From the outset, the critical response mostly ranged between enthusiastic and reverential. *Newsweek*, in the most famous review, declared, "Without ever moralizing *M*A*S*H* is the most moral entertainment on commercial television. It proposes craft against butchery, humor against despair, wit as a defense mechanism against the senseless enormity of the situation."[18] Critics quickly recognized and lauded the show as an evolutionary advance for the situation comedy. CBS frustrated the cast and crew by hopscotching *M*A*S*H* across different nights, deploying it like a search-and-destroy missile against shows displaying strength on the other networks, but its ratings were stellar anywhere it landed.

Reynolds and Gelbart had strong opinions but weren't as controlling as Lear. Both believed deeply in research; they collected hundreds of interviews with veterans of the conflict and visited Korea after the second season.[19] When Mike Farrell, who played surgeon B. J. Hunnicutt during the show's final eight seasons, joined the cast, Reynolds and Gelbart presented him with a thick book of interviews from doctors, nurses, and soldiers who had served not only in Korea but also in Vietnam.[20]

The cast remembers Gelbart as a genial presence who would bike down to the set from his office on the Fox lot whenever they needed to untangle a knot in the script.[21] Much like Lear with *All in the Family*, Gelbart with *M*A*S*H* found a voice more urgent and contemporary than he had ever displayed before. When Reynolds offered him what he called the "soapbox" of *M*A*S*H*, Gelbart said, "that let me combine what was obviously a dormant letter to the editor writer with . . . something that turned into a commercial success."[22] Gelbart was still brilliantly witty, but with *M*A*S*H*, he anchored that wit in a deeper recognition of life's absurdities, indignities, and inescapable losses. "A lot of those writers who came out of Sid Caesar and the Catskills comedians—they were not capable of doing anything but shtick," said Linda Bloodworth-Thomason, who wrote or cowrote five *M*A*S*H* episodes. "Larry could immediately come up with the most hilarious line that you would want to write down. People talk about the Algonquin [Round Table and its witticisms]. Larry said twenty-five of those a day. I don't care what you were talking about, he always had the best line. But . . . he was able to emerge so much beyond that."[23]

Key to that deepening was the intense connection between Gelbart and Alda. "They were into one another's head completely," Reynolds recalled.[24] Together the two men created in Hawkeye an iconic, if idealized, character. Though Gelbart and Alda had each been born well before World War II, Hawkeye embodied everything the liberal Baby Boomers thought best about themselves: he was smart, humane, highly competent, and driven by a deep personal sense of morality even as he displayed witty contempt for mindless bureaucracy, outdated rules, and rigid social strictures. Through a show set in the 1950s, he appealingly combined the suspicion of authority that germinated in the 1960s with the sensitivity that the women's movement increasingly demanded of men in the 1970s, especially as the show dialed back Hawkeye's womanizing after the first few seasons. Hawkeye was never afraid to fight authority or to show his emotions. Yet he was the wizard whom all his colleagues looked to in the toughest cases, not Maj. Frank Burns, his by-the-book bunkmate committed to traditional conceptions of patriotism and masculinity (though the show loaded the dice so much that Frank's efforts always ended in farce). Frank's lover, Margaret "Hot Lips" Houlihan (the head nurse played by Loretta Swit), was another stickler for protocol, yet even she turned to Hawkeye, not Frank, at moments of crisis in the operating room. Hawkeye was freer *and* better, exactly what the liberal side of the Baby Boom considered itself to be.

Alda, the show's undisputed center, set an inclusive tone. He was professional and grounded: during the show's eleven-year run, he flew home to New Jersey every weekend because he didn't want to uproot his family. In a process that seemed more a natural progression than an expression of star prerogative, he expanded from acting to also writing and directing. He did not have Carroll O'Connor's animosities about whether the show revolved enough around him or whether he was receiving enough credit for its success. "I always think of him as a very generous actor because he understood that while Hawkeye was the primary character in the show—which is why Wayne [Rogers] left, I'm sure—everybody really had to be developed, every character had to be given his shot, every character had to be full," said Farrell, whose character essentially replaced Wayne Rogers's Trapper John. "He made sure that happened because it could have gone another way. It could have been 'The Alan Alda Show,' which in fact it was in a way. But it was far more the group, 'The MASH,' than 'The Alan Alda Show.'"[25]

Nor did the show have too many conflicts with the network. After *All in the Family*, CBS was like a parent who doesn't have the stomach to reprise fights with the eldest son when a younger sibling comes along. On the big questions, Gelbart said CBS didn't challenge the lampooning of military authority or ask to dilute the unmistakable antiwar message.[26] "The most radical thing we did, obviously, was that we did a show that was against war while this country was at war," Gelbart reflected later.[27] And as the show became more successful, any network objections diminished in direct proportion. "They were eating out of our hands," Gelbart acknowledged.[28]

Still, CBS sometimes recoiled at the show's sharper edges. Reynolds and Gelbart were both determined to spike the comedy with stark reminders of the costs and futility of war. "We were always being urged by the network to keep it funny, . . . 'Nobody's really interested in that . . . sober stuff,'" Reynolds remembered being told.[29] Gelbart said, "We always fought for the right to make the show not less funny, but more serious, even while perhaps becoming funnier."[30] Both men were determined to skitter along the tightrope between comedy and drama.

Their intention may have first become fully apparent during the seventeenth episode of the first season, entitled "Sometimes You Hear the Bullet." That one episode functioned as a microcosm of their ambitions for the overall series. It started with pure sitcom slapstick between Frank and Margaret, but it turned sharply when a childhood friend of Hawkeye's, Tommy Gillis (played by James Callahan), appears in camp. He's a journalist who has enlisted to fight so he can write a book about the war from the perspective of a solider, not a correspondent. Gillis explains to Hawkeye that the book will puncture the myths about war sold in movies—among them, that doomed soldiers always hear the bullet that will kill them. He plans to title his book, *You Never Hear the Bullet*. Gillis goes back to the front, and Hawkeye returns to his usual pursuits, chasing a nurse and treating a suspiciously young soldier (played by *Andy Griffith*'s Ron Howard, billed as "Ronny") recovering from an appendectomy. But Hawkeye is soon summoned back to the operating room, where a badly wounded Gillis is among the casualties. Gillis, his life fading, tells Hawkeye that in fact he *did* hear the bullet that hit him, and Hawkeye, growing anxious, tells him he can change the title of his book. Despite Hawkeye's frantic exertions, his friend dies on the table, the first time an identified character dies in the operating room during the show.

Later, Hawkeye is in anguish when Henry Blake, the camp commander played by McLean Stevenson, finds him. "It's the first time I've cried since I came to this lousy place," Hawkeye says. "I've watched guys die almost every day. Why didn't I cry for them?" Blake responds that in his command training, he learned that "there are certain rules about a war. And rule number one is 'Young men die.' And rule number two is 'Doctors can't change rule number one.'" Hawkeye realizes that he can save one life, and he outs Ron Howard's underage soldier, sending him back home despite his protests. In the final scene, Hawkeye and Trapper steal a Purple Heart Frank has conspired to receive fraudulently and give it to Howard's character so he'll have evidence of the heroism he thinks will win him back his lapsed girlfriend at home.

The episode is a kaleidoscope of situation comedy conventions (pratfalls at the start, the perfect bow connecting the stories at the end), unusually sophisticated emotion (not only Hawkeye's despair over his friend's death, but his numbing to the deaths of so many others), and stark moral declaration (Henry Blake's rules of war). At the end, it was reasonable for viewers to ask whether what they had just seen was comedy, tragedy, or some mutable compound of both.

Gelbart executed his nuanced vision perhaps most powerfully in the final episode of the 1974/75 season, "Abyssinia, Henry." When McLean Stevenson wanted off the show, Gelbart saw it as an opportunity to underline his core belief that *M*A*S*H* was, as he later put it, "not about happy endings."[31] Gelbart assigned writers Everett Greenbaum and Jim Fritzell (each of whose television credits extended back to *Mister Peepers*, in the early 1950s)[32] to develop a script in which Stevenson's Henry Blake was transferred home to much ribbing from the *M*A*S*H* staff.[33] Then, in the final scene, came the twist: Radar appears in the operating room to announce that Henry's plane has crashed in the Sea of Japan and that he is dead. Gelbart, who directed the episode, so wanted the news to be a surprise to the actors that he kept the final scene's script from the cast until moments before they shot it. (The emotion survived a camera snafu that compelled them to shoot the scene twice.)[34] Stevenson was so moved that he couldn't leave his trailer during the season wrap party that followed the filming.[35] Many viewers were shocked. On the night the episode aired, Reynolds, alone late in his office, answered the phone. On the other end was an irate viewer from New York City, who had seen the East Coast feed of the show.[36] She was outraged that Blake had died. "'I don't know why you did it,'" Reynolds recalled her insisting. "'It was not necessary. It's just a little comedy show. We sit and we laugh at the show. You did not have to do this.'" But it was precisely the ambition to create something more than "just a little comedy show" that had led Gelbart and Reynolds to kill off Henry Blake and to interject so many other darker moments into the show's antic laughs.

Gelbart, who left the show after one more season, came to worry that *M*A*S*H* was normalizing war.[37] Just by its longevity—the show would run eleven seasons, concluding in the Reagan administration—it seemed to suggest that with enough pluck and the right buddies, anything could be survived. It was a reasonable concern. *M*A*S*H* also dulled its political punch by positioning itself more against war in general than against any specific war: in *M*A*S*H*, the Korean conflict seemed less an expression of specific policy choices by individual political leaders than an expression of endemic human failures, more a natural disaster than a human-constructed catastrophe. And at times, its humor depended on the handy crutch of anachronism, with Alda, as the prototypical sensitive man from the 1970s, clashing with the unenlightened sensibilities of the 1950s. But even with those limitations, *M*A*S*H* represented a transformative leap from the military comedies that preceded it. It was as funny as any show on television in that or any other era—Gelbart was one of the few television writers who truly deserved the title of genius—but it never let audiences relax into the assumption that war was a laughing matter. It proved so consequential largely because it showed consequences that television had never before displayed.

NONE OF THE KEY figures who created *Mary Tyler Moore* had as clear a sense of mission as Reynolds and Gelbart, much less Lear. Mary Tyler Moore and her husband, the elegant entertainment executive Grant Tinker, just wanted to revive her career, which had been drifting downward since her star turn as Laura Petrie, Dick Van Dyke's vivacious wife on his eponymous CBS show during the early 1960s. Nor were Allan Burns and James L. Brooks, the writers and producers whom Tinker and Moore hired to develop the show, looking to make a statement about society or politics. "The issue was never the king," Brooks said later.[38] To the extent the two men had a goal, it was to create a show more attuned than conventional situation comedies to the ways people interacted in daily life and how that was changing in the 1970s. Their instinct was to pursue small truths, not big declarations. Ultimately, this modest goal carried Brooks and Burns to great heights, as their tightly focused look at a single woman navigating love and career in her thirties caught the tailwind of a social upheaval about gender roles and relations. If *M*A*S*H* brought the sixties critique of war to television, *Mary Tyler Moore* opened the medium to the new attitudes about the role of women that emerged from the decade—albeit almost always in a gentle and cautious manner.

Burns and Brooks had good reason to want something more connected to contemporary life. They had trudged through all the stations of the cross of insipid sixties television. Each man had taken a hard road to success. Burns, who was talented as both a writer and an artist, spent a few years working on the classic cartoon *Rocky and Bullwinkle.* Even though the show was witty enough to move into prime time around when Burns joined the staff, he understandably grew restless. "I didn't want to be, um, writing for a moose when I was forty-five years old," he remembered later.[39] But even when he graduated from animation, he didn't get much closer to Strindberg: the first two shows he developed (along with a partner) were *The Munsters* and *My Mother the Car.*

Brooks made his way to Hollywood with even less of a plan. After a turn in the news division at CBS in New York, he took a job in Los Angeles, at his wife's urging, working on documentaries for producer David Wolper. Writing comedy had long intrigued Brooks—he had taken playwriting workshops and writing classes—but it never appeared to him a practical option. "It had been a dream that I always had that I couldn't pursue," he remembered.[40] After the job for Wolper ended, necessity made it more practical: Brooks started submitting unsolicited scripts for shows such as *Dick Van Dyke,* but he still found no takers. His breakthrough came when he met Burns at a 1966 New Year's Eve party.[41] When Brooks explained his ambitions, Burns arranged for him to rewrite a script on *My Mother the Car.* It wasn't *Dick Van Dyke,* but it got him off the mat. Assignments followed for *Andy Griffith, My Three Sons,* and *That Girl,* among others.

That work caught the attention of Gene Reynolds while he was creating his high school drama, *Room 222.* Reynolds hired Brooks to write the pilot. Once *Room 222* reached the air, Brooks returned Burns's favor from a few years earlier and invited him in.

Brooks and Burns took their next leap forward when their work on *Room 222* attracted interest from Grant Tinker, Mary Tyler Moore's husband and, at the time, vice president of Twentieth Century Fox Television. Though Moore was only in her thirties, her career clearly needed a refurbishing by 1970. Her role as Laura Petrie had made her a television icon: it didn't hurt that she and Dick Van Dyke, both elegantly slim and winning, looked a bit like Jack and Jacqueline Kennedy. But after *The Dick Van Dyke Show* finished its run in 1966, she had drifted through some bad movies before starring in a disastrous theatrical version of *Breakfast at Tiffany's* that closed before even reaching Broadway.[42] Moore was heading in the wrong direction when she reunited with Dick Van Dyke for an April 1969 CBS special (just weeks after Wood's appointment as network president) that proved to be a critical and commercial smash. CBS was so excited by the strong public reaction that they gave Moore a thirteen-week commitment for a new series without even identifying a premise.[43] That's when Tinker solicited Burns and Brooks to formulate an idea.

The two didn't have a strong political mission, but they did have strong views about television comedy. For one thing, they thought it would be exciting to have Moore play a character who was divorced. ("I think every writer in Hollywood had a script in his trunk about divorce, because probably most of the comedy writers in Hollywood were divorced," Burns said later.)[44] More modestly, they wanted her character to be tethered to the world outside by as many specifics as possible: a career, a social life, an identifiable age. Each of these ideas unnerved CBS. Perry Lafferty, CBS's West Coast production chief, told them, "Fellas, people are going to think she divorced Dick Van Dyke."[45] Lafferty even resisted specifying the character's age as early thirties. Brooks and Burns won the point about her age, but CBS absolutely drew the line at divorce.[46] At a hellish meeting in New York City with Michael Dann and other top CBS programming personnel, Mark Golden, the same executive who had loved the British show that inspired *All in the Family*, told Burns and Brooks that there were only four things that American viewers would not accept: New Yorkers, Jews, men with mustaches, and divorced women.[47] Grant Tinker rejected a demand from CBS to fire the writing duo (not even telling them about it until years later), but Brooks and Burns were forced to regroup.[48] Over the next few days, they rearranged the pieces: rather than a divorce, Mary would be rebounding from a broken relationship with a boyfriend who welched on marrying her after she put him through medical school and lived with him along the way. (Why living together was more acceptable than divorce remained an open question.) They also changed her profession. In their first scenario, Mary worked as the researcher for a powerful gossip columnist modeled on the *Los Angeles Times*'s fierce Joyce Haber.[49] Now they shifted Mary to a television newsroom, the fictional WJM in Minneapolis. These changes satisfied CBS enough for the show to secure a slot on its fall 1970 schedule.

With their training from Gene Reynolds, Brooks and Burns were committed to research. This closed a circle: Moore's aunt had been a secretary for Bob Wood, the CBS president, during his years at KNXT in Los Angeles.[50] So, they spent time soaking up the newsroom culture there. White-haired anchor Jerry Dunphy became the model for the fatuous Ted Baxter. Burns said Pete Noyes,[51] the producer of KNXT's pathbreaking *The Big News*, was one of the models for Lou Grant (though Brooks said Grant was based more on a CBS editor he had known in New York).[52] Filling out the cast wasn't easy. Ethel Winant, the CBS casting director, was an early supporter of the show and helped Brooks and Burns find many in the ensemble: Ted Knight, who played Ted Baxter; Valerie Harper, who incarnated the critical role of Rhoda Morgenstern; and Ed Asner, who actually had little experience in comedy, for the central role of Lou Grant. "That was a cast of people whose careers were not going so well," Winant said later.[53]

Brooks and Burns made two other key hires: Jay Sandrich, a young television veteran, became the principal director after John Rich, their first choice, rejected them for *All in the Family*. And as their first writer, they hired Treva Silverman, a brilliantly witty, if painstaking, New York transplant whose work on *The Monkees* and other shows, including *That Girl* and *Room 222*, established her as one of television's first female comedy writers. With her New York City background, Silverman became especially important in defining Rhoda as a more nuanced character than she emerged sometimes in Brooks's writing.

"I wrote her softer," Silverman remembered, "not so brash, [not] as sharp."[54]

The show received a break when Dann left CBS after failing to stop Wood's initial purge of rural, older comedies. Dann had consigned *Mary Tyler Moore* to a dead-end spot on Tuesday nights, against *The Mod Squad* and improbably squeezed between *To Rome with Love* and *Hee Haw*.[55] When Fred Silverman, who had succeeded Dann, saw the first episodes, he recognized the show as an example of the new tone Wood was seeking. The two men moved *Mary Tyler Moore* to Saturday nights, as part of an unusual, last-minute rearranging of the fall 1970 schedule.[56] Brooks and Burns would forever credit Wood in particular for saving the show from what could have been an anonymous slide toward cancellation on Tuesdays. "For a guy who was a . . . West Coast, USC sort of cheerleader, I mean 'rah-rah' conservative politically, all that stuff, [he] was daring," Burns said later. "And he was tough."[57]

Even so, *Mary* hardly took off. Like *M*A*S*H*, it drew only middling ratings its first year. Unlike *M*A*S*H*, it also drew mixed reviews. *Time*, the *New York Times*, and *TV Guide* all mostly panned the pilot episode.[58] But the show's consistent quality in writing, acting, and directing was impossible to miss, and it soared to tenth place in the Nielsen ratings for the 1971/72 season after Silverman turbocharged CBS's Saturday night by moving *All in the Family* to the critical starting slot at 8 p.m. Eastern. The next year, *Bob Newhart* (also produced by MTM Enterprises) and *Carol Burnett* joined the Saturday night schedule. In the fall of 1973, *M*A*S*H* spent its one season with the group, creating the formidable lineup (*All in the Family/M*A*S*H/Mary/Bob/Carol*) that some critics would call television's single greatest night.

Compared to the irresistible force that was *All in the Family*, and even *M*A*S*H*'s laugh-so-we-don't-cry moralizing, *Mary Tyler Moore*'s breakthroughs were easier to miss. Mary Richards was more independent and assured than Laura Petrie, but the changes were evolutionary, not revolutionary. What *Mary* shared with *All in the Family* and *M*A*S*H* was the determination to connect the show to contemporary life, "a grounding in reality that makes us feel like we're not completely selling out on this," as Burns later put it.[59]

Even small steps in the show were magnified by the backdrop of social change around it. "We were the beneficiaries of having the right character in the right place just as the nation was changing," Brooks said.[60] In one episode, it becomes clear that Mary is on the Pill. Lou Grant's wife leaves him because she doesn't know who she is without him. And though Burns and Brooks dilute the impact by having Mary nearly break down in Lou's office along the way, she does confront him in the first episode of season three over being paid less than the man who previously held her job. When Lou granted Mary the raise in the final scene, it was another step in her progression toward more assertiveness, authority, and independence; it was a striking departure from television convention that Mary Richards ended the show's seven-year run still single. Even *Mary*'s beloved theme song was rewritten after the first season ("You might just make it after all") into a more definitive statement that reflected the character's solidifying confidence ("You're gonna make it after all").

Inside the show, many considered Burns and Brooks a backstage parallel to Mary and Rhoda. Burns was Mary: calm, contained, and meticulous. Brooks, five years younger, was Rhoda: voluble, adventurous, and spontaneous. Brooks's undeniable brilliance increasingly made him the show's creative center. Compared to Lear or Gelbart, Linda Bloodworth-Thomason found Brooks more "novelesque" in his understanding of character and how to reveal it.[61] Other writers were awed by his ability to pace a room dictating long stretches of sparkling dialogue that would appear on-screen virtually unchanged. "Most people would have written twenty things before they got to that thing," Bloodworth-Thomason remembered. "His brain is like no other I've encountered in this business."

Burns and Brooks operated on a long leash. As with *M*A*S*H*, CBS interfered less as *Mary* grew more successful. And both Tinker and Moore deferred almost completely on creative issues. Moore did not express strong opinions about how Mary Richards should develop. Treva Silverman remembers her objecting only once, when a script had Mary visiting a doctor to remove a tattoo.[62] (As a Catholic, she didn't want to promote tattoos.) The only time Brooks remembers her complaining is when they somehow neglected to give her a speech in the final episode.[63]

The paradox is that for many of the show's most fervent female fans, Mary Richards was attractive precisely because she became more assertive than Mary Tyler Moore. Mary Kay Place, the writer and actress, remembers *Mary Tyler Moore* as her favorite show when she was working as a secretary at CBS. "I felt like she was a role model for me," she remembered. "She was not married, she wanted to have a career in the world and be her own person. Plus, it was hilarious. It reflected, I think, the culture at that time brilliantly."[64] Linda Bloodworth-Thomason, who became writing partners with Place, was likewise inspired. "*Mary Tyler Moore* did more for women than the Equal Rights Amendment, even if it [had] been passed, in terms of the public imagination and acceptance of women's equality," she said.[65]

Brooks had a complex relationship to such praise and to the show's growing identification as a symbol of feminism and social change. He always professed to be awed by *All in the Family*'s immersion in social controversy, and he was understandably appreciative of the huge lift it gave *Mary Tyler Moore* in the ratings. Yet neither he nor anyone on *Mary* sought to emulate Lear. "I can't speak for other people, but as far as I was concerned, *All in the Family* had nothing to do with us," Silverman said.[66] To Silverman, the subtle ways that Mary Richards changed in response to changing social attitudes "were the opposite of what Norman Lear was doing" with shows that loudly debated the changing attitudes themselves. Brooks took a more nuanced position. He did want to stay connected to the changes happening around him, but he resisted the idea of using the show to make a point. Shows lost their balance, Brooks believed, when they sacrificed character to polemic.[67] "There were feminists who wanted to politicize our show and make us stand for something, and we spent a lot of time just slapping all hands off the wheel," he said. "We used what happened [in the world], but there were so many attempts to make us express a distinct point of view, and we were not on any soapbox ever. We burned every soapbox anybody tried to bring in."[68]

The show absorbed plenty of criticism from liberals who thought

Mary still deferred too much to the men around her, especially Lou Grant. At a November 1975 conference at the University of Texas, Brooks, a reluctant public speaker at best, found himself facing criticism from no less than Gloria Steinem for Mary's continuing to call her boss "Mr. Grant" when the male characters called him "Lou."[69] But Mary Tyler Moore was uneasy from the other direction. A Republican in a very traditional marriage herself, Moore was never comfortable as a symbol of social change. She usually threw up clouds of indecipherable words whenever interviewers asked her about the feminist movement. "Mary at that point would not ever have called herself a feminist," Silverman recalled. "She led a pretty protected life. She was married to Grant Tinker, whom I adored, but she could have been out of a fifties marriage. He made the decisions."[70] In fact, the conflicted sentiments of both Mary Tyler Moore and Mary Richards may have made the character more relatable to a broader range of women than the zeal that Bea Arthur as Maude brought to renegotiating relations between men and women.

To the writers, the point was less that Mary Richards should symbolize any kind of social change than that she be a real person who grew and changed herself. "We were just true to our show and true to our characters," Brooks said.[71] He wanted Mary to call Lou "Mr. Grant" because that's what he believed her well-mannered small-town girl would do. "We didn't present issues. We presented what it was like to be a rather little bit shy but determined midwestern woman in the 1970s, and the issues that we would deal with would be, really, relationship issues," Silverman said.[72] In her eyes, it was natural for Mary Richards to grow more assertive as women around America did: the country, like the character, was in a different place by the show's finale than when it premiered. "We cared about being real," Brooks said. "We rebelled against the term *sitcom*, and it started to be character comedy for us."[73]

Maybe the best measure of how much the program modernized television's treatment of women came when CBS spun off Valerie Harper's character, Rhoda, for her own show, produced by Burns and Brooks. *Rhoda* started out well and drew very high ratings for a while, but Brooks and Burns felt it was in a creative rut. The wrong turn they believed came early in the run, when Fred Silverman pressured them to have Rhoda get married. The episode of her marriage indeed drew astronomical ratings, but the marriage slowly strangled the show, limiting comic opportunities for such a free-spirited character. After a few seasons, the producers, concluding that they needed to shake up the story line if the show was to survive, decided that Rhoda would divorce her husband. A few years earlier, CBS had refused even to consider that Mary Richards might be a divorcee. This time, CBS didn't blink. "I don't recall a single peep out of them," Burns said later.[74] Like so many of the other changes *Mary Tyler Moore* advanced, it was easy to miss, but when the show finally signed off in March 1977—in a sweet final episode in which all the newsroom except Ted is fired— television much more closely reflected the evolving lives of American women than it did when Mary Richards first walked into the WJM newsroom almost seven years before.

TWO MONTHS INTO THE fall 1974 season, a central component went missing from television's No. 1 show: its star Archie Bunker. The first two episodes of *All in the Family* for November 1974 concocted a plot about Archie disappearing on his way to a convention in Buffalo. The reason Archie had to appear missing was that Carroll O'Connor was, in fact, missing when those shows were filmed. In the summer of 1974, he went on strike, asking for more money and more control over the show.[75]

O'Connor's public dissatisfaction opened a window into the private discontent that shadowed *All in the Family*. The most influential show on television was also among the most tumultuous, trapped in endemic conflict between O'Connor, its star, and Lear, its creator. The show's phenomenal success by every measure (in ratings, critical response, and profitability) provided both sides enough incentive to slog through their differences, but it was rarely easy.

From the start, *All in the Family* fulfilled CBS president Robert Wood's greatest goal: it generated conversation. Critics didn't always revere the show, but almost all recognized it as something different. It provoked more discussion and debate outside newspapers' TV pages than any network show in years, perhaps ever. Rob Reiner, whose counterculture friends had derided his work even for the cutting-edge Smothers Brothers, received a very different reception for his new project. "Everybody at that point realized that we were doing something that had never been done before on American television," he remembered. "Everybody knew it. So, it was like the coolest thing to be a part of."[76]

The sharpest debate the show inspired was whether Archie's panoramic bigotry discredited or normalized prejudice. Reflecting Lear's own politics, the show's unspoken but unbreakable rule was that Archie could never win an argument, especially with minority antagonists. The show was a carousel of Archie encounters with minorities—Blacks, Jews, Puerto Ricans, gay men, even transvestites—who didn't conform to his stereotypes and ran rings about him rhetorically. "Every black man was smarter than Archie Bunker," John Rich, the director, said later. "Every Jewish character was smarter . . . every minority, whoever it was who came to grips with Bunker . . . always bested him."[77] But not all viewers saw it that way. Some were impressed with Archie saying out loud what they only muttered under their breaths. Reiner, as Mike, was Archie's most frequent antagonist, and he was almost always given better arguments, yet he often came across just as shrill and dogmatic as Archie. All this left even some of those who admired the show's artistry uneasy about its impact. Treva Silverman, the talented *Mary Tyler Moore* writer, remembers reaching the point where she could no longer watch *All in the Family*. "Archie Bunker's side is the bigot, and Rob Reiner's side is a liberal, but Archie was so fucking loveable," she remembers thinking. "I cringed at his attitudes, but he was kind of adorable, and I would worry that people would mix up the adorableness and his hatefulness. I got to the point where I didn't want to watch the show."[78]

The issue crystallized in a remarkable exchange through the pages of the *New York Times* in the fall of 1971, just as *All in the Family* moved to Saturday night and the top of the ratings. Novelist Laura Z. Hobson delivered a broadside against the show. Hobson, seventy-one at the time, was best known for her 1947 novel *Gentleman's Agreement*, which explored anti-Semitism and became the basis for a popular movie starring Gregory Peck. Her problem with Archie wasn't that he was too prejudiced; it was that he was not bigoted *enough*. She argued that Lear was domesticating Archie by sanitizing his language. Yes, he raged against "coons" and "black beauties" and "Hebes," but a real Archie Bunker, she argued, was more likely to use even harsher words: the N-word for Black people, *kikes* for Jews, and so on. "Everybody knows it," she wrote in the *Times* piece. "Then why doesn't this honest show use the real words that real bigots always use?" Her answer: to build a bigger audience. "Clean it up, deterge it, bleach it, enzyme it, and you'll have a show about a lovable bigot that everybody except a few pinko atheistic bleedin' hearts will love."[79] During her research for the article, Lear wouldn't talk to Hobson, whom he correctly suspected was on a mission to debunk. But he responded a month later with a lengthy rejoinder in the *Times* to what he called her "novella" attacking his show.[80] The essence of Lear's response was that Archie was motivated by fear of the future, not hatred, so he would be unlikely to use the harshest words Hobson identified. More fundamentally, Lear insisted that Hobson was wrong that a bigot couldn't be likeable; in fact, he argued, likeable bigots were a more common and thus greater problem than the sneering kind. For good measure, he argued that Hobson was too pessimistic about the capacity of lower-middle-class viewers to recognize Archie's failings. "Thus Mrs. Hobson raises the age-old specter of the intellectuals' mistrust of the lower middle classes," Lear wrote. "I submit there is a degree of prejudice in those feelings, Mrs. Hobson."

Hobson's arguments seem more persuasive than Lear's in retrospect, but the merits of this exchange were less important than its existence. A few weeks after Lear's duel with Hobson, *Newsweek* debated similar questions in a cover story about the show.[81] The following spring, the *New York Times Magazine* devoted another long story to the question "Can Archie Bunker Give Bigotry A Bad Name?"[82] (The author landed much closer to Lear than to Hobson.) Groups representing American Jews and Polish Americans weighed in. Whitney Young of the Urban League condemned the show. The NAACP defended it.[83] The ACLU, praising the show as a "breakthrough . . . in terms of presenting life as it really is," gave Lear its Freedom of the Press Award in 1973.[84] Elite publications, not to mention national organizations, had never debated the social impact of *The Beverly Hillbillies* or *Green Acres*. "Probably no show ever got more ink than Archie Bunker," Robert Wood exulted to a visiting Los Angeles television columnist. "We can't turn it off—not that we want to."[85]

Lear stoked this flame with an endless supply of topical kindling. Story ideas for *All in the Family* and, later, Lear's other shows began around a big conference table in his office; a microphone hung down from the ceiling, so an assistant down the hall could transcribe notes once the writers seriously started formulating a plot. Lear required his writers to keep up on the news. "Everybody was expected to read a couple of newspapers," he said. "We had the *New York Times*, *Wall Street Journal*, and the *Los Angeles Times* in the office, so anybody who missed something could read it."[86] On especially sensitive subjects, Lear would bring in outside experts to brief the writers.[87] From all these sources, Lear channeled a steady current of contemporary concerns into plots for *All in the Family* and his subsequent shows: Vietnam, draft deserters, racial tensions, gay rights, anti-Semitism, rape, abortion, miscarriage, menopause, impotence, inflation, layoffs, Watergate, Richard Nixon. "Whatever was going on we ripped from the headlines," Reiner remembered.[88] The list was endless. "It didn't take a lot of imagination," Lear said. "It just took looking around."[89]

For the cast and crew, the belief that they were exploring unchartered terrain was exhilarating, above all for Lear, perhaps because he had spent so many years producing more disposable entertainment. "Norman was the guiding light," Reiner remembered. "He was more than anything the force that pushed us to be better. Norman would force us to want to dig deeper, always dig deeper, dig deeper. He wanted it to go further."[90] But all the actors felt a strong connection to their characters. Reiner and O'Connor improvised some of their most memorable confrontations, including much of an episode where the two are locked in a storeroom and Archie explains how his bigoted views were instilled in him by his father. (O'Connor later called it his favorite episode.)[91]

From the start, *All in the Family* presented Lear with a two-front struggle. He banged against CBS's censors on one side and against the resentments of his star, Carroll O'Connor, on the other. As the show rocketed to the top of the Nielsen ratings in the fall of 1971 and then stayed there, Lear grew stronger on one front and more embattled on the other. In the show's early years, the battles with CBS were persistent and intense. "Lear was very strong willed, probably for the first year or two," Wood later reflected. The network, he acknowledged, might have been excessively cautious about the content at first because it was ruling on subjects it had not previously considered, but over time, CBS fought less with Lear, mainly because the shows he provided it were astonishingly successful. "Lear treated CBS like so many gnats on his back," Robert Wussler, a CBS producer and executive who became the network's president in 1976, said later. "He had the upper hand. The shows were good and successful."[92]

The best demonstration of Lear's growing leverage came in a story line he developed for *Maude*, his first spin-off from *All in the Family*. When Maude, played by the imposing Bea Arthur, discovered at age forty-seven that she was pregnant, she decided to have an abortion. The first episode of "Maude's Dilemma," as the two-part arc was called, appeared on November 14, exactly one week after Richard Nixon's landslide reelection and less than a month after the Supreme Court heard final oral arguments in *Roe v. Wade*, the case in which the Court established the nationwide legal right to abortion, in January 1973. Despite the explosive subject, CBS fought with Lear remarkably little over the episodes, a reflection both of its increasing tolerance for controversy and his growing clout. If anything, the network may have underestimated the response. Only two affiliates refused to air the episodes' initial broadcast (though, even that was an unusual breach). When the show returned for reruns that summer, though, *Roe* had legalized abortion and Catholic organizations mounted a tenacious boycott against the *Maude* abortion episodes. The pressure left a mark: nearly forty CBS affiliates this time refused to show the episodes when the network repeated them in August 1973, and national advertisers completely abandoned the programs.[93] Protesters lay down in front of William Paley's limousine one day as he pulled into Black Rock.[94] It was the most forceful example yet of Nixon's America pushing back against the sixties values surging into the networks' programming from Lear and the like-minded producers working near him in Los Angeles.

But not even this controversy could slow the conveyor belt from Lear's office to the CBS prime-time schedule: *Good Times*, which spun off Maude's African American maid, Florida, and her family into their own show, went on the air in February 1974, only a few months after the abortion boycott. *The Jeffersons* followed in January 1975. Through the winter of 1974/75, with four of his shows already in Nielsen's Top 10 and *The Jeffersons* poised to join them, Lear, at fifty-two, had reached an apex of influence in American popular culture matched by very few producers before or since. "We can all be proud of TV," Bob Hope said around this time, "and its owner, Norman Lear."[95]

BUT IF *ALL IN THE FAMILY'S* success cemented Lear's position at CBS, it only compounded O'Connor's resentments. Archie was the opportunity of a lifetime for O'Connor, but he always seemed focused less on what the role brought him than what he felt he was still being denied. Born in Manhattan and raised mostly in Queens, O'Connor was thoughtful and well read—he finished his undergraduate degree at University College in Dublin—but he had scuffled in his career: at thirty, he was still living with his mother.[96] After mixed success on Broadway, he worked steadily on television and in Hollywood during the 1960s, but he never advanced beyond supporting parts. (It was in such a role, as a bombastic general in the 1966 film *What Did You Do in the War, Daddy?*, that O'Connor caught Lear's eye as his Archie.) As O'Connor reached his late forties, Archie Bunker was by far the biggest opportunity of his career—yet the actor felt Lear slighted him over money, creative control, and credit for the show. From the outset, O'Connor viewed himself, not Lear, as the principal custodian of Archie Bunker. Off the set, he gave interviews offering extensive opinions on how Archie would react to current events and even developed a nightclub act around the conceit.[97] On set, he routinely complained that the scripts were unplayable.* O'Connor initially refused to participate in one of the most famous episodes because he didn't like a script that required Archie to help a Puerto Rican woman give birth in an elevator stuck between floors. He publicly revealed that he threatened to quit over an episode that suggested Archie might kiss Florence Jefferson, his African American neighbor, under the mistletoe because he thought it was unrealistic.[98]

O'Connor's response to the mistletoe argument opened a window into his skewed view about the show's overall hierarchy. He told one interviewer, "Suddenly, my resentment exploded and I thought: 'I'm the star of the number-one show on TV. I carry 75 percent of every episode. If I were somebody like Jackie Gleason, they'd all be ordered out on the street.' I couldn't imagine how anybody would set up this kind of argument with a big star like Jackie or Lucy. Why were they persisting in this thing when they knew Carroll O'Connor didn't want it?"[99] But of course, O'Connor on *All in the Family* wasn't Jackie Gleason or Lucille Ball on their eponymous shows. As Rob Reiner perceptively observed, it was Norman Lear's name on the marquee, not O'Connor's, no matter how many times the actor described it as "my show." Reiner, who had known Lear his entire life and quickly developed a close relationship with O'Connor, found himself in the difficult role of trying to keep the peace between two hardheaded men old enough to be his father. "Oddly enough, at age twenty-four or twenty-five, I was like the Henry Kissinger," Reiner recalled. "I was the diplomat." Lear and

---

* This attitude started early. O'Connor said the first script he read for the pilot was so inadequate—"I thought it was terrible," he said later—that he took it home and completely rewrote it; it was that script, O'Connor insisted, that became the basis for the show's pilot (O'Connor, Academy interview, August 13, 1999). Lear acknowledged that O'Connor disliked the script and offered revisions, but he insisted that his own original version was the one they used for the pilot (Lear, *Even This*, 224).

O'Connor were both stubborn, but their disagreement, as Reiner saw it, was more fundamental: "It was Norman's show, there's no getting around it, and Carroll wanted it to be *his* show."[100]

O'Connor's discontent became unavoidably public when he walked out in the summer of 1974, seeking more money and creative control. By his own account, he got the first but not the second.[101] Even after O'Connor returned, he continued to disparage Lear publicly. Indeed, O'Connor's resentments about Lear and the show ran even deeper than was apparent at the time. In an oral history interview after *All in the Family* completed its run, O'Connor complained about the show's heavily Jewish writing staff in terms that Archie Bunker would have recognized. "So, here were all these Jewish writers, and they were trying to write a script for a typical New York goy, an arch goy by the name of Archie," O'Connor said. "They didn't know that character. But I knew the character. And some of them might dispute that . . . but in a way, I was one. I wasn't really from Archie's background—I came from a well-to-do, educated background—but I sure was a white man, I sure was a Christian, and I sure understood Christian bias, and I understood how it came out of the Christian mouth, across the Christian dining table, and to the fellow Christians at work. My writers couldn't tell me that. I knew that. So, the rewriting went on more or less as a constant thing."[102]

Lear rarely responded to O'Connor's public baiting. Almost always, he insisted that O'Connor's performances more than compensated for the aggravation. "So worth it," Lear said. "You write a character like Archie Bunker, it's a lot of words . . . but Carroll O'Connor gave it life."[103] Still, O'Connor's bitterness only grew as the Lear family of successful spin-offs grew. "He spun these shows off my show; he never offered me a piece of any show," O'Connor said later. "And, of course, I'm very materialistic, which is a euphemism for greedy. So, since it's my show, and he's doing these things from my show, it's customary in this business to give a piece. As my friend Redd Foxx said, 'All I want is a little taste' . . . But on any of the shows that spun off from my show, no way, no way. He wouldn't give any money or any credit, anything."[104]

Lear and O'Connor never entirely reconciled over the show's nine-year run. Bob Daly, a business executive who had ascended through the ranks to become the CBS president, experienced the durability of the resentment when he flew to Los Angeles to negotiate with O'Connor over *Archie Bunker's Place*, the successor show that launched in 1979 after *All in the Family* went off the air.[105] Before Daly could talk any terms, O'Connor vented for two hours about Lear. Even after *Archie Bunker's Place* finished its own run on CBS, O'Connor and Lear remained distant. When O'Connor died in 2001—long after Archie and Edith's living room chairs had been accepted into the Smithsonian as a mark of their cultural impact, and after arbiters ranging from *TV Guide* to the Writers Guild of America had placed *All in the Family* near the top of their greatest-show-ever lists—the man forever remembered as Archie Bunker remained estranged from the producer who chose him for the role of his life.

EVEN AS THE PROCESSION of contemporary comedies reached their peak influence in the 1974/75 television season, *All in the Family* stood alone at the very pinnacle. Exactly why it struck the most powerful chord and attracted a larger audience than any of its contemporaries remains an enduring matter of debate. The most obvious reason is that the show represented such an extreme departure from what had come before it. Even decades later, early *All in the Family* episodes are stunning and, at times, shocking in both subject matter and language. To see them contemporaneously after *Hee Haw* must have felt like stepping from one decade to another. But more was involved than the show's originality: *M*A*S*H*, with its unprecedented intertwining of tragedy and comedy, was equally novel, and written, acted, and directed with comparable skill.

Fred Silverman, who championed *All in the Family*, thought it stood apart because Lear used topicality to entice audiences to tune in, and then gave them a classic situation comedy revolving around one of the genre's oldest tropes, a belligerent but ultimately loving family.[106] That may be closer to the explanation for its huge audiences. The ultimate stability of the family may have seemed a given for earlier comedy families, but by the early 1970s, it represented a form of triumph for the Bunker family to hold together despite all the disagreements separating Archie from Mike and Gloria (with Edith as a sort of noncombatant who loved both sides). Implicitly, *All in the Family* offered reassurance that America could bridge the generation gap: even with all the yelling (over Vietnam, race, drugs, sex), blood was thicker than politics for the Bunker family. For all the loud disagreements, everyone managed to coexist. As one critic noted, *All in the Family* became a kind of "Father Knows Least," in which Archie's love for his family increasingly overshadowed his retrograde attitudes.[107] The show ultimately promised integration, not division, between the generations, which is why some leftist critics came to believe it trivialized and domesticated the long list of social disputes that it hurled against the screen. For the same reason, though, the show remained popular with both younger and older viewers; unlike *The Smothers Brothers Comedy Hour*, which more overtly picked a team, it never narrowed its audience to just one side of the generation gap.

But if *All in the Family* promised generational reconciliation, it always signaled that it would come only on new terms. The show's most consistent political message was that Archie (and all those who thought like him) could not stop the social and cultural changes happening around them. The transformation unloosed by the 1960s was unstoppable and irreversible. In that way, the show precisely captured the paradox in the interplay between culture and politics during the early 1970s. On the one hand, Richard Nixon's forty-nine-state win in 1972 clearly demonstrated that the "silent majority" whom Archie symbolized remained the nation's political majority. But Archie's unease with change and his inability to reverse it captured how, even at that moment of triumph, the victors felt society slipping away from them. As one perceptive critic wrote in 1974, "A moment's listening identifies Archie as trapped and outraged, afraid and embittered, confused and resolute. The world is no longer his world, and America, land of the free and home of the brave, is teeming with pinkos, fags, meatheads, and intellectuals. Everything he sees and hears reminds him of what he has lost or is in danger of losing. . . . He curses anyone who would threaten even remotely what it took him a lifetime to earn and mouths every American slogan he can muster to convince himself all is not lost."[108] The overarching story of *All in the Family* and the other great contemporary comedies of the early 1970s was the terms of surrender from America's older generations as they conceded, week by week, episode by episode, to the cultural changes (new attitudes about sex, new roles for women, new assertiveness for racial minorities and gays) that the rising Baby Boomers advanced.

This central thread connecting all of the era's great contemporary comedies highlighted a second paradox about their success. Shows such as *All in the Family*, *M*A*S*H*, and *Mary Tyler Moore* provided television's first exposure to the critique of American life that emerged primarily from the youth protest movements of the 1960s, but as in the movie business, these stories were told almost entirely by an older generation. The three principal creative forces at the outset for *All in the Family* were Lear (born in 1922), O'Connor (1924), and director John Rich (1925). Lear quickly added two writers with roots as stand-up comics in the Catskills: Bernie West (born in 1918) and Mickey Ross (1919). Don Nicholl, the other key early writer for the show, was born in 1925.

At *M*A*S*H*, the dominant creative forces were Gene Reynolds (born in 1923) and Larry Gelbart (1928). One of the key directors on *M*A*S*H* was Hy Averback (born in 1920); Gelbart had met him when they both worked on *The Bob Hope Show* in 1948.[109] Only when Alan Alda (born in 1936) assumed a larger creative role did younger voices start to influence the show's direction. *Mary Tyler Moore* was the big exception, with Allan Burns (born in 1935) and James Brooks (1940) joined by younger writers such as Treva Silverman (born in 1936) and Ed Weinberger (1945).

In the Lear world especially, there were very few young people. The predominantly gray tint in the staff room for his shows reflected the balance that made Lear such a commercial success, even if it led to the complaint that he trivialized the big social conflicts he addressed. He almost invariably sided with the younger generations, but he saw their foibles, too. And he filtered all these ideas through the classic conventions of television comedy: throughout his career, the comedy that most inspired him remained vaudeville and the sketch shows of the 1950s. He aired the agenda of the Woodstock generation through the language and rhythms of the Catskills. Lear had one foot in the new and the other in the familiar, a stance that allowed millions on both sides of the generation gap to find their own footing in the world he created.

AS THE CONTEMPORARY COMEDIES reached the peak of their influence in the television season that began in September 1974, the man who, more than any other, had started that revolution was losing his will for the competition. For CBS president Robert Wood and his peripatetic programming chief Fred Silverman, the 1974/75 season was as much a critical and ratings triumph as all those before it. And while Wood's relationship with Lear remained ambivalent, the creators of *M*A*S*H* and *Mary Tyler Moore* each viewed him as a hero. "Each network, each major studio, each clothing company, each cosmetics firm . . . obviously reflects the taste of the person most entrusted with setting the direction for the company," Gelbart said later. "I was lucky to have fallen into the space [when] Wood was there and was encouraging more urbane material."[110]

And yet Wood felt the walls of his thirty-fourth-floor office at Black Rock closing in. Protest whipsawed him. The *Maude* abortion episodes generated a firestorm among conservatives. Then Wood infuriated liberals in March 1973 when he withdrew from the schedule, at the last minute, an anti–Vietnam War play by David Rabe.[111] Pressure from above increasingly grated on Wood. He complained to Frank Stanton, who had surrendered his president's position to become vice chairman in 1971, about constant second-guessing from Paley, and he would unburden to old friends about how difficult it was to satisfy CBS's mercurial chairman of the board.[112]

As president of CBS, Wood made a good salary, and he lived a comfortable life in tony Greenwich, Connecticut, but he grew increasingly frustrated that the producers of the breakthrough comedies he had fought to put on the air were making far more than he. "He was upset, not unlike Carroll O'Connor, that he [had] helped make all this money for Norman Lear, Grant Tinker, and all these people," Bob Daly recalled. "CBS didn't pay [executives] a lot of money compared to the creative side . . . and I think when we were redoing the deals all the time, and he was seeing how much money we paid out, he would think, You're going to give them what? He would go along with it because he had to, but he would have a little resentment. I think he resented Norman Lear, not creatively, but that 'Norman Lear made all this money, and I took the chance of putting *All in the Family* on the air.'"[113]

As Wood's frustration mounted, he began to lose focus and increasingly disengaged from decisions. Jack Schneider told Stanton that sometimes, during the day, he'd find Wood alone in a screening room watching old movies. At night, he arrived earlier and stayed later at the bar at 21. At company events, he would become visibly drunk less than an hour after arriving.[114]

As the pressures gathered on Wood, yet another challenge emerged. When Paley's first choice to succeed Stanton died after only a few months on the job, the CBS chairman hired Arthur Taylor, an ambitious young executive, as the company's president in 1972. Taylor wanted to make a mark not only in business but also in politics and society, and late in 1974 he began formulating an initiative that would inadvertently threaten Wood's greatest accomplishment. Taylor's idea was what he called "the family hour," and it would help to end the revolution in television comedy that Wood had ignited when he put *Mary Tyler Moore*, *All in the Family*, and *M*A*S*H* on the air.

10

OCTOBER

The (White) Boys' Club

In October, springtime in Hollywood finally arrived for Linda Blood-worth and her writing partner, Mary Kay Place. That month, a breezy script the two young women had written with the title "Springtime" aired on *M*A*S*H*. Less than two weeks after "Springtime" aired, their script "Gimme That Old Time Relation" appeared on the short-lived ABC television series *Paper Moon* (adapted from Peter Bogdanovich's movie and costarring a young Jodie Foster as Addie Pray). In December, *M*A*S*H* would air yet another script from the two women, entitled "Mad Dogs and Servicemen." Only a few days later, their script "The Groupie" would appear on the MTM Enterprises show *Paul Sand in Friends and Lovers*. For the multitalented Place, "Springtime" was a double triumph: it also marked her first acting appearance on *M*A*S*H*, as nurse Lt. Louise Simmons, a love interest for Gary Burghoff's ingenuous camp secretary, Radar O'Reilly.

Like most overnight success in Hollywood, the breakthrough for Bloodworth and Place had been germinating for years. Each of them had finished college in 1969 (Place at the University of Tulsa, Bloodworth at the University of Missouri) and had then pointed her ambitions toward Los Angeles. Each then spent years soldiering through other jobs as she worked to gain a foothold in television. The two became a writing team after meeting at a party—each thought the other funny during a game of charades.[1] In 1973, they notched their first significant credits, writing for *The Shape of Things*, a onetime variety special on ABC produced by *Laugh-In* creator George Schlatter that highlighted the talents of women performers, writers, and directors (including actress Lee Grant, who directed the show). Then, in December 1973, *M*A*S*H* aired a pathbreaking script the two women wrote entitled "Hot Lips and Empty Arms," which began Loretta Swit's transformation on the show from the one-dimensional "Hot Lips" to the more fully formed *Margaret* Houlihan. But it wasn't until the fall 1974 television season that the dam burst for them, with four of their scripts reaching the air over a period of just three months. "There were not many women comedy writers," remembered Bloodworth, who would become one of television's most celebrated producers after she created the situation comedy *Designing Women* in the mid-1980s.[2] (By then, she had married Harry Thomason, a writer, director, and producer, and was working professionally as "Linda Bloodworth-Thomason.") "We were such a novelty," she said of herself and partner Place. "We looked like young cheerleaders from the Midwest." Bloodworth recognized that this fact was not irrelevant to their expanding opportunities. "We got in the door for reasons we shouldn't have," she remembered. The men—and they were all men—running the shows thought, "They are fun and interesting and young and fresh," she recalled, "and we didn't seem like old bitter women, which is how they thought about some of the poor women who paved the way for us."[3]

This odd equation, an opening against sexist exclusion that itself relied upon sexist stereotypes, captured the precarious position of women in the entertainment industries of early 1970s Los Angeles. All these industries were transforming to respond to the shifting marketplace demands of a changing America. Film, television, and music alike were spotlighting new faces, new voices, and new stories that had previously been marginalized. Television shows and movies featuring anything other than white male protagonists were still the exception, but those exceptions became more common after the revolution in television engineered by Robert Wood and Norman Lear in 1971. *Sanford and Son*, *Good Times*, and *The Jeffersons*, all Lear-produced shows, became the first situation comedies since *Julia* in the late 1960s to center on African American families. Shows ranging from *Mary Tyler Moore* to *Rhoda* to *Maude* featured women characters who did not define themselves solely as wives, mothers, or singles desperately in search of a man. *Chico and the Man*, on NBC, starring the kinetic Freddie Prinze, brought television its first Hispanic star in the fall 1974 season. The change wasn't as pronounced in the film industry, but even there, the early 1970s surge in the hard-edged, usually violent, and frequently sexually explicit "blaxploitation" films exposed audiences to confident and commanding Black heroes (and antiheroes) ranging from Shaft and Superfly to Foxy Brown.

In all these ways, the stars in front of the curtain were slowly evolving to reflect a more diverse America. Still, behind the curtain, power in all the entertainment industries remained almost exclusively in the hands of white men. In television, Mary Kay Place quickly realized that even as more of the stories that television aired centered on the diverse experiences of modern women, the writers constructing those stories remained primarily older white men. "The one thing I noticed, which is why I was interested in trying to write screenplays and scripts, was that there were fifty-eight-year-old white men telling about what it was like to be a female," she remembered.[4] Even as a child, actress Jodie Foster, who would herself become a director years later, was likewise struck by the absence of women in any positions of authority. "There were no women anywhere, honestly," she said. Whenever she performed on a television show, she recalled, another woman would be around to play her mother, but beyond that, women were limited to "sometimes makeup and hair and script supervisor, but very often those were men as well. And other than that, they were all men, no women to be found anywhere. I think it was just subliminal. I think I thought, Oh well, that's not something I'll ever be able to do."[5] African Americans and other minorities (except on the blaxploitation films, aimed primarily at Black audiences) in positions of authority, either on individual film and television productions or at the networks and film studios that released them, were even rarer, as in virtually nonexistent. The near-complete absence of women and minorities in the rooms where decisions were made was so deeply ingrained that hardly anyone questioned or even noticed it. "It's something I didn't think about," said Anthea Sylbert, the brilliant costume designer who later became a studio executive and producer. "I thought, That's what it was. It wasn't even something that one wondered about."[6] The disparity became the social equivalent of the layer of thick, brown smog hanging over the city most days, a phenomenon so familiar that it had grown almost invisible—at least for the white men who exercised power. "We didn't even recognize it as an issue," remembers Tom Pollock, who was rising in prominence as the young attorney for the Movie Brat generation of filmmakers. "It was like, 'That's the way it is.'"[7] Tony Bill, the young producer of *The Sting* and other films in those years, agreed: "It was a given. It was the culture we inherited."[8]

For the woman and African American artists and executives seeking to upend that culture of exclusion, the early 1970s were a moment of transition. The white men in the corner offices of the entertainment industry remained largely obtuse to the demands for greater representation gathering around them. But so many talented new voices were pressing against the barriers that slowly, grudgingly, doors cracked open. For women and minorities, this was a period of enduring frustration but, also, encouraging breakthroughs. More pioneers from each group clawed their way to influence over the music, movies, and television Los Angeles produced over these years, even as they remained lonely exceptions.

MARY KAY PLACE WAS bursting with ambition and talent. The day after graduating from college, she pointed her Volkswagen Beetle toward the West Coast with the name of one contact at CBS in her pocket.[9] Place was creative and vivacious: she could sing *and* write songs; act *and* write dialogue. So, of course, she was offered only clerical jobs, and went through a series of them at CBS over the next few years. When *Maude*, the *All in the Family* spin-off, went on the air in 1972, Place became the secretary for the writing staff.

Her first opportunity to show she could do more than type came one day during *Maude*'s first season, when she was walking back from lunch with one of her colleagues.[10] The two were singing a funny song Place had written called "If Communism Comes Knocking at Your Door (Don't Answer It)." Some of the *All in the Family* writers overheard the two singing and told Lear about the song. After Place auditioned it for him, he put her and her friend on *All in the Family* to sing it in an episode that aired in January 1973. In a preview of her career to come, it became Place's first published song and her first television acting credit.

Her work in the hectic atmosphere of a weekly situation comedy provided her a crash course in scriptwriting. "Working with the writers was a seven-days-a-week, twenty-four-hours-a-day job," she remembered. "I was constantly typing every draft, every rewrite. I was in every note session with the writer. I was in the note sessions with the directors and the actors. I didn't go to graduate school, but this was a beautiful graduate school, because it was hands-on." Together with Barbara Gallagher, a young production assistant on the show, Place was responsible for incorporating into the scripts the inevitable changes made during the rehearsals held just days before the show was filmed before its live audience. The two would be handed a script scribbled with revisions at 11 p.m. and often stay in the office until daybreak retyping and cleaning it. With growing confidence, they substituted their own judgment for what the writing staff left unclear.[11] "They'd have maybe three different ideas for one line and kind of never really decided which one of those to use. They'd get distracted and go on to something else," Place remembered. "We'd go, 'This one's better,' and we'd put that one in, and they'd never know the difference." After a few months of this breakneck pace, Place felt ready to craft her own script.

In Linda Bloodworth, she found the right partner for the leap. Bloodworth hailed from a prominent family of lawyers, political activists, and newspaper editors in the southeastern corner of Missouri known as the Bootheel. In an area where racism was entrenched, the Bloodworths were outspoken liberals, especially about civil rights. Bloodworth grew up in a household where current events were served nightly with dinner and where the children were expected to contribute. "If you didn't have an opinion in my family, you had to go to your room," she recalled. After college, she moved to Los Angeles determined to become a writer. She first secured a job at a Los Angeles legal newspaper, where one of her initial assignments was to cover the murder trial of Charles Manson. ("He just picked me out, and he had that stare," she recalled of Manson. "I locked eyes with him every day.") After a few months at the newspaper, fired with idealism, Bloodworth quit to teach at a public high school in Watts. Then she met Place, who was looking for a writing partner.

Like many of the women hoping to find a seat in the writers' room, Place wanted above all to contribute to *Mary Tyler Moore*, with its strong roster of female characters. She had developed an idea for an episode—Mary's male colleagues ignore her warnings about a beautiful young intern who is constantly inserting herself into discussions and decisions where she doesn't belong—and she asked Bloodworth to join her in expanding it into a script. Working at night after each woman finished her day job, the two meshed smoothly and submitted a script within weeks. The MTM team passed—it had something similar already in development—but when Place showed the script to Stu Robinson and Bernie Weintraub, the agents for many of the writers on *Maude*, they immediately offered to represent her and Bloodworth.[12]

The first assignments trickled in, including their work for *The Shape of Things*, the pioneering 1973 television special about women. Their breakthrough came when they won an assignment from Larry Gelbart to write the "Hot Lips and Empty Arms" episode of *M*A*S*H*, in the show's second season. The episode features Loretta Swit's Margaret "Hot Lips" Houlihan snarling at everyone around her after receiving a letter from an old friend. When her married lover, Frank Burns, pushes for an explanation, she unloads. "She married a doctor I turned down, and now she has a beautiful home with a swimming pool, two adorable children, a two-car garage," Margaret cries. "Oh, Frank, that all could have been mine; that could have been me. But no, I married the Army. And what have I got to show for it? Rotten living conditions, surrounded by insolent doctors and nurses who don't give me an ounce of respect. . . . I have nothing, nothing." When Frank interjects, "Am *I* nothing, Margaret?" her rejoinder is devastating: "You're government issue, Frank . . . and after you're home, I'll only be a smile on your face your wife won't understand."

Larry Gelbart, *M*A*S*H*'s co-creator, was undoubtedly one of the most brilliant television writers ever, but these were complexities and subtleties (not to mention eloquence) he had never provided for Swit. In the show's early episodes, she had only two speeds: martinet and sex bomb. Place and Bloodworth wanted to give her something more. "Because we were the first women who were writing for *M*A*S*H*, we wanted to write something for Margaret," Bloodworth recalled. "We were just thinking about being so far from home, alone in that situation, and so little real love."[13] Once Place and Bloodworth developed the basic story line, Swit was closely involved in developing how "Hot Lips" would respond to the situation. "She was dying to have more humanity and to give the public more explanation of other sides of her than her affair with Frank," Bloodworth continued. "It's not to denigrate the characters; they were wonderful. But Alan [Alda] and the other actors were so beloved; Loretta wanted to get a little of that affability and depth into Margaret." The episode did exactly that, imbuing Houlihan with shadings and depth and establishing a foundation of respect between her and Alda's Hawkeye, respect that over the show's long run transformed Swit's character from a male fantasy into a role model whom women could admire. "Loretta did a hell of a job," said Mike Farrell, who played the show's earnest B. J. Hunnicutt. "I credit her with going from Hot Lips Houlihan to Margaret Houlihan over the period of the show. She fought for her character to have some significance rather than just be a sex symbol."[14] "Hot Lips and Empty Arms," Place and Bloodworth's first produced script, was the episode when that transformation began.

Women writers for television or movies remained so rare in the early 1970s that when Place and Bloodworth traveled to studio lots for meetings, men didn't know what to make of them. "We got stopped at the gate," Bloodworth recalled. "We looked like we were still in high school." When they went for lunch with producers, "people thought we were their secretaries," she said. "There were no women on the staff, no women anywhere. No one in a position of power."[15] When the Writers Guild of America West surveyed the fall 1973 television season, it found that women had written fewer than 1 in 14 of the scripts that reached the air.[16] Twenty-four of the 62 shows on the air had never used a woman writer, the survey found.[17] No woman had written any of the 139 episodes of the cop drama *Adam-12* or any of the 230 episodes of *FBI*. When the WGA conducted a follow-up survey for the 1974/75 season, it "indicated that very little progress had been made."[18] Apart from a few prominent exceptions, such as Jack Nicholson's old friend Carole Eastman (who crafted *Five Easy Pieces* under the pen name "Adrien Joyce"), few women writers had cracked the movie business, either.

Partnering with a man was a common requirement for aspiring female comedy writers. "The conventional wisdom then was that women aren't funny,"[19] said writer Treva Silverman, who refuted that sentiment almost anytime she spoke. Growing up on Long Island in the 1950s, she had idolized the fast-talking, sexy, and independent heroines of Hollywood comedies from the 1930s and '40s. Silverman had been toiling away in New York City playing the piano and writing comedy sketches when Carol Burnett, on the hunt for fresh voices, discovered and hired her. Then Bob Rafelson and Bert Schneider brought her to Los Angeles in 1966 as part of the initial group of writers they assembled for *The Monkees*.

Silverman quickly developed a reputation as very funny, very painstaking—it usually took her two months to complete a script, writing in longhand on legal pads—and skilled at generating not just punchlines but genuine emotions that humanized the characters.[20] These were all the qualities that James Brooks, whom she had met in New York, was seeking when he recruited her to write for *Room 222*, the high school comedy/drama he developed with Gene Reynolds. When Brooks created *Mary Tyler Moore*, Silverman was his first hire. "Jim called me," she remembered, "and he said, 'We just got the green light, and we'd like you to do as many episodes as you would like.'" She wrote the script for the first episode that aired after the pilot and ultimately contributed fifteen more through the 1973/74 season.[21] Brooks and Burns would often assign her to write the "Emmy script," the one show they would submit for consideration for an acting Emmy Award. Silverman won her own Emmy in 1974, for a pivotal episode in which Lou Grant's wife, Edie, leaves him, the first woman to win that recognition without a writing partner.[22] (One of the finalists Silverman beat was the writing team of Place and Bloodworth, who were nominated for "Hot Lips and Empty Arms.")[23] When the two producers elevated Silverman to executive story editor, she became the first female executive at a comedy show.

But apart from Treva Silverman, women contributed relatively little to the writing even of *Mary Tyler Moore*, the era's quintessential show about the changing role of women. Likewise on *Maude*, with its female lead, women wrote only about twenty of the episodes over six seasons. "It seemed really strange," said Elliot Shoenman, the youngest writer on *Maude*. "I was kind of shocked. The *All in the Family* staff was all men also. Everything was all men . . . and *older* men. Everybody was way older than I was."[24] Women were even more exotic on *M*A*S*H*, where no woman writer other than Place and Bloodworth was credited with a screenplay during the decade of the 1970s;[25] and on *All in the Family*, where women contributed little more than a dozen of the screenplay credits through the show's landmark nine-year run.[26]

The hardest part for these early women writers was getting in the door. The few women who were allowed inside mostly felt the men there respected them, cared about their opinions, and shared good advice on writing. Some experienced sexual harassment or belittling condescension, but those problems were not nearly as common for women writers as for actresses. Working with Brooks and Gelbart, two of the finest comedy writers ever, Bloodworth felt that "I was lucky to breathe their air in my twenties."[27] The problem, she thought, wasn't that the men running television were determined to exclude women; it was more that they never really noticed that they *were* excluding women or, for that matter, nonwhite writers. "I think all of these guys—because they were from a different era, they didn't have that perspective," she said. In some ways, that was more damning: even as they wrote the scripts that for the first time connected television to a changing America, the men behind the network renaissance of the early 1970s failed to recognize how deeply their own behavior remained stuck in the past.

IN THE EXECUTIVE SUITES at the production companies, television networks, and movie studios behind the shows, women's inroads were even more limited. Hardly any women held positions of authority. CBS did not name its first female vice president until 1973, when Robert Wood appointed Ethel Winant, the network's whiz casting director, as vice president for talent. The possibility of a female executive was so far beyond the expectation of the men running CBS that there was no women's restroom outside the dining room on the executive floor.[28] Winant had to leave her shoes next to the men's room door as a sign for the men to stay out.

It was no different in Hollywood. As late as the mid-1970s, Sherry Lansing and another woman executive at MGM studios had to lobby their male bosses to permit women to use the gym in the company building. Even then, the company initially only conceded to allow them to use the facility at scheduled times, when men weren't present.[29] This response left Lansing dumbfounded, but she also recognized that it was a form of progress that she had ascended high enough in the company to make the request at all. It was in her nature to focus more on the opportunity than the obstacle. In that, she was representative of the first generation of Hollywood women in the 1970s. Almost all seemed acutely aware that they were entering a man's world, and almost all, without exception, focused more on proving they could play by the rules the men had established than on questioning whether those rules were fair. "Most of us never thought about the obstacles," Lansing recalled. "We just wanted to do the work. I just felt, Okay, fine, I'll work twice as hard. And it changed."[30]

Lansing arrived in Los Angeles in 1966 as the young wife of a doctor she married after earning a degree in theater at Northwestern University.[31] Her initial ambition was to break in as an actress and model, partly because she was a movie buff who was tall and beautiful, slim and dark haired, but also because she could imagine no other possibility, given that there were no women succeeding in the entertainment industry in any other capacity. "Who were the women I looked up to?" she asked. "This is a terrible thing to say, but who were there? Who was I missing? I admired the actresses."[32]

Lansing stood out (literally) from the crowd with her five-foot, ten-inch frame, but her acting career progressed fitfully. After a few years in Los Angeles, she was ready for a change when producer Raymond Price offered her a job reading scripts for his production company. The job paid only five dollars an hour, not enough even for Lansing to initially quit her job as a substitute teacher, but she grabbed it as a chance to set a different course.[33]

After serving her apprenticeship with Price, she was hired as a story editor for Talent Associates, a high-powered television production company responsible for, among other things, *Get Smart* and *McMillan and Wife*.[34] From there she jumped to MGM after producer Dan Melnick, one of the partners in Talent Associates, was hired as the head of production for the studio; he brought Lansing along as a story editor, responsible for reading scripts and discovering new material.[35]

Lansing was following a well-worn path. Apart from work as a secretary or receptionist, reading scripts and manuscripts was one of the few points of entry available for women looking to crack Hollywood. Like many things about Hollywood in the late 1960s and even the early 1970s, this sexual division of labor seemed almost unchanged from the industry's founding. In fact, so many women were funneled into the early stages of film development that the industry had adopted the slightly demeaning shorthand for them of "D-girls," or development girls. "The job that was considered a woman's job, going back to Irving Thalberg, was that we were the readers," said Lansing. "We read and gave our synopses of the script so they [the executives] didn't have to read it themselves, unless they wanted to. That was considered a woman's job, and not just an entrance job, but an *ending* job. That's what you were supposed to do in the studio system."[36]

A few women found other roles in Hollywood. Marcia Nasatir, a former book editor who transitioned to Hollywood as an agent, broke through as the industry's first female vice president when United Artists hired her in 1974. Verna Fields and Marcia Lucas, the wife of George Lucas, worked regularly as respected film editors. The industry generally considered women well suited for work in public relations, partly because it was assumed that they could cope with temperamental stars more diplomatically than men could. Several women emerged as important go-betweens for the stars and the media, none of them more powerful than Pat Kingsley, a steely southerner who started as a secretary for legendary publicist Warren Cowan and launched her own company in 1971.[37] The only woman in LA with a more impressive client list may have been Sue Mengers, a vice president at the Creative Management Associates (CMA) talent agency. Bronx-born and unquenchably ambitious, Mengers tended to a roster of stars (Barbra Streisand, Ryan O'Neal, Diana Ross) and directors (Peter Bogdanovich, Arthur Penn, Bob Fosse) with an unrelenting intensity that sometimes seemed lifted from a Borscht Belt comic's parody of his overbearing mother. But she was an undeniable force, fabled for her exclusive parties and her relentlessness in pursuing opportunities for her clients.

Equally forceful was Julia Phillips, the producer who provided a druggy, sun-splashed clubhouse for the young generation of Hollywood filmmakers at the Malibu beach cottage she shared with her husband, Michael. Phillips was by far the most influential woman producer of the time, both before and after her split with her husband in July 1974. A native New Yorker who obtained an Ivy League dusting at Mount Holyoke, Phillips also found her way into Hollywood first as a reader, for Paramount in New York (after condensing books for the *Ladies' Home Journal*), and she had a reader's eye for good material. She and Michael jumped into producing in partnership with Tony Bill. Together they optioned two screenplays from a then-unknown writer named David Ward.[38] Those scripts became the partnership's first two movies: the forgettable *Steelyard Blues* and *The Sting*, which won the Oscar for Best Picture. Then Phillips picked up the script for *Taxi Driver*, from Paul Schrader, on a recommendation from Brian De Palma; both men were part of the regular circle at her weekend beach parties. In pursuing projects, Phillips was profane, resilient, and resourceful, disarming with her blunt candor. "Julia was extraordinarily bright, and she was outspoken and ahead of the curve in any conversation," Bill recalled. "That is potentially, and actually, threatening to a lot of people, but she is a great salesperson, and she had the taste to back it up. She was a younger equivalent of Sue Mengers, in some ways. It was time to speak up, and they spoke up. They also had a gift of humor which melts many men's souls."[39] Like Bert Schneider and Bob Rafelson a few years earlier, Julia and Michael Phillips became to the older generation of industry leaders "a ticket to what is young, hip, happening," as Phillips put it years later in her now-classic memoir, *You'll Never Eat Lunch in This Town Again.*[40]

For all these women, the price of admission into the rooms where decisions were made was accepting the rules set by the men who were already there. Unequal pay was a given. On one occasion at MGM, Lansing learned that a male colleague at the same level was earning more. "'Well, I understand why you feel you deserve it,'" she later recalled being told, "'but you're single, and he's married and has kids, so he deserves a raise, and you don't.'"[41] Lansing accepted the decision without argument, an indication of how tenuous she, like most women, considered her foothold in the system. This first generation of women felt enormous pressure to demonstrate their ability to fit in and to avoid seeming "threatening" to men. When they faced unwanted sexual advances in the workplace, they tried to defuse the situation, but rarely did they press for consequences. When powerful men mistook them for secretaries or assistants, they shrugged off the slights with laughs and jokes, however much they seethed on the inside. When they gave interviews to the press, they expressed opinions that upheld rather than challenged the prevailing values of the men around them.[*] The boys' club in Hollywood and television was so entrenched that even the few women who breached it mostly felt compelled to show they would not challenge its prejudices or rattle its hierarchy.

---

[*] In 1974, Mengers gave a bizarre interview with *Ms.* magazine in which she sweepingly dismissed the women's movement. "I don't have too much sympathy for a lot of the women who claim they're being discriminated against," she insisted. "They're discriminated against because they're *not that good*. Most of the Movement seems like a lot of *whining* to me. Just get out and do it. *I* did it" (Louise Farr, "And Now from Hollywood: The Sweetening of Sue Mengers," *Ms.*, June 1975). Jack Warner or even Robert Evans could hardly have said it any differently, which was probably why Mengers said it at all.

In this environment, women were more likely to see other women as rivals than as allies. "There was not a sense of sisterhood," Lansing said flatly.[42] She didn't seek friendships with the few other women emerging as studio executives; nor did they seek out her. Networking among women was almost nonexistent. Lansing, like others, internalized the unspoken but widespread assumption in Hollywood that in any room where decisions were made, there was space for only one woman (at most). "I don't know if it was one hundred percent reality," Lansing said, "but I can't remember [a meeting with] two women." And in fact, when Dan Melnick again brought Lansing with him to Columbia Pictures a few years later, Roz Heller, the other woman already in a senior position there, was forced out, partly to clear the way.[43] "All those years," said Lansing, "we thought there was only room for one at the table."[44] The men filling most of the chairs did nothing to dispel that notion.

DIRECTING WAS THE MOST difficult hill to climb for Hollywood women in the early 1970s. Very few occupied the director's chair in television or movies. Doors that flung open for the Movie Brat generation of young male directors (Scorsese, Spielberg, De Palma) remained closed to women. No woman ever directed an episode of *All in the Family* through its run, and none directed an episode of *M*A*S*H* until 1976. The problem, Treva Silverman thought, was straightforward: "What man wants a woman directing him, controlling him, in charge of him, telling him what to do?"[45] At one point, Dan Melnick considered bringing in Julia Phillips to supervise production at the television development company where he had hired Sherry Lansing as a reader, but in the end, he decided not to offer her the job and explained that he didn't think the crews on the sets would take orders from a woman.[46]

The one notable exception during this time was comedian Elaine May, formerly half of a celebrated late 1950s improvisational comedy duo with Mike Nichols. But May's experiences as director proved a cautionary tale. Paramount signed her in 1968 to write, direct, and star in a comedy, an unprecedented trifecta of responsibilities for a female artist, but the experience left both sides bruised.[47] Paramount considered May, a first-time director, unsteady on the set, and it sliced more than one third of the three-hour print she delivered of her film, *A New Leaf.* Though the movie received generally positive reviews, May was so outraged that she sued to have her name removed from it.[48] She took her next movie to Fox and rebounded with *The Heartbreak Kid* in 1972, a comedy she directed from a script by Neil Simon. Its success earned her enough credibility to return to Paramount in 1973 to direct her own script for a gangster buddy movie with Peter Falk and John Cassavetes, called *Mikey and Nicky*, but the reunion derailed her career. The film grew more expensive and more incomprehensible in tandem. With the budget soaring, Paramount fired May, then rehired her, and the two sides battled through another round of lawsuits after she finished shooting. The film didn't reach theaters until December 1976, where it instantly sank under the weight of brutal reviews.[49]

Some saw May's exile after *Mikey and Nicky* as evidence of a double standard. Certainly, no shortage of male directors had produced disjointed disasters and collected their next assignment more quickly than May, but no other woman received even as many chances as May did. The absence of woman feature film directors became so glaring that the American Film Institute, facing protests from feminist groups, established a workshop in the fall of 1974 intended to train more women to assume that role. The first class of fellows was glittering: Julia Phillips (who was hoping to direct Erica Jong's ode to sexual liberation, *Fear of Flying*), Lily Tomlin, and Lee Grant, who had directed *The Shape of Things* special for ABC the previous year.[50] But the program was threadbare, offering the women little more than "equipment that is one step above Mickey Mouse," as Grant put it, and the use of students as crews to produce sample videos.[51] More important, it could not address the fundamental problem women faced: the studios' refusal to finance movies with women directors.

Joan Tewkesbury, the writer who crafted *Nashville* for Altman, crashed against this very financing wall after she completed work on that epic in 1975. When the movie finished, Altman knew they would be riding a big wave, so he told both Tewkesbury and Alan Rudolph, his first assistant director, that if they had a project they wanted to move forward, this was the time to do so. Rudolph had a script for a *Nashville*-like story of intersecting doomed romances in Los Angeles called *Welcome to LA*.[52] Tewkesbury had a script called *Ever After*, a dark comedy about the dissolution of her marriage. But Altman ultimately found funding only for Rudolph. "Bob could get [Rudolph's] movie made," Tewkesbury remembered. "He couldn't get mine." The most common explanation she heard was that her movie too closely resembled *Diary of a Mad Housewife*, another story of a wife trying to emerge from the shadow of a domineering husband, but Tewkesbury recognized that more was involved. "I'm sure it had a little something to do with [my] being a girl," she said. Even Altman, she thought, "was much more comfortable working in that capacity as a producer with the men than with me."[53]

The first sustained breakthrough for a female director in early 1970s Hollywood came from an unlikely pioneer. Joan Darling wanted a career in entertainment from the time she was three, but acting was initially her focus. After moving to Los Angeles in 1969, Darling scratched out a few television parts, including a recurring role on *Owen Marshall, Counselor at Law*, a stolid ABC legal drama. She auditioned for the role of Rhoda on *Mary Tyler Moore* and came close to the part before the producers picked Valerie Harper.

Darling was hoping to leap from appearing in series television to the very hot new opportunity of made-for-TV movies when she wrangled a meeting with Norman Lear, a distant relation. Darling went to see Lear with an idea to star in a made-for-television movie about Golda Meir, the flinty Israeli prime minister. Lear wasn't much interested in that proposal, but he surprised her with an unexpected question: "How would you like to direct?"[54] Aware of how little opportunity his productions had provided to women behind the camera, he had been searching for a female director, particularly for a send-up of daytime soap operas that he had developed, called *Mary Hartman, Mary Hartman*. "He was looking for women," Darling said. "That was on his mind."[55] Darling had no experience directing anything except theater, but she felt the acting classes she had taught since arriving in

Los Angeles equipped her for the position. Besides, she was always up for a new challenge. She took the job and spent weeks in 1974 casting the show with Lear. (The cast, led by Louise Lasser in the title role, included Mary Kay Place as a country-singing neighbor, a role that highlighted her talent for both comedy and music.) Then Darling shot two pilot episodes.

Grant Tinker, at MTM, saw the tape of those two pilots and was impressed enough to make Darling an offer unprecedented for a female director in early 1970s Hollywood: he proposed to hire her for a full season to direct episodes across MTM's expanding stable of shows. When her agent excitedly relayed the news, Darling remembers first thinking, Wait, I'm an actress. But a second thought quickly displaced that one: "There is not a woman directing, and they think a woman can't direct for all the wrong reasons. I don't know if I was any good at it, but I do know I can deliver a job on time, so I am going to do this for one year, to show that a woman can direct."[56] For MTM, Darling directed episodes of the short-lived sitcom *Doc* and of the *Mary Tyler Moore* spin-offs *Rhoda* and *Phyllis*, all of which appeared in the fall of 1975.

These were solid efforts, but Darling made her name with the sole episode she ever directed of *Mary Tyler Moore*, "Chuckles Bites the Dust," which aired in October 1975. Written by David Lloyd, "Chuckles" was an edgier concept than the MTM show usually embraced: it centers on Mary giggling uncontrollably at the funeral of Chuckles the Clown, who hosted the children's show at the fictional WJM station, where she works. Three days into rehearsals, Mary Tyler Moore, who was even more proper than her character, stopped during a scene and openly wondered whether to proceed. "Do you think we should be doing this show?" she asked Darling. "It's about death, and it's funny."[57] Darling talked her down, persuading Moore that *Mary Richards*'s behaving so inappropriately would reassure anyone else who ever laughed at the wrong time in church or at the opera. "My absolute faith in her was like a floor for her to walk on," Darling said. It was typical of the no-nonsense style that allowed Darling to command the set at a time when so many male executives insisted that casts and crews would not accept direction from a woman. "I wasn't afraid to be a leader," Darling remembered. "As I say, having two older brothers is a perfect training ground for directing."[58] Moore aced the episode, which became perhaps the most beloved of all for the series and has won some polls as the greatest single episode of a situation comedy ever. The following spring, Lloyd won the Emmy for Outstanding Writing in a Comedy Series for "Chuckles," and Darling was named one of the finalists for Best Director.

This recognition only strengthened the wave of attention that descended on Darling in January 1976, when *Mary Hartman* finally reached the air to enormous critical acclaim. All the notice convinced producer Larry Turman, after some reluctance from Paramount, to hire her to direct *First Love*, an R-rated feature film love triangle that flashed plenty of skin.[59] Darling became the first of her contemporaries to scale that hill: incredibly, no other woman directed an American feature film in 1977.[60] Her ascension attracted plenty of media attention, but after *First Love* appeared to modest reviews and middling box office receipts, Darling's feature opportunities narrowed as quickly as Elaine May's had a few years earlier: she worked almost entirely in television through the fifteen-year remainder of her directing career.[61] Joan Tewkesbury likewise directed only for television after her first feature film was released in 1979. Lee Grant, after finally releasing her first feature in 1980, directed only one other in a career that kept her steadily directing for television over the next twenty-five years. It was another reminder of how narrow the ledge remained for women in Hollywood: it took only the slightest slip to fall off. "The boys got to do it again," said Tewkesbury, "but for the women, if you didn't score well, you did not get the opportunity to do your second feature. You had one shot, and everybody at the studios went, 'Whew, that's over and we can move on now.'"[62]

PROGRESS FOR AFRICAN AMERICANS in movies and television came, at best, only slightly faster during these years. Television featured very few minority characters through the early 1960s, but as the decade proceeded, a slow trickle began—starting in 1963 with African American Ossie Davis in a supporting role as a New York City police officer in the comedy *Car 54, Where Are You?*[63] A few Black actors and actresses expanded to leading roles, with Bill Cosby (*I Spy*), Clarence Williams III (*The Mod Squad*), Diahann Carroll (*Julia*), and Lloyd Haynes (*Room 222*). The burst of "relevant" situation comedies in the early 1970s brought a new wave of nonwhite leading characters, with *Chico and the Man* and the Lear-produced comedies *Sanford and Son, Good Times*, and *The Jeffersons*. Black action stars followed in *Get Christie Love, Tenafly*, and a television adaptation of the movie *Shaft* (though none of these shows survived for more than a season). When the U.S. Civil Rights Commission examined the composition of television casts, it found that most situation comedies and virtually all dramas in the 1973/74 season still did not have a single recurring nonwhite character.[64] Minorities represented only one in eight characters in the 1974 season, but even that modest presence was almost double the level in 1969.[65]

Behind the camera, the gains were more limited still. Even the shows that featured African American or Latino characters were typically owned by white producers, shaped by white directors, and crafted predominantly by white writers. The absence of Black directors and writers was a consistent source of tension, particularly in the shows centered on African American characters. Redd Foxx often complained about the lack of Black writers and directors on *Sanford and Son*, though those complaints were also a form of leverage in his endless financial struggles with Lear and Yorkin. The sharpest disputes came over *Good Times*. When Lear decided to create a new show around the character of Florida, the maid on *Maude* played by Esther Rolle, he initially hired two Black writers, Eric Monte and Mike Evans, who played Lionel Jefferson on *All in the Family*, to fill in the idea. They developed the basic characters and concept, but Lear didn't like their script, and he brought in Allan Manings to rewrite the pilot and take control as the showrunner.[66] Manings fit Lear's typical mold: a white comedy writer from the East Coast with a long television pedigree; he had written for *Leave It to Beaver* and *Petticoat Junction* as well as *Laugh-In*.[67] *Good Times* never entirely stabilized after that tumultuous birth. Over its bumpy six-year run, Lear repeatedly clashed with stars Esther Rolle and John Amos, who felt enormous pressure in their roles at the center of the first situation comedy about an African American family. The breakout popularity of Jimmie Walker as the family's elder son, J.J., in a role that many critics considered cartoonish and stereotyped, only heightened the tension, especially after Walker developed a catchphrase, "Dy-no-mite!" that the mostly white writing staff used too often when it needed a laugh. The friction bubbled into remarkable media interviews in which the show's stars publicly complained about its portrayal of Black families on the screen and the lack of Black faces behind it. Rolle virtually exploded in dismay to *Ebony* magazine about the writers' definition of the J.J. character, which she considered demeaning to young Black men: "Little by little . . . they have made him more stupid and enlarged the role," she complained.[68] Amos was so disgruntled about the show's direction that Lear wrote him out of it after its third season.[69] Lear did not face anything like this internal drama on his other comedy about a Black family, *The Jeffersons*, starring the Bunkers' upwardly mobile Black neighbors. But after that show reached the air in January 1975, it faced comparable questions as *Good Times* and *Sanford*, about its reliance on whites as producers, writers, and directors. When Lear won an award at an Urban League dinner in 1975, a group of Black screenwriters picketed his appearance.[70] The Congress of Racial Equality, a civil rights group, described its relationship with Lear's production company as a "state of cold war."[71]

From one angle, Lear could justifiably feel that he was being unfairly targeted—it wasn't as if other television producers were employing more Black writers or directors, and none matched him in developing shows centered on the Black experience—but precisely because he was breaking so much ground for Black performers onscreen, many critics found his limited progress off-screen especially glaring. The real issue, for many, wasn't so much that Lear, a white Jewish man in his fifties, had so much influence in interpreting the Black experience for the vast network television audience. The deeper problem was that no African Americans had comparable opportunities. As the fall 1974 season started, the Black actor Bernie Casey expressed this frustration when he told the *Los Angeles Times* that he considered the Black-themed network shows "a negative thing," given that they were still controlled by whites. "A black show is one written, produced and directed by blacks, so *Sanford and Son* is just another comedy," he complained. "Creatively, Hollywood has failed to encourage black talent—especially behind the camera."[72]

For all the tensions that surrounded Lear's African American comedies, the shows also represented undeniable progress. They embodied a two-pronged message of change. Most directly, they demonstrated increasing awareness inside the television networks that Black viewers represented an important component of their audience, especially as the Black middle-class slowly but irreversibly grew in the years following the passage of the Civil Rights Act of 1964. Equally important, the shows proved that a substantial white audience would watch programs with Black protagonists. The Hollywood studios during these years remained mostly unconvinced on that latter point: they were still skeptical that movies with Black stars (apart, perhaps, from Sidney Poitier) could attract large "crossover" white audiences. But the studios became even more intent than the networks on tapping Black America's growing buying power, and for a few years, this imperative ignited a dynamic but deeply controversial surge of Black filmmaking that became known as blaxploitation.

LONG INVISIBLE, BLACK STARS became indispensable to the movie industry for a brief window in the early 1970s. From 1971 to 1975, Hollywood released some two hundred movies centered on Black characters.[73] These films earned an estimated $450 million at the box office and proved instrumental in lifting the film industry from its financial doldrums of the late 1960s and early 1970s.[74] This tide of Black-themed films began when Warner Bros. in 1968 hired Gordon Parks Sr., a multitalented author, photographer, and composer, to write and direct an adaptation of his semi-autobiographical novel, *The Learning Tree*.[75] Parks became the first African American to direct a studio feature.[76] Columbia followed by hiring Melvin Van Peebles, another polymorphous talent, who had written novels and directed a film while living in France, to direct *Watermelon Man*, a comedy about a white bigot who wakes up Black. Around the same time, producer Sam Goldwyn Jr. tapped the veteran actor Ossie Davis to direct *Cotton Comes to Harlem*, an action comedy released by United Artists about a con man preacher in Harlem.

These three movies, which reached theaters in 1969 and 1970, represented the first trickle of opportunity for African American filmmakers. But the surge of Black films really began in 1971, when Van Peebles, who chafed at what he considered the studio's "benign, unconscious racism" during *Watermelon Man*, released his independently financed *Sweet Sweetback's Baadasssss Song*.[77] The story of a Black Southern California pimp who kills two racist cops for abusing a Black man, the movie mapped the coordinates for the blaxploitation films that followed. It mixed explicit violence and sex with a message of Black empowerment and stirred it all to the beat of a pulsing soundtrack (written, in this case, by Van Peebles himself and performed by Earth, Wind and Fire, which was little known at the time). *Sweetback* set another pattern: produced on a shoestring—Van Peebles had to borrow fifty thousand dollars from Bill Cosby to finish it[78]—it generated over ten million dollars in revenue off its five-hundred-thousand-dollar budget.[79]

The movie's success inevitably turned the heads of other studios, which responded with their own films targeted principally at Black audiences. In June 1971, MGM released *Shaft*, and the next year, Warner Bros. came out with *Super Fly*, and when both movies returned strong box office receipts, the doors were flung open. Movies about Black pimps (*The Mack*), gangsters (*Black Caesar*, *The Black Godfather*), detectives (*Cleopatra Jones* and two *Shaft* sequels), vigilantes (*Coffy* and *Foxy Brown*), and bounty hunters (*Truck Turner*) flowed into theaters.

Most of these movies were made on tiny budgets, with crude production values, but they provided an unprecedented pipeline of work for Black actors and actresses. Through the blaxploitation boom, Black men received more opportunities to direct than white women did in the same years. Black screenwriters remained rare (though former advertising copywriter Phillip Fenty wrote *Super Fly*, and Alex Haley, the novelist best known for *Roots*, wrote a less successful sequel), but after years of impenetrable racial exclusion in the Hollywood crafts, most of the Black directors elevated by the movement worked to include other Black employees, from cameramen and cinematographers to stagehands, on their productions.

The blaxploitation era also created opportunities for other Black-themed films that transcended the genre's narrow limitations of violence, sex, drugs, and crime. By demonstrating the buying power of the African American audience, the garish blaxploitation movies raised the studios' receptivity to films that portrayed the Black experience more accurately. Films such as *Lady Sings the Blues* (starring Diana Ross and Billy Dee Williams and executive-produced by Berry Gordy), *Sounder* (starring Cicely Tyson and Paul Winfield and written by Black playwright Lonne Elder III), *Buck and the Preacher* (directed by Sidney Poitier and starring Poitier and Harry Belafonte), and later *Cooley High* (directed by Michael Schultz and written by Eric Monte, two young Black veterans of network television) were all entirely different in tone and subject than the blaxploitation movies and of mixed quality themselves, but they all benefited from the growing awareness of the Black audience that the blaxploitation films generated in the studios. By 1975, two Black-owned production companies, Berry Gordy's Motown Productions and Poitier's Verdon Productions, were operating on the Universal Pictures lot, and a handful of other independent Black producers had negotiated distribution deals with the studios for individual films.[80] Apart from the solitary Julia Phillips, no white woman could match these inroads at the time.

In all these ways, the blaxploitation era created opportunities for Black artists and technicians that remained largely closed to them in television, but the films ignited a two-front war. From the outside, they faced condemnation from civil rights groups, who understandably accused them of projecting a distorted and demeaning view of Black life. Black protesters picketed showings of films such as *Super Fly*, waving signs that insisted "We Are Not All Pimps and Whores!"[81] The movies' defenders countered that the films also constituted a form of Black empowerment. The typical blaxploitation plot showed a confident, dynamic African American star (Roundtree's Shaft or Pam Grier's Coffy and Foxy Brown) conquering a complex and dangerous urban landscape while attracting Black and white lovers alike. To the extent that white society touched Black life at all, it was in the form of corrupt cops and politicians and sadistic mobsters, who make the big money while dribbling crumbs to the Black pimps and drug dealers. When Pam Grier's heroic nurse, Coffy, outwits and kills a bigoted white drug kingpin, after first dispatching the corrupt white cops on his payroll, she portrays a form of Black empowerment and retribution in the face of racism that Hollywood had rarely shown on-screen. Still, the case for blaxploitation films like *Coffy* as a form of social subversion was diminished by the fact that Grier also spent much of the movie with her top off and a good deal of her time tearing the tops from other prostitutes working for a "Super Fly"-like Black pimp and pusher who struts through the movie in a gold jumpsuit (until he's brutally murdered by the white kingpin).

Among Hollywood's small community of Black actors and filmmakers, the films stirred ambivalence. Many of those who found regular work for the first time defended the blaxploitation movies on both economic and social grounds. Gordon Parks Sr., who directed the first *Shaft*, wrote in the *New York Times* of encountering a crowd of young African Americans lining up to see a 4 a.m. showing of the film at a Manhattan theater soon after it opened. "The orchestra was filled," Parks wrote. "The balcony was filled. And everything was 'right on!' A new hero, black as coal, deadlier than Bogart and handsome as Gable, was doing the thing that everyone in that audience wanted to see done for so long. A Black man was winning."[82] But Parks, like most in Hollywood's modest community of African American filmmakers, also keenly felt the limits of Black control over the blaxploitation films. Black intellectuals who disliked the genre's lurid subject matter, he wrote in his *New York Times* article, must recognize "that we new black filmmakers are not yet running the big Hollywood studios." If the critics wanted movies to capture other aspects of Black life, he suggested, "they should bestow on us the means, or more bluntly, the money" to produce those films.[83]

Parks's retort spotlighted the second front in the debate over the blaxploitation films: frustration among Black filmmakers that whites were still receiving most of the benefits from these movies' success. Yes, the blaxploitation films undeniably created more opportunity for Black filmmakers than existed before, but even on these movies, white men still filled most of the important jobs, from screenwriter to director, not to mention producer and studio executive. "Of the approximately 200 [Black-themed] movies made during the five-year boom," the *Los Angeles Times* concluded in 1975, "few had any sort of significant input from blacks in their making."[84] And even at the height of the blaxploitation boom, Blacks (with the rare exception, such as Poitier) remained almost entirely absent, both in front of and behind the camera, in the major mainstream films aimed primarily at white audiences that the studios expected to dominate both the box office and the Academy Award ceremonies.

Henry Jaglom remembered that even his close friend Bert Schneider, despite his impassioned support for Huey Newton and the Black Panthers, never talked about producing a movie with a Black filmmaker. "From the perspective of today, you would have thought that Bert would have found somebody," Jaglom recalled. "But it never came up. We were acculturated in a way I didn't even realize at that point."[85] Likewise, Tom Pollock, a lawyer who rocketed to wealth and influence representing many of the "Movie Brat" generation of young white directors and writers, did not even really notice at the time that he had few clients who were racial minorities. "A few, but not many, because there weren't that many," Pollock recalled. "I was in the lucky position of being able to pick and choose who I wanted to represent and who I didn't. Everybody at that time wanted me, and I got to choose who I thought would be big. Guess where that left most of the people of color? And as I think about it, I'm getting a little ashamed. But it wasn't about 'Am I prejudiced?' It was more about 'Well, see, the industry isn't going to do that for this person, so what can I do [for them]?' It was more about realpolitik . . . But I wasn't leading the way, either."[86] In fact, it was difficult to identify anyone in the industry's upper reaches who did.

DURING ITS HEYDAY IN the years just before and through World War II, the sizzling jazz scene along Central Avenue in the predominantly Black neighborhoods south of downtown Los Angeles enticed a glamourous mixed-race crowd. Orson Welles, Ava Gardner, and other white celebrities made the trip across LA's entrenched color line to hear such jazz virtuosos as Charles Mingus and Dexter Gordon in the smoky clubs that clustered along Central.[87] But even then, African Americans from South Central, as the mostly Black neighborhoods were known, could not cross in the other direction to hear music in the still-segregated jazz clubs a few miles to the north, along Hollywood or Sunset Boulevards.

As the Central Avenue scene declined after World War II, the white and Black music worlds in Los Angeles steadily separated, especially once the center of the city's commercial music industry shifted in the early 1960s to the frothy pop of the white surf rock groups such as Jan and Dean and the Beach Boys. By the time the folk-rock and country-rock movements coalesced in the late 1960s, Black and white musicians in Los Angeles operated in almost entirely separate worlds. Though most of the artists who incubated at the Troubadour revered rhythm and blues, few African American musicians were part of the scene there. Music in Los Angeles, Linda Ronstadt recalled, "was more white than it should be."[88]

Lou Adler, the talented producer and executive, had a front-row seat for this separation. As a young songwriter in the 1950s, Adler and his partner, Herb Alpert (who went on to fame as a bandleader and trumpet player in the 1960s), cowrote the beautiful "Wonderful World" with Sam Cooke. Cooke was the great Black hope of the LA music business, a silky matinee idol–handsome former gospel singer who immediately enjoyed massive pop success. But once Cooke moved on to another record label and their lives drifted apart, Adler found less connection between the Black music community and his work in the mostly white world of Los Angeles pop music. "When I stopped doing that [with Cooke], nothing connected to the pop world that I was in," Adler remembered. "It just sort of stopped. My relationship with Sam and a couple of other people from that era [persisted,] but it never really crossed over. The attempt I made a couple of times of bringing gospel into the pop stream didn't really work."[89]

Even after this divergence, African Americans in Los Angeles entered the 1970s in a stronger position in the music industry than in films. While very few Black actors headlined a movie until the blaxploitation era, several Los Angeles–based African American recording artists established substantial national followings—Sly Stone; the Crusaders; Earth, Wind and Fire; and War all sold well—and compared to the movie business, Blacks also controlled more of their own institutions in the music industry. Clarence Avant, a shrewd and tenacious African American agent, initially moved to Los Angeles to cut deals for his client Lalo Schifrin to compose film and television scores.[90] (Schifrin, among other things, penned the *Mission: Impossible* theme.) Avant had Lew Wasserman–like brilliance at untangling problems, brokering alliances, and mentoring ambitious young people who grew into well-placed allies. In 1970 he formed his own record label, which he called Sussex Records, after the two things everyone wanted more of: success and sex.

If Sussex represented a foothill for African Americans in the music industry, the other major Black-owned label in LA constituted its own mountain. Motown Records, the commercial behemoth that poured hits off its assembly line through the 1960s as reliably as its Detroit neighbors Ford and General Motors turned out new Mustangs and Cadillacs, had gradually shifted its headquarters to Los Angeles after Berry Gordy, its founder, moved there in 1968.[91] During the first years in Southern California, Motown didn't miss a step: the company pounded out hits from Stevie Wonder, Marvin Gaye, Diana Ross, the Temptations, and Gordy's latest discovery, the Jackson 5. By 1974, *Black Enterprise* magazine identified Motown as the nation's largest Black-owned business of any sort.*[92]

---

* Over time, the move to LA did exact a higher price on Gordy's empire. Through the middle 1970s, Motown generated fewer hits and lost momentum. The fall came partly because of changing listening tastes and partly because the relocation separated it from the rich traditions in Black music that had nourished it in

Yet, as in television and movies, Blacks in the music industry operated in a mostly self-contained world. They were virtually invisible as executives at the major record labels or in any position, from agent to producer, around white artists. Maybe, Adler recalled, African Americans filled a role as "a couple of promo girls. Never a record producer, never an engineer, maybe a second or third engineer once or twice."[93] Among musicians, the interaction was only modestly greater. Lowell George's funky, southern-infused Los Angeles band, Little Feat, had two Black members. White artists, like the guitarist Danny Kortchmar, might jam with Black friends over beers and blunts at night, but they rarely found themselves working in the same studio the next morning.[94] Interaction in the other direction was rare, too. Motown was a monolith, but one that stood defiantly disconnected from the white Los Angeles music scene. "They were Motown, and they were *there*," remembered Adler, pointing off in the distance. "They had their writers, they had their producers, they had their stagers, choreographers, and everything. They were self-contained as far as the rest of the nation."[95] In a city renowned for its high-quality recording studios, Motown even built its own facility in Hollywood.[96]

Behind the many institutional and social barriers was an artistic divergence. During the early 1970s, LA's prominent Black artists mostly turned out groove-heavy music designed to move audiences onto the dance floor. They had less interest in the acoustic guitars and soul-unburdening lyrics of the singer-songwriters then ruling the city's white musical scene. "Black music was getting funkier," remembered Jackson Browne, who in his teens had gravitated more toward rhythm

---

Detroit. But the biggest reason for Motown's growing troubles in Los Angeles was that Gordy became distracted by his mostly unsuccessful efforts to crack the film industry. Like David Geffen, he found that eminence in one industry barely brought a personal parking spot in the other. "I loved making [movies] but had a lot to learn about how to make money at it," Gordy wrote in his memoir. "In the meantime, I had slipped in the business I *did* know something about—records" (Berry Gordy, *To Be Loved: The Music, the Magic, the Memories of Motown: An Autobiography* [New York: Warner Books, 1994], 353–54).

and blues than folk rock. "The singer-songwriter movement didn't really sweep Black people up in it."[97]

The biggest local exception was Avant's greatest discovery at Sussex Records.* Bill Withers was one of the most unlikely stars in the early 1970s Los Angeles music scene. An African American navy veteran, he taught himself to play guitar and started writing his own songs in the 1960s. He was working as a mechanic for Boeing (building toilets for 747 aircraft) when his self-produced demo tape, which all the major labels had rejected, found its way to Avant.[98] Recognizing the quality of Withers's songs, Avant signed him and sent him into the studio with Booker T. Jones (of Booker T. and the MG's). Initially, Withers thought Avant and Jones intended another vocalist to sing his songs. Instead, they surrounded him with a top-notch studio band (including Stephen Stills, a friend of Jones, on lead guitar) and turned out the 1971 album *Just as I Am* on a shoestring budget.[99] When the album's first single, the haunting "Ain't No Sunshine," took off, Withers became an unlikely star at age thirty-three.

The next year, Withers's second album, *Still Bill*, sold even better, behind his classic ode to friendship, "Lean on Me," and his brooding account of a doomed but delirious affair, "Use Me." A live album at Carnegie Hall in 1973 extended his critical and commercial success. Withers conquered the citadel of the Los Angeles music world with triumphantly reviewed stands at the Troubadour in 1971, 1973, and 1974.[100]

Withers represented a promising evolution of the Southern California sound. He combined the earthiness and grittiness of soul

---

* The most powerful African American contribution to the singer-songwriter movement in that era was crafted far from LA: Motown star Marvin Gaye's landmark 1971 album, *What's Going On*. Overcoming Gordy's resistance to a "protest album," Gaye wrote many of the songs on what became a panoramic portrayal of the racial, generational, and even environmental conflicts roiling America. Though Gaye completed the album's final mix in Los Angeles, he recorded it in Detroit, where he remained based, in defiance of Gordy's determination to move the Motown operation west.

music with the lyrical fluency and confessional tone of the singer-songwriters. But his career plateaued after those triumphant first three albums. A fourth record, released in April 1974, disappointed partly because Sussex itself was sinking into the bankruptcy that doomed it in 1975. When Sussex fell, Withers moved to Columbia, but after the intimacy of the Black-owned Sussex, he felt overlooked and misunderstood at a giant label where the decision makers remained all white.[101]

Despite some later hits, he never equaled his early success. As important, no other major Black singer-songwriters followed him onto the Troubadour stage. The potential bridge Withers offered between LA's Black and white musical traditions remained unfinished. "The scenes didn't coincide," as Browne concluded.[102]

THE BACKDROP FOR THE struggles over inclusion in the entertainment industry was the broader drive for racial equity in Los Angeles itself. For generations, Los Angeles had been a deeply segregated city in employment, education, and above all housing. The iron fist enforcing this separation was the Los Angeles Police Department, particularly under the long reign of Chief William Henry Parker. Under Parker, the LAPD policed minority communities with a heavy hand. Casual brutality was common, not only in Black but also Mexican American neighborhoods.

As in other major cities, tensions grew in Los Angeles through the 1960s over these interlocking tools of oppression. They erupted violently with the Watts uprising in August 1965. Parker adamantly rejected any suggestion that the LAPD's abusive treatment of Black neighborhoods contributed to the violence, and LA's boundlessly ambitious mayor, Sam Yorty, backed Parker unreservedly.[103]

This flinty response from Parker, Yorty, and the rest of the city's mostly white leadership lit the long fuse that eventually reordered the city's racial politics. Yorty unwittingly became the key figure in this transition (especially after Parker died in 1966). A folksy demagogue from Nebraska more accomplished at stoking fears than resolving them, Yorty improbably won election as Los Angeles mayor in 1961 and vaguely hinted that he would pressure Parker to treat Black residents with more respect.[104]

Once Yorty took office, that promise mostly fizzled, but the new mayor continued to solicit support in the Black community. In 1963, he backed the election of the first three African American members of the Los Angeles City Council. One of the three Black men elected was Tom Bradley, a former longtime LAPD officer, who was the only African American appointed to lieutenant during Parker's entire tenure as chief.[105] Born in Texas to sharecroppers, Bradley had moved to Los Angeles with his family before World War II, attended UCLA on a track-and-field scholarship, and joined the LAPD in 1940.[106] Tall, ramrod-straight, careful with language, and perpetually calm in manner, Bradley exuded reassuring professionalism. He quickly emerged as the leading voice on the council challenging Parker and Yorty and demanding change in the LAPD.[107]

A collision between Yorty and Bradley became inevitable following the Watts uprising. After the unrest, which flared just after Yorty won his second term in 1965, the mayor irrevocably cast his lot with the city's forces of white backlash. "Yorty became hostile to Blacks, especially after the 1965 riots," remembered Zev Yaroslavsky, at the time a young political activist and later a powerful member of first the Los Angeles City Council and then the Los Angeles County Board of Supervisors.[108]

Yorty's hard turn to the right solidified his support in many white neighborhoods, especially in the San Fernando Valley, but it alienated more liberal areas on the city's Westside, including many Jews and younger voters stirring into activism in the civil rights and antiwar movements. This discontent allowed Bradley to assemble a powerful coalition of Blacks and liberal whites when he eventually challenged Yorty in the 1969 mayoral contest. In the April 1969 primary, Bradley raced out to a stunning lead,[109] but Yorty stormed back to beat Bradley in the run-off election the next month after running an openly racist campaign that portrayed Bradley, a former police officer, as the tool of Black militants, stoked Jewish fears of Black anti-Semitism, and warned that half the city's (preponderantly white) police force would resign if their former colleague were elected.[110] Yorty's open stoking of racial anxiety and resentment won him that battle but cost him the war. His undisguised appeals to white bigotry embarrassed a wide array of city leaders hoping to grow Los Angeles into a global capital of commerce and finance.

Bradley never stopped running after his 1969 defeat. The spring 1973 rematch between him and Yorty inspired an outpouring of energy and activism, not only in the Black community but also among the white liberals ready to recommit to a new cause after George McGovern's landslide defeat a few months earlier. "The McGovern campaign sort of spilled over into the Bradley campaign," remembered liberal activist and journalist Harold Meyerson.[111] After initially modulating his racial rhetoric, Yorty reprised his tactics from 1969, portraying Bradley as hostile to the police and surrounded by Communists and Black militants.[112] This time the alarms failed. In May 1973, Bradley routed Yorty by almost one hundred thousand votes to become the first African American–elected mayor of a mostly white large city.[113] Once local television projected him as the likely winner shortly before 8 p.m. on Election Night, he relaxed by watching an episode of Norman Lear's *Maude*, on CBS.[114]

Bradley's election hardly resolved all the city's racial inequities. He proved particularly cautious about confronting the entrenched power of the LAPD, whose continued mistreatment of Black residents eventually culminated in the Rodney King beating and subsequent Black uprising in 1992, almost two decades after Bradley's election. But in ways large and small, his win toppled the hard, high wall of racial exclusion in Los Angeles and opened a path for greater progress for African Americans and Mexican Americans alike. Los Angeles, long a bastion of segregation, now placed itself at the forward edge of the change that would vastly expand minority representation in political office over the next generation, if more slowly and grudgingly than many hoped during the civil rights era in the 1960s. Much of the Los Angeles story in the early 1970s was that culture preceded politics in reflecting the changes remaking the country. But politics, in the form of Bradley's election, preceded culture in reflecting the dynamics that would imperfectly but inexorably carry more minorities to positions of authority in the years ahead.

LONG AFTER BRADLEY'S POLITICAL breakthrough, progress in Hollywood remained grudging and uneven for both African American and (white) women filmmakers. The tide of blaxploitation movies receded quickly after 1975. One reason was the sustained political controversy around these movies, but even more important was the studios' growing recognition that Black audiences were as attracted as their white counterparts to Hollywood's new generation of blockbusters, from *The Godfather* and *The Exorcist* to *Jaws* and *Star Wars*.[115] This undercut the incentive to produce movies whose overall financial ceilings were lower because they were tailored so heavily to Black audiences. Although few civil rights leaders mourned the demise of the blaxploitation films, their end did reduce the opportunities for Black actors and, especially, Black directors. Even the brightest stars of the blaxploitation era, such as Richard Roundtree, Ron O'Neal, and Pam Grier, though working regularly, rarely again scored roles of such visibility and style.

The environment for white women was more encouraging in some respects and more daunting in others. By the later 1970s, the funnel widened for white women in the upper reaches of the entertainment companies. This allowed a steadier flow of talented young women such as Dawn Steel and Paula Weinstein (formerly the agent for Jane Fonda) to move into executive positions in the movie studios; for costume designer Anthea Sylbert to transition into an executive role at Warner; for Sherry Lansing to become the first woman president of a major studio, at Fox, in 1980; and for Marcy Carsey, a former script reader and comedy programming executive, to rise to a vice president's role at ABC in 1979 and to be joined by other ambitious women in senior positions at the networks. But women writers and directors struggling to attain a foothold often complained that the women executives lacked either the authority or the interest to green-light productions from other women. "It did none of us any good because . . . they were in positions that had a great title and not very much decision-making power," said Joan Tewkesbury. "They certainly had opinions, but it didn't help women directors at all. The women executives couldn't really say to the studio, 'You've got to do this movie now.'"[116]

Was the more important lesson from Tewkesbury's experience that she could now sometimes make her case to a woman, or that those women could not deliver her the funding she needed to direct another feature? The ambiguous answer captured the mixed legacy for women and African Americans in the entertainment industry during those years. Their personal ambitions were often frustrated, yet their determination to advance in the industry cracked openings in the barriers blocking them. Opportunity for women and minorities in Hollywood and television remains constricted to this day, but the range of stories that the entertainment industry now tells, and the roster of storytellers who are empowered to tell them, is vastly more diverse than half a century ago—and the transition toward this panoramic world of widening options began in early 1970s Los Angeles, with the first female and Black pioneers who fought, inch by inch, to open the doors of the entertainment industry's white boys' club.

11

NOVEMBER

Breakthrough

Linda Ronstadt could relate to the difficult experiences of Mary Kay Place, Linda Bloodworth-Thomason, Sherry Lansing, and other women pioneers in the television and movie industries. If anything, the position of women in the music industry was even more fraught. As in movies and television, women in music faced an environment in which men held almost all the power in every facet of the business. But the music industry's sexual politics, shaped by the era's endemic groupie culture, seemed to especially encourage its men to believe that one of the perks of their position was the opportunity to have sex with almost any woman they met. "It was a very sexually charged atmosphere, the whole music scene," recalled Ellen Bernstein (now Ziffren), who worked as one of the very few women A&R (artists and repertoire) executives at Columbia Records in San Francisco and Los Angeles during the early 1970s.[1]

The industry's small circle of women was surrounded at every level by men. There were few women album producers or engineers, hardly any agents or managers (until Geffen's former assistant, Leslie Morris, set up her own shop), and no senior executives at any of the major record companies. Women assumed they would be routinely propositioned, or worse, by the men around them. "This was a time when the whole sexual music culture was pretty prevalent and accepted," remembered Bernstein, who, at twenty-four, had a brief romance herself with Bob Dylan in the summer and fall of 1974, while he was writing the songs for *Blood on the Tracks*.[2] Some of the female artists, such as

Ronstadt, Bonnie Raitt, and Emmylou Harris, built a friendly network that functioned as a kind of support group, but neither they nor the few women in the record companies seriously pressed for the inclusion of more women in positions of power. As in the television and movie industries, most women in the music business accepted male dominance of all the powerful positions as a permanent feature of the landscape. "It just seemed the way of the world,"[3] Ronstadt remembered. Bernstein felt the same way. "I didn't question it," she recalled.[4] "I didn't think there should be more women here. I thought, 'I'm here. That's cool.'" Even in bands, there were hardly any women musicians. Peter Asher, the producer and manager, recalled that when women singers toured, they would sometimes hire female backup vocalists or wardrobe managers just so they had someone to talk to on the road besides a man. "Girl singers all universally complained about one of the problems being that you're on a bus with a million guys, and it's kind of fun, but you really miss having girlfriends."[5]

From every direction, this imbalance compounded the struggle Linda Ronstadt faced to find her footing in the early 1970s. As she sought to create her distinctive synthesis of country and rock, to invigorate traditional sounds with a modern twist, she found that at every juncture, she had to convince men: executives, managers, producers, even bandmates. "It was daunting, believe me," she recalled.[6] No woman ever had the power to say yes to what she wanted to do; it was always, and only, men. Ronstadt's endemic insecurity, her often giggly presence onstage, and her tendency to fall into dependent romances with men she worked with all complicated her desire to assert authority over her career. But the larger problem was the industry-wide tendency to assume that those decisions properly belonged to men. And even as those men respected her talent as a singer, they tended to dismiss her perspective, seemingly on the assumption that someone so attractive could not be trusted with decisions, even about her own path. (Early in her career, her first manager even signed her to appear as a regular on a television series without consulting her, and then was infuriated when she rejected the job to focus on her music.)[7] Asher, who later worked with Ronstadt, said that soon after he started collaborating with her, he realized "how much of 'don't you worry your pretty head about it' had been going on, really, to an amazing degree."[8]

The challenge wasn't only in the studio. On the road, Ronstadt was the headliner, but she recognized that the boys (for it was always *boys*) in her band often bridled at following musical direction from a woman. "Backing up a girl wasn't cool at all," she said at the time. "They didn't want to do that. They wanted to be rock & rollers and have this sexual identity they get by being up onstage with their guitars."[9] It didn't make it easier for her to assert command when the road culture featured what amounted to hot- and cold-running women: for weeks, the boys in her band might not interact with any women beyond groupies they could sleep with. Operating in this environment, Ronstadt walked a narrow line. She didn't keep herself aloof from her traveling band and crew the way some other headliners did, but she did learn to establish a distance that preserved her authority. John Boylan, her producer, manager, bandmate, and former boyfriend, remembered "she developed a certain skin, in a way, to be one of the boys . . . but in the end, she was the CEO and ran everything."[10] Ronstadt didn't pass judgment on the nightly carousing unrolling around her, but she did set clear expectations. "What you had to do was make them relate to you through your music," she said. "Musicians were so single track. Musicians just care about music. I think they thought of me as the gig. All the guys in my band had girlfriends and wives at home, but I was the gig. We formed a camaraderie based on that, but no more than that."[11]

Both in the studio and on the road, Ronstadt often felt like she was being tested by the men she encountered. They often seemed surprised, she recalled, that she could contribute ideas about how to arrange and perform songs. "It's a little bit like that saying 'You throw like a girl,'" she remembered. "If you didn't throw like a girl, it was remarked upon. Girls weren't expected to be able to play an instrument, for instance. They weren't expected to be able to do their arrangements." She felt as if she gained more credibility each time one of her ideas produced a good result. "I had a lot of hand in my arrangements as the bossy girl singer," she said. "If the arrangement is good, nobody minds. Nothing succeeds like success."[12] Still, the idea of a female singer as anything more than an object of desire remained so foreign that when *Rolling Stone* profiled Ronstadt in early 1975, the writer asked all the men around her, from her band members to Asher, her new manager, whether they had tried to sleep with her.[13]

All these headwinds swirling around her own insecurities stalled Ronstadt as her career drifted through what she later called "the bleak years, when I was just grinding it out."[14] But in November 1974, she finally fulfilled the great expectations that had long surrounded her. Her long march at last produced a breakthrough so transcendent that her gifts became impossible to ignore. In the constellation of dazzling talents who had collected in Los Angeles, Ronstadt wasn't the only one to reach a new peak that month. So did her close friend Jackson Browne and her once-and-future boyfriend Jerry Brown. In November, each of them made commanding statements that provided a rousing crescendo for LA's landmark year of 1974.

LINDA RONSTADT HOPED FOR a fresh start when she left Capitol for David Geffen's Asylum Records in 1972, but old problems followed her to the new label. Working again with John Boylan, she started recording the album that became *Don't Cry Now*. She completed the two tracks that became the album's first singles, the ballad "Love Has No Pride" and "Silver Threads and Golden Needles," the Dusty Springfield song she had also included on her first solo album. But before long, Ronstadt and Boylan were clashing over her direction. "We argued a lot; we competed enormously in the studio," she recalled a few years later. "I just didn't trust him, I didn't trust anyone then, and I was always afraid that something was going to get pulled over me. I was punch-drunk from producers."[15]

Boylan developed an idea to break the rut. Ronstadt, with James Taylor, had contributed background vocals a few months earlier to Neil Young's breakout single "Heart of Gold." Now a mega-star, Young was beginning a tour that would carry him to arenas across America through early 1973. Boylan saw it as an opportunity to place Ronstadt before much larger audiences than she had ever attracted. "I said,

'The album's not finished, but this tour is great. Let's do this tour,'"
Boylan remembered.[16] He lobbied Elliot Roberts, Young's longtime
manager (and Geffen's partner), to put Ronstadt on the tour as the
opening act. Initially, Roberts refused because Young wanted to perform alone.[17] But after a few weeks, Young complained that this was
too tiring, and Roberts called Boylan offering to add Ronstadt as an
opening act. Then Ronstadt hesitated. She had played mostly small
clubs up to that point and was afraid she could not command arena-
size audiences, especially those impatiently waiting for the headliner.
"She didn't really want to do it," Boylan recalled. "She was scared."[18]
Boylan enlisted Geffen, who persuaded Ronstadt that the exposure of
appearing with Young was worth the stress. So, she jumped into the
deep end of the pool. With only a few days' notice, Ronstadt flew east
to open for Young at Madison Square Garden, the world's most famous arena, on January 23, 1973.

She picked a propitious show to join the tour: that was the night
Secretary of State Henry Kissinger reached the agreement in Paris of-
ficially ending American participation in the Vietnam War. (The formal documents were signed four days later.) Handed a notice during
his set, Young, characteristically terse, simply declared, "The war is
over," to raucous applause.[19] This was a rare moment of celebration for
Ronstadt. For the next few months, she found herself playing the nation's largest arenas with a band that, as she often said, wasn't "as loud
as the air-conditioning."[20] "It was one of those things where if you
want to play with the big boys, you'd better get your game up, and my
game wasn't up very high," she said, looking back. "I was a club act.
I got shoveled onto [the] stage at Madison Square Garden . . . and it
was pretty shocking. My naïveté: I didn't realize how different it was
going to be on one of those big stages. It's like jumping from a puddle
into a huge lake where you are a mile from shore and it's like three
hundred feet [of water] below you."[21] Ronstadt liked Young and found
him respectful when they interacted, but the dynamics of opening for
such a huge star could not have been more perfectly designed to trigger her insecurity. On the road, there was a clear caste system. "Everybody in Neil's band had priority over everybody [in mine] in the sound

check," she remembered. "And you know you had to stay in your place. There was a pecking order, and everybody obeyed it."[22] Jack Nitzsche, Young's keyboardist and old friend, mercilessly hazed Ronstadt with abusive, drunken rants that she wasn't up to the job of opening for their band. "What he did was inexcusable," remembered Boylan. To fortify herself, Ronstadt snorted enough cocaine that, by her account, she "had to have my nose cauterized twice."[23]

For all the stress, the tour served Boylan's purpose. Performing for the huge crowds that gathered for Young greatly raised Ronstadt's visibility. "It was tough for her, but she knocked them dead," remembered Boylan. "She thought she was not powerful enough to be on the stage with these people . . . like Neil Young. In fact, she was. It took her a while to figure that out."[24] After years mostly of running in place, the Young tour gave Ronstadt a burst of momentum. Another change in 1973 had an even greater effect. Ronstadt finally cemented her relationship with the man who would change her life, Peter Asher. An elfin, understated Englishman, Asher was a former child actor who had had pop success in the duo Peter and Gordon during the mid-1960s.[25] After the band broke up, he worked for the Beatles as a producer and then as an executive at their Apple Records. He soon relocated to Los Angeles to manage and produce James Taylor, whom he had signed (at the recommendation of guitarist Danny Kortchmar) at Apple.

When Ronstadt, at Boylan's suggestion, approached Asher about managing her, around 1971, he was initially enthusiastic. "I first heard her at the Bitter End, in New York," he remembered.[26] "Somebody told me, 'You have to go and see this girl. She's an amazing singer, she's incredible looking, sings barefoot, and wears short shorts, and she is really hot and sings like an angel.'[27] All of which is true. Then I met her and discovered her to be one of the most remarkably articulate and clever, amazing women I ever met." Within a few weeks, though, Asher backed out because he decided that taking on Ronstadt could create a conflict with his other client, Kate Taylor, James's sister.[28] Ronstadt remained in contact with Asher, sometimes attending the cozy dinner parties he threw for the rock elite with his wife, Betsy. When

Kate decided that she no longer wanted to pursue a touring career, she freed Asher from his commitment to her. Ronstadt approached Asher to manage her again, and this time he agreed.

His first job was to help her finish *Don't Cry Now*, as Geffen was growing impatient over the lengthening delay. Asher was different from Ronstadt's earlier producers. For one thing, in contrast to Boylan and J. D. Souther (whom Ronstadt briefly enlisted to produce after she dismissed Boylan), he never had a romance with her. Whatever temptations arose, their relationship was strictly business. "I think it's very difficult for a couple to work together," Asher said. "I know some of them figure out a successful way to do it. I think, given the role of a record producer to occasionally be critical or question decisions and stuff like that, being a boyfriend at the same time, it was much easier for Linda and I to work together and then go to our separate homes. It makes more sense."[29] Asher was also much less volatile than most people she had worked with and, for that matter, most people in the music business anywhere. For Ronstadt, finding the steady, professional Asher was like reaching a placid bay after crossing a rolling sea. "Peter was an intelligent person I could talk to and he would talk back to me like a person, not like somebody he wanted to ball, or somebody he thought was silly and could push around," she said at the time.[30]

With Asher's help, *Don't Cry Now* was released in September 1973. The process took Ronstadt over a year and about $150,000 in studio expenses.[31] With Geffen's promotional heft behind it, the album sold considerably more records than its predecessors, but it remained short of a breakout hit. It gave Ronstadt her first gold album but peaked at only No. 45 on the *Billboard* charts. Both the tracks she recorded with Boylan, "Love Has No Pride" and "Silver Threads and Golden Needles," reached a middling position on the singles charts in early 1974, but artistically, *Don't Cry Now* was another frustrating product, mixing her powerful voice with odd song choices—her barefooted earnestness clanged against Randy Newman's acerbic "Sail Away"—and syrupy arrangements.[32] Though it contained some moving moments (including an inspired cover of the Eagles' "Desperado" more compelling than the original), the best thing about *Don't Cry Now* was completing it. But with Asher now in her camp, Ronstadt looked forward with new optimism. "Let's face it," said Boylan, looking back, "Peter was at the top of his game."[33]

Asher didn't start with an answer to the question that so many people in LA were asking: Why hadn't Ronstadt, with all her gifts, achieved more success? "I didn't have a master plan in my head," he recalled, but he knew that part of the answer was providing more space for her to express her own eclectic musical ideas. "A lot of it was no one was listening to Linda," he said. "She had this reputation of being difficult, which was completely unjustified, and some of this is now cliché, but if you're a really good-looking woman, people don't take you seriously. I do think one of the things I did do that nobody was doing was sit down seriously and ask Linda, 'What do you think? What should we be doing?'"[34]

The pieces of a breakthrough came together month by month. Because she didn't write songs, Ronstadt had to find them. While some assumed that she relied on her producers, she herself selected the songs she recorded, and her ears were always open. "She was a great collector of songs," Jackson Browne recalled.[35] Through the frustrations of 1973, Ronstadt stockpiled the music that would carry her career to a new level. The first song that would anchor her next album came from Kenny Edwards, her old Stone Poneys bandmate. He introduced her to a rollicking rhythm-and-blues number called "You're No Good" that had first been a hit for Betty Everett in 1963.[36] Ronstadt used the song to close her sets during the Neil Young tour, and she delivered a scorching rendition, complete with a funky drum and bongo solo, on the nationally televised *Midnight Special* show that December. "You're No Good" went into her mental ledger.

While touring on her own in September 1973, Ronstadt had stopped in Atlanta to see the band Little Feat, headlined by the multitalented Lowell George. A Los Angeles native—his father worked in Hollywood—who played a brilliant slide guitar and crafted songs with a swampy southern funk, George had many admirers in LA's country-rock elite, but he was never a central part of it. Ronstadt had met him earlier in 1973, at a community festival in Topanga Canyon, where he played for her his masterpiece, "Willin'," a yearning, evocative ballad of a truck driver longing for his girl, "Dallas Alice," and getting by on "weed, whites and wine."[37] Ronstadt forgot about the song, but when she heard George perform it again, in Atlanta before a raucous crowd, she was understandably captivated. She asked George to teach it to her, and back in Los Angeles, he came over to her apartment with an acoustic guitar to work out an arrangement in a key she could sing.[38] "I didn't have any business trying to sing his songs," Ronstadt remembered, "but I liked them so much I had to try."[39] Another option went into the ledger.

Around the time Ronstadt saw Little Feat in Atlanta, the country-rock pioneer Gram Parsons succumbed to his demons and died of a drug overdose in Joshua Tree in September 1973. A few months earlier, during the Neil Young tour, Ronstadt had gone to see Parsons perform in a Houston honky-tonk. There she met his brilliant discovery, a young singer named Emmylou Harris, and Ronstadt, like many listeners, was blown away.[40] After Parsons's death, Ronstadt invited the grieving Harris out to sing with her for a set of shows she was performing that fall at the Roxy, the club that Lou Adler, Geffen, and their partners had recently opened on Sunset Boulevard. Among the songs the two women learned was the old Hank Williams ballad "I Can't Help It (If I'm Still in Love with You)." Ronstadt filed away that one, too.[41]

She found another new tune during the tour she began with Jackson Browne a few months after that, in January 1974. At a stop in Washington, DC, Ronstadt met a young songwriter named Paul Craft, who taught her his recently composed song, "Keep Me from Blowing Away." Ronstadt liked that one enough that she recorded a version of it in a nearby studio before she left the city.[42]

Earlier on the tour came a pivotal moment for her. During Ronstadt's years of uncertainty at Capitol, the symbol of her frustration was the label's refusal to let her record a song called "Heart Like a Wheel." "I just wanted to record that song more than anything," she recalled.[43] Written by Anna McGarrigle, part of a Canadian folk-singing duo with her sister, Kate, the aching "Heart Like a Wheel" captured the delicate, unfiltered emotions Ronstadt hoped to project in her music. "I found a song that was my sensibility," she said, looking back. "It expressed my taste exactly. What I thought about things and how I thought about them."[44] Ronstadt recorded a version for the self-titled album she did with John Boylan, but her manager and the record company thought it "too corny" and killed it. Disappointed, "I protected it in my back pocket and thought I'd hold it for another opportunity," Ronstadt remembered.[45] Initially, she didn't play it for Asher because she didn't want it to be rejected again. But the day before she and Jackson Browne appeared at Carnegie Hall, in February 1974, she heard Andrew Gold, the talented young guitarist in her band, strumming the introduction to the song during rehearsal.[46] She started singing along. Pleased with the result, Ronstadt added it to her set at the Carnegie Hall show.[47] Asher loved the song, too. "I fell in love with it the minute I heard it," he remembered. "She said that was when she knew I was the right person to produce her record."[48] Ronstadt became determined to finally record the song, on her next album.

Armed with these songs and a few others she had collected (some at Asher's suggestion), Ronstadt went into the Sound Factory studio in Hollywood to begin recording her next album in June 1974.[49] She was finally exercising more precise control over her prodigious but too often unfocused talent, and in Asher, she had found a sophisticated partner, both collaborative and decisive. "What Peter does," Ronstadt said later, "is to act as both editor and contributor. I might come up with five ideas, and four of them will be turkeys, and Peter will know instinctively which is gonna be the most appropriate one and how to latch on to some of these developing ideas in their embryonic stage and allow them to bloom."[50]

The album she ultimately entitled *Heart Like a Wheel* was a culmination not only for Ronstadt but for the entire ecosystem of musicians, singers, and songwriters who had developed in Southern California since the mid-1960s. "*Heart Like a Wheel* would not have happened without that pool of musicians," Ronstadt remembered.[51] An all-star team of Los Angeles luminaries joined the production. Glenn Frey played acoustic guitar and Don Henley contributed drums on "You Can

Close Your Eyes." (Timothy Schmit, then in Poco and later an Eagle, played bass on the track.) Ronstadt's old beau J. D. Souther contributed harmony vocals and acoustic guitar on a song he wrote, "Faithless Love." David Lindley, Jackson Browne's closest collaborator, picked a fiddle for "Heart Like a Wheel"; Russ Kunkel, Danny Kortchmar's good buddy, played drums on a rollicking update of the old Everly Brothers song, "When Will I Be Loved." "Sneaky" Pete Kleinow, who had played with the Flying Burrito Brothers and on earlier Ronstadt albums, contributed pedal steel to a few songs (including Lowell George's "Willin'"). Emmylou Harris reprised her harmonies from the Roxy on "I Can't Help It," and Ronstadt's friend Maria Muldaur contributed harmonies to "Heart." The album's secret weapon was the precocious Andrew Gold. A prodigy who could handle almost any instrument, Gold played guitar, electric piano, piano, drums, and percussion and worked with Asher and Ronstadt on the arrangements. Asher himself contributed background vocals, percussion, and on one song, even a cowbell.[52]

Recording proceeded steadily through the summer of 1974. Ronstadt and Asher didn't operate with a compass that pointed them toward a predetermined mix of country, rock, and blues. "We just figured it out song by song," he said.[53] "Heart Like a Wheel" was a tender ballad; "I Can't Help It," a rejuvenated country classic; "Willin'," a gender-bending triumph as Ronstadt put her own powerful stamp on George's tattered but tenacious truck driver. They experimented with different versions of the songs. Usually Ronstadt sang them live with the band, but sometimes Asher built the recordings one layer at a time, with each band member adding his parts separately. ("You're No Good" exemplified this approach.) The finished product spectacularly fulfilled Ronstadt's long-standing desire to "mush up the radio." Asher recognized that the core of her musical ambition was her desire to achieve what he called "genre-hopping . . . not just between albums but within an album."[54] *Heart Like a Wheel* took the idea one step further. Not only did it encompass different genres in its song selection, but it also mixed genres within the same song. The tendency was most apparent in "You're No Good." Ronstadt had tried to record

it on *Don't Cry Now*, but Asher didn't like the bongo-heavy arrangement she and Boylan had developed, and they could never agree on
an alternative approach. Late in the recording of *Heart Like a Wheel*,
they resurrected the song, simplifying the arrangement and highlighting Gold's Beatlesesque guitar solos.[55] The great backup singers
Shirley Matthews and Clydie King balanced Gold's exuberant AM-
friendly riffs with a gospel-infused groove.[56] "It was an R-and-B song
that Linda and I loved, and essentially we put all kinds of different
stuff in there, including a whole bunch of Beatles-ish guitars, quite
consciously," Asher recalled.[57] "We were aware that we were mixing
genres rather than idolizing one."[58] Other changes on the album were
subtler but no less consequential. The pedal steel from Ronstadt's earlier albums was still present, but it was more restrained, with less of
a country bite. Her own phrasing slightly muted the sharper country
twang on some of her earlier recordings. These changes were typical
of Asher's calibrated influence: he gently steered Ronstadt toward the
center of the rock fairway while maintaining the eclecticism and diversity that marked her. The difference, he thought, was measured in
"the rhythm of the thing, the way the drums were recorded, the punchi-
ness of it all."[59]

Perhaps most important, Asher's willingness to listen bolstered
Ronstadt's confidence in her own instincts. He encouraged her to contribute ideas and to shape the product. "I was no kind of early feminist, that's for sure," Asher said, "but at the same time, I was a normal,
sensible person who realized she was an intelligent being with a lot
to say, and [I] treated her accordingly, which made a big difference . . .
She'd be in the studio with ideas, and nobody would listen. I was listening out of self-interest. She had good ideas."[60] Even the album's cover
photo of Ronstadt, looking away contemplatively in moody shadow,
seemed much more adult. The image captured the moment: Ronstadt
turned twenty-eight during the recording, and with the completion
of *Heart Like a Wheel*, her apprenticeship in the music business was
finally over.

The album was released in November 1974 and proved an un-
equivocal commercial and critical smash for Ronstadt, the first of

her career. Reviewers recognized it as a huge leap forward for her. Typical was *Rolling Stone*: "One of the reasons *Heart Like a Wheel* is so impressive . . . is its expansion of repertoire beyond country and folk-rock. It also joins Ronstadt to her ideal producer, Peter Asher, who, with Andrew Gold, has provided ten well-chosen songs with full, distinctive sound settings, notable for the variety and imagination of their instrumentation," wrote Stephen Holden.[61] Robert Hilburn, at the *LA Times*, thought the album represented "the final artistic jump in her career."[62]

For years, Ronstadt had dreamed of transcending genres. Now she shattered those boundaries. "You're No Good," the first single from the album, reached No. 1 on the pop single charts on February 14, 1975.[63] "I Can't Help It," the flip side of the release,[64] peaked at No. 2 on the country album charts in March.[65] Later, her version of "When Will I Be Loved" reached No. 2 on the pop charts[66] and No. 1 on the country charts.[67] The album itself hit No. 1 on *Billboard*'s country charts on February 8, 1975,[68] and No. 1 on the pop charts one week later.[69] For years, Ronstadt had been frustrated by her inability to capture on vinyl the musical fusion she heard in her head. Now she had done something that none of the LA country rockers, not even the high-flying Eagles, had accomplished: produced a record that reached No. 1 on both the country and pop charts, and almost simultaneously at that. Ronstadt looked at the success more as relief than validation. "I was happy it was a hit, and I wanted to make another record," she said. "I didn't think, I told you so."[70]

Heart Like a Wheel proved to be Ronstadt's masterpiece because it captured her perfectly poised between her unvarnished past and her polished future. The record crystallized a moment in time, not only for her, but also for the great constellation of musicians operating around her. Something of the charm and innovation of Ronstadt's early years experimenting at the boundaries of country and rock was lost through the later 1970s, as she minted a succession of chart-topping singles and albums under Asher's skilled but sleek direction, but her power and energy remained irresistible. Ronstadt became the decade's biggest female artist.

Even after *Heart*'s massive success, Ronstadt continued to suffer from insecurity about her looks, her weight, and her talent, but she took steps to stabilize her life. She spent more time with her network of supportive women friends in the industry, Bonnie Raitt, Maria Muldaur, Wendy Waldman, Nicolette Larson, and Emmylou Harris.[71] She moved to the Malibu Colony, ditched her diet pills for a personal trainer, and started running on the beach. And on this new path, she eventually reconnected with an old boyfriend who had reached a big threshold of his own in November 1974.

JERRY BROWN HAD APPROACHED the primary for the Democratic gubernatorial nomination in June 1974 like a student studying for an exam. He was mostly on his best behavior throughout. He kept to his schedule; hit the daily messaging points his top adviser, Tom Quinn, typed up for him each day; and restrained his tendency to engage voters and reporters alike in obscure philosophical ruminations. He was rewarded with a decisive primary victory over his two more experienced opponents, Joseph Alioto and Bob Moretti.

Brown transitioned aggressively into the general election. On the same day as his primary victory in June, Republicans chose as their nominee for governor Houston Flournoy, who had served two terms as the state's controller and was an experienced but not intimidating opponent. A moderate in a party moving toward the right, Flournoy presented himself not as an heir to the staunchly conservative Reagan, but as a successor to the measured and bipartisan Earl Warren, who had served as California's governor before becoming chief justice on the U.S. Supreme Court. But although Flournoy was also relatively young (at forty-five), he seemed cast from a much earlier time than Brown. A chain-smoker who spoke in a "scholarly multisyllable style," he could have been the man in the gray flannel suit to a world that had exploded into Technicolor.[72] Beyond all these personal limitations, Flournoy faced the massive undertow for Republicans from the Watergate scandal. Polls through the summer of 1974 showed Brown with a substantial and steady lead in the race. Everything appeared aligned for him to become the state's youngest governor since the nineteenth century.

And then Jerry Brown started to lose the thread. His tendency to lose focus and drift toward untethered philosophizing reemerged. While Brown had (however reluctantly at times) mostly followed Quinn's straightforward political messaging during the primaries, in the general election he was drawn more to Jacques Barzaghi and other supporters who considered that approach too conventional and earthbound. "They liked the more saintly Brown, the ex-seminarian with the other-worldly approach," recalled Richard Maullin, Brown's pollster and senior adviser. "The stuff that Tom was churning out did not have the elements of radical-left quality to them. It was much more standard. A three-point plan for the environment. A seven-point plan for transportation."[73] The campaign staff would draw up a practical schedule for the week—an appearance before labor groups, a tour through Hispanic East Los Angeles, a visit to San Francisco—and Brown instead would show up on Monday morning "ruminating about some ethereal thing that Jacques had been talking about," recalled Chuck Winner, a longtime California consultant who had joined the campaign.[74]

After a relatively peaceful progression to the nomination, control of the campaign became contested into the fall. "It got to be a real conflict between Jerry and Tom, and Jerry began to rebel against Tom's direction," Maullin remembered.[75] The saintly clique thought Brown's principal advisers were furthering their own financial interests in steering him toward a traditional campaign centered on television advertising, daily media appearances, and the mobilizing of party interest groups. The political professionals in turn thought that Barzaghi and like-minded Brown friends were encouraging the candidate toward a dangerous level of abstraction and disconnection. Inside the campaign, Brown told his conventional political advisers that he didn't need to follow their plans, because Barzaghi had assured him he would win.[76] This was hardly reassuring to them, because Barzaghi had left some on the staff with the impression that he believed he could see into the future.[77] As during the primary, the campaign's managers could practically see Brown drifting away from them. He would spend less time announcing three-point plans and more time talking about transforming society, in terms that teetered between visionary and vacuous. "We have to generate a new consciousness, we have to restructure our lifestyle from the frontier style of profligate economic exploitation of resources," Brown told one audience of students. "We have to know that achieving social and economic justice is not a luxury anymore but today has become a necessity."[78]

WEAKENED BY THESE INTERNAL divisions, and Brown's own wavering focus, his campaign drifted through the summer and fall. He never entirely recaptured the dynamism he had displayed at his best during the primary.

In the campaign's final weeks, the California governor's race became the most prominent exception to the national current. Across the country, and even in California, the backlash against Watergate and Gerald Ford's decision to pardon Nixon in September was powering Democrats toward big gains. But in the governor's race, Flournoy's pollsters showed him gaining. On the morning before Election Day, Quinn, Maullin, and Faigin met over breakfast in San Diego before beginning the traditional final fly-around through the state's major media markets. All were glum over Maullin's tight final polling results from the night before. "We had been working so hard for so long, doing so well, and now the margin had come down," Faigin recalled. "So, the three of us were sitting there saying, 'Can you think of anything? Is there any stroke of genius we can come up with this last day to shift this, because it's a little too close?'"[79]

Election Day, on November 5, 1974, validated both Brown's breezy confidence and his advisers' mounting anxiety. Buoyed by Watergate and his own themes of reform and generational transition, Brown held on to win the race, but it was much closer than almost anything else on the ballot. He won by about 180,000 votes, the closest gubernatorial election in over fifty years;[80] Democratic senator Alan Cranston, by point of reference, won reelection on the same day by almost 1.5 million votes.[81] Voters nationwide had delivered landslide gains to the Democrats, but the general consensus in both parties was that if the California governor's race had continued for another week, Flournoy probably would have won.

Both the highs and lows of Brown's journey to the governorship revealed competing aspects of his personality. His troubles in the general election captured the airy, distracted side of Brown that would resurface even more prominently early in his gubernatorial term. But his race also showed qualities that would make him a national sensation during his first years as governor: His ability to cut through old debates with new perspectives and powerful symbolic gestures (like renouncing the governor's mansion) excited a broad range of voters. He struck a resonant chord with his promises of reform, fresh starts, and new ideas not bound to the rigid ideologies of the past. "He connected to [the] heartbeat in the voting population, and he became unbelievably popular," his sister Kathleen Brown noted.[82] It wasn't too much of a stretch to say that Jerry Brown in 1974 embodied both the best of the Baby Boom (its intelligence, creativity, and determination to rethink old assumptions) and the worst (self-absorption, a tendency to value theory over experience, and an aversion to discipline and focus).

Speculation about Brown as a possible presidential or vice-presidential candidate in 1976 began even before his election, and not just in the press; Maullin thought Brown was eyeing the White House before he ever reached Sacramento.[83] In late October 1974, *Time* magazine put Brown on the cover under the headline "New Faces, Key Races." But it was Tom Hayden, midway through his own transition from protester to politician, who most clearly recognized the implications of Brown's ascent.[84] Hayden, after working with his wife, Jane Fonda, for most of 1974 to organize congressional opposition against further American aid to South Vietnam, spent the last weeks of the campaign profiling Brown for *Rolling Stone*. Hayden's profile opened into a much broader rumination on how the protests of the 1960s might be reconfigured to meet the political and economic challenges of the 1970s. He correctly saw Brown as leading an emerging generation of political leaders grappling with that question. "With Jerry Brown and others like him, a Vietnam-to-Watergate generation is coming on the political scene," Hayden wrote perceptively. "They are as distinctive as the many Democratic groups who came to power after the New Deal and World War II and may as completely dominate the future of politics as did that earlier generation from Roosevelt to Ford. It's the arriving political establishment which will set the new rules under which a disordered and floundering American system will operate. They are a vanguard of the status quo, the men—and some women—who see themselves as 'modernizing rather than revolutionizing the social structure.'"[85]

That judgment likely carried some projection: Hayden also probably imagined himself in that "vanguard" now committed to "modernizing rather than revolutionizing" American society. But he was right to describe Brown's instincts that way, and to recognize how Brown embodied the larger generational transition under way as the Baby Boom moved into middle age. Brown wasn't offering the kind of revolution that Hayden had been touting only a few years earlier, but with his victory, aspects of the sixties critique of American life—that it was too consumerist, too environmentally destructive, too discriminatory against marginalized groups—were fastened onto mainstream politics as never before. He offered the political parallel to the triumph of those same ideas in the movies, television, and music produced in Los Angeles during those months. Brown, unlike Hayden and his friends during the 1960s, didn't want to dismantle capitalism or rethink the nuclear family, but he did want to promote clean energy, protect the environment, win more dignity and security for farmworkers, and achieve more representation for women and minorities in government. "Many of the conflicts expressed in the streets in the Sixties have now spread within institutions in the Seventies," Hayden wrote, "partly because of the growing up of that generation but more importantly because of the increased acceptance of what were labeled 'New Left' positions a decade ago."[86]

The lesson of Richard Nixon's forty-nine-state victory in 1972 had been that no one could win an election offering anything approaching the radical criticism of American society that Hayden and like-minded radicals had advanced for years. But Brown's victory just two years later showed that it was possible to incorporate important elements of that thinking, rephrased in a less threatening and dogmatic manner, into a broader package that a winning coalition of voters might accept. Brown's victory marked a milestone in the process of determining which ideas from the 1960s could survive in the stonier political soil of the 1970s and which would be shed. And almost exactly as Brown celebrated his victory, one of the Los Angeles singer-songwriters who most thoughtfully grappled with those same issues achieved a breakthrough of his own.

ON THE WEEK OF November 30, 1974, Jackson Browne celebrated a milestone. His third album, *Late for the Sky*, peaked on the *Billboard* album charts at No. 14, by far the highest ranking he had ever achieved.[87]

Browne had taken a circuitous road to that success. His first album had performed well, both critically and commercially, but like many artists, he found his second album much harder than the first. Browne was always a perfectionist with his songs. Songwriting, for him, he said, "was always really hard. It's hard now; it was hard then."[88] It was not unusual for him to spend a year tinkering before he felt comfortable with a composition. (Even some close friends thought his romance with Joni Mitchell foundered at least partly because he was frustrated that beautiful songs seemed to spring from her brain fully formed, like Athena from the head of Zeus.) All this generated an agonized production on his second record. Week after week, Browne took songs apart and reassembled them. In the end, he spent nine months in the studio, accumulating mounting costs and frustrating himself (and his musicians) nearly as much as he did Geffen.[89] Browne finished his first album in October 1971. His second, *For Everyman*, didn't reach stores until October 1973.[90]

After that long struggle, the record received a respectful but not rapturous reception. It mixed new compositions with several older songs Browne had allowed others to record first, including "These Days," the wise-beyond-his-years love lament he had written in high school (most recently covered by his good friend Gregg Allman), and "Take It Easy," his ode to the open road that had blasted the Eagles out of the gate on their first album. The album reached slightly higher on the *Billboard* charts than Browne's debut (although no single from the record approached the success of either "Doctor, My Eyes" or "Rock Me on the Water," from his first album). But like the Eagles' disappointing second album, *Desperado*, the record didn't produce a big leap forward for Browne, either commercially or artistically.

In the *LA Times*, Robert Hilburn, though generally a big Browne booster, felt *For Everyman* didn't appear as intimate or as personal as the confessional work of the era's best singer-songwriters. The big exception was its jaunty "Ready or Not." Over the exuberant electric fiddle of David Lindley, a multi-instrumental virtuoso, the song recounts in almost diary form the night Browne met the model Phyllis Major at the Troubadour bar. Raised in Greece and Europe, the beautiful but troubled Major had dated Keith Richards and singer Bobby Neuwirth by the time Browne, as he sang, "punched an unemployed actor defending her dignity."[91] The actor got up and decked Browne, but in life as in the song, "that girl came home with me." Soon Major was pregnant, and their son, Ethan, was born in November 1973, just after *For Everyman* was released. Browne relocated his budding new family into the Abbey San Encino, the fabled Mission-like home his grandfather had built in Highland Park.[92]

There, with his new life flowering around him, Browne started work on his third album. He struggled to balance his responsibilities to his family with the obligation he felt to his art. "I had a relationship and a kid all at once, and in the time it took to have the baby and to be moved into this old family house of mine, I sequestered," he remembered. "I mean all kind of things happened in my life that I wasn't . . . paying enough attention to."[93] He set up shop in the chapel his grandfather had built as part of the compound. Visiting Browne at the abbey for a *Rolling Stone* profile at the time, the precocious young journalist Cameron Crowe found him writing songs into an accounting ledger book propped up on a grand piano.[94] Browne remembers writing in the chapel while his infant son crawled contentedly on the floor. Reentering the world after long hours immersed in his words and melodies was always jarring, like stepping out into bright sunshine from a darkened room. "I remember discovering coffee," he recalled. "Like legal speed. I remember getting whacked out, like, drinking so much coffee. You might write all night or not have slept that much, and then

driving to go get Mexican food and bring it back to eat with the family,
and being on the freeway in the Valley, with [it] a hundred and ten
degrees out there, just tanked on coffee, the whole world sort of vibrat-
ing with a song in your head, and it was very much like the same kind
of thing that happens when you're taking drugs. You're using this to
create a focus and to maintain a focus, but it comes out of your life. It
takes a lot out of your life."[95]

Browne kept writing when he went out on his tour with Ronstadt
in January 1974. She remembers him sitting up late at night on one
of the hard benches in the bus scribbling into a notebook, sometimes
with Lowell George strumming along on guitar.[96] When their joint
tour concluded that spring, Browne returned home with a new idea
about how to approach his next album. With *For Everyman*, he, like
most of LA's artists in those years, tapped the city's remarkable pool of
session musicians. "Every song has a different sort of lineup," Browne
remembered of *For Everyman*'s recording. "With all of these different musicians, it was a wonderland, the session scene." But for his
third album, he wanted a more cohesive, integrated sound: "I decided
right around that time that I thought some of my favorite music was
made by people who have been playing together in a band for a long
time. Whether it's Creedence [Clearwater Revival] or the Beatles or the
Stones . . . you're able to explore this music as a unit instead of just
calling up the best session players you can find or the people that are
most interesting to you."[97]

Browne went to see Geffen with a new idea: he planned to use his
touring band on the next record, and he wanted to hire them to rehearse the songs for a few months before they went into the studio.[98]
Geffen did not like to give big advances on records, but Browne persuaded him to front ten thousand dollars so that Browne could hire
his bandmates from the road: David Lindley, on guitar and fiddle;
Doug Haywood, on bass and harmonies; Larry Zack, on drums; and
Jai Winding, who would join them on piano for Browne's next tour.
He brought all of them to the Abbey San Encino and, navigating past
the toys and baby wipes in the living room, they spent months rehearsing in his attic.

By summer, Browne was ready to enter the studio. And once again, he began the recording process without a producer. This was a distinctive component of his approach to recording. Unlike most artists, Browne did not use a producer when making his albums. Instead, he effectively produced them himself in partnership with a recording engineer, who executed his blueprint.* For this third album, he recruited the veteran engineer Al Schmitt, who had worked with him on some tracks during *For Everyman*. Schmitt had also done some work as a producer, but his principal experience was as an engineer stretching back to the 1950s. He wasn't one to challenge Browne's vision.

With the band primed on the material, Browne finished recording the album in only six weeks. He would have finished even faster, he remembers, if he had not caught a cold on week four. (He says he can still hear the effects on some of his vocals.) But the lack of a producer imposed a cost. "People talk about records being overproduced," said Jon Landau, the prominent critic who became the first full-scale producer to work with Browne on his next album, *The Pretender*. "Some of the feedback Jackson got on that record was [that it] was *under-produced*."[99] Browne remembers running into the singer Dave Mason after *Late for the Sky* reached the stores. "He said, 'Oh man, great bunch of songs, but, like, somebody needs to produce you,'" Browne remembered.[100] Browne was not entirely satisfied with the result, either. He was frustrated by his arrangement and performance on the album's two upbeat rockers, "The Road and the Sky" and "Walking Slow." "The biggest problem I had with this record is I didn't know how to make rock and roll happen," he recalled. "I was far outstripped in that area by the Eagles and Little Feat. I couldn't find my way into that kind of playing."[101]

None of this obscured the magnitude of Browne's achievement with *Late for the Sky*, which fulfilled all the expectations that had sur-

---

* Browne chose his engineers in part on the recommendations of Peter Asher, the skillful manager and producer who had taken on Linda Ronstadt. "He was the guy . . . I followed in his footsteps. I sort of jumped from studio to studio that he used, and engineer to engineer," Browne remembered.

rounded him since high school. It became his first gold record.[102] More important, the album's eight tightly written compositions confirmed Browne's place as the finest songwriter to emerge from the younger co-hort of Los Angeles musicians, the one second-generation talent most worthy of standing beside the early titans of the singer-songwriter movement, such as Joni Mitchell and Neil Young. On songs such as "Fountain of Sorrow" and "Late for the Sky," the album examined the fragility, futility, and elation of romantic relationships with a precision and world-weary wisdom belied by the impossibly youthful photo of the perpetually boyish Browne on the back cover. The songs resonated like reports from the front in the aftermath of the sexual revolution. Released when he was just twenty-six, with a new child and a part-ner he would marry the next year, the album captured Browne, like so many of his contemporaries, in the uneasy transition from cele-brating the freedom that revolution unlocked to tabulating its cost in impermanence and instability. Stephen Holden recognized this shift in his glowing *Rolling Stone* review of *Late for the Sky*: "No contempo-rary male singer/songwriter has dealt so honestly and deeply with the vulnerability of romantic idealism and the pain of adjustment from youthful narcissism to adult survival as Browne has in this album," he wrote. "*Late for the Sky* is the autobiography of his young manhood."[103]

If it was that alone, the album would have deserved its reputation as Browne's youthful masterpiece, but it was not only that. Browne addressed the fraying of not only personal but also political idealism. In each of his early records, he mined the space between the 1960s artists, who had overtly embraced collective social action, and the early 1970s singer-songwriters, who had turned inward to portray personal change as the only plausible path to changing society. The critic Janet Maslin had brilliantly captured Browne's unique position between those perspectives in her *Rolling Stone* review of *For Everyman*. Despite her other aesthetic objections to the record, to her it revealed Browne as "the first major songwriter to have emerged with the knowledge that the battles Bob Dylan depicted a decade ago are either over or too ambiguous to be worth fighting any more. But unlike most older writers, he is not yet ready to retreat into merely mining the realm of private problems for subject matter. He has internalized the remains of those larger struggles and still dares to hope for solutions."[104]

Each of Browne's first three albums offered one song that directly contemplated the state "of those larger struggles" to create a more just society. In each one, Browne surrounded personal reflection with biblical images of social and/or environmental disintegration. The trio of songs amounted to his apocalypse triptych, his attempt to measure what from the 1960s could be saved in the grinding environment of the 1970s.

"Rock Me on the Water," recorded for Browne's first album in 1971, when the social movements of the sixties were still fresh, is the most optimistic of the three. It's filled with images of judgment and disruption—walls are burning and towers are turning—but the apocalypse seems farthest away and the possibility of salvation greatest. It shows how strongly he still believes that collective action can avert disaster and create a more just world: "Oh people look among you, / It's there your hope must lie," Browne sings.[105] He holds out the possibility of rebirth (in part through sexual ecstasy). Yes, "the fires are raging hotter and hotter," but he will "get down to the sea somehow," where the "sisters of the sun" will "rock me on the water." The music, gospel-powered and propulsive, reinforces his message: Yes, it's late, but it's not too late. The song is less a lament than a call to arms.

The odds tilted somewhat by the time he recorded his second album's title track, "For Everyman." Browne wrote it largely in response to David Crosby's escapist vision. Crosby often told friends that if society fell apart or the arms race erupted into nuclear war, he would just "sail away into the distance" on his yacht.[106] (He expressed some of that perspective in the early Crosby, Stills and Nash song "Wooden Ships.") That was all well and good, Browne would answer in response to Crosby, but what about everyone who couldn't afford a yacht?[107]

In "For Everyman," Browne puzzled through his answer to his own question. The song begins with his friends planning to leave society because they "believe that they've heard their last warning." But Browne can't join them, because he's still waiting "for Everyman," his phrase for the social movements of the 1960s that sought change through collective action. Others may find their own escape, a private paradise, but he's not yet willing to withdraw from society or the hope of change. The song's final verse takes him to a plaintive place. Intellectually, he recognizes the mounting evidence that the possibility of social transformation is flickering, but he's not ready to inter the dreams of his youth. In a powerful image, he acknowledges that in clinging to those hopes, he may be only "holding sand."[108] But he clings to those hopes nonetheless and defines himself, as the song concludes, as "Just another dreamer / Dreaming 'bout Everyman."

The *Late for the Sky* album, written mostly in 1974 with the sixties receding further into memory and the Watergate scandal at high tide, catches Browne in a more pessimistic moment. He previews his mindset in the otherwise-upbeat rocker, "The Road and the Sky." This song first harkens back to his earlier celebrations of life on the road, such as "Take it Easy." He's got a girl and a Chevrolet and an open road, and that's all he needs. But this youthful reverie of freedom is unexpectedly interrupted by an ominous vision of "dark clouds gathering up ahead" that will "wash this planet clean like the Bible said."[109]

This image is expanded to cinematic scope in the album's concluding song, "Before the Deluge." Browne took the title for the song from an Otto Friedrich book about Berlin before World War II that Linda Ronstadt had given him, but its imagery was inspired by the darkest jeremiads of the emerging environmental movement.[110] In particular, Browne remembers being affected by a pamphlet called *Eco-Catastrophe*, by Stanford biologist Paul Ehrlich, who became renowned for his predictions of encroaching environmental doom driven mostly by overpopulation.[111] Ehrlich's influence was evident in Browne's gloomy prediction to Cameron Crowe in the spring of 1974: "I think the whole fucking thing is coming down," he declared. "I think it's all over. . . . When do I think it's all gonna come down? Seventies, Eighties, Nineties, it doesn't matter."[112]

That dark forecast proved too pessimistic, but at the time, it carried great power, and Browne transformed it into a poetic vision that merged environmental catastrophe with biblical retribution. Like "For Everyman," "Before the Deluge" begins with the few who are sufficiently attuned to the coming danger to seek an escape from civilization and a "journey back to nature."[113] But this time, Browne offers no prospect of escape. His perspective about his own generation has grown more critical. Now he sees his contemporaries replacing "their tired wings" with "the resignation that living brings." They will not escape the reckoning, either. While "Rock Me" centered on salvation, and even "For Everyman" stubbornly held to the dream of change, "Before the Deluge" offered less chance of renewal or even escape. Now, in Browne's telling, "when the sand was gone and the time arrived . . . only a few survived."

Tom Hayden and Jane Fonda, Jerry Brown, and other Baby Boomers who had marched in the 1960s could recognize the dialogue that Browne conducted with himself over these three albums. What of their sixties idealism could be preserved as their lives moved deeper into the bruising realities of the seventies? Looking back at these songs, Browne says he was not trying to bury the sixties. "I'm not trying to pronounce the dream dead," he said. "I'm trying to identify the part that lives on in us, and has to." He paused. "Or, at least, . . . I can look at my songs [now] and say that's what I was trying to do."[114]

Browne turned even further toward pessimism in his next record, *The Pretender*. That album was scarred by the death of his troubled wife, Phyllis Major, who committed suicide by overdosing on pills in March 1976 after the two had married in December 1975.[115] In the wake of such a tragedy, personal and social renewal, not surprisingly, receded further on *The Pretender*'s title song, when Browne asked, "What became of the changes / we waited for love to bring" and ruefully wondered if those hopes of renewal were "only . . . fitful dreams."[116]

And yet, much like Hayden and Fonda and Jerry Brown, and untold millions of their contemporaries, Browne through the mid-1970s found a way to look forward more often than he looked back. Over time, it became clear that the guarded optimism of "Rock Me on the Water" and the stubborn determination of "For Everyman" more reflected the convictions that guided his life than the tempest-tossed pessimism of "Before the Deluge" and "The Pretender." Rather than lament the flickering of the old dreams, Browne, as he reached his peak commercial success into the early 1980s, plunged himself into new causes: the environment, human rights, opposition to nuclear energy. It was easy in the early 1970s, he recalled, for those who responded to "the idealism of the sixties" to feel "a kind of disappointment and deflated" because change had not come as fast or as comprehensively as people had hoped. "But the thing is, that struggle continues," Browne went on. "That's why I say in 'The Pretender' 'Were they only the fitful dreams of some greater awakening?' I've always been trying to express, from 'For Everyman' to 'The Pretender' and even some recent songs, the idea of arriving someplace with more consciousness and with more purpose than we have had in the past. So, if I was talking about something that was burning out and flickering, it was people's hope or ideals. But you don't give up that kind of thing."[117]

BROWNE'S BRILLIANT *LATE FOR THE SKY* capped the quartet of breakthrough albums for Southern California artists in 1974: Joni Mitchell's incisive *Court and Spark*, the Eagles' propulsive *On the Border*, and Linda Ronstadt's genre-defying *Heart Like a Wheel*. Behind all of them stood the driven management of David Geffen. All those artists except Mitchell would go on to enjoy huge commercial success through the remainder of the 1970s, but 1974 was the moment of maximum cultural influence for the Southern California sound. Emerging new voices in 1975 would shift the center of the rock world back to New York City, and then to London, for a grittier, less polished sound. And as that axis turned, the movie and television industries faced their own transition, as they retreated from the biting social criticism of their parallel awakenings earlier in the decade. As 1974 dissolved into 1975, across each of these industries, darkness encroached on what had been Los Angeles' golden hour.

12

DECEMBER

Transitions

When CBS hired Arthur Taylor as its president in July 1972, he had no experience in broadcasting, apart from some work on his college radio station at Brown.[1] But it was the heyday of the conglomerate in American business, and CBS's aging founder, William Paley, thought Taylor could effectively manage the company's steadily diversifying portfolio of assets. Taylor, though just thirty-five when CBS picked him, was well suited for that responsibility. As vice president and executive vice president of International Paper, he had earned a reputation as a financial wizard. Taylor applied those skills immediately to CBS, streamlining operations, shedding assets (including the New York Yankees, which he sold to a group of investors led by George Steinbrenner), directing some targeted acquisitions, and delivering solid financial returns that quickly made him a favorite on Wall Street.

But Taylor aspired to more than burnishing the bottom line. He was a man of varied and diverse interests, someone who had risen from a blue-collar background to obtain an undergraduate degree in Renaissance history and a master's degree in economic history at Brown University. At CBS, Taylor pursued the role of corporate statesman that the company's legendary president Frank Stanton had played for so many years before he left the position in 1971. Taylor's colleagues widely believed he hoped someday to run for office or hold a cabinet position. "He was extraordinarily ambitious," remembered Jack Schneider, CBS's acerbic number-three executive. "He genuinely wanted to be, in this order, President of the United States, Secretary of State, or U.S. Senator from New Jersey."[2]

Whether because of those ambitions or his own convictions, Taylor felt deeply that broadcasting was not upholding what he considered its public responsibility. In private, he lamented the "cynicism" of the industry and even of his own colleagues, the willingness to put anything on the air that generated ratings. He believed that television's programming needed to uphold the public good, however hazily that was defined. A deeply religious man, Taylor was especially concerned about the impact of television violence on children, believing that it encouraged some children toward violent behavior themselves. And while he always insisted that he was not concerned about the increasingly frank discussions of sex in the network's breakthrough comedies of the early 1970s, he did make clear that he considered some of what reached the air beneath the dignity of CBS as the so-called "Tiffany network." (The camera's prominent attention to Cher's navel on *The Sonny and Cher Comedy Hour* particularly irritated him.)[3] Taylor's moralizing alienated many of the CBS executives who worked beneath him. Jim Rosenfield, a CBS business executive who later became the network's president, spoke for many inside the company's Manhattan headquarters at Black Rock when he said, "Arthur Taylor was bright but a real jerk. He was an elitist and out of touch with people. He had his own agenda."[4]

None of this dissuaded Taylor. Month by month, he perceived a growing backlash against the increased freedom in tone and subject that television, like the movie industry, had enjoyed since the late 1960s. From Washington, DC, came growing complaints about violence on television from some conservative members of the House and Senate, which in turn generated pressure on the Federal Communications Commission to act. In confrontations like the uproar over the 1972 *Maude* episodes (soon after his arrival at CBS) in which Bea Arthur's forty-seven-year-old character has an abortion, Taylor saw a grassroots uprising among cultural conservatives, a movement that represented one of the first stirrings of what would soon become known as the religious right. Taylor's desire to respond to these complaints may have annoyed or even horrified many of his colleagues, who thought he was placing his own personal ambition over the interests of the creative community or even those of CBS itself. But Taylor believed that CBS, and the industry more broadly, could not ignore these pressures, and in December 1974, he took a fateful step that hastened the end of the golden age of television that Robert Wood and Norman Lear had opened when they partnered to place *All in the Family* on the air in January 1971.

CULTURAL ERAS DON'T PRECISELY follow the calendar. The creative renaissance in Los Angeles did not begin on January 1, 1974 (or even January 1, 1967). It did not abruptly end on December 31, 1974. But the dynamics that rejuvenated culture and politics in Los Angeles reached their fullest expression through 1974. And as the year transitioned into 1975, forces gathered momentum that would end the city's revival in movies, music, television, and politics. The most important of these was a shift in cultural preferences that reduced America's appetite for popular entertainment that relitigated the arguments of the 1960s and ignited the backlash against the greater freedom of expression that worried Arthur Taylor. Not surprisingly, it was the television networks, the component of the entertainment industry most dependent on the broadest mass audience, that felt these tremors first.

ROBERT WOOD WAS GROWING unhappy as president of the CBS network even before Arthur Taylor started grousing about the impact of violence on television. Wood found the pressure for ratings and profits grueling; no matter the results he produced, Paley always wanted more. Wood and his top programming lieutenant, Fred Silverman, still achieved sterling outcomes: CBS shows held nine of the eleven top spots in the Nielsen ratings[5] for the 1974/75 season, but those successes did nothing to alleviate the squeeze Wood felt from Silverman's desire for more compensation, Taylor's insistence on cutting costs, and Wood's own frustration that the producers of the shows he greenlit for the air took home a dollar to every dime of his own. "Much of the time, he was visibly tired, irritable," Robert Wussler, a producer and executive who eventually succeeded Wood as CBS's president, later remembered. Wood had been a dynamic and gregarious presence during his first years as CBS president, but to Wussler, it now appeared that he "had dialed out."[6]

Wood's exhaustion probably made it easier for Taylor to pursue his growing passion for retrenching violence on television. Taylor's colleagues may have thought him obsessed with the issue, but the backlash against television's greater freedom was real and growing. The noise from Washington picked up through 1974, particularly from the chairman of the FCC, a relatively centrist Republican named Richard E. Wiley. NBC, either oblivious or arrogant, chose that moment to air a television movie in September 1974 called *Born Innocent*, starring Linda Blair, fresh from her *Exorcist* fame. Blair played a teenager in reform school who is raped with a mop by a gang of other girls in the shower.[7] The understandable complaints about *Born Innocent* escalated the simmering controversy over television content into a raging blaze when a group of teenagers committed what appeared to be a copycat crime against a young girl in San Francisco.[8] A few weeks after *Born Innocent* aired, Wiley delivered a speech warning that federal regulation of sex and violence on television might be unavoidable if the industry did not act voluntarily.[9] He then summoned the presidents of CBS, NBC, and ABC to his office in Washington to discuss the issue in late November 1974.

Taylor was outraged by *Born Innocent*, but also initially infuriated by Wiley's demand for a meeting, which seemed to him government censorship.[10] But to Wiley's delight, Taylor agreed at the meeting that explicit content on television represented a real problem.[11] Wiley suggested to the executives that the networks issue a joint statement agreeing that they would not air before 9 p.m. in the East any programming that parents might find objectionable.[12] That was the beginning of what became known as "the family hour."

Taylor's CBS colleagues initially reacted coolly when he brought back the idea of barring "sensitive" programming before 9 p.m. "We had endless meetings over this subject," remembered Bob Daly, a senior CBS executive at the time who also later became the network's president. "The programmers were ballistic over this, and the creative community was ballistic over this, [but] he was very strong on it. He took a lot of heat for this, but he didn't seem to care."[13] An aide to Taylor developed the idea of institutionalizing the family hour by recommending that the National Association of Broadcasters adopt it as part of its code of conduct for the broadcasting industry.

On the Monday before Christmas 1974, Taylor gathered CBS's senior leadership, including Bill Paley, for a meeting that placed them all on the record supporting the proposal to create a family viewing hour in the first hour of prime time, between 8 and 9 p.m.[14] The meeting was almost perfunctory, with very little discussion. "Paley, for whatever reason, went along with it," recalled Daly.[15] On the last day of 1974, the Television Code Review Board of the National Association of Broadcasters announced that it would call a special meeting to respond to Taylor's proposal,[16] and in early February 1975, the board approved a policy statement requiring that, before 9 p.m., "entertainment programming inappropriate for viewing by a general family audience should not be broadcast."[17]

For years thereafter, Taylor insisted that his target in pushing the family hour was violence on television, not explicit sexuality, much less the handling of sexually related subjects on topical comedies such as *All in the Family*, *Mary Tyler Moore*, and their many spin-offs. Though unenthusiastic about the family hour, CBS programming executives considered it acceptable because they thought it would most disrupt the schedule for ABC, which relied heavily on action shows in the 8 p.m. hour. But as the networks met to translate the broad dictates of the family hour into specific guidelines, ABC argued that the guidelines should also exclude "permissiveness" in topical comedy.[18] CBS initially resisted this suggestion, but concluded that it could not be seen defying a policy that its own president, Arthur Taylor, in interviews that spring, was proudly proclaiming to have fathered.

The trap that Taylor had set for his own network was sprung in April 1975, when Robert Wood called Norman Lear in Paris, where he was vacationing. As the highest-rated show on television, *All in the Family* was the foundation, from its time slot at 8 p.m., of CBS's powerhouse Saturday night. But when the CBS Program Practices Department analyzed the twenty-three scripts from the show's 1974/75 season, it concluded that two dealt with themes that were completely unacceptable for the new family hour and that language in twenty of the remaining twenty-one would need to be altered.[19] To the CBS executives, this foreshadowed a grueling year of perpetual conflict with Lear, who bridled against all attempts at censorship. That prospect prompted Wood to ask Lear if he would consider toning down the show for the season beginning in September 1975, the first to be covered by the family hour. When Lear refused, Wood swiftly moved *All in the Family* to Monday nights at 9 p.m.

The practical impact of *All in the Family*'s move was mixed. Even in its new time slot, it remained the year's top-rated show for the 1975/76 season, but the move had a real cost. None of the formerly top-rated CBS shows left behind on Saturday night (*Mary Tyler Moore*, *Bob Newhart*, and *Carol Burnett*) finished higher than nineteenth in the Nielsen ratings. The verdict on the family hour itself was similarly equivocal. Rather than reducing violence on television, it merely concentrated the most violent shows in the 9 and 10 p.m. hours. And it created new headaches and uncertainty for the producers of the topical comedies that had transformed television in the early 1970s. Shows such as *Rhoda*, *Phyllis*, and *M*A*S*H*, on CBS, and the new *Barney Miller*, on ABC, all of which aired during the family hour, faced heightened scrutiny over potentially objectionable material. The writers of the topical situation comedies eventually won most of these skirmishes, but they were so offended by the intensified monitoring—not to mention the implication that their work was corrupting the morals of young America—that many enlisted when Lear organized a lawsuit against the family hour. "It was egregious, what they were doing," Lear recalled. "It was stupid and egregious, and it was hurtful to open dialogue."[20] In October 1975, the Writers Guild of America filed suit against the policy as a violation of the First Amendment. After an extensive trial, a federal district court judge in Los Angeles ultimately invalidated the family hour in November 1976, two days after Jimmy Carter's election as president.[21]

Hollywood's producers and writers welcomed the family hour's demise, but its fall did not revive the topical comedies that proliferated during the early seventies. The family hour, it turned out, was more a symptom than a cause of a cultural and political shift. It wasn't only pressure groups and government officials pushing back against television's advance into edgier and more contemporary content. A large slice of the viewing audience was ready for a break, too.

This larger change was symbolized by the unlikely challenger that finally dislodged *All in the Family* from its extended hold on the No. 1 ranking in the Nielsen ratings. *Happy Days*, set in 1950s Milwaukee, virtually inverted *All in the Family*, offering social consensus, intergenerational harmony, and an escape from all the national tensions that the Bunker household each week condensed into a single living room. *Happy Days* traced its origin to television executive Michael Eisner's search for a response to the powerful CBS lineup of contemporary situation comedies. Eisner, who had moved from New York to Los Angeles in 1973 to take charge of ABC's prime-time programming, was by nature a counterpuncher. "Anytime it looked like everybody was doing one thing, I was interested in doing something else," he recalled.[22]

Eisner, a little older than the Baby Boomers, had not much engaged with the political and cultural tumult of the 1960s as he ascended the corporate ladder at ABC. This probably encouraged his belief that a sizable audience of Americans no longer wished to continue relitigating the arguments from that decade, even for laughs. "Too many people are playing to the great angst," Eisner remembers thinking.[23] The television revolution that Wood ignited at CBS had buried the toothless and often mindless comedies that ruled the airwaves through the 1960s, yet Eisner thought that, with a modest updating, shows of similar intent would now be received as comfort food by a nation tired of conflict. To move past the sixties, Eisner wanted to reach back *before* it. "My point was nobody is doing *Green Acres, Father Knows Best, Brady*

Bunch," he remembered. "So, I was going to bring back the family drama."[24]

The idea crystallized for him one day when he was snowed in at Newark airport with Tom Miller, a top development executive at Paramount. The two killed the time by spitballing ideas for possible programs, sharing their admiration for the warm, if bland, family dramas of their youth, such as *Father Knows Best*. Based on their conversation, Eisner wrote a short memo called "New Family in Town," framing his idea for a gentle family comedy set in an earlier time. Eisner and Miller recruited Garry Marshall, who had adapted *The Odd Couple* for television, to develop the idea. Marshall suggested setting the show in the 1950s (which Eisner and Miller liked) and situating it in the Bronx (which they didn't; the borough seemed too "ethnic" for universal appeal). Eisner proposed, instead, placing the program somewhere in the Midwest, and the three settled on Milwaukee.[25]

Marshall produced a script for the project now known as *Happy Days*, but Eisner could not sell his colleagues at ABC on financing a pilot. He regrouped by converting the idea into an episode of *Love, American Style*, an anthology show that Paramount produced for ABC.[26] But even after the episode aired to generally positive reaction, ABC still would not approve the project as a series. Eisner's salvation came when the young George Lucas, then just beginning his own exercise in pre-sixties nostalgia, asked to see the "Happy Days" episode of *Love, American Style*. For Richie Cunningham, the earnest all-American teen at the center of *Happy Days*, ABC had cast Ronny Howard, the red-haired former child actor who had played Opie on *The Andy Griffith Show*. Lucas cast Howard as one of the leads in *American Graffiti*, and that film's critical and commercial success generated the tailwind Eisner needed to finally push *Happy Days* into production (while also demonstrating how shifting cultural dynamics reinforced one another, given that *American Graffiti* itself had followed the success of *Grease*, an equally nostalgic Broadway musical about the fifties). *Happy Days* joined the ABC schedule in January 1974 as a midseason replacement.

Even then, the show started slow. It gained more traction in its second season, as it elevated the role of Arthur "Fonzie" Fonzarelli,

Henry Winkler's leather-jacketed greaser with a heart of gold. Fonzie was mildly rebellious but more domesticated than disruptive, and the show celebrated rather than challenged the simple virtues of the white, mid-American nuclear family that often seemed the butt of the joke in the Lear comedies. ABC's market research in 1975 concluded that after Watergate and Vietnam, viewers had tired of "social issue or confrontation comedy" and craved a return to "the traditional values" of an earlier time.[27] *Happy Days* gave them exactly that (albeit with some modern shadings, such as a modestly more assertive role for Mrs. Cunningham than the mothers in the fifties comedies). In the 1976/77 season, *Happy Days* reached No. 1 in the Nielsen ratings, finally ending *All in the Family*'s five-year run as America's most highly watched program.[28] Finishing second was *Laverne and Shirley*, an equally mild *Happy Days* spin-off about the misadventures of two young brewery workers, played by Cindy Williams (who had also starred in *American Graffiti*) and Penny Marshall, Garry's younger sister. *All in the Family* tumbled all the way to twelfth in the ratings that year.

Happy Days surpassing *All in the Family* as the nation's top-rated show almost too perfectly marked the end of an era. *All in the Family* regained a place in Nielsen's Top 10 during the next two seasons, its final ones on the air, but it no longer set the pace for television. After Fred Silverman, Wood's top programming lieutenant, left CBS for the top job at ABC in the spring of 1975, that network led the ratings with programs that uniformly and unashamedly offered escapism: the nostalgia of *Happy Days* and *Laverne and Shirley* and the leering sexuality of "jiggle" shows, which included comedies such as *Three's Company* (the story of a young man who feigns being gay so he can share an apartment with two sexy young women) and dramas such as *Charlie's Angels* (about three impossibly glamorous female detectives). It was a schizophrenic strategy, with Silverman dividing his prime-time offerings between inanity for kids and titillation for adults—but it fit the time. The escapist ABC comedies of the late 1970s dominated the ratings as thoroughly as CBS's topical comedies had done earlier in the decade. These shows, and the network offerings that followed into the

1980s, accepted the new social rules that the sixties had established—with greater tolerance of premarital sex; less deference to authority; and more respect for gays, people of color, and other marginalized groups—but they resurrected the network belief from the years before *All in the Family* that television's principal role was to comfort and even numb, not to challenge or provoke. The family hour notwithstanding, what succeeded *All in the Family* was not a return to traditional values but, rather, a retreat from social engagement of any sort.

In this new environment, Wood hung on for a while at CBS, though he was deeply stressed and increasingly disengaged. He quit in April 1976, three days after the trial for the writers' lawsuit against the family hour began.[29] Taylor followed him out the door in October 1976, when Paley unexpectedly and summarily dismissed him.[30]

Wood returned to Los Angeles with a cushy four-year deal from CBS to develop programming, but his heart wasn't in it; he spent too much time on the golf course and produced nothing of quality.[31] His final years in New York had disillusioned and depleted him. Pete Noyes, his old KNXT colleague, remembers having lunch with Wood after he returned to Los Angeles. "He was a bitter man," Noyes recalled. "He never got in motion when he came back. It was all downhill for him. I was shocked at the different Bob Wood I met that day, who once had all the enthusiasm and the get-up-and-go mentality. He was now just out of it."[32] Wood died in 1986 at age sixty-one, only a decade after he returned to LA.[33] By then, relatively few in the industry remembered his pivotal role in transforming the face of television.

The credit for television's rebirth in the early 1970s had always tilted more toward his partner in the transformation, Norman Lear. Lear's breakthrough shows justifiably made him an icon in the entertainment industry, where he remained a force well into his nineties, some seven decades after he first arrived in Los Angeles. But he, too, never again shaped the culture as powerfully as he did in the early 1970s. *One Day at a Time*, about a divorced mother and her two precocious daughters in Indianapolis, became Lear's last big network comedy hit when it reached the air in 1975, and even that was much more of a conventional situation comedy than his landmark earlier programs. Lear displayed his old talent for disruption the next year with *Mary Hart-man, Mary Hartman,* a brilliant send-up of soap operas that held up an unforgiving (and often very funny) mirror to American consumerism and the social impact of television itself. But the show, under the relentless pace required to produce episodes five nights a week, lasted only two seasons.[34] Starting in 1978, Lear shifted his focus away from television, first toward movies and then toward politics; in 1981 he founded an organization called People for the American Way, to defend free speech and combat the influence of the growing religious right, which he had skirmished with since the early 1970s.[35]

Larry Gelbart and James L. Brooks, the two contemporaries who most closely rivaled Lear in skill and influence, also shifted their focus from television to film through the mid- and late 1970s. *Mary Tyler Moore* went off the air in 1977, with a sweet and beloved final episode. *M*A*S*H* hung on until 1983 (although Gelbart departed years before) and also went out with a bang: an emotional final episode that for many years was the most highly watched television program ever. It may have been coincidental that Robert Wood, Norman Lear, Larry Gelbart, and James Brooks all stepped away from network television in the second half of the 1970s, but the migration nonetheless reflected a larger reality: the window that all these men had opened around 1971, allowing for the entrance of a different and more daring kind of television, had closed. Television produced some great shows in the 1980s and '90s (from *Hill Street Blues* to *Seinfeld*), but few people would look to television again as a source of social insight and cultural commentary until the era of "peak TV" began around 2000, with cable shows such as *The Sopranos* and *The Wire*, followed by *Mad Men, Breaking Bad,* and then the bottomless buffet of options delivered to viewers' living rooms by the streaming revolution that began a few years later. Each glittering point in the modern constellation of great television had its own unique origins, but all these shows shared a root in the conviction that television could be a form of art at all, a lens through which to examine and understand the society around it. And in that way, all of them carried a debt to the great innovators in early 1970s

Los Angeles who inherited a television landscape of Jed Clampett, Andy Griffith, and Gomer Pyle and replaced it with one populated by Mary Richards, Hawkeye Pierce, and Archie Bunker.

THROUGHOUT 1974, CONVENTIONAL WISDOM in Hollywood anointed *Chinatown* as the favorite to win the Best Picture Academy Award. Then, on December 12, Francis Ford Coppola challenged that assumption when he unveiled *The Godfather Part II* at a splashy New York City premiere. Coppola initially wanted no part of a sequel to *The Godfather*, a massive critical and commercial success, but the offer of a staggering million-dollar payday and the promise of no studio interference from Paramount ultimately swayed him. Coppola had always been interested in crafting a movie that would parallel the stories of a father and son across two different time periods; this inspired the film's unique structure, which juxtaposes the rise of the young Vito Corleone (played by Robert De Niro) with the ascent of his son Michael. Coppola and Mario Puzo, the novel's author, holed up in a Reno casino to finish the script, and shooting on the film began in October 1973.[36]

Awarded unchallenged control, Coppola confidently executed a compelling vision. The final product stood as a landmark in early 1970s cinema, one of the era's most searching deconstructions of American society. Coppola justifiably viewed even his first *Godfather* as a commentary on the corruption rotting American life in the guise of a genre film.[37] In *Part II*, he deepened that critique by directly contrasting the stories of the young Don and his son. Compared to the father, Michael is more polished, but also more soulless, even arranging the murder of his own brother (who has unwittingly betrayed him) at the movie's end. Michael is the Mafia equivalent of "the best and the brightest"; like the Vietnam-era national security planners immortalized in the classic David Halberstam book of that name, he is a man of unquestioned skill and capacity who lacks the ethical compass to truly reckon with the collateral damage of his actions. Swimming through a tide of corruption in business and politics, he was the metaphor to Coppola of a nation whose moral standing sank precisely as its military and economic might swelled. "I wanted to make a definitive statement about power," Coppola said soon after the sequel was released. "The finished film . . . says that this country is in danger of losing its soul, like Michael did. That power without humanity is destructive."[38]

This same astringent message also infused *Chinatown*, in the character of John Huston's Noah Cross, the monstrous father of Faye Dunaway's Evelyn Mulwray. These two towering works dominated the race for the 1975 Academy Awards; when the Academy announced the nominations in February 1975, each film received eleven, including for Best Picture, Best Director (for Coppola and Roman Polanski), Best Actor (Al Pacino and Jack Nicholson), and Best Screenplay (Robert Towne in the original screenplay category and Coppola and Puzo for an adapted work).[39] The competition was uncomfortably intimate. Both *Chinatown* and *The Godfather Part II* were released in 1974 by Paramount, as was Coppola's *The Conversation*, a small jewel of early seventies paranoia that won him a second nomination for Best Picture. *The Godfather Part II* and *Chinatown* had even overlapped in their shooting schedules at the studio; Fred Roos, Coppola's co-producer, remembers Jack Nicholson, wearing his 1930s suit and nose bandage from *Chinatown*, wandering over to sit in the gallery during the climactic Senate hearing scene in *Godfather II*.[40] Coppola and Towne had been friends since their days with Roger Corman; Coppola had enlisted Towne to write the great garden scene between Marlon Brando and Al Pacino in the first *Godfather*.

The A-list crowd filing into the Dorothy Chandler Pavilion on a rainy night in April 1975 considered *Chinatown* the favorite for the night's top prizes, as it had swept the Golden Globes, winning Best Picture, Director, Actor, and Original Screenplay.[41] "Oscar night, they were the odds-on favorite to win Best Picture," said Roos. "Everybody said it was a slam dunk."[42] But instead, *Godfather II* dominated the night. Coppola won the Oscars for Best Picture and Best Director and shared the award with Puzo for Best Adapted Screenplay; Robert De Niro won as Best Supporting Actor for his portrayal of the young Don. Among *Chinatown*'s eleven nominees, only Towne won, for Best Original Screenplay. "I just remember feeling bad that I was the only one who won," he recalled.*[43]

Even Nicholson was passed over for Best Actor (though, so was Pacino, with sentimental favorite Art Carney winning the prize for his role in the slight *Harry and Tonto*). Nicholson finally captured an Oscar the next year for his portrayal of Randle McMurphy, the rebellious mental institution patient in *One Flew Over the Cuckoo's Nest*. That film was brilliantly constructed by Milos Forman, a Czech-born director who joined Nicholson in capturing an Oscar for his work on the movie. *Cuckoo* extended the extraordinary run of early 1970s films from the older generation of directors—Forman was born in 1932—that delivered piercing commentaries on American life. Through 1975 and 1976, directors (and often writers) born in the 1920s and '30s released a sunburst of great works, including Altman's *Nashville*; *Shampoo*, from Warren Beatty, Towne, and Hal Ashby; *Network*, from director Sidney Lumet and writer Paddy Chayefsky; Alan Pakula's *All the President's Men*; and *Rocky*, from John Avildsen (albeit with a defining contribution from Baby Boomer Sylvester Stallone, the film's writer and star).

BUT EVEN AS THIS crescendo of powerful films from the older generation of moviemakers reached the screen, the movement in Hollywood was tilting away from their kind of moviemaking. A younger generation of filmmakers was steering the film industry toward its future by returning it to old verities of compelling stories, big stars, and engrossing effects. The sheer filmmaking bravura of their work entranced audiences, and produced box office returns so vast as to make the new direction irresistible to the studios.

---

* *Chinatown*'s makers could console themselves with history's verdict, which solidified over time that their film ranked with *The Wizard of Oz*, *The Grapes of Wrath*, and *Citizen Kane* as among the very greatest movies that did not win a Best Picture Oscar. Robert Evans blamed himself for the results, insisting that the picture suffered because of a backlash against his unusual dual role producing the movie while serving as Paramount's production chief (Robert Evans, *The Kid Stays in the Picture* [New York: itBooks, 2013], 290).

Jaws, released in June 1975 after its laborious production in the summer of 1974, represented the pivotal moment in this transition. Even more emphatically than the other mega hits of the early 1970s (*The Godfather*, *The Exorcist*, and *The Sting*), *Jaws* demonstrated that the Hollywood roulette wheel could pay out much bigger prizes than ever before. Spielberg's shark story surpassed *The Godfather* as Hollywood's highest-grossing movie up to that point in just sixty-four days.[44] It made Spielberg a millionaire. Richard Zanuck, the film's co-producer, said he made more money from *Jaws* than his father, Darryl Zanuck, one of the industry's founding moguls, made in his entire career.[45] Two years later, in May 1977, George Lucas raised the stakes again when he finally completed his long struggle to bring *Star Wars* to the screen. Within months of its release, *Star Wars* surpassed *Jaws* as the highest-grossing movie of all time.

It escaped no one in Hollywood that the top of the all-time box office lists was increasingly populated by films that appealed to a youth population that remained enormous in size as the final Baby Boomers moved into their teens and early twenties. The possibility of generating returns as large as *Jaws* or *Star Wars*, particularly by attracting young people, changed how studios invested their money. Franchises and packages built around name stars and directors became more attractive; one-off films, especially with quirky perspectives, less so. Movies that lacked the qualities (stars, spectacle, special effects) to sustain a mass domestic opening faced increasing skepticism. The emergence of greater foreign film markets compounded the effect, because the movies that could appeal to audiences across national boundaries were usually the same kind of big-budget thrill rides that could fill shopping mall multiplexes in every town across America. A light saber, a shark, and, later, a superhero crossed cultural barriers more easily than one of Robert Altman's conflicted antiheroes.

The rise of Creative Artists Agency as Hollywood's most powerful institution both reflected and accelerated these new dynamics. CAA also traced its roots to late 1974, when a group of five agents at William Morris reached their limit over its hidebound ways. The rebellion at Morris was another front in Hollywood's generational struggle during the early 1970s. Morris was a cobweb of rules and hierarchies, a gerontocracy that bestowed all its rewards, from titles to compensation, based on seniority, not production. "It was an old, soft, corrupt place," Michael Ovitz, the driven young agent who became the central figure at CAA, wrote later.[46] Through the final months of 1974, Ovitz and his close friend Ron Meyer, another young agent, plotted to form their own agency; soon they joined forces with three equally frustrated agents from the television department.

Although it was hardly apparent at the time, CAA's launch in early 1975, like the release of *Jaws* a few months later, marked a milestone in Hollywood's transition (or, more accurately, reversion) toward mass-market filmmaking. It was never entirely clear whether CAA was a cause or a symptom of the change; the answer was probably some of both. In its first years, it subsisted mostly by signing clients in television, where its partners had the most experience. But led by Ovitz, as ruthless and relentless in his own way as Spielberg's great white shark, the agency moved into film during the late 1970s, and it proved the perfect vehicle to both propel and profit from Hollywood's shift toward the blockbuster. CAA's contribution, as it built its client list, was to perfect "the package." It would assemble directors, stars, and a writer around a proposed film and then present the entire slate as a take-it-or-leave-it proposition to the studios. CAA controlled so many of the most highly sought talents in every aspect of filmmaking that studios could not easily bypass the agency. All roads led back to Ovitz. "We eclipsed everybody," Ovitz said, looking back. "Ten years in, we had everybody. So, if you want to do a character piece that requires Hoffman, De Niro, Pacino, you're coming to us. We have all three. It was unheard of."[47] At one point, the agency represented forty-five of the fifty highest-grossing directors.[48]

The movies produced by this process were, with rare exceptions, not quirky, idiosyncratic, or experimental. They were, by design, mainstream star vehicles intended to generate the biggest-possible salaries (and commissions) for as many clients on the CAA roster as possible.[49] The movies constructed through CAA's assembly line included *Tootsie, The Natural, Rain Man, Gandhi, Ghostbusters, Out of Africa,* and

Jurassic Park. These were all films of great skill and craft—though Ovitz was a ferocious empire builder, he also loved movies—but they reinforced Hollywood's return in the late 1970s and beyond toward big-budget, mainstream productions that aimed to captivate audiences, not challenge them. These movies recalled Hollywood's mainstream offerings before the 1960s, with one important concession to the industry's increased reliance on a young audience. "The big movies were different," Ovitz recalled. "They had young people in them."[50]

The older generation of directors did not go quietly into the night as this push for younger audiences nudged them toward the exit. Mike Nichols, Hal Ashby, Alan Pakula, and Roman Polanski, among others, all produced fine work through the remainder of their careers. Warren Beatty, operating as always on his own clock, worked more fitfully, but he still had notable achievements with *Reds*, his ambitious epic about John Reed and the Russian Revolution, in 1981, and *Bulworth*, the inspired (and underrated) political satire he wrote, directed, and starred in seventeen years later. Altman, after stumbling through years of decline following *Nashville*, enjoyed a late-career renaissance after critics revered his 1992 version of the dark Hollywood comedy *The Player.*

Yet almost all these works, however excellent, felt like the epilogue to earlier triumphs. The world of mega blockbusters left less room for the personal movies the older directors formulated during Hollywood's decade of maximum experimentation. The generation of directors born from the 1920s through the mid-1930s never matched the cultural influence they achieved from 1967 through 1976. They had found a moment that matched their sensibility, and when the moment ended, their work never again resonated with the same impact.

Spielberg and Lucas went on to rule the box office, separately and together. *Star Wars* became perhaps the most successful franchise of all time, though Lucas's critical reputation might as well have been hit by the Death Star after the negative responses to his trilogy of prequel films. Spielberg produced an iconic roster of science-fiction and adventure hits, including *Close Encounters of the Third Kind*, *E.T.*, *Jurassic Park*, and the *Indiana Jones* movies that he made in partnership with

Lucas. Lucas never displayed much interest in social commentary; he remained guided by his Modesto manifesto: he wanted to make movies that caused people to feel better when they left the theater than when they arrived. Paul Schrader remembered seeing *Star Wars* and telling a mutual friend, "Thank God, George has got that Buck Rogers shit out of his system. Now he can go back to being a filmmaker."[51] But in fact, Lucas never did return to movies with a critical edge. "George wasn't that person, was he?" said Tom Pollock, his lawyer (and later the chairman of Universal Studios). "George had a few stories he wanted to tell, and that's all he ever wanted to tell."[52]

Spielberg started that way, too, but eventually he broadened his perspective. Later in life, he became a political activist close to both Bill Clinton and Barack Obama, and he also produced more works that sought to comment on his times—at first, awkwardly (*The Color Purple*), and later, with more confidence (*Saving Private Ryan*, *The Post*, and above all, *Schindler's List*). But those movies came well after Spielberg's youthful success encouraged Hollywood to revert from commentary to spectacle.

Among the generation that emerged in the 1970s, only Scorsese achieved the long-term influence of Lucas and Spielberg. In *Taxi Driver*, his partnership with Paul Schrader released in 1976, the director painted an unsettling portrait of alienation and social disintegration that matched the best of the older generation's statements. But after *Taxi Driver*, Scorsese produced few films that were seen as comments on contemporary American life. Instead, he crafted a powerful succession of stylistically brilliant movies that illuminated more timeless questions about masculinity and honor, often against a backdrop of organized crime (especially Italian American organized crime). Unlike Coppola with *The Godfather*, Scorsese never sought to frame the Mafia as a metaphor for the ruthlessness of American capitalism. Nor did he show much interest in exploring the changing dynamics of relationships between men and women. His canvas was the relationship between men, their dreams and delusions, their loyalties and betrayals.

Scorsese's sustained brilliance captured a larger truth. Excellence in Hollywood, like excellence on television, did not end after the early 1970s: great moviemakers in every decade continued to produce films of enormous skill, insight, and emotion. What did change after the early 1970s was the idea of Hollywood as a central source of social commentary on the changing American society. The film studios largely renounced that role, as if shedding a skin, beginning around 1975. The change in movies followed almost precisely the transition in television. The movie industry, even more enthusiastically than television, absorbed the major cultural changes championed by the social movements of the 1960s: greater freedom in sexual relations (and more explicit portrayal of sex on-screen), more independence for women, more skepticism of authority in business and government, and in a more halting process, more respect for marginalized groups. But after the early 1970s, Hollywood more rarely produced works akin to *Easy Rider*, *Five Easy Pieces*, the two *Godfather* films, or *Chinatown*, that is, films that fundamentally challenged America's self-image as an equitable society and a force for good in the world. The biggest movies rarely argued the opposite; they just sidestepped the argument altogether to revert to the undemanding (if often enthralling) entertainment that had guided the industry before the revolution of the late 1960s. And when filmmakers returned in larger numbers to the terrain of social commentary starting around the turn of the twenty-first century, it was far more through the medium of cable and then streaming television than on film (notwithstanding such exceptions as Jordan Peele's biting allegory *Get Out*).

The changes that transformed both television and movies in the twenty-first century make clear that the two generations that competed for supremacy in early 1970s Hollywood had started distinct bloodlines. The descendants of the great socially aware films from the older generation are today almost entirely found on the television screen in binge-worthy shows that examine modern life in unsparing detail (*Breaking Bad*, *The Wire*, *Fleabag*, *Atlanta*). By contrast, the movie screen still remains predominantly in thrall to the kind of spectacle and rousing entertainment that characterized the younger generation of 1970s filmmakers, particularly Spielberg and Lucas. On each side of this new equation, the competing visions that collided in Hollywood's generational transition during the 1970s still shape the entertainment that Americans consume nearly half a century later.

JERRY BROWN TOOK THE OATH[53] as California's thirty-fourth governor in Sacramento on January 6, 1975, and in almost every way, he presented the stylistic opposite of Ronald Reagan, the man he succeeded.Reagan was orderly, punctual, structured. He kept banker's hours, arriving in the governor's office at 9 a.m. and leaving promptly at 5 p.m. with a clean desk. He followed direction from his advisers, left almost all details to his staff, and maintained a cordial professional relationship with the legislature. None of that could be said of Brown.

His first years in office, much like his general election campaign for governor, featured a heavy dose of chaos. Brown resisted structure, constantly sent mixed signals to the legislature, reversed positions, left key jobs unfilled for months, obsessed over details, and because he had no family commitments, he thought nothing of convening meetings that would sprawl long past midnight and drift through hours of unfocused speculation that carried a whiff of the dorm room. His relationship with the state legislature was especially chaotic, and his legislative accomplishments throughout his governorship were skimpy.

And yet Brown as governor was a sensation from the start, first in California and, before long, nationally as well. Polls showed his approval rating among voters in the state soaring. "He is the most interesting politician in the United States," Richard Reeves concluded flatly in the *New York Times* a few months after Brown took office.[54] Brown didn't look, sound, or act like a typical politician. Not only had he rejected the lavish governor's mansion Reagan constructed, choosing to live in a sparsely furnished apartment near the Capitol, and renounced the governor's usual car and driver, ferrying himself in a blue Plymouth, but he also returned all gifts, no matter how small or personal. He didn't give long speeches—his inaugural address was just eight minutes[55]—or offer flowery promises, and he talked at least as much about what government could not do as what it could. The skepticism of government that he projected both symbolically and substantively struck a perfect note in a country that had emerged bruised and wary from Vietnam and Watergate.

Brown never fit entirely into any single category. His goal was not just to shrink government, the way conservatives such as Reagan had, but rather, to improve it so it could more effectively advance the traditional liberal goals: uplifting the needy, constraining the power of business, expanding the circle of opportunity. And he married his flinty attitude toward spending with a warm embrace of the political causes and social changes of the 1960s. He reflected the changes in cultural attitudes by supporting legislation to decriminalize sex acts between consenting adults and the possession of small amounts of marijuana. He appointed unprecedented numbers of women and racial minorities to executive branch and judicial positions. As important, he filled many jobs with idealistic young experts (many of them, like him, lawyers from Yale) drawn from the institutional side of the movements that emerged from the 1960s: environmental groups, public interest law firms, antipoverty organizations.[56] The figures Brown appointed to government positions from those movements generally didn't drift as far into radical politics during the 1960s as, say, Tom Hayden did, but they were moving along the same trajectory as Hayden in 1974, from protest to participation. Brown, to a degree unmatched at that point, provided a bridge for the outsiders of the sixties to become insiders in the seventies and beyond. For all the disorder that surrounded him, Brown seemed to live with one foot in the future.* "If you were willing to go with the flow, it was certainly a very exciting place to be," said Bill Press, an aide in the state senate who joined the administration to direct Brown's Office of Planning and Research. "You knew you were working with the most popular,

---

* Early on, Brown recognized the seismic implications of the computer revolution that such innovators as Steve Jobs and Steve Wozniak were beginning in Silicon Valley, and he may have been the nation's only prominent political leader who went to see *Star Wars* immediately after it was released in May 1977 (Miriam Pawel, *The Browns of California: The Dynasty that Transformed a State and Shaped a Nation* [New York: Bloomsbury, 2018], 260).

the most famous, the most intelligent politician in the country at the time."[57]

It didn't take long for a politician with these ambitions and skills to look beyond Sacramento. On March 12, 1976, weeks after Jimmy Carter, the former Georgia governor, had established himself as the clear front-runner for the Democratic nomination, and barely a year after Brown took office in Sacramento, Brown casually told a group of reporters in his office that he planned to run for president.[58] Presidential candidates usually spend years traveling the country to build networks of donors and political supporters. When Brown recruited the former legal services lawyer Mickey Kantor to run the campaign, Kantor quickly learned that there was no staff, no financing committee, no organization, nothing on the ground in any state.[59]

Still, however improbably, Brown's campaign instantly ignited. His unorthodox mix of conservative and liberal themes attracted voters from both camps, and his promise of generational change and reform struck as powerful a chord in other states as it did in California. Inspiring but vague, earnest in manner but slippery in his political commitments, Brown seemed something like a real-life version of the fictional third-party candidate Hal Phillip Walker from Robert Altman's *Nashville* (an impression deepened when Ronee Blakley and Keith Carradine, from the movie, campaigned with him).[60] In the campaign's final weeks, Brown (or delegate slates sympathetic to him) stormed past Carter to victory in primaries in Maryland, Nevada, Rhode Island, New Jersey, and California. "He was hot," remembered Kantor. "There's no other way to say it. He was hot, and everywhere he went, people wanted to see him. He'd pack the house."[61] Brown's star was so bright that it attracted even other stars. One day, Kantor was sitting in his small campaign office when Eagles' manager Irving Azoff; Jerry Weintraub, the music manager and producer of *Nashville*; and another music executive named Paul Drew walked in.[62] They wanted to stage a concert for Brown with the Eagles, Jackson Browne, and Linda Ronstadt. The resulting sold-out concert in the Washington, DC, suburb of Largo, Maryland, raised nearly one hundred thousand dollars for Brown's campaign, helped propel him to his first big victory in the Maryland primary, and rekindled his acquaintance with Linda Ronstadt. Not long after, the two began a more serious romance than their brief encounter in the early 1970s.[63]

Though Brown had entered the race far too late to stop Carter, the young California governor emerged from the campaign a new star, glowing with unlimited possibility. This proved a false dawn. The meteoric 1976 race represented Brown's zenith over the next three decades. He won reelection as California's governor in 1978, but a series of political missteps tarnished his image—particularly his mishandling of a suburban uprising over property taxes that year and the outbreak in 1980 of a Mediterranean fruit fly (the medfly) that threatened the state's agricultural production.[64] An approach to governing that initially appeared eclectic increasingly seemed erratic. Critics portrayed him as a flake. This image was crystallized in newspaper columnist Mike Royko's dismissive description of Brown as "Governor Moonbeam." Royko eventually came to regret the label as unfair, but it completed the shift in Brown's image from an inspiring symbol of change to the embodiment of unfulfilled youthful promise. Brown drew an embarrassingly meager level of support when he challenged Carter in the Democratic presidential primaries in 1980 and then lost a race for a U.S. Senate seat from California in 1982.

Brown receded from view through the 1980s, before returning to his roots by launching a long-shot bid for the 1992 Democratic presidential nomination as a champion of political reform. He lost that race, too (to Bill Clinton), and then lowered his sights. He moved to Oakland and, somewhat like Hayden almost three decades before, started a commune.[65] Brown had more success with it: he used it as a springboard to win election two times as Oakland's mayor. From there, he followed in his father's footsteps to win election as California's attorney general in 2006. He then completed his improbable reinvention by convincingly winning the governorship again, in 2010, nearly four decades after he first captured the seat. Brown won reelection by an even greater margin in 2014. After his often-chaotic terms in the 1970s, this time he drew stellar reviews for his measured, steady leadership. By 2020, some Democrats were lamenting that Brown, who turned eighty during his final year as governor, thought himself too old to seek the presidency.

No individual life encompasses a generation's experience, but the extraordinarily long arc of Brown's career did provide a yardstick to measure the enduring impact of the social and political movements that inspired him during the 1960s. Many of the causes Brown championed over his career emerged from those movements. Ideas that seemed novel or threatening when Brown first raised them (more inclusion of women and people of color, greater tolerance of gay rights, more emphasis on sustainable living and renewable power) have become mainstream. Those were undeniable gains, but they represented only one side of the ledger. The ascent of the Baby Boomers, which became the largest cohort of eligible voters in 1984 and held that title until the Millennial generation surpassed them in 2020, never produced the larger political transformation that youthful leftist activists such as Tom Hayden once anticipated. Instead, a decades-long struggle between the liberal wing of the Baby Boom, which dominated the generation's identity during the 1960s, and its more conservative and traditional elements, which grew more assertive over time, fueled the heightening polarization that reshaped American politics after the 1960s.[66] The liberal Baby Boomers, on most fronts, won the war over changing the culture, but they never achieved a lasting political victory. It was telling that the four Baby Boomers who (so far) have won the presidency are divided between two Republicans (Donald Trump and George W. Bush, born three weeks apart in June and July 1946) and two Democrats (Bill Clinton, born only a few weeks after them, in August 1946, and Barack Obama, born nearer the boom's end, in August 1961).

Jerry Brown never won the White House, and he was, in any case, a few years older than the oldest Boomers, but no one did more than Brown to integrate concerns of the sixties activists into the mainstream political system. At the same time that the brilliant collection of early 1970s music, television, and movie artists operating in Los Angeles were embedding those ideas in popular culture, Brown provided a beachhead for them in the world of politics and governance.

He never achieved all he sought, but he left the country a different place than he found it. The same words could apply as the final assessment on the political movements of the 1960s that inspired Brown and so many others.

THE 1974 EAGLES TOUR that began in the spring, a few weeks before the massive California Jam festival in Ontario, finally rumbled to its conclusion in December. The marathon had carried the band to new heights. They played to their largest audiences ever, sharing bills with artists ranging from Neil Young and Linda Ronstadt to the Beach Boys and the Allman Brothers.[67] On New Year's Eve 1974, the Eagles celebrated the tour's completion with an exuberant final show at Los Angeles' Shrine Auditorium, during which they were joined onstage by J. D. Souther, Jackson Browne, Ronstadt, and Joe Walsh (who would enter the band as a permanent member a few years later). It was a rousing conclusion to a miraculous year in LA music.

The Eagles tour, prolonged as it was, still only hinted at the scale of opportunity that now existed for rock concerts as the huge youth population expanded the ticket-buying audience. Two other 1974 tours mapped those new possibilities. The reunion tour for Bob Dylan and the Band that David Geffen and Bill Graham engineered in the winter of 1974 set records for ticket sales and revenues. Just a few months later, the Crosby, Stills, Nash and Young reunion tour that Geffen, Graham, and Elliot Roberts organized for the summer of 1974 shattered those marks.

Dylan and the Band played big indoor arenas, such as New York's Madison Square Garden and Los Angeles' Forum, during their tour. The CSNY reunion topped that by playing mostly in outdoor baseball and football stadiums that could hold three or four times as many fans as the indoor venues. Other bands had occasionally played outdoor stadiums—mostly, notably, the Beatles during their abbreviated 1966 American tour—but no act had tried to fill as many stadiums, in as many cities, as the CSNY tour booked for the summer of 1974. The gamble, in financial terms, paid off spectacularly.

Everything about the tour was massive. Starting in Seattle in July, the band drew enormous crowds all summer long: 90,000 people over two nights in Oakland; 60,000 each in Denver and Dallas; 82,000 in Cleveland; 52,000 in Milwaukee; 70,000 in Atlantic City; 77,000 on Long Island for the final American show in September.[68] Always politically engaged, the group was riveted that summer as the House of Representatives moved toward impeaching Nixon; as his resignation approached, the band made "Ohio," Neil Young's searing response to the Kent State shootings, a fixture of its nightly encores. The foursome was onstage at Roosevelt Stadium in New Jersey on the night of Nixon's resignation; after Nash announced the news, the band broke into a crackling version of Crosby's "Long Time Gone."[69]

But the tour was also defined by stupefying levels of rock star excess and bottomless bickering among the band. (Nash remembers they had one crew member whose only job was to supply them with cocaine.)[70] The shows had moments of excellence, but the drugs, the squabbling, the deficiencies of the sound systems at the time, and the tendency of Young and Stills to express their disagreements by pounding out ever-louder and longer guitar solos all sabotaged the performances. The tour set the template for gargantuan rock shows to come by proving that the huge youth population could support itineraries of an unprecedented scale, but it was with good reason that Crosby labeled the shows the "Doom Tour."

For a younger generation of musicians, the leviathan nature of the CSNY tour symbolized all that had gone wrong with rock. "Music had just become so bloated," Richard Hell, cofounder of the pioneering punk band Television, said later. "It was all these leftover sixties guys playing stadiums, you know, being treated like they were very important people, and acting like they were very important people. It wasn't rock & roll, it was like some kind of stage act."[71] The smooth Southern California country-rock aristocracy of singer-songwriters, what some at the time called the "Avocado Mafia," became a special target of derision for the circuit of rougher-edged musicians coalescing a continent away in Lower Manhattan. "There was this thing coming from the West Coast, they called it the Avocado Mafia—the Eagles and 'Blue Bayou' and all that," remembered Elda Stiletto (née Gentile), the founder of another early punk band called the Stilettos (which featured a young Deborah Harry, later to go on to fame in Blondie). "And here we were, a bunch of New York people, living in the art scene, going, 'Wow, that sounds really boring.'"[72]

Far from the spotlight and the riches enjoyed by the top LA artists, a cohort of aspiring younger New York musicians wrote an alternative history of the early 1970s. Their music evoked crowded urban avenues, not open desert highways. While the LA stars retreated to mansions in Malibu and Bel Air, the young New York musicians subsisted in tenement walk-ups on the Lower East Side. LA was patched jeans and cowboy boots; New York was torn jeans and combat boots. Gays and transvestites were as central to the emerging New York City scene as winsome blond groupies were in LA. The first signs of a New York alternative to the chart-ruling sounds from Los Angeles emerged in the early 1970s, in the work of the New York Dolls, a flamboyant cross-dressing glitter band, and the mesmerizing performances that a young singer and poet named Patti Smith delivered in venues around the city. The movement coalesced and gained momentum after the opening of the club CBGB & OMFUG (for "Country, Bluegrass, Blues and Other Music for Uplifting Gourmandizers") in a space below a flophouse in the Bowery in December 1973. The club would incubate the developing punk and New Wave scene as lovingly as the Troubadour had nurtured the LA singer-songwriter and country-rock movements. Patti Smith and Television, the Ramones, Blondie, Talking Heads, and Mink DeVille, all of whom performed at CBGB, would bring an elemental ferocity to their frenzied performances that stripped rock back to its rebellious roots.

Along with the emergence of Bruce Springsteen, who filled the space between LA's polished professionalism and CBGB's anarchic energy, the blossoming punk movement captured the turn of the cultural wheel. The California dream of the early 1970s was really a sixties dream of peace, love, and personal liberation, however hazily those terms were defined. By the time Springsteen released his landmark *Born to Run* album in August 1975 and the punk movement fully flowered in 1976 and 1977, America was reeling under economic recession, the oil embargo, gasoline lines, defeat in Vietnam, scandal in Washington, rising crime rates, persistent racial tensions, and urban decay in cities around the country. Both Springsteen and the punk bands were shaped by New York City at its absolute nadir in the mid-1970s, the period when *Taxi Driver*, from Martin Scorsese and Paul Schrader, justifiably portrayed the city as a hell on earth, complete with stygian steam rising from the manhole covers. The bright, breezy optimism of the early 1970s California sound seemed too gossamer for the grim realities of this harsher world.

The California artists were not immune to this reassessment. Jackson Browne's *The Pretender*, released in 1976, offered a much darker take than his earlier work on modern America and the ebbing of the sixties dream. The Eagles, as the embodiment of the "Avocado Mafia," were often brittle and defensive about the new sounds emerging from New York; they scoffed at the New York Dolls, and after *Born to Run*, Henley improbably insisted "our songs have more to do with the streets than Bruce Springsteen's."[73] But the Eagles felt the shifting mood, too, and in 1976 the band also moved from sunshine to darkness with the release of their masterpiece, *Hotel California*. "Every band has its peak," Henley said later, "and that was ours."[74] Timed to appear during the nation's bicentennial, the album was a brilliant exploration of the price of fame and the end of the California dream. With songs both intimate ("Wasted Time") and cinematic ("Life in the Fast Lane" and "Hotel California"), *Hotel California* projected an enveloping sense of loss, a mood set by the haunting cover photo of the Beverly Hills Hotel at twilight. The band seemed acutely conscious that it was burying the youthful political dreams of many Baby Boomers, most directly when Henley sang of California on the title track, "We haven't had that spirit here since 1969." Speaking to Robert Hilburn of the *Los Angeles Times* around the time of the album's release, Henley portrayed it as an alarm bell for a nation that had tuned out the sixties' demands for reform and renewal. "The '70s have seemed unusually decadent," Henley lamented. "There has been a lot of escapism and apathy. We're trying to say 'Get out of your house, hang out, vote. . . . [D]o something.'"[75] It was a shout in the wind during the same year *Happy Days* surpassed *All in the Family* as the nation's top-rated television show.

Hotel California nonetheless was a huge commercial and critical hit for the Eagles (despite some niggling carping in *Rolling Stone*).[*76] Its success underscored the continued commercial power of the big Los Angeles artists through the decade's second half. Linda Ronstadt worked the most diligently, producing, under Peter Asher's careful direction, perfectly composed chart-topping albums on an almost yearly schedule, albeit with less of the untamed charm that marked her early 1970s records. Jackson Browne followed *The Pretender* with *Running on Empty* in 1977. Recorded on the road, the album became a huge hit that captured his mounting disillusion with the rock star life. Browne's new albums continued to sell well in the 1980s, though the rapturous early critical reception for his work cooled substantially. Joni Mitchell moved in the opposite direction as she shed her poppy melodies of the early 1970s to produce challenging records infused with her growing fascination with jazz. Her commercial audience dwindled even as critics often loved the work.

But while most of the great LA artists retained a loyal audience among their Baby Boom contemporaries, the sense that they represented the edge of musical innovation plummeted after the mid-1970s. Big sales and AM hits for the Eagles or Linda Ronstadt did not stop the movement of musical influence from Los Angeles to New York and from then on to London, as the Sex Pistols, the Clash, and the bands orbiting them put a sharper class-conscious edge on the first punk stirrings from the Lower East Side. For all the disillusionment that suffused *Hotel California*, it still used the sixties as its jumping-off point. The lyrics of the American (as opposed to British) punk bands didn't carry much political content, but on both sides of the

---

[*] In 2018, the Recording Industry Association of America certified *Hotel California* as the third-highest-selling album of all time. Ranking No. 1 was the early-career Eagles' *Greatest Hits* collection that David Geffen released in 1976 over the band's objections (RIAA rankings, https://www.riaa.com/riaa-awards-eagles-1–3-top-certified-albums-time/).

Atlantic, the movement in attitude and affect seemed more connected to the economic and social problems that mounted through the 1970s. In that world, the California sound, even when projecting disillusion, struck many younger musicians and critics as too pretty and polished.

Even some of the LA music scene's leading lights concluded that it had reached an impasse by the mid-1970s. "I thought that the LA sound had painted itself into a corner," remembered Danny Kortchmar, the thoughtful guitarist who moved from New York to LA in the late 1960s. "There's only so much you can do with banjos and steel guitars and acoustic guitars." The punk and New Wave bands that emerged in 1975 and 1976 "were coming out and giving us all the finger," Kortchmar continued. "It had to happen, because things had gotten stagnant. 'Enough already. Let's bust out. Let's try some other stuff. Let's get rid of these clothes, bell bottoms and promo T-shirts and shaggy hair. Enough already. Let's have some fun, this is dreary.'"[77]

BY THE FINAL MONTHS of 1974, the LA renaissance in television, movies, and music faced the common external threat of a shift in consumer preferences and political attitudes. But there was also a threat from within, and that threat, like so much else about life in Los Angeles, initially arrived bearing promises of liberation and pleasure.

Drugs had always been part of the social scene in the entertainment industry—marijuana and then LSD had lubricated LA parties through the 1960s—but the city's relationship with drugs transformed when cocaine arrived in force in the early 1970s. The storm never hit as hard in the television business, whose tight deadlines left less leeway for dysfunctional behavior. But with cocaine's ascent, drug use in the music and movie industries became both more widespread and more debilitating. "By 1974, it was everywhere," remembered Jonathan Taplin, the producer and road manager who crossed between the movie and music worlds. "You would go into meetings in offices, and the executives would pull out a little vial and put it on the coffee table."[78] Cocaine entered Los Angeles mostly through the music industry, becoming as ubiquitous in recording studios as guitars and amps, but like a wildfire crossing a highway, it quickly jumped the border into Hollywood, and before long, it was burning through both industries. "There was so much cocaine at those times, it was insane," remembered Graham Nash. "It was literally insane. I remember one friend of Stephen [Stills]'s coming into the studio one night and just pouring out a pound of cocaine on the desk. Not a gram, not a little white packet, a *pound* of cocaine."[79] Too much was never enough. "I know guys," recalled John Boylan, the manager and producer for Linda Ronstadt, "who snorted their houses, basically."[80]

Early 1970s Los Angeles soon became known as the place where stars could go to misbehave. John Lennon, one of the biggest of them all, arrived in October 1973, ostensibly to record an album of classic fifties rock-and-roll songs with the erratic Phil Spector, but his deeper purpose was to escape his fraying marriage to Yoko Ono, and he careened through the Los Angeles nightlife like a vintage sports car that had burned out its brakes.[81] In March 1974, Lennon and Harry Nilsson, both drunk to the point of belligerence, were tossed out of the Troubadour for heckling the Smothers Brothers (of all people).[82] Lennon even lost his trademark round spectacles in the scuffle. Later, in a drunken rage, he smashed all the gold records on the wall of the house belonging to producer Lou Adler, who had allowed him to stay there when he first arrived in LA. "He was so wild, and he was just crazed," Adler remembered. "Alcohol and drugs—totally unruly."[83]

Lennon's lost weekend, as it became known, captured the descent into decadence encroaching on the LA renaissance. Others followed in his footsteps. David Bowie spent a similarly drug-addled ten months in Bel Air in 1975, while starring in the trippy Nicolas Roeg movie *The Man Who Fell to Earth* and recording his album *Station to Station*. Bowie later called his LA stay "singularly the darkest days of my life."[84]

The cycle of excess kept spinning until it reached perhaps its peak (or nadir) in March 1977. That's when director Roman Polanski returned after years in Europe following the release of *Chinatown*. He'd come back to the States to finish the screenplay for a detective thriller he was set to direct, *The First Deadly Sin*, but he had also convinced *Vogue Hommes* to let him design a photo spread on adolescent girls.[85]

It wasn't surprising that Polanski had chosen that topic. His fixation on teenage girls was long-standing. He wrote openly in his memoir about cruising outside "finishing schools" to pick up teenage girls in Gstaad, Switzerland, where he had retreated after wife Sharon Tate's murder in 1969.[86] When he finally returned to the States in 1973 to film *Chinatown*, his attraction to very young girls "began to be a significant problem for those few of us who knew about it," recalled Peter Bart, the Paramount executive at the time.[87] Back in Europe, Polanski in 1976 had begun an affair with Nastassja Kinski when she was just fifteen.[88]

Soon after Polanski returned to the Beverly Wilshire hotel in February 1977 to complete the *First Deadly Sin* script, he drove out into the San Fernando Valley to meet with a potential model for the *Vogue Hommes* shoot whom a friend had suggested.[89] After some preliminary sessions, Polanski, by his later account, brought the girl to his friend Jacqueline Bisset's house on Mulholland Drive on March 10 and shot a few photos by the pool. With shadows lengthening, he then took her to Jack Nicholson's house, on the other side of Mulholland Drive, where the light would last longer. Nicholson was away, but a housekeeper let Polanski in. Polanski served the girl some champagne from Nicholson's refrigerator[90] and, by the girl's later account, also gave her a Quaalude.[91] He took some pictures of her inside the house, then some photos of her naked in Nicholson's Jacuzzi. Then he brought her into a ground floor room and had sex with her.[92] She was thirteen.[93]

The encounter ended when Anjelica Huston, who was in the process of collecting her belongings after breaking up with Nicholson, arrived at the house. Polanski and the girl had put their clothes back on by the time they came out to see Huston, and Huston recalled that she didn't think anything of it. The next day, acting on a complaint from the girl's mother, LAPD detectives arrested Polanski at his hotel. A search warrant in hand, they drove to Nicholson's house, where Huston was still collecting her belongings. Though she wasn't a target, they found pot in an ashtray and cocaine in her handbag and arrested her along with Polanski.[94] The charges against Huston were dropped, but Polanski eventually pleaded guilty to one count of unlawful sexual intercourse and spent forty-two days in prison.[95] He fled the United States for London on February 1, 1978, when it appeared the judge might sentence him to more time, and he never returned.[*][96]

To this day, Huston seems less amazed that she found Polanski with a thirteen-year-old girl than that he was arrested for being so. "Those were the days where everybody thought that was just great," she remembered. "Everybody was operating with immunity. . . . Somebody takes the fall, and I think Roman probably took the fall for a lot of immunities. A lot of people I know at the time were going out with extremely young women, maybe not on a regular basis, but he certainly wasn't the only person around town who was sleeping with very young women."[97]

It was a measure of how thoroughly the cloud of decadence had settled onto the Los Angeles scene by the mid-1970s that it didn't strike Huston as particularly unusual to find Polanski with a girl that young. Among the stars glittering in LA, the vices varied, but the costs were consistent. Anyone comparing photos of Glenn Frey and Don Henley in 1972 and, say, 1977 could track the price of the years of drugs and high living. Julia Phillips's drug addiction incinerated her Hollywood career. Martin Scorsese barely survived his own cocaine addiction in the mid-seventies. Since the days of *Bonnie and Clyde* and *The Graduate*, Los Angeles had sold a vision of personal liberation. A decade later, liberation had curdled into license. The theme song for Los Angeles in the buoyant early 1970s could have been "Take It Easy" or "Rock Me on the Water." But by 1976, when the Eagles released *Hotel California*, the mood of lengthening shadows was more precisely captured by their rueful "Life in the Fast Lane."

---

* In January 2018, Los Angeles prosecutors announced that they had received another allegation from a minor claiming that Polanski had sexually abused her in 1975, but they declined to prosecute because the statute of limitations had run out (Richard Winton, "Polanski Won't Face New Charges," *Los Angeles Times*, January 9, 2018).

THE MAN WHO HAD lifted many of the LA artists to stardom also fell victim to the darkening mood after 1974. David Geffen began 1975 in a deep depression. Cher had left him after meeting Gregg Allman (while on a date with Geffen). Dispirited by the breakup and worn down by his conflicts with Dylan and the Eagles, Geffen sought a fresh start by pushing Warner Communications chairman and CEO Steve Ross to move him from Elektra/Asylum to the Warner Bros. movie studio. Ross rejected Geffen's pleas to run the studio, but he agreed to name Geffen as its vice chairman. The move proved perhaps the worst professional decision of Geffen's career. Accustomed to running his own operation, and wealthier than Ted Ashley, the man he worked for, Geffen bristled through an uncomfortable year at the studio before he was fired in November 1976.[98] His life then took a bizarre turn. In August 1977, he received a mistaken diagnosis of bladder cancer at Cedars-Sinai Hospital. Fearful that he didn't have long to live, at least not without the discomfort of a urostomy bag, he moved back to New York to spend what he believed were his remaining months of good health in pursuit of sex and pleasure as a gay man. In January 1978, he left Los Angeles for Manhattan, where he became a fixture on the sybaritic Studio 54 scene.[99]

Geffen had always been a controversial figure in the Los Angeles music world, even for many of his clients—the Eagles in particular bridled against him and spent years in litigation seeking the return of their music publishing rights—but his departure from LA hastened the end of the city's musical moment. Though the bands he had promoted continued to sell well, when he left, the escalator that seemed to run from the bar at the Troubadour to the top of the charts abruptly stopped. The impact on the LA scene of his taste, and his skill at building a mass audience for his artists, was fully apparent only when it was removed. The next wave of indigenous Los Angeles acts were bands such as the Runaways and X, influenced by the punk and New Wave movements, who never approached the commercial success of the Asylum artists from a few years earlier.

When Geffen finally learned that he had been incorrectly diagnosed with bladder cancer, he decided to return to music. In a triumphant second act, he moved back to Los Angeles in 1980, founded Geffen Records, and had another huge run of success that propelled his wealth into the stratosphere when he sold the new company to Lew Wasserman's MCA in 1990.[100]

Ironically, among the artists who made Geffen Records a powerhouse during the 1980s was Don Henley. Henley reinvented himself as a solo act after the Eagles finally succumbed to their internal tensions around the time that Geffen, their old patron and antagonist, returned to the music business. After the massive success of *Hotel California*, the conflict among the band members made it almost impossible for them to function together. The guitarist Don Felder was the most conspicuous malcontent, but even the once-indivisible alliance between Frey and Henley cracked. Creatively and emotionally, the band had reached a dead end. The Eagles broke up in July 1980 after Frey and Felder erupted into a screaming match at a fund-raiser for California senator Alan Cranston. "Don Felder and cocaine broke up the band," Irving Azoff says flatly.[101]

The Eagles' demise, like the dethroning a few years earlier of *All in the Family* as the nation's top-rated television show, seemed to mark an era's end almost too perfectly. By the time the Eagles collapsed, most remnants of the early 1970s Los Angeles musical scene had faded from view, like ruins covered by shifting sands. The Troubadour was struggling to survive: the circle of friends who had conspired and commiserated in their scuffling days, who had shared confidences in its bar, and who had polished new songs in Laurel Canyon living rooms, now saw one another only rarely. "Every now and then people would say, 'God, we never see each other anymore,'" remembered Jackson Browne. "We didn't hang around. We weren't single."[102] Even when the old friends could see each other perform, it was in an arena, not the "intimate settings," as Ronstadt recalled, where they had worked through their music a decade earlier. "If they were all in town, we'd visit," Ronstadt remembered. "Jackson would come out to the beach with J. D. [Souther], and we'd play music. We saw each other, but it wasn't as tight. We weren't as tight with each other because we knew other people. [But] we were the only people we knew in those early days. We were each other's resources."[103]

The days of music echoing through the canyon, boozy dinners at Dan Tana's, and spontaneous sing-alongs in the Troubadour bar all seemed very far away by the time the Eagles finally completed their long-delayed follow-up to *Hotel California*. *The Long Run* was the last album the band released before its split. The recording had been a joyless and laborious process, and the musicians didn't finish the record until 1979, far from their Hollywood haunts, at a studio in Miami.[104] On the record's elegiac closing ballad, the Eagles looked back at that earlier time. In a nod to a Carson McCullers short story, they called the song "The Sad Café." In it, Henley, Frey, J. D. Souther, and Joe Walsh, who are all credited as cowriters, mourn the decline of the Troubadour, for them "the Sad Café." In a voice as tender as he ever summoned, Henley laments the loss of "a holy place" that once seemed "protected by amazing grace." Once, the friends who gathered at the Sad Café "would sing right out loud" their hope to "change this world." Now, many months and miles later, that dream has "washed away" in the "softly falling" rain.

It was the last new music the Eagles would release together for fifteen years.

ON DECEMBER 31, THE final day of 1974, the veteran drummer and band leader Mick Fleetwood called producer Keith Olsen, whom Fleetwood had grown friendly with since relocating to Los Angeles a few months earlier. He wanted to know if one of Olsen's clients, a talented young musician named Lindsey Buckingham, might consider joining his group, Fleetwood Mac, which had just lost its lead guitarist and principal vocalist. Olsen told Fleetwood that Buckingham would not join the band without his musical (and romantic) partner, Stevie Nicks. It was an audacious response. Buckingham and Nicks, who had met and first played together in Northern California but had migrated, like so many others, to the buzzing music scene in LA, had released an eponymous album the previous year that quickly disappeared. Both were struggling financially and personally; after their record label dropped them, Nicks was even working as a waitress to help pay their bills.[105] Still, Olsen knew they constituted an all-or-nothing package. He told Fleetwood, "'Well, you know they're kind of a pair,'" Olsen recalled later.[106]

On New Year's Eve, as the city's rock aristocracy gathered for the final show of the Eagles tour at the Shrine Auditorium, Buckingham and Nicks had invited a few friends to mark the final hours of 1974 in the small West Hollywood apartment they shared with an engineer from the studio. The year's end was a bittersweet milestone for the couple. Nineteen seventy-four had been the apex of LA's artistic reawakening, but Nicks and Buckingham had been excluded from that feast. For them, 1974 had been largely a lost season; as they sat in their small apartment awaiting the New Year, their careers had less momentum than they had twelve months before. This changed when Olsen walked through the door with a big smile. He had news that would upend their lives—and thrill audiences for the rest of the decade and beyond. "Hey," Olsen told an astonished Buckingham and Nicks, "Fleetwood Mac want you to join them."[107] Los Angeles, and then the world, was about to discover its next superstars.

The last day of 1974 lowered the curtain on LA's golden year. Amid all the forces that coalesced in 1975 and beyond, in music, movies, television, and politics, the glow faded from the Los Angeles renaissance. And yet, in that small Hollywood apartment, as two unknown musicians moved toward their glittering future on the year's final day, a new spark ignited. As one chapter closed, another opened.

In the final moments of 1974, as they contemplated a new life in Fleetwood Mac, Lindsey Buckingham and Stevie Nicks stepped into the timeless procession of young talents elevated by LA's unending process of discovery and reinvention. Warren Beatty and Jack Nicholson; Don Henley and Glenn Frey; Linda Ronstadt and Jackson Browne; Steven Spielberg, George Lucas, and Martin Scorsese; Clarence Avant and Bill Withers; Norman Lear, Larry Gelbart, and James L. Brooks; Jane Fonda and Tom Hayden; Lou Adler, David Geffen, and Irving Azoff; even Jerry Brown and Tom Bradley—all had once stood in the same place, cradling the same dreams. For a few years, they came together in Los Angeles to form a historic constellation of inspiration, collaboration, and achievement. And then, just as an older generation had ceded the stage to them, in time they gave way to younger voices with new perspectives telling the stories of their own experiences.

As the years passed, fewer of those young people remembered the revolutionary contributions of the breakthrough Los Angeles artists during the early 1970s. This oversight was a measure of the earlier generation's success: the big ideas that they channeled from the social movements of the 1960s into popular culture and politics (suspicion of authority, greater personal freedom, more respect for marginalized groups, and increased tolerance of difference) had become so embedded in the nation's mental assumptions that later generations could hardly imagine a time before them. But there was such a time—and it was the lasting legacy of the talents who gathered in the nourishing sun of LA's golden hour to lead America beyond it.

ACKNOWLEDGMENTS

Every author incurs many debts. My biggest one is to the more than 100 people who made this book possible: the actors, musicians, writers, directors, producers, and politicos from Los Angeles in the early 1970s who gave me hours of their time and who often welcomed me into their homes to remember the city in those dynamic years.

All of them were generous and insightful. A few were particularly gracious in providing their time, answering my questions, tracking down information and photos, and often introducing me to other sources. I especially want to thank Linda Ronstadt, Jackson Browne, Graham Nash, Danny Kortchmar, Jon Landau, Peter Asher, John Boylan, Lou Adler, Danny Goldberg, Jonathan Taplin, and Irving Azoff; Warren Beatty, Jane Fonda, Anjelica Huston, Jodie Foster, Howard (Hawk) Koch Jr., Sherry Lansing, Mike Medavoy, Michael Ovitz, Barry Diller, Bob Rafelson, Toby Rafelson, Henry Jaglom, Peter Bogdanovich, Joan Tewkesbury, Jeremy Larner, Peter Bart, Tony Bill, Sean Daniel, Peter Davis, Paul Schrader, Fred Roos, Robert Towne, and the late Tom Pollock; Norman Lear, Rob Reiner, James L. Brooks, Linda Bloodworth-Thomason, Joan Darling, Mary Kay Place, Elliot Shoenman, Treva Silverman, Mike Farrell, Pete Noyes, James Rosenfield, Jack Schneider, and Bob Daly; Richard Maullin, Doug Faigin, Mickey Kantor, Tom Quinn, Bill Press, Vic Fazio, Henry Waxman, Howard Berman, Zev Yaroslavsky, and Kathleen Brown; Bill Zimmerman, Joan Andersson, Bruce Gilbert, Larry Levin, and Ira Arlook. Ira not only provided great insight on the work of Tom Hayden and Jane Fonda against the Vietnam War but also made critical introductions to other sources. Tom passed before I began writing this book, but I learned—and enjoyed—much from my occasional breakfasts with him in Venice before his death.

Brandon Bub was a thorough, careful, and creative research assistant. His tenacity in unearthing obscure sources about pop-culture events that occurred long before he was born (and his patience in listening to my attempts to explain them) greatly enriched the book. He was a true partner in every sense. Cynthia Colonna cheerfully and reliably produced accurate transcripts of dozens of interviews, often on very tight deadlines.

I spent seventeen very happy years at the *Los Angeles Times*, and several of my former colleagues there were extremely generous with their time, offering insights, contact information, and introductions when I needed them. Particularly helpful were Bill Boyarsky, Kenneth Turan, Randy Lewis, and the legendary Robert Hilburn, who was as central a figure in the cultural life of early 1970s Los Angeles as any of the rockers or movie stars I write about. The *LA Times* coverage of Los Angeles in those years was indispensable to my understanding of the period. On politics, I benefited enormously from the great work of Bill Boyarsky, Richard Bergholz, William Endicott, George Skelton, Jerry Gillam, and Al Martinez; on movies, Kevin Thomas, Gregg Kilday, Charles Champlin, and Dale Pollock (also author of a terrific George Lucas biography); and on music, Dennis Hunt, Leonard Feather, and Robert Hilburn, whose coverage of the rock scene in LA's golden hour really needs to be collected between hard covers for posterity. (His bedazzled December 11, 1971, review of Linda Ronstadt's first appearance at the Palomino alone would justify the collection.) The newspaper's fierce gossip columnist Joyce Haber was a great (if barbed) guide through the schemes and dreams of the city's elite. I also admired the pathbreaking efforts by reporters such as Hollie L. West, Renee Ward, Mary Murphy, and others to document the emerging position of women and African Americans in the film industry. The deeply reported and poetic accounts of Venice in those years from Dave Smith were riveting. Some of these great journalists were my colleagues when I worked at the paper, but I came to view even those I did not know as my collaborators in this book. Half a century later, the quality of their work still shines.

Several authors and scholars went above and beyond to provide me access to their own research material from the era, including interviews with key figures who have passed in the years since. Sally Bedell

Smith shared transcripts from her extraordinary conversations with all of the key television figures from the 1960s and 1970s, even driving out to a storage facility to fish out transcripts for me of the revealing interviews she conducted for her landmark biographies of Fred Silverman (*Up the Tube*) and Bill Paley (*In All His Glory*). No author could have possibly been more generous toward another. Todd Gitlin granted me access to the transcripts of his probing conversations for his book *Inside Prime Time* with many of the people who shaped television of that era. Geoff Cowan shared his insights over the "family hour" struggle, which he definitively chronicled in his own book, *See No Evil*. The great movie and celebrity photographer Steve Schapiro graciously welcomed me to his home and shared his remarkable photographs from the set of *Chinatown*, which are as emotionally revealing as they are aesthetically pleasing. Maureen Dowd, Lara Bergthold, and Tim Robbins facilitated critical introductions.

Dozens (if not hundreds) of books have been written about the various strands of this story, and I learned something from all of the (very) many that I read. But some authors were especially valuable guides to these times: Peter Biskind and Mark Harris on Hollywood; Barney Hoskyns, Marc Eliot, and Tom King on the music industry; Todd Gitlin and Sally Bedell Smith on television; and Miriam Pawel on Jerry Brown and his family. Josh Ozersky's slim but incisive volume, *Archie Bunker's America*, provided important insights. Documentaries by Lyn Goldfarb (on Tom Bradley), Reginald Hudlin (on Clarence Avant), Rob Epstein and Jeffrey Friedman (on Linda Ronstadt), and Alison Ellwood (on the Eagles) vividly brought to life central characters in my story. I thank them all for chronicling this period in such a stylish and thoughtful way.

The staff at the University of Southern California's Southern California Library, Special Collections, Los Angeles and Southern California Regional History, not only led me through Jerry Brown's papers as Secretary of State and governor but also produced an extremely helpful file of clippings about one of the university's famous alums, Bob Wood. Equally helpful were Nora Bates and Jenni Matz at the Television Academy Foundation's incredible oral history project *The*

Interviews, which has valuably documented the experiences of hundreds of central figures who have shaped the medium that shapes all of our lives. Librarians at the Los Angeles Public Library were diligent and reliable in tracking down my book requests, and the online data base that the library maintains of the *Los Angeles Times* and other relevant publications (such as the *Los Angeles Sentinel*, which focused on the city's Black community) is a tremendous public service. At a critical moment, my former *LA Times* colleague Cary Schneider pointed me toward this valuable asset.

Throughout this process, the team at HarperCollins proved welcoming partners. Jonathan Jao was an encouraging editor who also had the discipline and insight to help me find the essence of my story and trim any undergrowth in the way. He balanced support and direction in perfect proportions. Sarah Haugen led me through the production process with good humor, efficiency, and patience when the 2020 election demanded my attention. Robert Barnett, my agent, believed in this project from the beginning and found it a good home with his customary skill and dedication.

Family, friends, and colleagues sustained me during this process. My editors at *The Atlantic* (particularly Jeffrey Goldberg and Nora Kelly Lee) and CNN (Rachel Smolkin, Z. Byron Wolf, Beryl Adcock, and Brooke Brower) make me a better writer, thinker, and reporter every day—and also were understanding when scheduled interviews and other book obligations occasionally collided with deadlines. Jake Tapper, engaged in his own literary work about LA in a slightly earlier period, was always up for comparing notes. Mary Beth LaRue helped to keep me grounded (and flexible) throughout.

My sons, Danny and Taylor, and Taylor's wife, Katie, listened patiently to my soliloquies about the relevance to their lives *right now* of music, movies, and television from decades ago. I don't think they ever once rolled their eyes at me, but I do know they make me proud and happy every day. My brother, Harold, and sister, Lenore, provided long-distance support throughout. Matt Moser read chapters, offered encouragement, and listened patiently to my inevitable authors' complaints. Morris was a steadfast, if furry, companion during the writing.

My wife, Eileen, whose own musical upbringing ran more toward the Cure and the Smiths, learned to sing along with "Take It Easy," "Already Gone," and "Rock Me on the Water" and sat through the good, the bad, and the ugly of endless screenings of early 1970s movies and sitcoms. Seven years ago, she took a leap of faith to move to Los Angeles, a city that I loved but where she had never lived, and she has embraced our California adventure with the joy, enthusiasm, and grace that infuse everything she does. She truly is my dazzling LA Woman, and this book, like everything I do, would not exist without her.

This book often felt like a refuge from my day job of chronicling the dark conflicts of modern American politics amid the terrible suffering that the coronavirus pandemic brought to so many American families. It was a joyful labor to spend time with these transcendent LA artists at their creative peak. But grief reached into the process when my great friend Howard Schneider passed as the manuscript was being completed. Howard was a spring breeze of a man who made a friend in every room he entered. Whenever I hold a copy of this book, I will always think of his friendship and encouragement at every step of its creation—and at every triumph and trial of my life. To paraphrase a Bruce Springsteen song we both loved, I just want to say one last time, I miss you brother, good luck, good-bye.

Finally, I want to thank my adopted home, Los Angeles. I am a New Yorker by birth (Queens at that) and fiercely proud of it, but no city has ever moved me as Los Angeles does. It is open and welcoming, diverse and creative, soothing and exhilarating. LA has many flaws and inequities, but to me it is the capital of the future in American life, the place that more than any other always points the way to what America is becoming. *Rock Me on the Water* is my love song to the city at its golden hour in the early 1970s. There are many more magical hours in LA to come, and I am excited and grateful for the chance to watch the new generation of dreamers and visionaries who are creating them.

Ronald Brownstein
Los Angeles, November 2020

NOTES

PROLOGUE: Magic Hour in Los Angeles

1. Robert Hilburn, "Frosting on Geffen's Cake," *Los Angeles Times*, February 23, 1974.
2. Graham Nash, interview with author, February 10, 2018.
3. Linda Ronstadt, interview with author, January 29, 2018.
4. Irving Azoff, interview with author, January 31, 2018.
5. Michael Ovitz, interview with author, July 17, 2018.
6. Joe Bosso, "Session King/Producer Danny Kortchmar on 12 Career-Defining Records," *Music Radar*, November 4, 2013, https://www.musicradar.com/news/guitars/session-king-producer-danny-kortchmar-on-12-career-defining-records-587265.
7. Census Bureau, Historical Statistics of the United States, Colonial Times to 1970, Series A29-42, https://www.census.gov/library/publications/1975/compendia/hist_stats_colonial-1970.html.
8. Census Bureau, Historical Statistics of the United States, Colonial Times to 1970.
9. Anjelica Huston, *Watch Me* (New York: Scribner, 2014), 5.
10. Anjelica Huston, interview with author, November 28, 2018.
11. Huston, author interview.
12. Azoff, author interview.
13. Ronald Brownstein, "The Rage Unifying Boomers and Gen Z," *The Atlantic*, June 18, 2020.
14. Brownstein, "The Rage Unifying Boomers."
15. Jackson Browne, interview with author, July 24, 2019.

1 JANUARY: Hollywood's Fall and Rise

1. Patrick McGilligan, *Jack's Life: A Biography of Jack Nicholson* (New York: W.W. Norton, 2015), 252.
2. Warren Beatty, interview with author, April 21, 2018.
3. McGilligan, *Jack's Life*, 252.
4. Robert Evans, *The Kid Stays in the Picture* (New York: itBooks, 2013), 262.
5. Huston, author interview.
6. Huston, author interview.
7. Jeremy Larner, interview with author, April 28, 2018.
8. Howard Koch Jr., interview with author, December 6, 2018.
9. Paul Schrader, interview with author, September 18, 2018.
10. Beth Ann Krier, "Costume Designer for Famous," *Los Angeles Times*, August 4, 1974.
11. Huston, author interview.
12. David Yaffe, *Reckless Daughter: A Portrait of Joni Mitchell* (New York: Sarah Crichton Books/Farrar, Straus and Giroux, 2017), 168–69.
13. Sheila Weller, *Girls Like Us: Carole King, Joni Mitchell, Carly Simon, and the Journey of a Generation* (New York: Washington Square Press, 2008), 345, 360, 367.
14. Robert Towne, interview with author, March 20, 2018.
15. Huston, author interview.

16. Mark Harris, *Pictures at a Revolution: Five Movies and the Birth of the New Hollywood* (New York: Penguin Press, 2008), 214–15.

17. Larner, author interview.

18. Towne, author interview.

19. Lawrence Bietz, "Raymond Chandler's L.A.," *Los Angeles Times*, December 14, 1969.

20. Towne, author interview.

21. Peter Biskind, *Star: How Warren Beatty Seduced America* (New York: Simon and Schuster, 2010), 185.

22. Towne, author interview.

23. Towne, author interview.

24. Beatty, author interview.

25. McGilligan, *Jack's Life*, 69.

26. McGilligan, *Jack's Life*, 84–85.

27. Towne, author interview.

28. Towne, author interview.

29. Interview: Jack Nicholson, *Playboy*, April 1972.

30. Fred Roos, interview with author, September 13, 2018.

31. Nicholson, *Playboy* interview. Names also cited in John L. Scott, "Coffeehouse New After-Dark Lure," *Los Angeles Times*, November 29, 1958.

32. Nicholson, *Playboy* interview.

33. Roos, author interview.

34. Roos, author interview.

35. Peter Bogdanovich, interview with author, August 15, 2018.

36. Roos, author interview.

37. Biskind, *Star*, 31.

38. Beatty, author interview.

39. Beatty, author interview.

40. Beatty, author interview.

41. Rex Reed, "Will the Real Warren Beatty Please Shut Up?" *Esquire*, August 1967.

42. Beatty, author interview.

43. Beatty, author interview.

44. Towne, author interview.

45. Beatty, author interview.

46. Charles Higham, *Hollywood at Sunset* (New York: Saturday Review Press, 1972), 96.

47. Higham, *Hollywood at Sunset*, 104.

48. Towne, author interview.

49. Harris, *Pictures at a Revolution*, 171.

50. Mike Medavoy, interview with author, May 24, 2017.

51. Barry Diller, interview with author, October 30, 2017.

52. Motion Picture Association of America, *US Theatrical Statistics 1946–2011*, provided by MPAA.

53. Beatty, author interview.

54. Beatty, author interview.

55. Harris, *Pictures at a Revolution*, 138.

56. Harris, *Pictures at a Revolution*, 252.

57. Biskind, *Star*, 84.

58. Towne, author interview.

59. Biskind, *Star*, 88.

60. Towne, author interview.

61. Beatty, author interview.

62. Biskind, *Star*, 94.

63. Harris, *Pictures at a Revolution*, 340.

64. Harris, *Pictures at a Revolution*, 341–42.
65. Harris, *Pictures at a Revolution*, 369.
66. Beatty author interview.
67. Biskind, *Star*, 128.
68. Ronald Brownstein, *The Power and the Glitter: The Hollywood-Washington Connection* (New York: Pantheon, 1990), 242.
69. Aljean Harmetz, "Jack Ransacks the Cupboards of His Past," *Los Angeles Times*, March 31, 1974.
70. Bob Rafelson, interview with author, February 13, 2019.
71. Towne, author interview.
72. Bob Rafelson, author interview.
73. Harris, *Pictures at a Revolution*, 382.
74. Schrader, author interview.
75. Higham, *Hollywood at Sunset*, 179.
76. Diller, author interview.

2 FEBRUARY: The Republic of Rock and Roll

1. Browne, author interview.
2. Ronstadt, author interview.
3. Linda Ronstadt, *Simple Dreams* (New York: Simon and Schuster, 2013), 61–62.
4. Jon Landau, "Joni Mitchell: A Delicate Balance," *Rolling Stone*, February 28, 1974.
5. Concert tour schedule accessed at https://jonimitchell.com/chronology/tour.cfm?id=3.
6. Tom King, *The Operator: David Geffen Builds, Buys, and Sells the New Hollywood* (New York: Random House, 2000), 214.
7. Howard Sounes, *Down the Highway: The Life of Bob Dylan* (New York: Grove Press, 2011), 276.
8. Browne, author interview.
9. Ronstadt, author interview.
10. Judith Sims, "Performance: Jackson Browne," *Rolling Stone*, February 14, 1974.
11. Cameron Crowe, "A Child's Garden of Jackson Browne," *Rolling Stone*, May 23, 1974.
12. Jonathan Taplin, interview with author, August 3, 2017.
13. Azoff, author interview.
14. Ronstadt, *Simple Dreams*, 2.
15. Ronstadt, author interview.
16. Ronstadt, author interview.
17. Crowe, "A Child's Garden."
18. Crowe, "A Child's Garden."
19. Mike Boehm, "Most Likely to Secede: If Nothing Else, Jackson Browne's Orange County Days Gave Him a Place to Move Away From," *Los Angeles Times*, August 25, 1994.
20. Boehm, "Most Likely to Secede."
21. Boehm, "Most Likely to Secede."
22. Boehm, "Most Likely to Secede."
23. Browne, author interview.
24. Ronstadt, *Simple Dreams*, 30.
25. Ronstadt, *Simple Dreams*, 32.
26. Browne, author interview.
27. Browne, author interview.
28. Neil Young, *Waging Heavy Peace* (New York: Plume, 2012), 125.
29. Danny Kortchmar, interview with author, March 30, 2018.
30. Danny Goldberg, interview with author, October 26, 2017.

31. Chart history accessed at *Billboard* archives, https://www.billboard.com/archive /charts.

32. Jimmy McDonough, *Shakey: Neil Young's Biography* (New York: Anchor Books, 2003), 158.

33. McDonough, *Shakey*, 160.

34. David Crosby and Carl Gottlieb, *Long Time Gone* (Santa Monica, CA: Crosby and Gottlieb, 2007), 116–19.

35. McDonough, *Shakey*, 229.

36. Nash, author interview.

37. Graham Nash, *Wild Tales: A Rock and Roll Life* (New York: Three Rivers Press, 2013), 130.

38. Nash, author interview.

39. Kortchmar, author interview.

40. Barney Hoskyns, *Waiting for the Sun: A Rock 'n' Roll History of Los Angeles* (Milwaukee, WI: Backbeat Books, 2009), 193.

41. Nash, author interview.

42. Nash, author interview.

43. Nash, author interview.

44. Ronstadt, author interview.

45. Lou Adler, interview with author, February 22, 2018.

46. Ronstadt, author interview.

47. Ronstadt, *Simple Dreams*, 49.

48. Hoskyns, *Waiting for the Sun*, 167.

49. Browne, author interview.

50. Ronstadt, author interview.

51. Ronstadt, author interview.

52. Ronstadt, author interview.

53. John Boylan, interview with author, January 12, 2018.

54. Robert Hilburn, "Linda Ronstadt in Her Palomino Bow," *Los Angeles Times*, December 11, 1971.

55. Ronstadt, author interview.

56. Ronstadt, author interview.

57. Ronstadt, author interview.

58. Boylan, author interview.

59. Boylan, author interview.

60. Ronstadt, author interview.

61. Marc Eliot, *To the Limit: The Untold Story of the Eagles* (Boston: Da Capo Press, 2005), 60.

62. Ronstadt, *Simple Dreams*, 74.

63. Ronstadt, author interview.

64. Chart history accessed at *Billboard*, https://www.billboard.com/music/linda-ronstadt.

65. Boylan, author interview.

66. Boehm, "Most Likely to Secede."

67. Dave Thompson, *Hearts of Darkness: James Taylor, Jackson Browne, Cat Stevens, and the Unlikely Rise of the Singer-Songwriter* (Milwaukee, WI: Backbeat Books, 2012), 59.

68. Thompson, *Hearts of Darkness*, 119–20.

69. Robert Hilburn, "Linda Ronstadt Sings Country at Troubadour," *Los Angeles Times*, September 19, 1969.

70. Browne, author interview.

71. Jon Landau, interview with author, October 28, 2017.

72. Thompson, *Hearts of Darkness*, 148.

73. Browne, author interview.

74. Cameron Crowe, "Jackson Browne Earns His Letter in Music," *Los Angeles Times*, March 3, 1974.

75. Crowe, "Jackson Browne Earns His Letter in Music."

76. Thompson, *Hearts of Darkness*, 146–47.

77. Nash, author interview.

78. Ronstadt, author interview.

79. Boylan, author interview.

80. Weller, *Girls Like Us:*, 191.

81. Weller, *Girls Like Us*, 328.

82. Browne, author interview.

83. *History of the Eagles, Part 1*, documentary, directed by Alison Ellwood (2013; Jigsaw Productions).

84. Browne, author interview.

85. Browne, author interview.

86. Thompson, *Hearts of Darkness*, 209.

87. Thompson, *Hearts of Darkness*, 212.

88. Browne, author interview.

89. Author's interview with confidential source.

90. Lyrics accessed at AZLyrics, https://www.azlyrics.com/lyrics/jacksonbrowne/lookingintoyou.html.

91. Chart history accessed at *Billboard*, https://www.billboard.com/music/jackson-browne.

92. Thompson, *Hearts of Darkness*, 231.

93. Nash, *Wild Tales*, 207.

94. Ben Fong-Torres, "Linda Ronstadt: Heartbreak on Wheels," *Rolling Stone*, March 27, 1975.

95. Ronstadt, author interview.

96. Ronstadt, author interview.

97. Miriam Pawel, *The Browns of California: The Dynasty that Transformed a State and Shaped a Nation* (New York: Bloomsbury, 2018), 67.

98. Robert Pack, *Jerry Brown: The Philosopher Prince* (New York: Stein and Day, 1978), 1.

99. Kathleen Brown, interview with author, February 2, 2018.

100. Tom Quinn, interview with author, July 27, 2017.

101. Quinn, author interview.

102. "The Political Record of Edmund G. Brown Jr.," undated document, Box B-29-3, Edmund G. Brown Jr. Papers, Governor's Office, 1975–1983, Miscellaneous, Llew Werner Files, 1973–1983, Special Collections: Los Angeles and Southern California Regional History, University of Southern California Library, Los Angeles.

103. Pack, *Jerry Brown*, 35.

104. *Californians for Brown* newsletter, Nov.–Dec. 1973, San Francisco Elections file, Joseph Alioto Papers, San Francisco Public Library, San Francisco, CA.

105. Jerry Brown memo to Ralph Martig, March 24, 1971, Box B-23-10, Secretary of State, Memos, 1971–73, Personal papers, Jerry Brown Papers, University of Southern California, Los Angeles.

106. Jerry Brown, "MEMO EGB TO ALL STAFF MEMBERS," March 5, 1971, Box B-23-10, Secretary of State, Personal papers, Memos 1971–73, Jerry Brown Papers, University of Southern California, Los Angeles.

107. Quinn, author interview.

108. Pack, *Jerry Brown*, 44.

109. Quinn, author interview.

110. Willie Brown, interview with author, April 27, 2018.

111. Pack, *Jerry Brown*, 57.

112. Browne, author interview.
113. Peter Asher, interview with author, January 10, 2018.
114. Nash, author interview.
115. Asher, author interview.
116. Asher, author interview.
117. Kortchmar, author interview.
118. Nash, author interview.
119. Asher, author interview.
120. Nash, author interview.
121. Boylan, author interview.
122. Weller, *Girls Like Us*, 360.
123. Boylan, author interview.
124. Ronstadt, author interview.
125. Ronstadt, author interview.
126. Ronstadt, author interview.
127. Barney Hoskyns, *Hotel California: The True-life Adventures of Crosby, Stills, Nash, Young, Mitchell, Taylor, Browne, Ronstadt, Geffen, the Eagles, and Their Many Friends* (Hoboken, NJ: John Wiley and Sons, 2006), 135.
128. Landau, author interview.
129. Browne, author interview.

3 MARCH: The Greatest Night in Television History

1. Tim Brooks and Earle Marsh, *The Complete Directory to Prime Time Network and Cable TV Shows, 1946–Present* (New York: Ballantine Books, 2007).
2. Brooks and Marsh, *Complete Directory to Prime Time Network and Cable TV Shows*.
3. Rob Reiner, interview with author, August 10, 2017.
4. Linda Bloodworth-Thomason, interview with author, February 14, 2018.
5. James L. Brooks, interview with author, August 30, 2018.
6. Norman Lear, interview with Academy of Television Arts and Sciences Foundation, February 26, 1998. Video for all Academy interviews available at https://interviews.televisionacademy.com/About.
7. Brooks, author interview.
8. Reiner, author interview.
9. Ella Taylor, *Prime Time Families: Television Culture in Postwar America* (Berkeley: University of California Press, 1989), 77.
10. Lear, Academy interview.
11. Norman Lear, *Even This I Get to Experience* (New York: Penguin Press, 2014), 24.
12. Lear, *Even This*, 22.
13. Lear, *Even This*, 95–96.
14. Lear, Academy interview.
15. Lear, *Even This*, 116.
16. Lear, *Even This*, 119.
17. Lear, *Even This*, 120.
18. Rob Reiner, interview with Academy of Television Arts and Sciences Foundation, November 29, 2001.
19. Lear, *Even This*, 140.
20. Norman Lear, interview with author, May 19, 2017.
21. Lear, *Even This*, 176.
22. Lear, *Even This*, 177.
23. Bud Yorkin, interview with Academy of Television Arts and Sciences Foundation, August 9, 2000.
24. Ovitz, author interview.

25. Les Brown, *Televi$ion: The Business Behind the Box* (New York: Harcourt Brace Jovanovich, 1971), 48.

26. USC press release, May 27, 1966, and untitled CBS document dated July 1971, Robert Wood Files, Special Collections: Los Angeles and Southern California Regional History, University of Southern California Library, Los Angeles.

27. Hal Humphrey, "Policy Sought on Editorials for TV," *Los Angeles Times*, December 6, 1966.

28. Pete Noyes, interview with author, July 25, 2018.

29. Howard Williams, interview with author, August 3, 2018.

30. Williams, author interview.

31. Memorandum from Squinn, Re: Letters for the Radio-TV News Association luncheon, January 18, 1962, provided by Richard Nixon Presidential Library and Museum, Yorba Linda, CA.

32. KNXT editorial, "The Chaos at Berkeley," December 4, 1964, https://oac.cdlib.org/ark:/13030/kt8d5nb337/?brand=oac4.

33. "CBS Names Wood to Top Post," *Los Angeles Times*, February 15, 1969.

34. James Rosenfield, interview with author, February 9, 2018.

35. John Sutton, interview with author, June 28, 2018.

36. Rosenfield, author interview.

37. Rosenfield, author interview.

38. Sally Bedell, *Up the Tube: Prime-Time TV and the Silverman Years* (New York: Viking Press, 1981), 25.

39. Bedell, *Up the Tube*, 35.

40. Reiner, Academy interview.

41. Reiner, author interview.

42. David Bianculli, *Dangerously Funny: The Uncensored Story of "The Smothers Brothers Comedy Hour"* (New York: Touchstone, 2009), 307.

43. Josh Ozersky, *Archie Bunker's America: TV in an Era of Change, 1968–1978* (Carbondale: Southern Illinois University Press, 2003), 51.

44. Cecil Smith, "Scene 70: The New Season," *Los Angeles Times TV Times*, 9/13–19/70 in Robert Wood Papers, University of Southern California Library, Los Angeles.

45. Gene Jankowski, interview with author, January 18, 2018.

46. Bob Daly, interview with author, January 26, 2018.

47. Jankowski, author interview.

48. Daly, author interview.

49. Ovitz, author interview.

50. Irwin Segelstein, interview with Sally Bedell, March 1979, provided by Sally Bedell Smith.

51. Arnold Becker, interview with Todd Gitlin, undated. Gitlin interviews are collected in his files for *Inside Prime Time*, available at Rare Book and Manuscript Library, Columbia University, New York (hereafter "Gitlin interviews").

52. Rosenfield, author interview.

53. Ozersky, *Archie Bunker's America*, 52.

54. Robert Wood, interview with Sally Bedell, August 1979, provided by Sally Bedell Smith.

55. Jack Gould, "Here's to Relevance—But Will It Sell?" *New York Times*, March 1, 1970.

56. Perry Lafferty, interview with Academy of Television Arts and Sciences Foundation, December 4, 1997.

57. Donna McCrohan, *Archie and Edith, Mike and Gloria: The Tumultuous History of "All in the Family"* (New York: Workman Publishing, 1987), 12–13.

58. Segelstein, Bedell interview.

59. Yorkin, Academy interview.

60. Lear, author interview.
61. Lear, *Even This*, 221.
62. Lear, *Even This*, 221.
63. Lear, author interview.
64. Lear, author interview.
65. Lear, *Even This*, 224.
66. Lear, *Even This*, 224.
67. Lear, *Even This*, 225.
68. Michael Eisner, interview with author, September 7, 2017.
69. Eisner, author interview.
70. Bedell, *Up the Tube*, 43.
71. Yorkin, Academy interview.
72. Segelstein, Bedell interview.
73. Todd Gitlin, *Inside Prime Time: How the Networks Decide About the Shows that Rise and Fall in the Real World Behind the TV Screen* (New York: Pantheon Books, 1985), 212.
74. Fred Silverman, interview with Sally Bedell, March 1979.
75. Rosenfield, author interview.
76. Becker, Gitlin interviews, undated.
77. Reiner, Academy interview.
78. John Rich, interview with Academy of Television Arts and Sciences Foundation, August 3, 1999.
79. Reiner, author interview.
80. Interview: Carroll O'Connor, *Playboy*, January 1973.
81. Lear, author interview.
82. Lear, author interview.
83. Rich, Academy interview.
84. Rosenfield, author interview.
85. Bedell, *Up the Tube*, 45.
86. Robert Metz, *CBS: Reflections in a Bloodshot Eye* (Chicago, IL: Playboy Press, 1975), 333.
87. McCrohan, *Archie and Edith*, 33.
88. Reiner, author interview.
89. Lear, *Even This*, 237.
90. McCrohan, *Archie and Edith*, 31.
91. Lear, *Even This*, 237.
92. Rich, Academy interview.
93. *Hee Haw* lineup, https://www.ranker.com/review/roger-miller-and-peggy-miller/6 2482662?ref=wiki_287572.

4 APRIL: Already Gone

1. Robert Hilburn, "California Jam Aims at Rock Record," *Los Angeles Times*, March 30, 1974.
2. California Jam Fan Club, Video of Eagles, "Already Gone," April 6, 1974, https://www .facebook.com/279833373059/videos/eagles-already-gone-1974-california-jam /1232051733902/.
3. David Shaw, "'California Jam' Is Just That—But 200,000 Have a Nice Day," *Los Angeles Times*, April 7, 1974.
4. Shaw, "'California Jam.'"
5. Shaw, "'California Jam.'"
6. David Allen, "California Jam Festival Rocked Ontario in 1974," *Inland Valley Daily Bulletin*, April 4, 2014.
7. Don Felder with Wendy Holder, *Heaven and Hell: My Life in the Eagles, 1974–2001* (Hoboken, NJ: John Wiley and Sons, 2008), 126–27.

8.   Eagles setlist, April 6, 1974, Ontario Speedway, https://www.setlist.fm/setlist/eagles
      /1974/ontario-motor-speedway-ontario-ca-6bdba6de.html.
9.   Eliot, *To the Limit*, 29.
10.   Judith Sims, "Meet the Eagles," *Rolling Stone*, August 17, 1972, reprinted in *Rolling
      Stone Special Edition: Eagles—The Ultimate Guide.*
11.   Charles M. Young, "Hell Is for Heroes," *Rolling Stone*, November 29, 1979, reprinted
      in *Rolling Stone Special Edition: Eagles—The Ultimate Guide.*
12.   Browne, author interview.
13.   *History of the Eagles, Part 1.*
14.   *History of the Eagles, Part 1.*
15.   Eliot, *To the Limit*, 21.
16.   Eliot, *To the Limit*, 21.
17.   Eliot, *To the Limit*, 58.
18.   Cameron Crowe, "Across the Border," *Rolling Stone*, September 25, 1975, reprinted
      in *Rolling Stone Special Edition: Eagles—The Ultimate Guide.*
19.   Ronstadt, author interview.
20.   Sims, "Meet the Eagles."
21.   King, *The Operator*, 46–47.
22.   King, *The Operator*, 60.
23.   King, *The Operator*, 119.
24.   Nash, author interview.
25.   Nash, author interview.
26.   Browne, author interview.
27.   King, *The Operator*, 137.
28.   Adler, author interview.
29.   Taplin, author interview.
30.   Asher, author interview.
31.   Browne, author interview.
32.   Landau, author interview.
33.   "Full Talent Line-Up for Atl, Geffen Label," *Billboard*, September 11, 1971.
34.   Browne, author interview.
35.   David Browne, "Eagles: The Debut Set a New Bar for Country Rock and Open-Road
      Optimism," in *Rolling Stone Special Edition: Eagles—The Ultimate Guide.*
36.   Browne, author interview.
37.   Robert Hilburn, "The Eagles: Hatched in a Barroom," *Los Angeles Times*, April 14,
      1974.
38.   Stan Cornyn with Paul Scanlon, *Exploding: The Highs, Hits, Hype, Heroes, and Hus-
      tlers of the Warner Music Group* (New York: HarperCollins, 2003), 221, 191.
39.   Taplin, author interview.
40.   Simon Frith, "The Industrialization of Popular Music," https://condor.depaul.edu
      /dweinste/MM/frith.html.
41.   Recording Industry Association of America (RIAA), U.S. Sales Database, is source
      of all revenue figures. See also https://www.riaa.com/u-s-sales-database/.
42.   Motion Picture Association of America, *US Theatrical Statistics*, undated, provided
      by MPAA. RIAA database.
43.   Cornyn with Scanlon, *Exploding*, 239.
44.   King, *The Operator*, 178.
45.   King, *The Operator*, 196.
46.   Robert Hilburn, "Holzman and Geffen to Communication Posts," *Los Angeles Times*,
      August 16, 1973.
47.   Azoff, author interview.
48.   Eliot, *To the Limit*, 101.

49. Azoff, author interview.
50. Robert Hilburn, "Roxy: Pop-Rock Takes a Step Uptown," *Los Angeles Times*, September 22, 1973.
51. Adler, author interview.
52. Azoff, author interview.
53. Landau, author interview.
54. Taplin, author interview.
55. Cornyn with Scanlon, *Exploding*, 221.
56. Sounes, *Down the Highway*, 275.
57. King, *The Operator*, 207.
58. Huston, author interview.
59. Chart positions from *Billboard*, https://www.billboard.com/charts/billboard-200/1974-03-09.
60. Nash, author interview.
61. Nash, author interview.
62. Beatty, author interview.
63. Robert Hilburn, "Frosting on Geffen's Cake," *Los Angeles Times*, February 23, 1974.
64. Adler, author interview.
65. Ronstadt, author interview.
66. Browne, author interview.
67. Ronstadt, author interview.
68. Hoskyns, *Hotel California*, 150.
69. Young, "Hell Is for Heroes."
70. Boylan, author interview.
71. Ronstadt, author interview.
72. Browne, author interview.
73. Cameron Crowe, "The Heart of an Eagle," in *Rolling Stone Special Edition: Eagles—The Ultimate Guide*.
74. Boylan, author interview.
75. David Browne, "Desperado: The Band Plunged Itself Forward by Immersing Itself in the Old West," in *Rolling Stone Special Edition: Eagles—The Ultimate Guide*.
76. Browne, author interview.
77. Crowe, "Across the Border."
78. Eliot, *To the Limit*, 101.
79. Azoff, author interview.
80. Azoff, author interview.
81. Taplin, author interview.
82. King, *The Operator*, 225.
83. Sounes, *Down the Highway*, 278.
84. Julie Baumgold, "The Winning of Cher," *Esquire*, February 1975.
85. Browne, author interview.
86. Browne, author interview.
87. Eliot, *To the Limit*, 111.
88. Azoff, author interview.
89. Eliot, *To the Limit*, 102.
90. Azoff, author interview.
91. Azoff, author interview.
92. King, *The Operator*, 217.
93. Azoff, author interview.
94. Young, "Hell Is for Heroes."
95. Crowe, "Across the Border."
96. Felder, *Heaven and Hell*, 115–16.

97. Azoff, author interview.

98. Azoff, author interview.

99. For RIAA ranking, see https://www.grammy.com/grammys/news/riaa-eagles-greatest -hits-has-outsold-michael-jacksons-thriller#:~:text=The%20battle%20for%20 the%20top,s%20Thriller%20at%2033x%20platinum.

100. Azoff, author interview.

101. David Browne, "On the Border: The Eagles Took Control of Their Increasingly Expansive Sound," in *Rolling Stone Special Edition: Eagles—The Ultimate Guide.*

102. *History of the Eagles, Part 1.*

5 MAY: The Ballad of Tom and Jane

1. Jeffrey Toobin, *American Heiress: The Wild Saga of the Kidnapping, Crimes, and Trial of Patty Hearst* (New York: Anchor Books, 2017), 210.

2. Toobin, *American Heiress*, 204.

3. Toobin, *American Heiress*, 210.

4. Al Martinez and Robert Kistler, "Suspected SLA Hideout Stormed, 5 Die," *Los Angeles Times*, May 18, 1974.

5. Martinez and Kistler, "Suspected SLA Hideout Stormed."

6. Tom Hayden, "An Activist Radical Views the SLA," *Los Angeles Times*, May 26, 1974.

7. Ira Arlook, interview with author, June 23, 2018.

8. Tom Hayden, "At Issue: Peaceful Change or Civil War," *New York Times*, November 14, 1970.

9. Bill Zimmerman, interview with author, March 23, 2018.

10. Zimmerman, author interview.

11. Hayden, "An Activist Radical."

12. Jane Fonda, interview with author, February 15, 2019.

13. Jane Fonda, *My Life So Far* (New York: Random House Trade Paperbacks, 2006), 192, 195.

14. Interview: Jane Fonda and Tom Hayden, *Playboy*, April 1974.

15. Fonda and Hayden, *Playboy* interview.

16. Tom Hayden, *Reunion: A Memoir* (New York: Collier Books, 1988), 327–28.

17. Bruce Gilbert, interview with author, July 27, 2018.

18. Sara Davidson, "The Images Constantly Reversing," *New York Times*, June 2, 1974.

19. Gilbert, author interview.

20. Hayden, *Reunion*, 423.

21. Gilbert, author interview.

22. Jack Nicholl, interview with author, June 3, 2018.

23. Hayden, *Reunion*, 421.

24. Nicholl, author interview.

25. Carol Kurtz, interview with author, June 3, 2018.

26. Fonda, author interview.

27. Fonda, author interview.

28. Fonda, *My Life*, 222.

29. Brownstein, *The Power and the Glitter*, 251.

30. Mary Hershberger, *Jane Fonda's War: A Political Biography of an Antiwar Icon* (New York: The New Press, 2005), 12–14.

31. Hershberger, *Jane Fonda's War*, 52.

32. Hershberger, *Jane Fonda's War*, 51.

33. Hershberger, *Jane Fonda's War*, 22.

34. Fonda, author interview.

35. Fonda, *My Life*, 231.

36. Fonda, author interview.

37. Hershberger, *Jane Fonda's War*, 48.
38. Brownstein, *The Power and the Glitter*, 252.
39. Brownstein, *The Power and the Glitter*, 252.
40. Peter Knobler, "Hanoi Jane," in *Very Seventies, A Cultural History of the 1970s from the Pages of "Crawdaddy,"* ed. Greg Mitchell and Peter Knobler (New York: Fireside, 1995), 39.
41. Knobler, "Hanoi Jane," 34.
42. Barbara Zheutlin and David Talbot, *Creative Differences: Profiles of Hollywood Dissidents* (Boston: South End Press, 1978), 140–41.
43. Brownstein, *The Power and the Glitter*, 253.
44. Brownstein, *The Power and the Glitter*, 252.
45. Brownstein, *The Power and the Glitter*, 252.
46. Fonda, author interview.
47. Fonda, *My Life*, 280.
48. Hayden, *Reunion*, 426.
49. Dave Smith, "Death in Venice—the Lonely Wait," *Los Angeles Times*, November 8, 1971.
50. Joan Andersson, interview with author, August 6, 2018.
51. Andersson, author interview.
52. Larry Levin, interview with author, January 17, 2019.
53. Levin, author interview.
54. Levin, author interview.
55. Hayden, *Reunion*, 434.
56. Levin, author interview.
57. Hayden, *Reunion*, 436.
58. Art Seidenbaum, "Off Their Pedestals," *Los Angeles Times*, January 7, 1970.
59. Hayden, *Reunion*, 444.
60. Hayden, *Reunion*, 445.
61. Hayden, *Reunion*, 446.
62. Fonda, author interview.
63. Levin, author interview.
64. Andersson, author interview.
65. Fonda, author interview.
66. Fonda, author interview.
67. Fonda, *My Life*, 290.
68. Fonda, author interview.
69. Fonda, *My Life*, 319.
70. Steven J. Ross, *Hollywood Left and Right: How Movie Stars Shaped American Politics* (New York: Oxford University Press, 2011), 240–42.
71. Fonda, *My Life*, 318.
72. Fonda, *My Life*, 304.
73. Fonda, author interview.
74. Brownstein, *The Power and the Glitter*, 257.
75. Brownstein, *The Power and the Glitter*, 258.
76. Brownstein, *The Power and the Glitter*, 258.
77. Levin, author interview.
78. Gilbert, author interview.
79. Tom Hayden, "The Indochina Peace Campaign: A Working Paper," March 1973, 29.
80. Hayden, "Indochina Peace Campaign," 1.
81. Hayden, *Reunion*, 449.
82. Fonda, *My Life*, 335.
83. Fonda, author interview.

84. Fonda, author interview.
85. Associated Press, "Jane Fonda and Hayden Are Married on Coast," *New York Times*, January 22, 1973.
86. Bill Zimmerman, *Troublemaker: A Memoir from the Front Lines of the Sixties* (New York: Anchor Books, 2012), 380.
87. Gilbert, author interview.
88. Kenneth Reich, "The Bloody March that Shook L.A.," *Los Angeles Times*, June 23, 1997.
89. Brownstein, *The Power and the Glitter*, 203–4.
90. Fonda, author interview.
91. Michele Willens, interview with author, April 5, 2018.
92. Zimmerman, author interview.
93. Zimmerman, author interview.
94. Brownstein, *The Power and the Glitter*, 260.
95. Nicholl, author interview.
96. Fonda, author interview.
97. Brownstein, *The Power and the Glitter*, 260.
98. Ross, *Hollywood Left and Right*, 246.
99. "Move to Censure Jane Fonda Killed by City Council," *Los Angeles Times*, June 28, 1973.
100. Arlook, author interview.
101. Gilbert, author interview.
102. Fonda, author interview.
103. Fonda, author interview.
104. Fonda, *My Life*, 341.
105. Fonda, author interview.
106. Fonda, *My Life*, 347.
107. Fonda and Hayden, *Playboy* interview.
108. Fonda and Hayden, *Playboy* interview.
109. Fonda, author interview.
110. Kurtz, author interview.
111. Fonda, *My Life*, 347.
112. Paul Ryder, interview with author, May 5, 2018.
113. Zimmerman, author interview.
114. Kurtz, author interview.
115. Nicholl, author interview.
116. Zimmerman, author interview.
117. Brewster Rhoads, interview with author, July 1, 2018.
118. Levin, author interview.
119. Tom Daschle, interview with author, July 20, 2018.
120. Robert Kistler and Patt Morrison, "850 Attend 2 LA Rallies Calling for Nixon's Impeachment," *Los Angeles Times*, January 21, 1974.
121. Associated Press, "250 Antiwar Protesters Fail to Present 'Award,'" *New York Times*, January 27, 1974.
122. Levin, author interview.
123. Levin, author interview.
124. Arlook, author interview.
125. Fonda and Hayden, *Playboy* interview.
126. Fonda and Hayden, *Playboy* interview.
127. Fonda and Hayden, *Playboy* interview.
128. Hayden, *Reunion*, 467.
129. Gilbert, author interview.
130. Zheutlin and Talbot, *Creative Differences*, 136.

6 JUNE: From *Chinatown* to Jerry Brown

1. Towne, author interview.
2. Paul D. Zimmerman, "Blood and Water," *Newsweek*, July 1, 1974.
3. Zimmerman, "Blood and Water."
4. Koch, author interview.
5. Towne, author interview.
6. Alex Simon, "Forget It, Bob, It's Chinatown: Robert Towne Looks Back on 'Chinatown's' 35th Anniversary," *The Hollywood Interview*, February 1, 2013, http://thehollywoodinterview.blogspot.com/2009/10/robert-towne-hollywood-interview.html.
7. Towne, author interview.
8. "The New Movies," *Newsweek*, December 6, 1970.
9. McGilligan, *Jack's Life*, 277.
10. Simon, "Forget It, Bob."
11. Evans, *The Kid Stays in the Picture*, 278.
12. Evans, *The Kid Stays in the Picture*, 279.
13. Martin Kasindorf, "Hot Writer," *Newsweek*, October 14, 1974.
14. Simon, "Forget It, Bob."
15. Robert Towne, "It's Only L.A., Jake," *Los Angeles Times*, May 29, 1994.
16. Carey McWilliams, *Southern California: An Island on the Land* (Salt Lake City, UT: Peregrine Smith Books, 1983), 183–91.
17. Towne, author interview.
18. Towne, author interview.
19. Writers Guild Foundation, "The Writer Speaks: Robert Towne Part One," August 8, 2013, https://www.youtube.com/watch?v=P6r7exIYOo8&feature=youtu.be.
20. Towne, author interview.
21. Towne, "It's Only L.A., Jake."
22. Simon, "Forget It, Bob."
23. Simon, "Forget It, Bob."
24. Peter Bart, interview with author, April 18, 2018.
25. Paul Iorio, "Sleuthing 'Chinatown,'" *Los Angeles Times*, July 8, 1999.
26. Roman Polanski, *Roman by Polanski* (New York: William Morrow and Company, 1984), 346.
27. Polanski, *Roman*, 347.
28. Polanski, *Roman*, 346–47.
29. Polanski, *Roman*, 347–48.
30. Charles Higham, "Polanski: 'Rosemary's Baby' and After," *New York Times*, September 23, 1973.
31. Anthea Sylbert, interview with author, July 3, 2018.
32. Towne, author interview.
33. Iorio, "Sleuthing 'Chinatown.'"
34. Iorio, "Sleuthing 'Chinatown.'"
35. Polanski, *Roman*, 348.
36. Iorio, "Sleuthing 'Chinatown.'"
37. Koch, author interview.
38. Koch, author interview.
39. Huston, author interview.
40. Sylbert, author interview.
41. Sylbert, author interview.
42. Towne, author interview.
43. Sylbert, author interview.
44. Polanski, *Roman*, 352. Also, Koch, author interview.
45. Interview: Roman Polanski, *Playboy*, December, 1971.

46. Sylbert, author interview.
47. Bart, author interview.
48. Faye Dunaway, *Looking for Gatsby: My Life* (New York, Simon and Schuster, 1995), 257.
49. Jesse Kornbluth, "Faye Fights Back," *Vanity Fair*, August 1987.
50. Huston, author interview.
51. Richard Sylbert and Sylvia Townsend, *Designing Movies: Portrait of a Hollywood Artist* (Westport, CT: Praeger, 2006), 127.
52. Sylbert, author interview.
53. Koch, author interview.
54. Sylbert, author interview.
55. Dunaway, *Looking*, 251.
56. Huston, author interview.
57. Diller, author interview.
58. Sylbert, author interview.
59. Evans, *The Kid Stays in the Picture*, 287.
60. Towne, author interview.
61. Sylbert, author interview.
62. Koch, author interview.
63. Towne, author interview.
64. Beatty, author interview.
65. Peter Biskind, *Easy Riders, Raging Bulls: How the Sex-Drugs-and-Rock 'n' Roll Generation Saved Hollywood* (New York: Simon and Schuster Paperbacks, 1998), 51.
66. Beatty, author interview.
67. Beatty, author interview.
68. Biskind, *Star*, 116.
69. Brownstein, *The Power and the Glitter*, 244.
70. Biskind, *Star*, 175–76.
71. Beatty, author interview.
72. Towne, author interview.
73. Bart, author interview.
74. Towne, author interview.
75. Beatty, author interview.
76. Biskind, *Star*, 191.
77. Sylbert, author interview.
78. Tony Bill, interview with author, August 1, 2018.
79. Sylbert, author interview.
80. Sylbert, author interview.
81. Sylbert and Townsend, *Designing Movies*, 139–140.
82. Sylbert, author interview.
83. Sylbert and Townsend, *Designing Movies*, 136.
84. Towne, author interview.
85. Beatty, author interview.
86. Towne, author interview.
87. Towne, author interview.
88. Krier, "Costume Designer for the Famous."
89. Bill Boyarsky, interview with author, January 23, 2018.
90. George Skelton, "Trouble for Democrats in Governor Race Seen," *Los Angeles Times*, March 1, 1974.
91. Grover McKean, interview with author, February 16, 2018.
92. Doug Faigin, interview with author, January 23, 2018.
93. McKean, author interview.
94. "Alioto Lays Out Some 'Facts,'" *Modesto Bee*, May 15, 1974.

95.   Kenneth Reich, "Alioto Calls Brown Insincere, Charges He 'Hid' Oil Firm Gift," *Los Angeles Times*, March 27, 1974.

96.   McKean, author interview.

97.   Chuck Winner, interview with author, March 1, 2018.

98.   Shana Alexander, "The Art of Negative Politics," *Newsweek*, October 15, 1973.

99.   Quinn, author interview.

100. Faigin, author interview.

101. George Skelton, "Zen and the Art of Advising Gov. Brown," *Los Angeles Times*, April 4, 1977.

102. Faigin, author interview.

103. Richard Maullin, interview with author, February 2, 2018.

104. David Broder, "Candidate Brown: A Politician of the 70s?" *Los Angeles Times*, May 9, 1974.

105. Mickey Kantor, interview with author, February 1, 2018.

106. Kathleen Brown, author interview.

7 JULY: Hollywood's Generational Tipping Point

1.   Edith Blake, *On Location . . . On Martha's Vineyard: The Making of the Movie 'Jaws'* (Edgartown, MA: Edith Blake, 1974), 40.

2.   Blake, *On Location*, 89.

3.   Carl Gottlieb, *The Jaws Log: 25th Anniversary Edition* (New York: Newmarket Press, 2001), 146.

4.   Jan Stuart, *The Nashville Chronicles: The Making of Robert Altman's Masterpiece* (New York: Simon and Schuster, 2000), 126.

5.   Interview: Robert Altman, *Playboy*, August, 1976.

6.   Joan Tewkesbury, interview with author, July 19, 2018.

7.   Bart, author interview.

8.   Mitch Tuchman, "Close Encounter with Steven Spielberg," in *Steven Spielberg: Interviews*, ed. Lester D. Friedman and Brent Notbohm (Jackson: University Press of Mississippi, 2000), 38.

9.   Bill, author interview.

10.   Bart, author interview.

11.   Ovitz, author interview.

12.   Medavoy, author interview.

13.   Bill, author interview.

14.   "David Picker Named as UA President," *Los Angeles Times*, June 5, 1969.

15.   "Medavoy at UA," *Los Angeles Times*, April 9, 1974.

16.   Biskind, *Easy Riders, Raging Bulls*, 125.

17.   Dennis McLellan, "John Calley Dies at 81; Honored Studio Chief and Movie Producer," *Los Angeles Times*, September 14, 2011.

18.   Taplin, author interview.

19.   Schrader, author interview.

20.   Bart, author interview.

21.   Digby Diehl, "Q&A Peter Bogdanovich," *Los Angeles Times*, April 2, 1972.

22.   Foster Hirsch, "Why Feel Sorry for These Hoods?" *New York Times*, December 30, 1973.

23.   Gilbert, author interview.

24.   Stephen Farber, "Coppola and 'The Godfather,'" *Sight and Sound* (Fall 1972).

25.   Stephen Farber, "Where Has All the Protest Gone?" *New York Times*, March 31, 1974.

26.   Biskind, *Easy Riders, Raging Bulls*, 204.

27.   Bogdanovich, author interview.

28.   Diehl, "Q&A Peter Bogdanovich."

29. Bogdanovich, author interview.

30. Bogdanovich, author interview.

31. Dale Pollock, *Skywalking: The Life and Films of George Lucas* (New York: Harmony Books, 1983), 37.

32. Pollock, *Skywalking*, 94.

33. Pollock, *Skywalking*, 86.

34. Biskind, *Easy Riders, Raging Bulls*, 98.

35. Tom Pollock, interview with author, June 28, 2018.

36. Pollock, *Skywalking*, 33.

37. Sean Daniel, interview with author, April 16, 2018.

38. Alan Crawford, "'American Graffiti' Makes Kids Real Again," *Human Events*, December 8, 1973.

39. Pollock, *Skywalking*, 104.

40. Joseph McBride, *Steven Spielberg: A Biography* (Jackson: University Press of Mississippi, 2010), 127.

41. Julia Phillips, *You'll Never Eat Lunch in This Town Again* (New York: Random House, 2017), 156.

42. McBride, *Steven Spielberg*, 37.

43. Joan Darling, interview with author, July 20, 2018.

44. David Helpern, "At Sea with Steven Spielberg," in *Steven Spielberg: Interviews*, 6.

45. Helpern, "At Sea with Steven Spielberg."

46. Tuchman, "Close Encounter," 41.

47. Biskind, *Easy Riders, Raging Bulls*, 262.

48. McBride, *Steven Spielberg*, 264.

49. Biskind, *Easy Riders, Raging Bulls*, 262.

50. Richard Thompson, "Screen Writer: Taxi Driver's Paul Schrader," *Film Comment*, March–April 1976.

51. Thompson, "Screen Writer"; and Schrader, author interview.

52. Schrader, author interview.

53. Schrader, author interview.

54. Schrader, author interview.

55. McBride, *Steven Spielberg*, 232.

56. Gottlieb, *The Jaws Log*, 53.

57. Gottlieb, *The Jaws Log*, 33.

58. McBride, *Steven Spielberg*, 234.

59. McBride, *Steven Spielberg*, 44.

60. Blake, *On Location*, 112.

61. Blake, *On Location*, 116.

62. McBride, *Steven Spielberg*, 238.

63. Joyce Haber, "The Man Who Bit the Bullet on 'Jaws,'" *Los Angeles Times*, July 13, 1975.

64. "Summer of the Shark," *Time*, June 23, 1975.

65. McBride, *Steven Spielberg*, 241.

66. Daniel, author interview.

67. McBride, *Steven Spielberg*, 244.

68. Gottlieb, *The Jaws Log*, 179.

69. Tewkesbury, author interview.

70. Mitchell Zuckoff, *Robert Altman: The Oral Biography* (New York: Vintage Books, 2010), 273.

71. Stuart, *Chronicles*, 39.

72. Tewkesbury, author interview.

73. "Visual History with Joan Tewkesbury," interviewed by Katt Shea, Directors Guild of

America, December 5, 2006, https://www.dga.org/Craft/VisualHistory/Interviews/Joan-Tewkesbury.aspx.

74. Tewkesbury, author interview.
75. Tewkesbury, author interview.
76. Tewkesbury, author interview.
77. Tewkesbury, author interview.
78. Tewkesbury, author interview.
79. Zuckoff, *Altman*, 278.
80. Tewkesbury, author interview.
81. Stuart, *Chronicles*, 85–86.
82. Richard Baskin, interview with author, September 26, 2018.
83. Baskin, author interview.
84. Baskin, author interview.
85. Stuart, *Chronicles*, 130.
86. Tewkesbury, author interview.
87. Stuart, *Chronicles*, 162.
88. Baskin, author interview.
89. Baskin, author interview.
90. Tewkesbury, author interview.
91. Charles Michener with Martin Kasindorf, "Altman's Opryland Epic," *Newsweek*, June 30, 1975.
92. Tewkesbury, author interview.
93. Tewkesbury, author interview.
94. Stuart, *Chronicles*, 190.
95. Stuart, *Chronicles*, 205.
96. Stuart, *Chronicles*, 258.
97. Pauline Kael, "The Current Cinema: Coming: 'Nashville,'" *New Yorker*, March 3, 1975.
98. Alan Crawford, "The Ego Trip Called Nashville," *Human Events*, November 8, 1975.
99. Robert Mazzocco, "Letter from Nashville," *New York Review of Books*, July 17, 1975.
100. Altman, *Playboy* interview.
101. Altman, *Playboy* interview.
102. Connie Byrne and William O. Lopez, "Nashville," *Film Quarterly* 29, no. 2 (Winter 1975/76), 13–25.
103. John Getze, "'Jaws' Swims to Top in Ocean of Publicity," *Los Angeles Times*, September 28, 1975.
104. Gary Arnold, "In the Terrifying Grip of a Sensational 'Jaws,'" *Washington Post*, June 15, 1975.
105. Stephen Farber, "'Jaws' and 'Bug'—The Only Difference Is the Hype," *New York Times*, August 24, 1975.
106. McBride, *Steven Spielberg*, 254.
107. Bill, author interview.

8 AUGUST: The Icarus of Los Angeles

1. Candice Bergen, *Knock Wood* (New York: Simon and Schuster, 1984), 186.
2. Fonda, author interview.
3. Huston, author interview.
4. Beatty, author interview.
5. Nash, *Wild Tales*, 219.
6. Azoff, author interview.
7. Ryder, author interview.
8. Bo Burlingham, "Politics Under the Palms," *Esquire*, February 1977.

9.   Zimmerman, author interview.
10. Suzan Asycough, "Ex-Col Titan Schneider Dies," *Variety*, April 23, 1993.
11. Burlingham, "Under the Palms."
12. Toby Rafelson, interview with author, February 13, 2019.
13. Bob Rafelson, author interview.
14. Biskind, *Easy Riders, Raging Bulls*, 61.
15. Bob Rafelson, author interview.
16. Richard Wechsler, interview with author, July 21, 2018.
17. Henry Jaglom, interview with author, June 18, 2018.
18. Jaglom, author interview.
19. Bob Rafelson, author interview.
20. Biskind, *Easy Riders, Raging Bulls*, 75.
21. Taplin, author interview.
22. Bob Rafelson, author interview.
23. Bogdanovich, author interview.
24. Bob Rafelson, author interview.
25. Alexander Horwath, "A Walking Contradiction (Partly Truth and Partly Fiction),"
     in *The Last Great American Picture Show: New Hollywood Cinema in the 1970s*, ed.
     Thomas Elsaesser, Alexander Horwath, and Noel King (Amsterdam: Amsterdam
     University Press, 2004), 95.
26. Roos, author interview.
27. Jaglom, author interview.
28. Wechsler, author interview.
29. Roos, author interview.
30. Bogdanovich, author interview.
31. Toby Rafelson, author interview.
32. Jaglom, author interview.
33. Jaglom, author interview.
34. Toby Rafelson, author interview.
35. Bob Rafelson, author interview.
36. Bergen, *Knock Wood*, 186.
37. Bergen, *Knock Wood*, 191–95.
38. Bergen, *Knock Wood*, 195.
39. Bergen, *Knock Wood*, 211.
40. Bergen, *Knock Wood*, 190.
41. Joyce Haber, "'First True Love' for Candy Bergen," *Los Angeles Times*, October 18,
     1971.
42. Bergen, *Knock Wood*, 210.
43. Peter Davis, interview with author, September 17, 2018.
44. Davis, author interview.
45. Davis, author interview.
46. Bergen, *Knock Wood*, 198.
47. Bergen, *Knock Wood*, 199.
48. Toby Rafelson, author interview.
49. Toby Rafelson, author interview.
50. Bob Rafelson, author interview.
51. Larner, author interview.
52. Bogdanovich, author interview.
53. Larner, author interview.
54. Toby Rafelson, author interview.
55. Jaglom, author interview.
56. Burlingham, "Under the Palms."

57. Burlingham, "Under the Palms."
58. Burlingham, "Under the Palms."
59. Bergen, *Knock Wood*, 212.
60. Jaglom, author interview.
61. Ross, *Hollywood Left and Right*, 235.
62. Hayden, "At Issue."
63. Hugh Pearson, *The Shadow of the Panther: Huey Newton and the Price of Black Power in America* (Reading, MA: Addison-Wesley, 1994), 241–43.
64. Jaglom, author interview.
65. Bob Rafelson, author interview.
66. Bob Rafelson, author interview.
67. Kate Coleman, "True Hollywood Story: The Producer and the Black Panther," *Salon*, June 9, 2012.
68. Bergen, *Knock Wood*, 212.
69. Julian Smith, "Look Away, Look Away, Movie Land," *Journal of Popular Film* (Winter 1973): 36.
70. Fonda, author interview.
71. Davis, author interview.
72. Jack Gould, "The Unselling of the Pentagon," *New York Times*, March 7, 1971.
73. Jack Gould, "House Panel Bids C.B.S. Yield Films," *New York Times*, April 7, 1971.
74. Davis, author interview.
75. Davis, author interview.
76. Davis, author interview.
77. Davis, author interview.
78. Davis, email to author, August 29, 2019.
79. Davis, author interview.
80. Davis, author interview.
81. Davis, author interview.
82. Peter Davis, "Remembering Bert Schneider," *Huffington Post*, February 27, 2012; and Davis, author interview.
83. Davis, "Remembering."
84. Davis, "Remembering."
85. Davis, author interview.
86. Stephanie Harrington, "First an Undeclared War, Now an Unseen Film," *New York Times*, November 17, 1974.
87. Harrington, "First an Undeclared War, Now an Unseen Film."
88. Pearson, *Shadow of the Panther*, 264.
89. Pearson, *Shadow of the Panther*, 266.
90. Pearson, *Shadow of the Panther*, 267.
91. Burlingham, "Under the Palms."
92. Biskind, *Easy Riders, Raging Bulls*, 272.
93. Zimmerman, author interview.
94. Joshuah Bearman, "The Big Cigar," *Playboy*, December 2012.
95. Zimmerman, author interview.
96. Zimmerman, author interview.
97. Zimmerman, author interview.
98. Zimmerman, author interview.
99. Zimmerman, *Troublemaker*, 387.
100. Burlingham, "Under the Palms."
101. Bearman, "The Big Cigar."
102. Zimmerman, author interview.
103. Zimmerman, author interview. Zimmerman's description of Newton's arrival in

Cuba and his reception there was based on conversations with Newton after he returned to the United States.

104. Gregg Kilday, "The Skirmishing Over Hearts," *Los Angeles Times*, November 15, 1974.
105. Harrington, "First an Undeclared War, Now an Unseen Film."
106. Davis, author interview.
107. Jaglom, author interview.
108. Jaglom, author interview; and Gregg Kilday, "'Hearts, Minds' Finds a Home," *Los Angeles Times*, December 16, 1974.
109. "'Hearts, Minds' Opens to Qualify for Oscars," *Los Angeles Times*, December 20, 1974.
110. Roger Ebert, "Hearts and Minds," https://www.rogerebert.com/reviews/hearts-and-minds-1974.
111. Vincent Canby, "The Ten Best Films of 1975," *New York Times*, December 28, 1975.
112. Harrington, "First an Undeclared War, Now an Unseen Film."
113. Davis, author interview.
114. "Peter Davis" and "Bert Schneider," in Academy Award Acceptance Speech database, April 8, 1975, http://aaspeechesdb.oscars.org/.
115. "Peter Davis" and "Bert Schneider."
116. Charles Champlin, "The Real World Ruffles the Oscar Ritual," *Los Angeles Times*, April 10, 1975.
117. Burlingham, "Under the Palms."
118. "Davis Defends 'Hearts & Minds,'" *Variety*, April 16, 1975.
119. Bob Rafelson, author interview.
120. Pearson, *Shadow of the Panther*, 314–15.
121. Toby Rafelson, author interview.
122. Jaglom, author interview.
123. Jaglom, author interview.

9 SEPTEMBER: Three Roads to Revolution

1. Jack Gould, "C.B.S. Line-up for Fall Omits Once-Prized Country Comedies," *New York Times*, March 17, 1971.
2. Elliot Shoenman, interview with author, March 23, 2018.
3. Darling, author interview.
4. Larry Gelbart, interview with Academy of Television Arts and Sciences Foundation, May 26, 1998.
5. Reiner, author interview.
6. Darling, author interview.
7. Jodie Foster, interview with author, September 10, 2018.
8. Ovitz, author interview.
9. Diller, author interview.
10. Lear, author interview.
11. Lear, author interview.
12. Bedell, *Up the Tube*, 69.
13. Gene Reynolds, interview with Academy of Television Arts and Sciences Foundation, August 22, 2000.
14. Gelbart, Academy interview.
15. Gelbart, Academy interview.
16. Reynolds, Academy interview.
17. Gelbart, Gitlin interviews, April 21, 1981.
18. Cyclops, "Mashed Morality," *Newsweek*, April 23, 1973.
19. Gelbart, Academy interview.

20. Mike Farrell, interview with author, August 18, 2017.
21. Alan Alda, interview with Academy of Television Arts and Sciences Foundation, November 17, 2000.
22. Gelbart, Academy interview.
23. Bloodworth-Thomason, author interview.
24. Reynolds, Academy interview.
25. Farrell, author interview.
26. Gelbart, Academy interview; also, Gelbart, Gitlin interviews.
27. Gelbart, Gitlin interviews.
28. Gelbart, Gitlin interviews.
29. Reynolds, Academy interview.
30. Gelbart, Gitlin interviews.
31. Gelbart, Academy interview.
32. For Greenbaum's credits, see https://www.imdb.com/name/nm0338456/?ref_=fn_al_nm_1#writer; Fritzell credits accessed at https://www.imdb.com/name/nm0296091/?ref_=ttfc_fc_wr2#writer.
33. Gelbart, Academy interview.
34. Gelbart, Academy interview.
35. Gelbart, Academy interview.
36. Reynolds, Academy interview.
37. Gelbart, Gitlin interviews.
38. James L. Brooks, interview with Academy of Television Arts and Sciences Foundation, January 2, 2003.
39. Allan Burns, interview with Academy of Television Arts and Sciences Foundation, February 18, 2004.
40. Brooks, author interview.
41. Jennifer Keishin Armstrong, *Mary and Lou and Rhoda and Ted: And All the Brilliant Minds Who Made the "Mary Tyler Moore" Show a Classic* (New York: Simon and Schuster, 2013), 24.
42. Armstrong, *Mary and Lou*, 19.
43. Bedell, *Up the Tube*, 63.
44. Burns, Academy interview.
45. Burns, Gitlin interviews.
46. Burns, Academy interview; also, Bedell, *Up the Tube*, 64.
47. Bedell, *Up the Tube*, 64.
48. Brooks, Academy interview.
49. Armstrong, *Mary and Lou*, 38.
50. Brooks, author interview.
51. Burns, Academy interview.
52. Brooks, Academy interview.
53. Ethel Winant, interview with Academy of Television Arts and Sciences Foundation, August 7, 1996.
54. Treva Silverman, interview with author, March 29, 2018.
55. Gould, "Here's to Relevance—But Will It Sell?"
56. Brown, *Televi$ion*, 252.
57. Burns, Gitlin interviews.
58. Armstrong, *Mary and Lou*, 100–101.
59. Burns, Academy interview.
60. Brooks, Academy interview.
61. Bloodworth-Thomason, author interview.
62. Treva Silverman, author interview.
63. Brooks, Academy interview.

64. Mary Kay Place, interview with author, March 2, 2018.
65. Bloodworth-Thomason, author interview.
66. Treva Silverman, author interview.
67. Brooks, Academy interview.
68. Brooks, author interview.
69. Brooks, Academy interview; also, Armstrong, *Mary and Lou*, 181–82.
70. Treva Silverman, author interview.
71. Brooks, author interview.
72. Treva Silverman, author interview.
73. Brooks, author interview.
74. Burns, Academy interview.
75. Joyce Haber, "Stifling Those Archie Bunker Rumors," *Los Angeles Times*, August 5, 1974.
76. Reiner, author interview.
77. John Rich, interview with Academy of Television Arts and Sciences Foundation, August 3, 1999.
78. Treva Silverman, author interview.
79. Laura Z. Hobson, "As I Listened to Archie Say 'Hebe' . . . ," *New York Times*, September 12, 1971.
80. Norman Lear, "As I Read How Laura Saw Archie . . . ," *New York Times*, October 10, 1971.
81. "TV: Speaking About the Unspeakable," *Newsweek*, November 29, 1971.
82. Arnold Hano, "Can Archie Bunker Give Bigotry A Bad Name?" *New York Times*, March 12, 1972.
83. Hano, "Can Archie Bunker Give Bigotry a Bad Name?"
84. McCrohan, *Archie and Edith*, 185.
85. Earl Wilson, "This TV Boss' Wish," *Los Angeles Herald-Examiner*, May 11, 1972, Robert Wood Files, Special Collections: Los Angeles and Southern California Regional History, University of Southern California Library, Los Angeles.
86. Lear, author interview.
87. Lear, author interview.
88. Reiner, author interview.
89. Lear, author interview.
90. Reiner, author interview.
91. Carroll O'Connor, interview with Academy of Television Arts and Sciences Foundation, August 13, 1999.
92. Robert Wussler, interview with Sally Bedell, April 1979, provided by Sally Bedell Smith.
93. Kathryn C. Montgomery, *Target, Prime Time: Advocacy Groups and the Struggle Over Entertainment Television* (New York: Oxford University Press, 1990), 47.
94. Lear, *Even This*, 265.
95. Richard M. Levine, "Norman Lear—Daring the Sitcom Audience," *New York Times*, May 18, 1975.
96. O'Connor, *Playboy* interview.
97. O'Connor, *Playboy* interview.
98. O'Connor, *Playboy* interview.
99. O'Connor, *Playboy* interview.
100. Reiner, author interview.
101. O'Connor, Academy interview.
102. O'Connor, Academy interview.
103. Lear, author interview.
104. O'Connor, Academy interview.

105. Daly, author interview.
106. Fred Silverman, Bedell interview.
107. Ozersky, *Archie Bunker's America*, 79.
108. Howard F. Stein, "'All in the Family' as Mirror of Contemporary American Culture," *Family Process* 13, no. 5 (September 1974): 281.
109. Gelbart, Academy interview.
110. Gelbart, Gitlin interviews.
111. "Disputed Antiwar Play Rescheduled by CBS," *Los Angeles Times*, July 16, 1973.
112. Frank Stanton, interview with Sally Bedell, August 18, 1986, provided by Sally Bedell Smith.
113. Daly, author interview.
114. Stanton, Bedell interview.

10 OCTOBER: The (White) Boys' Club

1. Bloodworth-Thomason, author interview.
2. Bloodworth-Thomason, author interview.
3. Bloodworth-Thomason, author interview.
4. Place, author interview.
5. Foster, author interview.
6. Sylbert, author interview.
7. Pollock, author interview.
8. Bill, author interview.
9. Place, author interview.
10. Place, author interview.
11. Place, author interview; and Barbara Gallagher, interview with author, May 8, 2018.
12. Place, author interview.
13. Bloodworth-Thomason, author interview.
14. Farrell, author interview.
15. Bloodworth-Thomason, author interview.
16. U.S. Commission on Civil Rights, *Window Dressing on the Set: Women and Minorities in Television*, August 1977, U.S. Commission on Civil Rights, Washington, DC, 24–25.
17. U.S. Commission on Civil Rights, *Window Dressing on the Set*, 24.
18. U.S. Commission on Civil Rights, *Window Dressing on the Set*, 25.
19. Treva Silverman, author interview.
20. Treva Silverman, author interview.
21. For writing credits for Treva Silverman at *The Mary Tyler Moore Show*, see https://www.imdb.com/name/nm0798988/?ref_=fn_al_nm_1#writer.
22. Armstrong, *Mary and Lou*, 160.
23. For Emmy results, see https://www.emmys.com/awards/nominees-winners/1974/outstanding-writing-for-a-comedy-series.
24. Shoenman, author interview.
25. For writing credits for *M*A*S*H*, see https://www.imdb.com/title/tt0068098/full credits/?ref_=tt_ov_st_sm.
26. For writing credits for *All in the Family*, see https://www.imdb.com/title/tt0066626/fullcredits/?ref_=tt_ov_st_sm.
27. Bloodworth-Thomason, author interview.
28. Winant, Academy interview.
29. Sherry Lansing, interview with author, August 24, 2018.
30. Lansing, author interview.
31. Stephen Galloway, *Leading Lady: Sherry Lansing and the Making of a Hollywood Groundbreaker* (New York: Crown Archetype, 2017), 26.

32. Lansing, author interview.
33. Galloway, *Leading Lady*, 55.
34. Galloway, *Leading Lady*, 56.
35. Galloway, *Leading Lady*, 58.
36. Lansing, author interview.
37. Jerry Parker, "Lady Press Agents," *Cosmopolitan*, September, 1974.
38. Phillips, *You'll Never Eat Lunch in This Town Again*, 109.
39. Bill, author interview.
40. Phillips, *You'll Never Eat Lunch in This Town Again*, 164.
41. Galloway, *Leading Lady*, 55.
42. Lansing, author interview.
43. Galloway, *Leading Lady*, 69.
44. Lansing, author interview.
45. Treva Silverman, author interview.
46. Phillips, *You'll Never Eat Lunch in This Town Again*, 139.
47. Manohla Dargis, "The Marvelous Ms. Elaine May," *New York Times*, January 21, 2019.
48. Maya Montañez Smukler, *Liberating Hollywood: Women Directors and the Feminist Reform of 1970s American Cinema* (New Brunswick, NJ: Rutgers University Press, 2019), 83.
49. Jay Cocks, "Cinema: Hit Men," *Time*, January 31, 1977.
50. Mary Murphy, "AFI Women: A Camera Is Not Enough," *Los Angeles Times*, October 27, 1974.
51. Murphy, "AFI Women."
52. Tewkesbury, author interview.
53. Tewkesbury, author interview.
54. Lear, *Even This*, 294.
55. Darling, author interview.
56. Darling, author interview.
57. Darling, author interview.
58. Darling, author interview.
59. Robert Lindsey, "A Woman Directing in Hollywood? Isn't It About Time?" *New York Times*, March 30, 1977.
60. Joan Mellen, "Hollywood Rediscovers the American Woman," *New York Times*, April 23, 1978.
61. For Darling's directing credits, see https://www.imdb.com/name/nm0201375/?ref_=fn_al_nm_1#director.
62. Tewkesbury, author interview.
63. Marilyn Diane Fife, "Black Image in American TV: The First Two Decades," *The Black Scholar* 6, no. 3 (November 1974): 11.
64. U.S. Commission on Civil Rights, *Window Dressing on the Set*, 39.
65. U.S. Commission on Civil Rights, *Window Dressing on the Set*, 30.
66. Lear, *Even This*, 269.
67. For Allan Manings's writing credits, see https://www.imdb.com/name/nm0542425/?ref_=fn_al_nm_1#writer.
68. Louie Robinson, "Bad Times on the 'Good Times' Set," *Ebony*, September 1975.
69. Lear, *Even This*, 274.
70. Faith C. Christmas, "'Good Times' Rift Denied," *Los Angeles Sentinel*, May 20, 1976.
71. U.S. Commission on Civil Rights, *Window Dressing on the Set*, 23.
72. Celeste Durant, "Blacks on TV: Projecting an Unreal Image?" *Los Angeles Times*, September 18, 1974.
73. Renee Ward, "'The Crossover' Goes Beyond Blaxploitation," *Los Angeles Times*, December 28, 1975.

74. Ward, "'The Crossover.'"
75. Betty Martin, "Parks Will Direct 'Tree,'" *Los Angeles Times*, April 1, 1968.
76. Charles Champlin, "The Negro's Place in Film World," *Los Angeles Times*, April 9, 1968.
77. George Alexander, *Why We Make Movies: Black Filmmakers Talk About the Magic of Cinema* (New York: Harlem Moon, 2003), 22.
78. Mikel J. Koven, *Blaxploitation Films* (Harpenden: Kamera Books, 2010), 19.
79. Hollie L. West, "Makers of Black Films Stand at Crossroads," *Los Angeles Times*, January 28, 1973.
80. Ward, "'The Crossover.'"
81. Josiah Howard, *Blaxploitation Cinema: The Essential Reference Guide* (Surrey: FAB Press, 2008), 12.
82. Gordon Parks, "Black Movie Boom—Good or Bad?" *New York Times*, December 17, 1972.
83. Parks, "Black Movie Boom—Good or Bad?"
84. Ward, "'The Crossover.'"
85. Jaglom, author interview.
86. Pollock, author interview.
87. Kevin Starr, *Golden Dreams: California in an Age of Abundance, 1950–1963* (New York: Oxford University Press, 2009), 386.
88. Ronstadt, author interview.
89. Adler, author interview.
90. *The Black Godfather*, documentary directed by Reginald Hudlin (2019; Netflix).
91. Berry Gordy, *To Be Loved: The Music, the Magic, the Memories of Motown: An Autobiography* (New York: Warner Books, 1994), 278–79.
92. Robert A. Wright, "The Dominant Color Is Green," *New York Times*, July 7, 1974.
93. Adler, author interview.
94. Kortchmar, author interview.
95. Adler, author interview.
96. Gordy, *To Be Loved*, 295.
97. Browne, author interview.
98. Leonard Feather, "Withers Strikes Gold with First Record," *Los Angeles Times*, October 10, 1971.
99. Feather, "Withers Strikes Gold with First Record."
100. Leonard Feather, "Singer-Author Withers Performs at Troubadour," *Los Angeles Times*, September 16, 1971; also, Dennis Hunt, "Withers Comes Back to the Troubadour," *Los Angeles Times*, September 7, 1974.
101. Andy Greene, "Bill Withers: The Soul Man Who Walked Away," *Rolling Stone*, April 14, 2015.
102. Browne, author interview.
103. *Bridging the Divide: Tom Bradley and the Politics of Race*, documentary directed by Lyn Goldfarb (2015; Our L.A.).
104. John C. Bollens and Grant B. Geyer, *Yorty: Politics of a Constant Candidate* (Pacific Palisades, CA: Palisades Publishers, 1973), 132.
105. Lou Cannon, *Official Negligence: How Rodney King and the Riots Changed Los Angeles and the LAPD* (Boulder, CO: Westview Press, 1999), 70.
106. Cannon, *Official Negligence*, 64.
107. *Bridging the Divide*.
108. Zev Yaroslavsky, interview with author, March 29, 2018.
109. Bollens and Geyer, *Yorty*, 166.
110. Bollens and Geyer, *Yorty*, 166–68.
111. Harold Meyerson, interview with author, January 20, 2018.

112. Richard Bergholz, "Yorty Says Hidden 'Radicals' Are Working in Bradley Camp," *Los Angeles Times*, May 17, 1973.
113. Bill Boyarsky, "Bradley Defeats Yorty in Landslide," *Los Angeles Times*, May 30, 1973.
114. Boyarsky, "Bradley Defeats Yorty in Landslide."
115. Novotny Lawrence, *Blaxploitation Films of the 1970s: Blackness and Genre* (New York: Routledge, 2008), 97; and Howard, *Blaxploitation Cinema*, 16.
116. Tewkesbury, author interview.

11 NOVEMBER: Breakthrough

1. Ellen Ziffren, interview with author, August 9, 2018.
2. Ziffren, author interview.
3. Ronstadt, author interview.
4. Ziffren, author interview.
5. Asher, author interview.
6. Ronstadt, author interview.
7. Ronstadt, author interview.
8. Asher, author interview.
9. Fong-Torres, "Linda Ronstadt: Heartbreak on Wheels."
10. Boylan, author interview.
11. Ronstadt, author interview.
12. Ronstadt, author interview.
13. Fong-Torres, "Linda Ronstadt: Heartbreak on Wheels."
14. Fong-Torres, "Linda Ronstadt: Heartbreak on Wheels."
15. Fong-Torres, "Linda Ronstadt: Heartbreak on Wheels."
16. Boylan, author interview.
17. Boylan, author interview.
18. Boylan, author interview.
19. Ronstadt, *Simple Dreams*, 77.
20. Boylan, author interview.
21. Ronstadt, author interview.
22. Ronstadt, author interview.
23. Fong-Torres, "Linda Ronstadt: Heartbreak on Wheels."
24. Boylan, author interview.
25. Ben Fong-Torres, "Peter Asher Presents James Taylor and Linda Ronstadt," *Rolling Stone*, December 29, 1977.
26. Asher, author interview.
27. Asher, author interview.
28. Ronstadt, *Simple Dreams*, 67.
29. Asher, author interview.
30. Fong-Torres, "Linda Ronstadt: Heartbreak on Wheels."
31. Fong-Torres, "Linda Ronstadt: Heartbreak on Wheels."
32. For *Don't Cry Now*'s chart history, see https://www.billboard.com/music/linda-ronstadt/chart-history/TLP/song/829591.
33. Boylan, author interview.
34. Asher, author interview.
35. Browne, author interview.
36. Ronstadt, *Simple Dreams*, 96; also, Boylan, author interview.
37. Ben Fong-Torres, *Willin': The Story of Little Feat* (Boston: Da Capo Press, 2013), 75–76.
38. Ronstadt, *Simple Dreams*, 86.
39. Ronstadt, author interview.
40. Ronstadt, *Simple Dreams*, 79.
41. Ronstadt, *Simple Dreams*, 84.

42. Ronstadt, *Simple Dreams*, 92.
43. Ronstadt, author interview.
44. Ronstadt, author interview.
45. Ronstadt, author interview.
46. Ronstadt, *Simple Dreams*, 89; also, Ronstadt, author interview.
47. Ronstadt, *Simple Dreams*, 89.
48. Asher, author interview.
49. Liner notes, *Heart Like a Wheel*, Capitol Records, 1974.
50. Fong-Torres, "Peter Asher Presents."
51. Ronstadt, author interview.
52. All contributions from liner notes, *Heart Like a Wheel*.
53. Asher, author interview.
54. Asher, author interview.
55. Fong-Torres, "Linda Ronstadt: Heartbreak on Wheels."
56. Fong-Torres, "Linda Ronstadt: Heartbreak on Wheels."
57. Asher, author interview.
58. Asher, author interview.
59. Asher, author interview.
60. Asher, author interview.
61. Stephen Holden, "Heart Like A Wheel," *Rolling Stone*, January 16, 1975.
62. Robert Hilburn, "Linda Ronstadt: She Who Hesitated Has Won," *Los Angeles Times*, December 15, 1974.
63. For "You're No Good"'s pop chart history, see https://www.billboard.com/music/linda-ronstadt/chart-history/HSI/song/337928.
64. Ronstadt, *Simple Dreams*, 97.
65. For "I Can't Help It"'s country chart history, see https://www.billboard.com/linda-ronstadt/chart-history/country-songs/song/838509.
66. For "When Will I be Loved"'s pop chart history, see https://www.billboard.com/music/linda-ronstadt/chart-history/HSI/song/338121.
67. For "When Will I Be Loved"'s country chart history, see https://www.billboard.com/music/linda-ronstadt/chart-history/country-songs/song/346544.
68. For "Heart Like a Wheel"'s country chart history, see https://www.billboard.com/music/linda-ronstadt/chart-history/country-albums/song/317371.
69. For *Heart Like a Wheel*'s pop chart history, see https://www.billboard.com/music/linda-ronstadt/chart-history/TLP/song/317371.
70. Ronstadt, author interview.
71. Hilburn, "Linda Ronstadt: She Who Hesitated."
72. George Skelton, "Flournoy Promises to Wage Hard-Hitting Race for Governor," *Los Angeles Times*, July 27, 1974.
73. Maullin, author interview.
74. Winner, author interview.
75. Maullin, author interview.
76. Winner, author interview.
77. Winner, author interview.
78. Tom Hayden, "Jerry Brown: The Mystic and the Machine," *Rolling Stone*, December 19, 1974.
79. Faigin, author interview.
80. Pack, *Jerry Brown*, 69.
81. Pack, *Jerry Brown*, 69.
82. Kathleen Brown, author interview.
83. Charles T. Powers, "Jerry Brown: The Son Also Rises," *Los Angeles Times*, October 31, 1974.

84. Hayden, "The Mystic and the Machine."
85. Hayden, "The Mystic and the Machine."
86. Hayden, "The Mystic and the Machine."
87. For Jackson Browne's album chart history, see https://www.billboard.com/music/jackson-browne.
88. Browne, author interview.
89. Thompson, *Hearts of Darkness*, 233.
90. Crowe, "A Child's Garden."
91. For lyrics, see https://www.azlyrics.com/lyrics/jacksonbrowne/readyornot.html.
92. Crowe, "A Child's Garden."
93. Browne, author interview.
94. Crowe, "A Child's Garden."
95. Browne, author interview.
96. Ronstadt, *Simple Dreams*, 91.
97. Browne, author interview.
98. Browne, author interview.
99. Landau, author interview.
100. Browne, author interview.
101. Browne, author interview.
102. Rich Wiseman, *Jackson Browne: The Story of a Hold Out* (Garden City, NY: Dolphin Books, 1982), 104.
103. Stephen Holden, "Manchild in the Promised Land: Late for the Sky," *Rolling Stone*, November 7, 1974.
104. Janet Maslin, "For Everyman," *Rolling Stone*, November 22, 1973.
105. For lyrics, see https://www.azlyrics.com/lyrics/jacksonbrowne/rockmeonthewater.html.
106. Crosby and Gottlieb, *Long Time Gone*, 276.
107. Crosby and Gottlieb, *Long Time Gone*, 276.
108. For lyrics, see https://www.azlyrics.com/lyrics/jacksonbrowne/foreveryman.html.
109. For lyrics, see https://www.azlyrics.com/lyrics/jacksonbrowne/theroadandthesky.html.
110. Browne, author interview.
111. Browne, author interview.
112. Crowe, "A Child's Garden."
113. For lyrics, see https://www.azlyrics.com/lyrics/jacksonbrowne/beforethedeluge.html.
114. Browne, author interview.
115. Wiseman, *Jackson Browne*, 118.
116. For lyrics, see https://www.azlyrics.com/lyrics/jacksonbrowne/thepretender.html.
117. Browne, author interview.

12 DECEMBER: Transitions

1. Geoffrey Cowan, *See No Evil: The Backstage Battle Over Sex and Violence in Television* (New York: Touchstone, 1978), 65–66.
2. Jack Schneider, interview with Sally Bedell, August 1979, provided by Sally Bedell Smith.
3. Arthur Taylor, interview with Sally Bedell, undated, provided by Sally Bedell Smith.
4. Rosenfield, author interview.
5. Brooks and Marsh, *Complete Directory to Prime Time Network and Cable TV Shows*.
6. Wussler, Bedell interview.
7. Cowan, *See No Evil*, 67.
8. Cowan, *See No Evil*, 69.

9. Cowan, *See No Evil*, 93.
10. Cowan, *See No Evil*, 81.
11. Cowan, *See No Evil*, 96.
12. Cowan, *See No Evil*, 94.
13. Daly, author interview.
14. Cowan, *See No Evil*, 108.
15. Daly, author interview.
16. "Code Board to Meet on Family TV Fare," *New York Times*, January 1, 1975.
17. Cowan, *See No Evil*, 113.
18. Bedell, *Up the Tube*, 101; also, Cowan, *See No Evil*, 32–33.
19. Cowan, *See No Evil*, 36–37.
20. Lear, author interview.
21. Cowan, *See No Evil*, 230.
22. Eisner, author interview.
23. Eisner, author interview.
24. Eisner, author interview.
25. Kim Masters, *The Keys to the Kingdom: How Michael Eisner Lost His Grip* (New York: William Morrow, 2000), 39.
26. Masters, *The Keys*, 39; also, Eisner, author interview.
27. Bedell, *Up the Tube*, 122–23.
28. Brooks and Marsh, *Complete Directory to Prime Time Network and Cable TV Shows*.
29. Cowan, *See No Evil*, 201.
30. Les Brown, "CBS Ousts Taylor as Its President," *New York Times*, October 14, 1976.
31. Les Brown, "The Rewards of Being a Network Ex-President," *New York Times*, May 9, 1976.
32. Noyes, author interview.
33. Peter J. Boyer, "Robert Wood, Former Head of CBS Television Network," *New York Times*, May 22, 1986.
34. UPI, "'Mary Hartman' Canceled," *New York Times*, April 27, 1977.
35. Brownstein, *The Power and the Glitter*, 280.
36. David Canfield, "'It Changed My Life': Francis Ford Coppola Reflects on 'The Godfather' Book's 50th Anniversary," *Entertainment Weekly*, March 5, 2019.
37. Farber, "Coppola and 'The Godfather.'"
38. Joseph Gelmis, "The Midwifing of 'Godfather II,'" *Los Angeles Times*, January 2, 1975.
39. Wayne Warga, "Two Movies Receive 11 Oscar Nominations Each," *Los Angeles Times*, February 25, 1975.
40. Roos, author interview.
41. Joyce Haber, "The Sound of One Hand Clapping," *Los Angeles Times*, April 10, 1975.
42. Roos, author interview.
43. Towne, author interview.
44. McBride, *Steven Spielberg*, 254.
45. McBride, *Steven Spielberg*, 259.
46. Michael Ovitz, *Who Is Michael Ovitz?* (New York: Portfolio/Penguin, 2018), 47.
47. Ovitz, author interview.
48. Ovitz, *Who Is Michael Ovitz?*, 120.
49. Ovitz, *Who Is Michael Ovitz?*, 118.
50. Ovitz, author interview.
51. Schrader, author interview.
52. Pollock, author interview.
53. Jerry Gilliam, "OK Seen for Many Bills Brown Seeks," *Los Angeles Times*, January 7, 1975.
54. Richard Reeves, "And Why Is He So Popular?" *New York Times*, August 24, 1975.

55. Gilliam, "OK Seen."

56. Pack, *Jerry Brown*, 141–50.

57. Bill Press, interview with author, March 23, 2018.

58. Jerry Gilliam and Richard West, "Brown Enters Presidential Race," *Los Angeles Times*, March 13, 1976.

59. Kantor, author interview.

60. Al Martinez, "Brown's Style-Youth, Women Turn On," *Los Angeles Times*, May 18, 1976.

61. Kantor, author interview.

62. Kantor, author interview.

63. Maureen Orth, "Linda Ronstadt Opens for Presidential Candidate Jerry Brown," *Newsweek*, May 31, 1976, https://maureenorth.com/1976/05/linda-ronstadt-opens -for-presidential-candidate-jerry-brown/.

64. Pawel, *The Browns of California*, 218.

65. Pawel, *The Browns of California*, 333.

66. Ronald Brownstein, "After 2016 Election, Will Millennials Know How to Use Their New Power?" *National Journal*, May 12, 2015.

67. Eagles tour dates and accompanying bands from Randy Meisner Concert Chronology, http://www.angelfire.com/rock3/deliverin/MEISNER/randyconcerts.htm.

68. Pete Long, "Crosby, Stills, Nash & Young 1974," 43–71, in *CSNY 1974*, CD set, Rhino Records, 2014.

69. Long, "Crosby, Stills, Nash & Young 1974," 57.

70. Andy Greene, "The Oral History of CSNY's Infamous 'Doom Tour,'" *Rolling Stone*, June 19, 2014.

71. Legs McNeil and Gillian McCain, *Please Kill Me: The Uncensored Oral History of Punk*, Twentieth Anniversary Edition (New York: Grove Press, 2016), 118.

72. Steven Blush, *New York Rock: From the Rise of the Velvet Underground to the Fall of CBGB* (New York: St. Martin's Griffin, 2016), 83.

73. Eliot, *To the Limit*, 155.

74. David Browne, "Hotel California: Rock's Ultimate Statement on West Coast Excess—and the Eagles Biggest Hit," in *Rolling Stone Special Edition: Eagles—The Ultimate Guide*.

75. Robert Hilburn, "The Eagles: Denials of the Promised Land," *Los Angeles Times*, December 12, 1976.

76. Charley Walters, "Hotel California," *Rolling Stone*, February 14, 1977.

77. Kortchmar, author interview.

78. Taplin, author interview.

79. Nash, author interview.

80. Boylan, author interview.

81. Geoffrey Giuliano, *Lennon in America: Based in Part on the Lost Lennon Diaries, 1971–1980* (New York: Cooper Square Press, 2000), 55.

82. Giuliano, *Lennon in America*, 56.

83. Adler, author interview.

84. Gustavo Turner, "The Man Who Fell to Los Angeles: David Bowie's Lost L.A. Year," *LA Weekly*, January 13, 2016, https://www.laweekly.com/the-man-who-fell-to-los -angeles-david-bowies-lost-l-a-year/.

85. Polanski, *Roman*, 381.

86. Polanski, *Roman*, 327.

87. Bart, author interview.

88. Polanski, *Roman*, 377.

89. Polanski, *Roman*, 384–85.

90. Polanski, *Roman*, 391.

91. Polanski, *Roman*, 400.
92. Polanski, *Roman*, 393.
93. Polanski, *Roman*, 408.
94. Huston, *Watch Me*, 81.
95. Bill Farr, "Polanski Skips Sentencing in Sex Case, Flees to London," *Los Angeles Times*, February 2, 1978.
96. Farr, "Polanski Skips Sentencing in Sex Case."
97. Huston, author interview.
98. King, *The Operator*, 275.
99. King, *The Operator*, 286.
100. King, *The Operator*, 452–56.
101. Azoff, author interview.
102. Browne, author interview.
103. Ronstadt, author interview.
104. Young, "Hell Is for Heroes."
105. Stephen Davis, *Gold Dust Woman: The Biography of Stevie Nicks* (New York: St. Martin's Griffin, 2017), 46.
106. *Stevie Nicks: Through the Looking Glass*, documentary directed by Elio Espana (2013; Prism Films).
107. Davis, *Gold Dust Woman*, 61.

INDEX

ABOUT THE AUTHOR

RONALD BROWNSTEIN, a two-time finalist for the Pulitzer Prize for his coverage of presidential campaigns, is a senior editor at *The Atlantic*, and a senior political analyst for CNN. He also served as the national political correspondent and national affairs columnist for the *Los Angeles Times* and covered the White House and national politics for the *National Journal*. He is the author of six previous books, most recently *The Second Civil War: How Extreme Partisanship Has Paralyzed Washington and Polarized America*.